DATE DUE

			PRINTED IN U.S.A.

SOMETHING ABOUT THE AUTHOR

SOMETHING ABOUT THE AUTHOR

Facts and Pictures about Contemporary Authors
and Illustrators of Books for Young People

Anne Commire

VOLUME 7

GALE RESEARCH
BOOK TOWER
DETROIT, MICHIGAN
48226

Also Published by Gale

CONTEMPORARY AUTHORS:
A Bio-Bibliographical Guide to
Current Authors and Their Works

(Now Covers More Than 40,000 Authors)

Special acknowledgment is due to the members of the *Contemporary Authors* staff (particularly Mary Reif Stevenson) who assisted in the preparation of this volume, and to Gale's art director, Chester Gawronski.

Library of Congress Catalog Card Number: 70-127412
ISBN 0-8103-0062-1

GRATEFUL ACKNOWLEDGMENT

is made to the following publishers, authors, and artists, for their kind permission to reproduce copyrighted material. ■ **ABINGDON PRESS.** Illustration by George Wilde from *Andy and Mr. Wagner* by Gina Bell. Copyright © 1957 by Abingdon Press. Reprinted by permission of Abingdon Press. ■ **ADDISON-WESLEY PUBLISHING CO., INC.** Illustration by Willi Baum from *Baron Munchausen* retold by Doris Orgel. Illustrations copyright © 1971 by Willi Baum. /Illustration by Tom Funk from *The Terrible Trick or Treat* by Edith Battles. Copyright © 1970 by Edith Battles, a young Scott Book. /Illustration by Leonard Kessler from *Oodles of Noodles* by Lucia and James L. Hymes, Jr. Illustrations copyright © MCMLXIV by Leonard Kessler. All reprinted by permission of Addison-Wesley Publishing Co., Inc. ■ **ATHENEUM PUBLISHERS.** Illustration by Margery Gill from *The Little Dark Thorn* by Ruth M. Arthur. Copyright © 1971 by Ruth M. Arthur. /Illustration by Kay Chorao from *My Mama Says There Aren't any Zombies, Ghosts, Vampires, Creatures, Demons, Monsters, Fiends, Goblins, or Things* by Judith Viorst. Illustrations copyright © 1973 by Kay Sproat Chorao. /Illustration by Bret Schlesinger from *Roam the Wild Country* by Ella Thorp Ellis. Copyright © 1967 by Ella Thorp Ellis. /Illustration by Velma Ilsley from *She, the Adventuress* by Dorothy Crayder. Copyright © 1973 by Dorothy Crayder. /Illustration by Carl Anderson from *Matilda Investigates* by Mary Anderson. Copyright © 1973 by Mary Anderson. /Illustration by Ray Abel from *The Edge of Nowhere* by Lucy Johnston Sypher. Copyright © 1972 by Lucy Johnston Sypher. /Illustration by Kelly Oechsli from *Seeds of Time* by Bernice Grohskopf. Copyright © 1963 by Bernice Grohskopf and Kelly Oechsli. All reprinted by permission of Atheneum Publishers. ■ **THE BOBBS-MERRILL CO.** Illustration by Jan Pyk from *Luap* by June Rachuy Brindel. Illustrations copyright © 1971 by Jan Pyk. Reprinted by permission of The Bobbs-Merrill Co., Inc. ■ **BRADBURY PRESS.** Illustration by Emily McCully from *Finders Keepers* by Alix Shulman. Copyright © 1971 by Emily McCully. Reprinted by permission of Bradbury Press. ■ **CHILDRENS PRESS.** Illustration by William Neebe from *Those People in Washington* by David Flitner. Copyright © 1973 by Regensteiner Publishing Enterprises, Inc. /Illustration by Henry Luhrs from *Good Times on Boats* by Will Hayes. Copyright © 1963 by Melmont Publishers, Inc., Chicago, Ill. Both reprinted by permission of Childrens Press. ■ **COWARD, McCANN & GEOGHEGAN, INC.** Illustration by Richard Lebenson from *When the World's on Fire* by Sally Edwards. Copyright © 1972 by Sally Edwards. /Illustration by Michael Hampshire from *A Cow for Jaya* by Eva Grant. Illustrations copyright © 1973 by Michael Hampshire. Cover by David Brown from *A Hero Ain't Nothin' but a Sandwich* by Alice Childress. Copyright © 1973 by Alice Childress. /Illustration by Joan G. Robinson from *Mary Mary Stories* by Joan G. Robinson. Copyright © 1965 by Joan G. Robinson. All reprinted by permission of Coward, McCann & Geoghegan, Inc. ■ **THOMAS Y. CROWELL CO.** Illustration by Anne Ophelia Dowden from *Wild Green Things in the City* by Anne Ophelia Dowden. Copyright © 1972. /Illustration by Victor G. Ambrus from *Beyond the Weir Bridge* by Hester Burton. Copyright © 1969 by Hester Burton. Both reprinted by Thomas Y. Crowell Co. ■ **CROWELL-COLLIER PRESS.** Illustration by Paul Giovanopoulos from *The Real Tin Flower* by Aliki Barnstone. Copyright © 1968 by Macmillan Publishing Co., Inc. Reprinted by permission of Macmillan Co. ■ **CROWN PUBLISHERS, INC.** Illustration by Marilyn Hirsh from *George and the Goblins* by Marilyn Hirsh. Copyright © 1972 by Marilyn Hirsh. Reprinted by permission of Crown Publishers, Inc. ■ **THE JOHN DAY CO., INC.** Illustration by Chiyo Ono from *The Boy and the Bird* by Tamao Fujita, translated from the Japanese *The Lost Parrot*. Copyright © 1970 by Shiko-Sha Ltd. Reprinted by permission of The John Day Co., Inc. **DELACORTE PRESS.** Illustration by Paul Bacon from *Zanballer* by R. R. Knudson. Copyright © 1972 by R. R. Knudson. /Illustration by Imero Gobbato from *Foma the Terrible* by Guy Daniels. Illustrations copyright © 1970 by Imero Gobbato. Both reprinted by

PHOTOGRAPH CREDITS

RICHARD ADAMS

ADAMS, Richard 1920-

PERSONAL: Born May 9, 1920, in Newbury, Berkshire, England; son of Dr. Evelyn George Beadon and Lilian Rosa (Button) Adams; married Barbara Elizabeth Acland, September 20, 1949; children: Juliet, Rosamond. *Education:* Attended Bradfield, 1933-38; Worcester College, Oxford, M.A., 1948. *Religion:* Church of England. *Home:* 26 St. Paul's Place, London N1 2QG, England. *Agent:* David Higham Associates Ltd., 5-8 Lower John St., London W1R 4HA, England.

CAREER: British Higher Civil Service, 1948-74, assistant secretary, Department of Environment. *Military service:* British Army, 1940-45. *Awards, honors:* Guardian Award for children's literature, and Carnegie Medal, both 1973, for *Watership Down.*

WRITINGS: Watership Down, Rex Collings, 1972, Macmillan, 1974; *Shardik,* Allen Lane, 1974.

SIDELIGHTS: "I should be very sorry if people tried to read deeper meanings into *Watership Down.*"

HOBBIES AND OTHER INTERESTS: "My great passion is Shakespeare. I took him through 5½ years of war."

FOR MORE INFORMATION SEE: Horn Book, June, 1973, August, 1974; *New York,* March 4, 1974; *Publishers' Weekly,* April 15, 1974.

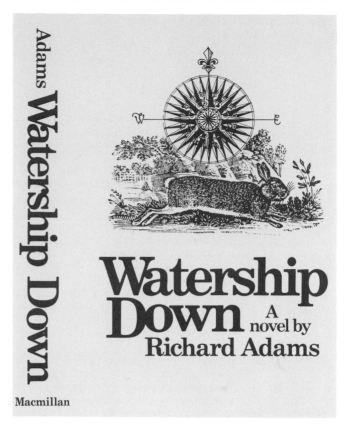

Rabbits above ground, unless they are in proved, familiar surroundings close to their holes, live in continual fear. If it grows intense enough they can become glazed and paralyzed by it —"tharn," to use their own word. ■ (From *Watership Down* by Richard Adams.)

ADELBERG, Doris
See ORGEL, Doris

AINSWORTH, Ruth (Gallard) 1908-

PERSONAL: Born October 16, 1908, in Manchester, England; daughter of Percy Clough (a Methodist minister) and Gertrude (Fisk) Ainsworth; married Frank Lathe Gilbert (now managing director of chemical works), March 29, 1935; children: Oliver Lathe, Christopher Gallard, Richard Frank. *Education:* Attended Ipswich High School and Froebel Training Centre, Leicester, England. *Politics:* Labour. *Home:* West Cheynes, Corbridge, Northumberland, England.

CAREER: Writer.

WRITINGS—All juveniles: Tales About Tony, Epworth, 1936; *Mr. Popcorn's Friends,* Epworth, 1938; *The Gingerbread House,* Epworth, 1938; *The Ragamuffins,* Epworth, 1939; *Richard's First Term: A School Story,* Epworth, 1940; *All Different* (poems), Heinemann, 1947; *Five and a Dog,* Epworth, 1949.

Listen with Mother Tales, Heinemann, 1951; *Rufty Tufty the Golliwog,* Heinemann, 1952; *The Evening Listens* (poems), Heinemann, 1953; *The Ruth Ainsworth Readers,* Books 1-12, Heinemann, 1953-55; *Rufty Tufty at the Sea-*

side, Heinemann, 1954; *Charles Stories, and Others* (selected from BBC radio program, "Listen with Mother"), Heinemann, 1954; *More About Charles, and Other Stories* (selected from "Listen with Mother" program), Heinemann, 1954; *Three Little Mushrooms* (four puppet plays), Heinemann, 1955; *More Little Mushrooms* (four puppet plays), Heinemann, 1955; *The Snow Bear,* Heinemann, 1956; *Rufty Tufty Goes Camping,* Heinemann, 1956; *Rufty Tufty Runs Away,* Heinemann, 1957; *Five Listen with Mother Tales About Charles,* Adprint, 1957; *Nine Drummers Drumming* (stories), Heinemann, 1958; *Rufty Tufty Flies High,* Heinemann, 1959.

Cherry Stones (fairy stories), Heinemann, 1960; *Rufty Tufty's Island,* Heinemann, 1960; *Lucky Dip,* Penguin, 1961; *Rufty Tufty and Hattie,* Heinemann, 1962; *Far-Away Children,* Heinemann, 1963, Roy, 1968; *The Ten Tales of Shellover,* Deutsch, 1963, Roy, 1968; *The Wolf Who Was Sorry,* Heinemann, 1964, Roy, 1968; *Rufty Tufty Makes a House,* Heinemann, 1965; *Daisy the Cow,* Hamish Hamilton, 1966; *Horse on Wheels,* Hamish Hamilton, 1966; *Jack Frost,* Heinemann, 1966; *The Look About You Books,* Heinemann, Book 1: *In Woods and Fields,* 1967, Book 2: *Down the Lane,* 1967, Book 3: *Beside the Sea,* 1967, Book 4: *By Pond and Stream,* 1969, Book 5: *In Your Garden,* 1969, Book 6: *In the Park,* 1969; *Roly the Railway Mouse,* Heinemann, 1967, published in America as *Roly the Railroad Mouse,* Watts, 1969; *The Aeroplane Who Wanted to See the Sea,* Bancroft & Co., 1968; *Boris the Teddy Bear,* Bancroft & Co., 1968; *Dougal the Donkey,* Bancroft & Co., 1968; *More Tales of Shellover,* Deutsch, 1968, Roy, 1969; *Mungo the Monkey,* Bancroft & Co., 1968; *The Old Fashioned Car,* Bancroft & Co., 1968; *The Rabbit and His Shadow,* Bancroft & Co., 1968; *The Noah's Ark,* Lutterworth, 1969; *The Bicycle Wheel,* Hamish Hamilton, 1969; *Look, Do and Listen* (anthology), Watts, 1969; (editor) *Book of Colours and Sounds,* Purnell Juvenile, 1969; *The Ruth Ainsworth Book* (stories), Watts, 1970; *The Phantom Cyclist,* Deutsch, 1971; *Fairy Gold,* Heinemann, 1972; *Another Lucky Dip,* Puffin, 1973.

Educational books with Ronald Ridout: *Look Ahead Readers,* Books 1-8 (includes supplementary readers for each book), Heinemann, 1956-58; *Books for Me to Read,* six volumes, Bancroft & Co., 1964; *Bancroft Red Books* (includes *Jill and Peter, House of Hay, Come and Play, Name of My Own, Duck That Ran Away,* and *Tim's Hoop*), Bancroft & Co., 1965; *Bancroft Blue Books* (includes *At the Zoo, What Are They?, Colors, Silly Billy, Jane and John,* and *Pony, Pony*), Bancroft & Co., 1965; *Bancroft Green Books* (includes *Susan's House, What Can You Hear?, Tim's Kite, Flippy the Frog, Huff the Hedgehog,* and *A House for a Mouse*), Bancroft & Co., 1965, each book also published separately by Initial Teaching Publishing Co., 1968. Writer of puppet plays and stories for television. Contributor of stories to British Broadcasting Corp. programs (also broadcast in Australia and New Zealand), "Listen with Mother" and "English for Schools."

SIDELIGHTS: "I am told that I began making up poems when I was three, and wrote an exercise book of fairy tales when I was eight. Throughout my childhood I enjoyed writing, whether diaries, school essays or stories. I had a poem in a national daily when I was fifteen, and in my late 'teens there was poetry published in *The Spectator, Country Life* and other journals. I wrote for children's magazines which bought my stories for a song.

"My father died when I was a baby and we moved to a Suffolk backwater. This may be why so many of my stories have a seaside setting. My characters play on the beach as I did, with few other distractions. When I was seventeen we moved to Leicester where there was a good library, which added another dimension to life. I won a Gold Medal for original work and had some poems printed as part of the prize.

"My first break came when Heinemann published a book of my children's poetry, *All Different,* and I began writing regularly for 'Listen with Mother'. Heinemann published my *Listen with Mother Tales* which are still in print, and included stories about a little boy called Charles. He kept his treasures in a useful bag, and I heard that many children demanded useful bags for themselves.

"I now had a husband, and three sons to whom I told endless stories. They soon began to tell me wonderful stories, too. Books followed steadily, including a series of eight books about *Rufty Tufty the Golliwog,* who proved as popular as Charles. He went camping—stayed by the sea—got carried away by a kite—found buried treas-

RUTH AINSWORTH

ure—and had other adventures, accompanied by his friend Rose. It is true that he started school, but in most respects Rose and he stayed about the age of five throughout.

"I write in a relaxed position, using a biro. Later, with less enthusiasm, I type the manuscript rather badly. I bought my first typewriter when I was eighteen and had earned thirty dollars. I carried it home in triumph and then spent ages poring over the instruction book, unable even to insert a sheet of paper. I was, and have remained, totally unmechanical. Perhaps this is why Rufty Tufty never visited the moon.

"My sons maintain that they can recognize much of their own childhood in my stories and now I have grandchildren among my readers, including an imaginative six year old who fills notebook after notebook with stories and poems.

"If I live long enough to write stories for my great-grandchildren, I suppose my characters will behave much as they have always done, building sandcastles, making houses, and meaning well, though this sometimes turns out badly. They experience the anguish of separation and disappointment, but there is usually a comforting, solid figure near at hand, an eternal Mrs. Golliwog.

They saw lovely sandy beaches and great, black rocks bearded with green seaweed. A seagull flew right past their faces and they could see his pink feet tucked underneath him. ■ (From *The Ruth Ainsworth Book* by Ruth Ainsworth. Illustrated by Shirley Hughes.)

"Children find magic in the everyday life of play and family. My sources spring from just that. Only children and birds.

> 'Know the sweetness of cherries,
> The goodness of bread.'

"Books, especially poetry when I was younger, have always been among my purest pleasures. Writing is a pleasure too and I seem to write from a top layer of happiness. If this is lacking, writing becomes more of a routine, less of a joy."

FOR MORE INFORMATION SEE: Brian Doyle, *The Who's Who of Children's Literature,* Schocken, 1968; *Books for Young Children,* November, 1972.

ANDERSON, Mary 1939-

PERSONAL: Born January 20, 1939, in New York, N.Y.; daughter of Andrew Joseph and Nellie (DeHaan) Quirk; married Carl Anderson (a commercial artist), March 1, 1958; children: Lisa, Maja, Chersteen. *Residence:* New York, N.Y. *Agent:* Curtis Brown Ltd., 60 East 56th St., New York, N.Y. 10022.

CAREER: Actress in Off-Broadway productions, New York, N.Y., 1956-58; secretary in advertising and television fields, New York, N.Y., 1956-59.

WRITINGS—For young people: (With Hope Campbell, pseudonym of Geraldine Wallis) *There's a Pizza Back in Cleveland,* Four Winds, 1972; (illustrated by husband, Carl Anderson) *Matilda Investigates,* Atheneum, 1973; *Emma's*

Already there were lady Prime Ministers, lady astronauts—even a lady rabbi. . . . There was no time to wait if she was going to be the first female detective in the world (well, New York City, anyway). ■ From *Matilda Investigates* by Mary Anderson. Illustrated by Carl Anderson.)

Search for Something, Atheneum, 1973; *I'm Nobody! Who Are You?,* Atheneum, 1974; (illustrated by husband) *Just The Two of Them,* Atheneum, 1974.

WORK IN PROGRESS: Sequel to *Emma's Search for Something,* "which will feature Freddie the Cat in a more prominent role. The very tentative title is *F.T.C. Superstar.*"

SIDELIGHTS: "The main motivation behind my work is to recreate for others (and myself) the pleasure I received from reading as a child. Children's books are one of the last strongholds in literature where optimism, joy, compassion, and a sheer wonder for the world are still being portrayed successfully."

HOBBIES AND OTHER INTERESTS: Interior decoration, biking, making miniature doll furniture, sewing.

FOR MORE INFORMATION SEE: Horn Book, June, 1973; *Junior Literary Guild Catalogue,* March, 1974.

MARY ANDERSON

4

Mandy slowly turned her head and saw a chair, a fireplace, a table in one corner of the room with bottles and glasses and a thermometer on it. A pretty coverlet was on her bed. ■ (From *Mandy* by Julie Edwards. Illustrated by Judith Gwyn Brown.)

Something about the Author

JULIE ANDREWS

ANDREWS, Julie 1935-
(Julie Edwards)

PERSONAL: Born October 1, 1935; name originally Julia Elizabeth Wells, took the surname of her stepfather when her mother married music hall singer, Edward Andrews; daughter of Edward C. Wells (a schoolteacher known as Ted Wells) and Barbara (a pianist; maiden name, Ward) Wells Andrews; married Tony Walton (a theatrical designer), May 10, 1959; married second husband, Blake Edwards (a producer and director), November 12, 1969; children: (first marriage) Emma Kate Walton. *Education:* Educated privately by tutors; studied voice with Madame Stiles-Allen. *Office:* C/o Gadbois Management Co., 9201 Wilshire Blvd., Los Angeles, Calif. 90210. *Agent:* (Theatrical) Chasin-Park-Citron, 10889 Wilshire Blvd., Los Angeles, Calif. 90024.

CAREER: Her singing in a bomb shelter at the age of eight led to professional training and a debut at twelve at the Hippodrome in London in the revue, "Starlight Roof"; had the title role in "Humpty Dumpty," 1948, "Red Riding Hood," 1950, and "Cinderella," 1953, and played in other revues and pantomimes in England before making a Broadway debut at the Royale Theatre in "The Boy Friend," September, 1954; played Eliza in the Broadway production of "My Fair Lady," 1956-60, and Guinevere in "Camelot," 1960-62. Appeared opposite Bing Crosby in the television version of "High Tor," 1956, and in the television remake of Rodgers and Hammerstein's "Cinderella," 1957. Her first screen role was in the Academy Award-winning "Mary Poppins," 1964, followed by "The Americanization of Emily," 1964, "Torn Curtain," 1966, "The Sound of Music," 1966, "Hawaii," 1966, "Star," 1966, "Thoroughly Modern Millie," 1968, "Darling Lili," 1971, "The Tamarind Seed," 1974, "The Return of the Pink Panther," 1975. Recordings include the original cast records of "My Fair Lady" and "Camelot," "Julie Andrews and Carol Burnett at Carnegie Hall," and other albums. Television includes specials and the "Julie Andrews Hour" on A.B.C., 1972-73.

AWARDS, HONORS: New York Drama Critics Award for "My Fair Lady," 1956; Academy of Motion Picture Arts and Sciences "Oscar" as best actress for "Mary Poppins," 1964; named best actress of the year and world's favorite actress by Hollywood foreign press, 1967; Silver Rose Montreaux, for "Julie Andrews Hour," 1973.

WRITINGS—Under name Julie Edwards: *Mandy* (juvenile), Harper, 1971; *The Last of the Really Great Whangdoodles,* Harper, 1974.

WORK IN PROGRESS: A novel, as yet untitled.

SIDELIGHTS: Ms. Andrews' second book for children, a fantasy, began with a trip to the dictionary. "I was looking up a word, and suddenly I saw 'Whangdoodle.' I thought to myself, that's a sensational word, and the title of my book occurred to me immediately.

"Once I started writing, I enjoyed myself so much I couldn't wait to get back to Whangdoodleland every day. My own children became as involved as I was, and naturally there is a lot of them in Lindy, Tom and Ben."

FOR MORE INFORMATION SEE: Christian Science Monitor, November 11, 1971: Lee Bennett Hopkins, *More Books by More People,* Citation, 1974.

ARTHUR, Ruth M. 1905-

PERSONAL: Born May 26, 1905, in Glasgow, Scotland; daughter of Allan (an electrical contractor) and Ruth M. (Johnston) Arthur; married Frederick N. Huggins (a lawyer), September 2, 1932; children: two sons, four daughters. *Education:* Froebel Training College, diploma, 1926. *Religion:* Church of Scotland. *Home:* 46 Victoria Ave., Swanage, Dorset, England. *Agent:* Curtis Brown Ltd., 60 East 56th St., New York, N.Y. 10022; Curtis Brown Ltd., Craven Hill, London W23EW, England.

CAREER: Kindergarten teacher in Glasgow, Scotland, 1927-30, in Loughton, Essex, England, 1930-32; writer of stories for children and novels for teen-agers. *Member:* Society of Authors, National Book League, Children's Writers Group, P.E.N.

WRITINGS: Carolina's Holiday, Harrap, 1956; *The Daisy Cow,* Harrap, 1957; *Carolina's Golden Bird,* Harrap, 1958; *A Cottage for Rosemary,* Harrap, 1959; *Carolina and Roberto,* Harrap, 1960; *Dragon Summer,* Hutchinson, 1962, Atheneum, 1963; *Carolina and the Sea Horse, and Other Stories,* Harrap, 1963; *My Daughter Nicola,* Atheneum, 1965; *A Candle in Her Room,* Atheneum, 1966; *Requiem for a Princess,* Atheneum, 1967; *Portrait of Margarita,* Atheneum, 1968; *The Whistling Boy* (Junior Literary Guild selection), Atheneum, 1969; *The Saracen Lamp,* Atheneum, 1970; *The Little Dark Thorn,* Atheneum, 1971; *The Autumn People,* Atheneum, 1973; *After Candlemas,* Atheneum, 1974.

SIDELIGHTS: "I am the mother of two sons and four daughters, now all married, and we have eight grandchildren. My husband, a retired solicitor, and I live quietly on the southwest coast of England. We walk a good deal along the beautiful wild coast line, and we travel abroad as much as we are able to, often by car, and sometimes with a small trailer caravan. We see our grandchildren and have them stay with us as often as we can.

"I have always written stories, poetry, diaries, and when I was young and teaching in Glasgow, I used to broadcast many of them on the radio. I began to write more seriously when our youngest daughter was six, and I followed her up, and started writing books for young teenagers when she

I can remember the very first time I came to Aunt Emma's house. ■ (From *The Little Dark Thorn* by Ruth M. Arthur. Illustrated by Margery Gill.)

was eleven. I find eleven-to-fourteen the most interesting age to write for, although people a little younger and much older seem to enjoy my books. I try to introduce my young readers to the grown-up problems but at their own level, and this means a lot of research and checking up on facts and reading around the subjects I write about. I find this very interesting. I always choose a real house and a real village or rural area for the setting of my story, and a great many of the experiences I write about have been my own personal ones, although of course, there are fictitious happenings as well.

"It takes me at least a year, sometimes two or three years to collect data for a book, to think about it and mull it over before I start writing it. I write in long hand, and when I have finished the first copy I put it away for a month or two, then re-write most of it. Once I have begun a book I try to write a bit every day, although some days are easier than others. Once I am well into a book I can write anywhere—train, bus, outside or inside. It takes me at least a year to write each book. I do not illustrate ever, but Margery Gill who illustrates my books, is a friend and we meet and discuss the story before she starts her drawings. She makes sketches first of the real place where the story is set."

HOBBIES AND OTHER INTERESTS: Travel, country living, theatre, music, cooking, people.

FOR MORE INFORMATION SEE: Horn Book, October, 1971, June 6, 1973.

ARUEGO, Ariane
See DEWEY, Ariane

RUTH M. ARTHUR

ANN ATWOOD

ATWOOD, Ann (Margaret) 1913-

PERSONAL: Born February 12, 1913, in Heber, Calif.; daughter of Howard Catlin (a doctor of osteopathy) and Marie (Jones) Atwood. *Education:* University of Redlands, B.A., 1934; Art Center School, Los Angeles, Calif., photography student, summer, 1935.

CAREER: Owner and manager of Ann Atwood Studio of Children's Portraiture in Riverside, Calif., 1937-40, San Marino, Calif., 1940-60, and South Laguna, Calif., 1960-67. Founder and director of adult education class in poetry writing in Riverside, Calif., 1938-40; adult night school poetry teacher in Hollywood, Calif., 1943-44. *Member:* Sierra Club, Wilderness Society.

AWARDS, HONORS—For books: University of California at Irvine annual book award, 1967, for *The Little Circle; New Moon Cove* won Horn Book Award for illustration from *Boston Globe* and *School Library Journal* award in 1969, and Southern California Council on Literature for Children and Young People award for illustration, 1970; *School Library Journal* award, 1970, for *The Wild Young Desert;* University of California at Irvine special award, 1970, for *New Moon Cove; Haiku: The Mood of Earth* won Horn Book award, 1971, and Southern California Council on Literature for Children and Young People award, *School Library Journal* award, and University of California at Irvine annual book award, all in 1972.

Awards for filmstrips: •''The Little Circle'' won silver medal in International Film and Television Festival of New York, 1970, and media award of Southern California Social Science Association, 1972; ''Haiku: The Mood of Earth'' won Chris Award from Columbus Film Festival and silver medal from International Film and Television Festival of New York in 1971, and award for distinguished contribution for fusion of poetry and photography from Southern California Council on Literature for Children and Young People, and Ann Corneille award from National Educational Film Festival (Oakland, Calif.) in 1972; silver medal from International Film and Television Festival of New York, 1972, for ''The Gods Were Tall and Green''; Jack London Award from National Educational Film Festival (Oakland, Calif.), and gold medal from Atlanta International Film Festival, 1973, for ''Haiku: The Hidden Glimmering.''

WRITINGS—Books of photographs for children all published by Scribner: *The Little Circle,* 1967; *New Moon Cove* (*Horn Book* Honor List), 1969; (with Elizabeth Hazelton) *Sammy: The Crow Who Remembered,* 1969; *The Wild Young Desert,* 1970; *Haiku: The Mood of Earth* (*Horn Book* Honor List), 1971; *The Kingdom of the Forest,* 1972; *My Own Rhythm,* 1973; (with Erica Anderson), *For All that Lives,* 1974.

Author and photographer of film strips—all produced by Lyceum Productions: ''Sea, Sand and Shore,'' in three parts, 1969; ''The Little Circle,'' 1970; ''The Wild Young Desert,'' in two parts, 1970; ''Haiku: The Mood of Earth,'' in two parts, 1971; ''The Gods Were Tall and Green,'' in two parts, 1972; ''Haiku: The Hidden Glimmering,'' 1973. Photographer for filmstrips written by Elizabeth Baldwin Hazelton and produced by Lyceum Productions: ''Tahiti Is My Island,'' 1969; ''Sammy the Crow,'' 1970; ''Teeka the Otter,'' 1971; ''My Forty Years with Beavers,'' 1974.

WORK IN PROGRESS: Another book and film on haiku; two filmstrips on wild beavers, two filmstrips for Lyceum.

SIDELIGHTS: ''As far as I know, it would be hard to think of a place that has influenced my life less than that barren lonely spot at the southern tip of California where I was born; a place called Heber.

''But certainly my early years were greatly enriched by my father, who was both by temperament and training an artist and photographer, and who, after putting up a stubborn and futile battle to farm untold acres of desolate desert, moved his family to what was then a scantily populated area, the town of Newport Beach. At the age of five, I and my two older brothers, were literally transported from Inferno into Paradise. That year spent between the crashing surf and the quiet bay, boating across the water in search of clams and mussels, learning how to dodge the power of breaking waves while tasting their salt, running the long, uninterrupted beaches filled with countless treasures—all of this made me an incurable follower of the sea.

''There were to be many years, all of them within a radius of sixty miles, before I could return to what I always knew was my true home. First of all, my early schooling in Riverside extending through junior college, then a B.A. in English from the University of Redlands, a photography course at the Art Center School in Los Angeles.

"Then the summer of 1939 which began as magic and ended in terror. A three-month trip through England, Scotland, Holland, Belgium, Germany, into Switzerland, Italy, and back through Germany with the borders closing behind us, into the chaos of France and Americans frantically trying to get home while ship after ship was cancelled. But before that . . . cycling through those enchanting countries with a camera as a constant companion! Sleeping in hostels with young people from all over the nearby countries (25c a night included breakfast!).

"Later that year, I started a class in the Riverside Adult Education Program on poetry writing, published a book of poems illustrated with my photographs, and opened a studio in child portraiture.

"I have always had an obsession, not with children, but with the quality of childhood expressed in the faces of children. I felt this quality to be a tangible thing that could be transferred onto film. There were many successful years, most of them in my studio in San Marino. Finally it seemed feasible to take the financial risk and move the studio to the seaside, where I had longed to live ever since childhood. South Laguna offered the most beauty, though the least possibility from a business point of view. But there comes a time when first things must come first, and when you know what those first things are, everything falls into place.

"For me, they fell into place in an unpredictable fashion. After spending several years establishing the business, my health suddenly forced me to close it. Even during that period of comparative physical uselessness, the two great interests of my life were converging—my fascination with the sea, and my preoccupation with the quality of childhood.

"*The Little Circle* began with some joyful observations on a bubble in the foam, and progressed into a full circle of my own interrupted self-discovery, and I hope that it conveys some of the excitement that comes to every man and every child with the sense of his own identity.

"*New Moon Cove* was a continuation of that early love-affair with the sea, and perhaps the impressions of light, textures, shapes and patterns were fresher for having been denied so long, and picked up again at that point where childhood broke off. The two books of haiku gave me the opportunity for new forms of poetic expression in both writing and photography, and a deep sense of the unity that exists between the two.

"But I don't mean to imply that creating a book is all that easy and delightful. For me, every sentence is painfully tedious and slow, I learned much from a fine editor, and I am grateful to Scribner's for being willing to publish books for young readers with photographs in full color. How very fortunate for me!

"Travel is a necessary part of my life. *The Wild Young Desert* depended completely on long trips through our deserts for film-material, and much research on a subject of which I knew very little. (This is true of everything I work on!)

"For recreation I like to walk the beaches, and always think I will leave my camera behind me, but I never can

bring myself to do so and have yet to be sorry that I accepted the burden of its presence!

"I limit my reading to books that will enrich my studies and to books or articles which bring me only the deepest satisfaction. Among the authors who do are Loren Eisley, Gerald Heard, and many fine nature writers, philosophers and poets too numerous to name.

"When I have finished a book I have invested so much in time and film that I utilize that material in filmstrips. I've become closely associated with Lyceum Productions, a filmstrip company here in Laguna, and have been able to enlarge both meaning and content of book material into packages containing usually two strips and the book. This is an exciting concept and gives me a chance to slant my work for curriculum use, and also it is a great challenge to mold films and text in this medium.

"As for the satisfactions! I think every writer will agree that each book is its own reward. There is no happiness like the happiness of travelling with a camera to explore the light of new valleys or the shadows of new forests. And there is no peace that equals the relief when one is through with the struggle of fusing words and pictures into a tightly knit whole. Few things are as thrilling as opening that long-awaited cardboard carton and leafing through the first copies of a book of your own, letting yourself rejoice in it for a little while.

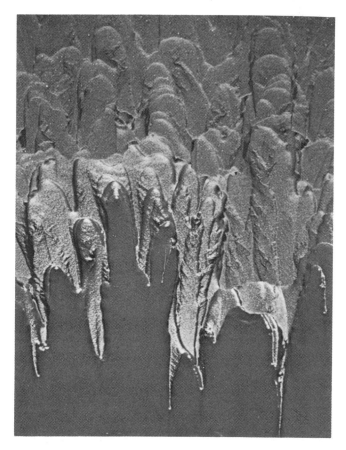

Often, too, sculpture is created where the sea and shore meet.
■ (From *New Moon Cove* by Ann Atwood. Photograph by the author.)

"And then once more there is that Nothingness where dim and shapeless images are stirring—and this is the deepest joy of all."

FOR MORE INFORMATION SEE: New York Times Book Review, November 5, 1967, May 3, 1970; *Horn Book,* August, 1969, December, 1971, June, 1974; *Library Journal,* March 5, 1970, May 15, 1970.

AUSTIN, Oliver L(uther), Jr.   1903-

PERSONAL: Born May 24, 1903, in Tuckahoe, N.Y.; son of Oliver Luther (a physician) and Elizabeth (Wise) Austin; married Elizabeth Schling (an author), September 10, 1930; children: Anthony, Timothy. *Education:* Berkshire School, Sheffield, Mass., student, 1921-22; Wesleyan University, Middletown, Conn., B.S., 1926; Harvard University, Ph.D., 1931. *Home:* 205 Southeast Seventh St., Gainesville, Fla. 32601. *Office:* Florida State Museum, Seagle Building, University of Florida, Gainesville, Fla. 32601.

CAREER: U.S. Department of Agriculture, Bureau of Biological Survey, Washington, D.C., assistant biologist, 1930-35; Austin Ornithological Research Station, Wellfleet, Mass., director, 1932-57; U.S. Department of the Army, technical consultant in Tokyo, Japan, 1946-50; Air University, Maxwell Air Force Base, Ala., research and education specialist at Arctic, Desert, Tropic Information Center, Research Studies Institute, 1953-57; Florida State Museum, Gainesville, curator of birds (ornithology), 1957—. *Military service:* U.S. Naval Reserve, active duty, 1942-46; became commander.

OLIVER L. AUSTIN JR.

MEMBER: American Ornithologists' Union (fellow), British Ornithologists' Union, Ornithological Society of Japan, Nuttall Ornithological Club, Cooper Ornithological Club, Wilson Ornithological Society, Eastern Bird-Banding Association, Explorers Club (New York). *Awards, honors:* Guggenheim fellowship, 1952-53; Distinguished Alumnus Award, Wesleyan University, 1966; (with Elizabeth Austin) Arthur A. Allen medal of the Cornell Laboratory of Ornithology, 1973.

WRITINGS: The Birds of Newfoundland and Labrador, Nuttall Ornithological Club, Harvard University, 1932; *The Birds of Korea,* Museum of Comparative Zoology, Harvard University, 1948; (with Nagahisa Kuroda) *The Birds of Japan,* Museum of Comparative Zoology, Harvard University, 1953; *Birds of the World: A Survey of the 27 Orders and 155 Families,* edited by Herbert S. Zim, Golden Press, 1961; (editor) *Life Histories of North American Birds,* U.S. National Museum, 1968; (editor) *Antarctic Bird Studies,* American Geophysical Union, 1968; (with wife, Elizabeth S. Austin) *The Random House Book of Birds* (juvenile), Random House, 1970; *Families of Birds,* Golden Press, 1971. Contributor of about one hundred papers to ornithological journals. Editor, *Auk* (quarterly publication of American Ornithologists' Union), 1968—.

WORK IN PROGRESS: With Arthur Singer, *Field Guide to Birds of the Oceans.*

HOBBIES AND OTHER INTERESTS: Growing orchids, gardening.

AVERY, Gillian (Elise)   1926-

PERSONAL: Born September 30, 1926; daughter of Norman Bates (an estate agent) and Grace Elise (Dunn) Avery; married Anthony Oliver John Cockshut (a university lecturer and writer), August 25, 1952; children: Ursula Mary Elise. *Education:* Attended schools in England. *Religion:* Anglican. *Home:* 32 Charlbury Rd., Oxford, OX2 6UU, England.

CAREER: Writer. *Awards, honors: Guardian* award and Carnegie Medal runner-up, 1972, for *A Likely Lad.*

WRITINGS: The Warden's Niece, Collins, 1957, Penguin, 1963; *Trespassers at Charlcote,* Collins, 1958; *James Without Thomas,* Collins, 1959; *The Elephant War,* Collins, 1960, Holt, 1971; *To Tame a Sister,* Collins, 1961, Van Nostrand, 1964, Viking, 1973; *Mrs. Ewing,* Bodley Head, 1961, Walck, 1964; *The Greatest Gresham,* Collins, 1962; *The Peacock House,* Collins, 1963; *The Italian Sprint,* Collins, 1964, Holt, 1972; (with Angela Bull) *Nineteenth Century Children: Heroes and Heroines in English Children's Stories,* Hodder & Stoughton, 1965; *Call of the Valley,* Collins, 1966, Holt, 1968; (contributor) *The Eleanor Farjeon Book,* Hamish Hamilton, 1966; (contributor) *Winter's Tales for Children 2,* Macmillan, 1966; *Victorian People in Life and Literature,* Holt, 1970; (with others) *Authors' Choice,* Hamish Hamilton, 1970, Crowell, 1971; *A Likely Lad,* Holt, 1971; *Ellen's Birthday,* Hamish Hamilton, 1971; *Ellen and the Queen,* Hamish Hamilton, 1971, Nelson, 1974; *Jemima and the Welsh Rabbit,* Hamish Hamilton, 1972; (contributor) *Allsorts 5,* Macmillan, 1972;

(contributor) *Rudyard Kipling*, Weidenfeld & Nicolson, 1972; *The Echoing Green: Memories of Regency and Victorian Youth*, Viking, 1974; *Childhood's Pattern*, Brockhampton, 1975.

Editor: *The Sapphire Treasury of Stories for Boys and Girls*, Gollancz, 1960; *In the Window-Seat: A Selection of Victorian Stories*, Oxford University Press, 1960, Van Nostrand, 1965; (and author of introduction) *Unforgettable Journeys*, Watts, 1965; *School Remembered: An Anthology for Young Adults*, Gollancz, 1967, Funk, 1968; *The Hole in the Wall, and Other Stories*, Oxford University Press, 1968; (and author of introduction) *Gollancz Revivals* (12 volumes of 19th century children's books, reissued) Gollancz, 1967-70, of which *Victorian Doll Stories* was published in America, Schocken, 1969; *Strange and Odd*, Longmans, 1975. Author of introductions to reissues of Victorian children's books, Faith Press.

SIDELIGHTS: "My interest in Victorian children's books originated, when I was fourteen or so, from Mrs. Ewing's *A Flat Iron for a Farthing*. It was one of a bundle of books which we housed for a friend during the Second World War, and after the war, alas, its owner demanded it back. But by this time I was working in London, I had a little spare cash, and I used to wander round the bookshops near Charing Cross road and pick up a few cheap, battered old books, choosing ones that looked as though they might be interesting to read, rather than collectors' items.

GILLIAN AVERY

She was wearing the same rusty clothes that he remembered, and the squashed bonnet on her head, now at a tipsy angle, as though it had slipped there after long months of living in it, day and night. ▪ From *A Likely Lad* by Gillian Avery. Illustrated by Faith Jaques.)

"But it was not until I was married that I acquired much knowledge of Victorian literature, and all I have learned of this I owe to my husband's specialist interest in the period. When I first met him I was living in Oxford and working at the University Press. He was a junior research fellow at Balliol College in the university, and writing a critical study of Trollope's novels. We spent two years in Oxford, and then moved up to Manchester. In a bitter moment of homesickness one cold February day in 1955, I sat down in the study and, looking out at the frozen garden and the heavy gray Manchester skies, began to write about a small girl who wanted to live in Oxford and be a professor of Greek. I made her a Victorian child because I seemed to know more by that time of how children of 1875 felt than I did about 1955 children, and besides, in many ways they resembled me and my contemporaries with our meek acceptance of the power of the adult world more than the post-war generation, with their bounce and assurance. That book, *The Warden's Niece*, was the forerunner of other books about Oxford and the Oxfordshire country, all set in Victorian times. It was an escape from the weeping Manchester skies and the raw fogs, and I would settle down each January to write another.

"Then, in 1964, my husband was appointed to an Oxford lectureship in 19th century studies. We moved back, and I found I no longer wanted to write about the place. Instead I wrote about Manchester, first with dislike in *The Call of the Valley,* where I sent a Victorian Welsh country boy to work there, and then with affection in *A Likely Lad,* for by this time I was remorseful about my lack of appreciation of the city when I lived in it.

"Access to the University—(the Bodleian)—Library broadened my interests. I found myself becoming more and more absorbed by social and local history: Victorian biography, pamphlets, memoirs—anything that threw light on how ordinary people thought and lived in the 19th century. I still kept my interest in children's books of the period, but more for the insight they gave into fashions of upbringing and education. My most recent books, therefore, have been a collection, drawn from memoirs, of episodes from the lives of children during the last century, and a study of how the ideal child in children's fiction has varied between 1770 and 1970."

FOR MORE INFORMATION SEE: New Statesman, November 3, 1967; Young Readers' Review, April, 1968; Best Sellers, April 1, 1968; Books and Bookmen, May, 1968, October, 1970; Book World, June 2, 1968; Library Journal, July, 1968; New Yorker, December 14, 1968; Brian Doyle, The Who's Who of Children's Literature, Schocken, 1968; Horn Book, August, 1971, April, 1972; Authors' Choice, Crowell, 1971; Guardian, March 23, 1972.

BAASTAD, Babbis Friis
See FRIIS-BAASTAD, Babbis

BABBIS, Eleanor
See FRIIS-BAASTAD, Babbis

BAKER, (Mary) Elizabeth (Gillette) 1923-

PERSONAL: Born November 14, 1923, in Rochester, N.Y.; daughter of Charles L. and Ruth (Otis) Gillette; married Morton H. Baker, 1947; children: Margaret, Maria, Stephen. Education: University of Rochester, A.B., 1945. Home: 284 Heath's Bridge Rd., Concord, Mass. 01742.

CAREER: Houghton Mifflin Co., Boston, Mass., advertising department, 1945-48. Now housewife and writer. Louisa May Alcott Memorial Association, member; Concord Antiquarian Society, member. Member: League of Women Voters of Concord. Awards, honors: Weekly Reader fellowship to Bread Loaf Writers' Conference, 1959.

WRITINGS: Tammy Camps Out, 1958, Treasures of Rattlesnake Hill, 1959, Fire in the Wind, 1961, Tammy Climbs Pyramid Mountain, 1962, Tammy Goes Canoeing, 1966, Stronger than Hate, 1969, Tammy Camps in the Rocky Mountains, 1970, This Stranger, My Son, 1971 (all published by Houghton).

SIDELIGHTS: "Breaking the barriers of limitations is in my opinion the chief business of living. I don't mean by this the breaking of the sound and proven laws of the Ten Commandments which have governed and protected civilization for millenia but the hedges which such things as fear, timidity, hate and rebellion put around children and which keep them from adventuring into new paths and enjoying a fuller life and happier relationships. This is the philosophy which I try to express in my writing for children.

"The events in my books usually have strong ties to incidents and situations in our family life. My husband and I and our three children camped, canoed and hiked together for many years when the children were in grade school. We often visited on a family farm in the Berkshire Hills of Massachusetts and were captured by the history of this

ELIZABETH BAKER

12

Something about the Author

once-thriving pocket of the state. We suffered and enjoyed through the teen-age years with our children and we shared with them the turmoil and soul-searching which swept over this country during the height of the civil rights conflicts. Each book has been a distillation of personal experience into what I hope at the same time is a positive, true-to-life and interesting piece of children's fiction.''

HOBBIES AND OTHER INTERESTS: Canoeing, hiking, and tennis.

FOR MORE INFORMATION SEE: Lowell Sunday Sun, Lowell, Mass., April 23, 1961; *Concord Free Press,* Concord, Mass., May 10, 1962.

BARTH, Edna   1914-

PERSONAL: Born March 13, 1914, in Marblehead, Mass.; daughter of Charlton Lyman (a writer) and Elizabeth

EDNA BARTH

"She was beautiful, dressed in white, with soft fiery brown eyes and a mass of auburn hair. . . ." ■ (From *I'm Nobody! Who Are You?* by Edna Barth. Illustrated by Richard Cuffari.)

(Bateman) Smith; married Julius Weiss, August 22, 1938 (divorced, 1966); married George Francis Barth (a writer and lecturer), November 19, 1966; children: (first marriage) Elisabeth Weiss Fein, Peter J., Paul J. *Education:* Radcliffe College, B.A., 1936; Simmons College, B.S. (library science), 1937. *Politics:* Independent. *Religion:* Episcopalian. *Home:* 85 Fourth Ave., New York, N.Y. 10003. *Agent:* Ms. Josephine Rogers, Collins-Knowlton-Wing,

Inc., 60 East 56th St., New York, N.Y. 10022. *Office:* Lothrop, Lee & Shepard Co., 105 Madison Ave., New York, N.Y. 10016.

CAREER: Lothrop, Lee & Shepard Co., New York, N.Y., vice-president and editor-in-chief, 1971—. Associate editor of children's books for Thomas Y. Crowell Co. and McGraw-Hill Book Co. Children's Book Council, member of board of directors. *Member:* Authors' Guild, National Organization of Women, Radcliffe Club of New York.

WRITINGS—For children: *Sally Saucer,* Houghton, 1956; *Truly Elizabeth,* Houghton, 1957; *The Rainbow,* Nelson, 1960; *Lilies, Rabbits, and Painted Eggs,* Seabury, 1970; *The Day Luis Was Lost,* Little, Brown, 1971; *I'm Nobody: Who Are You?–The Story of Emily Dickinson,* Seabury, 1971; *Holly, Reindeer, and Painted Eggs,* Seabury, 1971; *Witches, Pumpkins, and Grinning Ghosts,* Seabury, 1972.

WORK IN PROGRESS: Hearts, Cupids, and Red Roses and *Jack O'Lantern.*

SIDELIGHTS: "Since childhood I had wanted to be an author and/or an editor, but was past forty and the mother of three before realizing either ambition.

"My stories always seem to come from experiences I have had with people within a year or two of the writing. Whether children or adults, they had made a deep impression, and from this impression a story would begin to grow. The settings, too, are always ones I have visited or lived in fairly recently."

FOR MORE INFORMATION SEE: Horn Book, April, 1970, December, 1971, February, 1974; *New York Times Book Review,* October 29, 1972.

BARTHELME, Donald 1931-

PERSONAL: Born April 7, 1931, in Philadelphia, Pa.; son of Donald (an architect) and Helen (Bechtold) Barthelme. *Home:* 113 West 11th St., New York, N.Y. *Agent:* Lynn Nesbit, Josephson Associates, 1271 Avenue of the Americas, New York, N.Y. 10020.

CAREER: Worked as a newspaper reporter and a museum director; was managing editor, *Location,* an art and literature review. Now full-time writer. *Military service:* U.S. Army, served in Korea and Japan. *Awards, honors:* Guggenheim fellowship, 1966; National Book Award, 1972, for *The Slightly Irregular Fire Engine* (also a Children's Book Showcase title); M.D. Zabel Award from the National Institute of Arts and Letters, 1972.

WRITINGS: Come Back, Dr. Caligari (stories), Little, Brown, 1964; *Snow White* (novel; first published in *The New Yorker,* February 18, 1967), Atheneum, 1967; *Unspeakable Practices, Unnatural Acts* (stories), Farrar, Straus, 1968; *City Life* (stories), Farrar, Straus, 1970; *The Slightly Irregular Fire Engine* (children's), Farrar, Straus, 1971; *Sadness* (stories), Farrar, Straus, 1972.

We tell him that if he just tends to his knitting, he'll be all right. So that's what he does, tends to his knitting. ■ (From *The Slightly Irregular Fire Engine* by Donald Barthelme.)

FOR MORE INFORMATION SEE: New York Review of Books, April 30, 1964, August 24, 1967, April 25, 1968; *New Republic,* May 2, 1964, June 3, 1967; *New York Times Book Review,* September 27, 1964, May 21, 1967, May 12, 1968, November 7, 1971, September 3, 1972, December 23, 1973; *Books,* April, 1967; *Book Week,* May 21, 1967; *Newsweek,* May 22, 1967, May 6, 1968; *Time,* May

BURIED JEWELS
Oceanic Dredging Company

26, 1967; *Life,* May 26, 1967; *Kenyon Review,* spring, 1967; *Christian Science Monitor,* June 1, 1967; *Nation,* June 19, 1967; *Hudson Review,* autumn, 1967; *Commonweal,* December 29, 1967, June 21, 1968; *Publishers' Weekly,* March 18, 1968; *New York Times,* April 24, 1968; *New York Times Magazine,* August 16, 1970; *Horn Book,* October, 1972.

DONALD BARTHELME

BATTLES, (Roxy) Edith   1921-

PERSONAL: Born March 29, 1921, in Spokane, Wash.; daughter of Rosco Jiriah (a caterer) and Lucile Zilpha (Jacques) Baker; married Willis Ralph Dawe Battles (a petroleum chemist); children: Margaret Elizabeth, Ralph Willis, Laura Lucile, *Education:* Bakersfield College, A.A., 1940; Long Beach State College (now California State College, Long Beach), B.A., 1959; graduate study at La Verne College, University of Southern California, University of California, Los Angeles, and Pepperdine College. *Home:* 560 South Helberta Ave., Redondo Beach, Calif. 90277. *Office:* Torrance Unified School District, Torrance, Calif.

CAREER: Free-lance writer. Elementary school teacher in Torrance, California, 1959—. Also teaches adult education courses in writing to sell, and has appeared in lecture series on television through Pepperdine University. California Car Bed Co., advertising writer. *Member:* National Education Association, Authors Guild, Southern California Council on Literature for Children and Young People, Southwest Manuscripters, California Teacher's Association, Torrance Education Association.

*WRITINGS—*Juvenile: *Over the Rickety Fence,* with teacher's manual, Fearon, 1967; (illustrated) *The Terrible Trick or Treat,* W. R. Scott, 1970; (illustrated with photographs) *501 Balloons Sail East* (Child Study Association book list), W. R. Scott, 1971; (illustrated) *The Terrible Terrier* (Junior Literary Guild selection), W. R. Scott, 1972; *One to Teeter-Totter*, A. Whitman, 1973; *Where Are the Elephants, Eddie?*, A. Whitman, 1974. Author of column appearing in *Manhattan Tide*. Contributor of humor, research articles, photographs, reviews, short stories, and verse to magazines and newspapers, including *Saturday Evening Post, New York Times, Highlights for Children, American Girl, Westways, Outdoor World, Reader's Digest,* and education and religious journals.

SIDELIGHTS: "I was a depression child nurtured on comic books and public libraries. A book of my own was a rare and treasured thing. My first *own* book was a paperback excerpt of the 'Pooh' stories which I was much too serious to find the least bit funny.

"I read library books with a balanced appetite, loving Grimm and Twain and any book at all about boarding schools. I felt it would be very nice to abandon my life as a middle child of seven and become the most popular girl at the boarding school. There I would star at all the games I was notably bad at. No one there would dare to choose me last or—worse—offer me to the other team as a kind of negative bonus. (As a fifth-grade teacher, I find my heart going out to these non-athletic bookworms who more and more infrequently people my class. The bookworms aren't diminishing, but their game skills are picking up.)

EDITH BATTLES

"I knew at age five I would be a writer. I had learned to read, and *somebody* wrote those words. So I wrote a poem:
> Poppies are sweet.
> They grow down by my feet.
My unimaginative first grade teacher wanted to edit it by omitting 'down by' and inserting 'at' but I insisted my way was better. In my maturer years I have let the editor do what she wants.

"I became a selling writer when I had to look busy at a desk job. The typewriter was handy for short spurts, so I typed a lifetime accumulation of light verse and began peddling it. I moved into magazine articles and fiction by degrees, then shelved the whole avocation to complete teacher training. For the first few teaching years I was using all my creativity on middle-graders, but I sold a few minor things when I had holiday time to write.

"The children in my classes are encouraged to do a lot of creative writing, and I used to give myself the same assignment. My second book came out of a class assignment—'When I got home on Halloween night, I looked in my trick-or-treat bag and found. . . .' *The Terrible Trick or Treat* was my own contribution to a very funny collection of treats. The fact that there was a *real* Christopher to an almost-real story was incidental.

"*The Terrible Terrier* combined my real Christopher and a pair of dogs from my own childhood. It is a funny book, I think, but it does just the opposite of what I intended. I wanted the very young reader to enjoy the naughty dog vicariously; instead, the very little children take it with the same grim seriousness that I took Pooh. Older children have agreeable hysterics over it, but it scares the blue blazes out of their little brothers.

"A very rewarding memory lives for me in *501 Balloons Sail East,* for all five hundred children in my school helped me in the balloon lift and posed for the pictures. They were featured later on a *Weekly Reader* cover for their efforts and the book was widely reviewed, even getting two columns in *Scientific American!* The school closed its doors to children in 1973 and became an adult center, so our little book is one of the lasting records of our days together there.

"Work habits? Sometimes I write on weekends and sometimes only during vacations and sometimes not at all. I become sporadic, reform and go great guns, and then slow to a stall. Since I have been teaching writing to adults, I urge them to set me a good example. Indeed they have done so. Like my younger students (who average twenty stories during the school year) my adult students are prolific. I have god-mothered some very good books and the entire spectrum of ephemeral material.

"Writing takes space. Teaching takes space. My husband's hobbies take space. Our keeshond dog takes space. A house that was once full of children (not *seven*, of course!) is much too small for all that must now fit inside. Our flower beds have more grass and our lawns have more weeds than those of the neighbors from orthodox homes. For *time*, too, is as precious as space. (And, truthfully, I

The door opened. Christopher said, "A big trick or . . ." ■ (From *The Terrible Trick or Treat* by Edith Battles. Illustrated by Tom Funk.)

am as good at housekeeping chores as I once was at fifth grade games). So the domestic frills are lacking. Most good ambitions require a sacrifice of other ambitions. I'd *like* to be a superlative homemaker just as I once would have been the most popular girl at a boarding school. But I like to be a writer even more.

"My neighbors may frown at the fine crop of gazania infiltrating the parkway grass, but *they* don't know the satisfactions that override my own distress. They haven't any young readers who write to say they liked a story that I wrote instead of weeding the yard.

"Weeds can wait."

FOR MORE INFORMATION SEE: Junior Literary Guild Catalogue, March, 1972.

BAUDOUY, Michel-Aime 1909-

PERSONAL: Surname pronounced "Bo-Doo-EE"; born April 1, 1909, in Le Vernet, Ariege, France; children: three. *Education:* Studied at Ecole Normale Superieure de l'Enseignement Technique in Paris, University of Toulouse, and Sorbonne, University of Paris. *Religion:* Roman Catholic. *Home:* 15 Rue Cave, Levallois-Perret, Seine, France.

MICHEL-AIME BAUDOUY

Frost had come, hard and sudden, seizing the earth, freezing the grass, stripping the trees of their brilliant autumn color. ▪ (From *Old One-Toe* by Michel-Aime Baudouy. Illustrated by Johannes Troyer.)

CAREER: Novelist and writer for young people; professor of literature at Lycee Raspail, Paris, France. *Member:* Societe des Gens de Lettres, Societe des Auteurs et Compositeurs Dramatiques. *Awards, honors:* Prix de la Tribune de Paris, 1953, for children's literature; Prix Enfance du Monde, 1957; Prize, 1957, for play, "Pitie pour le Heros"; Prix de la Societe des Auteurs et Compositeurs Dramatiques, 1958; Honor Book award, Hans Christian Andersen International Children's Book Medals awards, 1960.

WRITINGS—Adult: *Nous n'etions que des hommes* (stories), Editions Stock, 1946; *Tandis que les peres* (novel), Calmann-Levy, 1948; *Le Ciel est bleu* (novel), Calmann-Levy, 1954; *La Quadrille Sarda* (novel), Plon, 1957; *J'ai vu naitre le France,* Editions du Temps, 1961; *Civilisation contemporaine: Aspects et problemes,* A. Hatier, 1965; *Europe, mon pays,* Editions de l'Amitie, 1967.

Youth books: *L'Enfant aux aigles,* translation by Audrey Clark published in England as *Noel and the Eagles,* Dent, 1955; *Bruno, roi de la montagne,* Editions de l'Amitie, 1953, translation by Marie Ponsot published as *Bruno, King of the Mountain,* Harcourt, 1960 (published in England as *Bruno, King of the Wild,* Bodley Head, 1962); *Les Vagabonds de la Marisma,* Editions de l'Amitie, 1955, translation by Gerard Hopkins published in England as *The Children of the Marshes,* Bodley Head, 1958, and in America under same title, Pantheon, 1959; *Les Princes du vent,* Rageot, 1956; *Le Seigneur des Hautes-Buttes,* Editions de l'Amitie, 1957, translation by Marie Ponsot published as *Old One-Toe,* Harcourt, 1959; *Mick et la P. 105,* Editions de l'Amitie, 1959, translation by Marie Ponsot published as *More than Courage,* Harcourt, 1961 (published in England as *Mick and the P. 105,* Bodley Head, 1961); *Le Chant de la voile,* Editions de l'Amitie, 1960; *Flashes sur le France,* Editions de l'Amitie, 1961, translation by Fanny Louise Neago published as *Deception at St.-Nazaire,* Harcourt, 1963 (published in England as *Tom and the S.S. France,* Bodley Head, 1964); *Mystere a Carnac,* Editions de l'Amitie, 1962, translation by Anne Carter published as *Secret of the Hidden Painting,* Harcourt, 1965; *Le "Onze" de mon village,* Editions de l'Amitie, 1963; *Zabo,* La Bacconniere, 1966; *Le Garcon du barrage,* translation by Thelma Niklaus published as *The Boy Who Belonged to No One,* Harcourt, 1967 (published in England as *The Boy on the Dam,* Brockhampton Press, 1970).

Plays: "Pitie pour le Heroes," first performed in Paris at Comedie de Paris, 1957. Also author of four plays produced on French radio and television.

SIDELIGHTS: Baudouy wrote *L'Enfant aux aigles* while a prisoner of war in Germany in 1942. His books, translated into many languages, have brought him letters from young readers all over the world; he says that he has corresponded with a number of them.

FOR MORE INFORMATION SEE: Third Book of Junior Authors, edited by de Montreville and Hill, H. W. Wilson, 1972.

BELL, Gina
See IANNONE, Jeanne

BELL-ZANO, Gina
See IANNONE, Jeanne

BELVEDERE, Lee
See GRAYLAND, Valerie

BERRIEN, Edith Heal
See HEAL, Edith

BERRY, B. J.
See BERRY, Barbara J.

BERRY, Barbara J. 1937-
(B. J. Berry)

PERSONAL: Born February 17, 1937, in Westfield, N.Y.; married Warren J. Berry (a purchasing agent), July 13, 1957. *Education:* Jamestown Community College, A.A., 1957. *Address:* Box 231, Ashville, N.Y.

CAREER: Journal Press, Inc., Jamestown, N.Y., proof reader, 1958-61. *Member:* Authors Guild.

BARBARA J. BERRY

WRITINGS—Youth books: *Shannon* (fiction), Follett, 1968; (under name B.J. Berry) *Just Don't Bug Me* (fiction), Follett, 1971; *Let 'er Buck! The Rodeo* (nonfiction), Bobbs, 1971; *A Look of Eagles* (fiction), Bobbs, 1973; *The Thoroughbreds* (nonfiction), Bobbs, 1974. Contributor of dog stories and nonfiction to *Sports Afield.*

WORK IN PROGRESS: Research for a book on Saddlebred horses.

SIDELIGHTS: "I grew up the only child in a farming neighborhood, thus early becoming a reader and a 'pretender,' which I suppose is what most writers are to start with. And in my lone condition I came to love animals as well as books, these two constituting my friends. Horses, especially, and the dream of owning one in particular, became an obsession—not unusual in young girls. Moreover, I think the fact that for various good and sufficient reasons (but to me, of course, unacceptable!), I could not realize my dream, led me eventually to write about horses. Perhaps had I realized my dream I would have felt no need to write, later. I'm sure this helps me to identify with my readers, most of whom share this desire. (I don't consciously concern myself with the reader identifying with my characters—if I can identify, first, I feel that the rest will follow.) I really just write the kind of thing that I would have liked to read at that age.

"But I was 'that age' quite a while ago, which sometimes makes me wonder about the future, if any, of the plain old 'horse story,' and the related question, Do children as a rule get the books *they* want to read?

"I think it's fine that children (say, 10 to 14) are now being offered books that concern themselves with such 'real' things as drug addicts, abortion, their legal rights, and so forth. But sometimes I worry that in the rush to out-do one another in being 'with it,' publishers might eliminate the horse story kind of book altogether. And that the adults involved in buying and popularizing children's books—the librarians, reviewers, etc.—might overlook or misunderstand or disregard what the children really want. That more and more book manuscripts might be returned, as one of mine once was, with the chilling comment, 'The kids would *love* this, but . . .' I forget, now, what the 'But' was, but no matter. If the kids would love it, why not print it? (Somebody eventually did, but the chill remains!) And, most alarming to me of all, what if, in order to get published, writers give in and write for librarians, reviewers, etc., instead of for the kids? Write a book about a drug addict, say, when they would *rather* write a 'horse story?'

"But, thank goodness, children do still have some say in the matter. And after many hours spent visiting fifth and sixth grades and talking with the kids, I'm convinced that as far as they are concerned, anyway, the horse story is still very much acceptable. I think they do like some variety, some 'new things.' But after being enlightened about the problems involved in abortion and so on, I believe that they appreciate going back to the more familiar and less frightening, too. As an example from my own books, *Shannon*, is strictly a horse story—emotionally involving, 'sentimental,' happy ending and all. The other two novels, while horses are important in them, are really 'boy stories'—'problem books'—and though the endings are hopeful, they are not 'happy.' *Shannon*, I find, is by far the favorite among the groups I've talked with.

"In short, I'm all for realism in children's books, as long as it *is* real—and as long as, therefore, a realistic mix is available to the kids . . . 'good news' as *well* as bad news.'"

FOR MORE INFORMATION SEE: New York Times Book Review, May 2, 1971.

DONALD BISSET,
in BBC2's "Rural Rides," 1972

BISSET, Donald 1910-

PERSONAL: Born August 30, 1910, in London, England; divorced; children: one son. *Education:* "Negligible". *Home:* 33 Andrewes House, Barbican, London EC2Y 8AB, England. *Agent:* A.M. Heath & Co. Ltd., 40-42 William IV St., London WC2N4DD, England.

CAREER: Actor; appeared with the National Theatre and Royal Shakespeare Theatre companies, and in the television film, "Henry VIII," in New York, 1971, later that year played in "The Great Waltz" at Drury Lane Theatre, London. Writer of children's books. *Military service:* British Army, 1940-46; became lieutenant.

WRITINGS: Anytime Stories, Faber, 1954, Transatlantic, 1955; *Sometime Stories,* Methuen, 1957; *Next Time Stories,* Methuen, 1959; *This Time Stories,* Methuen, 1961; *Another Time Stories,* Methuen, 1963; *Little Bear's Pony,* Benn, 1966; *Hello Lucy,* Benn, 1967; *Talks with a Tiger,* Methuen, 1967; *Kangaroo Tennis,* Benn, 1968; *Nothing,* Benn, 1969; *Upside Down Hand,* Progress Publishing House (Moscow), 1969; *Time and Again Stories,* Methuen,

1970; *Benjie the Circus Dog,* Benn, 1970; *Barcha the Tiger,* Benn, 1971; *Tiger Wants More,* Methuen, 1971; *Yak and the Sea Shell,* Methuen, 1971; *Yak and the Painted Cave,* Methuen, 1971; *Yak Goes Home,* Methuen, 1971; *Father Tingtang's Journey,* Methuen, 1973; *The Happy Horse,* Benn, 1974; *The Story of Mandy Duck,* Methuen, 1974; *The Story of Smokey the Horse,* Methuen, 1975; *Baby Crow Learns to Fly,* Benn, 1975; *"Oh Dear!" Said Tiger,* Methuen, 1975. Writer of television serial, "Yak," produced in color cartoons, 1971.

WORK IN PROGRESS: Sound Cassettes and video cassettes of his stories.

SIDELIGHTS: Bisset's books have been translated into sixteen European languages.

HOBBIES AND OTHER INTERESTS: Horseback riding.

FOR MORE INFORMATION SEE: Times Literary Supplement, April 16, 1970.

BOGGS, Ralph Steele 1901-

PERSONAL: Born November 17, 1901, in Terre Haute, Ind.; son of Harry and Edna Earl (Patterson) Boggs; married Marian Wells, 1929 (divorced 1948); married Edna Garrido, June 24, 1948; children: (first marriage) Ralph Karl. *Education:* University of Chicago, Ph.B., 1926, Ph.D., 1930. *Religion:* Baptist. *Home:* 536 Altara Ave., Coral Gables, Fla. 33146.

CAREER: University of Puerto Rico, Rio Piedras, instructor in English, 1926-28; University of North Carolina, Chapel Hill, began as assistant professor, became associate professor and professor of Spanish and folklore, 1929-50; University of Miami, Coral Gables, Fla., visiting professor, 1948-49, professor of Spanish and folklore, 1950-67, professor emeritus, 1967—Visiting professor, University of Santo Domingo, 1944, National University of Mexico, 1945-46, University of New Mexico, 1948, University of California, Los Angeles, 1963, University of California, Berkeley, 1970. *Member:* Sociedad Folklorica de Mexico (founding), American Folklore Society (fellow), Phi Beta Kappa. *Awards, honors:* Medalha Sylvio Romero from Brazil

WRITINGS: (With N. B. Adams) *Spanish Folktales,* F. S. Crofts & Co., 1932; (with Carlos Castillo) *Leyendas epicas de Espana,* Heath, 1935; (with Mary Gould Davis) *Three Golden Oranges and Other Spanish Folktales,* Longmans, Green, 1936; *An Outline History of Spanish Literature,*

As the gypsy bent over to fill her pitcher at the fountain she saw the face of the girl reflected in the water, and jealousy of the the beauty of that face filled her. ■ (From *Three Golden Oranges* by R. S. Boggs and M. G. Davis. Illustrated by Emma Brock.)

Heath, 1937; *Bibliography of Latin American Folklore,* Wilson, for Inter-American Bibliographical and Library Association, 1940; *Bosquejo historico de la literatura espanola,* Editorial Independence (Uruguay), 1945.

Spanish Pronunciation Exercises, Latin American Institute Press, 1954; (with R. J. Dixson) *English Step by Step with Pictures,* Latin American Institute Press, 1956, revised, 1971; (with Dixson) *Sound Teaching: A Laboratory Manual of American English,* Regents Publishing Co., 1959; (with M. A. Jagendorf) *The King of the Mountains; A Treasury of Latin American Folk Stories,* Vanguard, 1960; (with J. I. Andujar) *Sound Teaching: A Laboratory Manual of Everyday Spanish,* Regents Publishing Co., 1961; *Spanish Word Builder: 2000 Basic Spanish Words to Increase Your Vocabulary,* Latin American Institute Press, 1963; *Basic Spànish Pronuniciation,* Simon & Schuster, 1970.

Contributor: *The Biography of a Spanish and Folklore Bibliography,* Wilson, for Inter-American Bibliographical and Library Association, 1938; *Folklore Library Resources of the University of North Carolina,* edited by Charles E. Rush, University of North Carolina Press, 1945; *Homenjae a don Luis de Hoyos Sainz,* [Madrid], 1949; *Mark the Boat; Romance Studies presented to William Morton Dey,* University of North Carolina Press, 1950; *The Caribbean: Contemporary Trends,* edited by A. Curtis Wilgus, University of Florida Press, 1953; (author of foreword) Aurora Lucero White, *Literary Folklore of the Hispanic Southwest,* Naylor, 1953; *Homenje a Fritz Kruger,* Universidad

RALPH STEELE BOGGS

nacional de Cuyo, 1954; *Responsible Freedom in the Americas,* edited by Angel del Rio, Doubleday, 1955; *Miscelanea de estudios dedicados a Fernando Oritz,* [Havana], 1956; *Humaniora: Essays in Literature, Folklore, Bibliography, Honoring Archer Taylor,* 1960; *Estudos e ensaios folcloricos em homenagem a Renato Almeida,* [Rio de Janeiro], 1960.

Booklets and bulletins: *Practical Phonetics of the American Language,* University of Puerto Rico Press, 1927; *Folklore: An Outline for Individual and Group Study,* University of North Carolina Press, 1929; *The Halfchick Tale in Spain and France,* Academia Scientiarum Fennica (Finland), 1933.

American collaborator, *Volkskundliche Bibliographie,* volumes for years 1925-26, 1927, 1928, 1929-30, 1931-32, 1933-34, Walter de Gruyter, 1935-39. Also contributor: *Handwoerterbuch des deutschen Marchens,* Volume II, Walter de Gruyter, 1935; "Handbook of Latin American Studies" series, Harvard University Press, 1936-48; *Encyclopedia of Literature,* Philosophical Library, 1946; *Funk and Wagnalls Standard Dictionary of Folklore, Mythology, and Legend,* Funk, 1950; contributor to published reports, proceedings, and yearbooks.

Compiler of annual folklore bibliography for *Southern Folklore Quarterly,* 1937-58. Contributor of more than one hundred articles and reviews to folklore and literary journals in Latin America and in United States. Editor and director of *Folklore Americas,* 1940-65.

SIDELIGHTS: Speaks Spanish, reads Portuguese, French, Italian, and German.

FOR MORE INFORMATION SEE: Folklore Americas, December, 1951; *Orlando Sentinel,* Orlando, Fla., March 11, 1962.

BOLLIGER, Max   1929-

PERSONAL: Born April 23, 1929, in Glarus, Switzerland; son of Jacques and Maria Regula (Durst) Bolliger. *Education:* Studied in Switzerland at progymnasium, 1943-46,

MAX BOLLIGER

He ran after the lion, grabbed it and snatched back the bleating lamb. David was not afraid. ■ (From *David* by Max Bolliger. Illustrated by Edith Schindler.)

Seminar Wettingen, 1946-51, and University of Zurich, 1958-61; also studied in London, England, 1956. *Home:* Bergstrasse 157, 8032, Zurich, Switzerland.

CAREER: Teacher in Kallern, Switzerland, 1951-54, Meisterschwanden, Switzerland, 1954-56, and in Luxembourg, 1957; school psychologist in Adliswil, Zurich, Switzerland, 1961—. *Awards, honors:* National German Children's Book Award for *David,* 1966; *Noah and the Rainbow* was a Children's Book Showcase Title, 1973.

WRITINGS: Verwundbare Kindheit (stories), Tschudy, 1957; *Ausgeschickte Taube* (poems), Eirene Verlag, 1958; *Knirps* (picture book), Comenius Verlag, 1963; *David* (juvenile), Otto Maier Verlag, 1965 (English translation published under same title, Delacorte, 1967); *Joseph,* Otto Maier Verlag, 1967, translation by Marion Koenig published under same title, Delacorte, 1969; *Daniel* (juvenile), Otto Maier Verlag, 1968, Dell, 1970; *Marios Trompete,* Otto Maier Verlag, 1968; *Fireflies* (juvenile), Atheneum, 1970; *Golden Apple* (juvenile), Atheneum, 1970; *Der Regenbogen,* Artemis, 1972, translation by Clyde Robert Bulla published as *Noah and the Rainbow,* Crowell, 1973. Author of several scripts for Swiss television.

FOR MORE INFORMATION SEE: HORN BOOK, February, 1971, February, 1973.

BONHAM, Barbara (Thomas)   1926-

PERSONAL: Born September 27, 1926, in Franklin, Neb.; daughter of Laroy Oscar and Ethel (Dependehner) Thomas; married Max Bonham (now a grain-elevator operator), December 24, 1950. *Education:* University of Nebraska, student, one year. *Politics:* Independent. *Religion:* Agnostic. *Home:* Naponee, Neb. 68960. *Agent:* Scott Meredith Literary Agency, Inc., 580 Fifth Ave., New York, N.Y. 10036.

BARBARA BONHAM

CAREER: Writer. *Member:* Franklin County Historical Society.

WRITINGS: *Diagnosis: Love,* Monarch, 1964; *Challenge of the Prairies* (juvenile), Bobbs, 1965; *Army Nurse,* Bouregy, 1965; *Nina Stuart, R.N.,* Bouregy, 1966; *Crisis at Fort Laramie* (juvenile), Duell, 1967; *To Secure the Blessings of Liberty* (juvenile), Hawthorn, 1970; *Willa Cather* (juvenile), Chilton, 1970; *Heroes of the Wild West* (juvenile), Whitman, 1970. Editor of Franklin County Historical Society's county history, 1966.

BOONE, Pat 1934-

PERSONAL: Real name Charles Eugene Boone; born June 1, 1934, in Jacksonville, Fla; son of Archie A. (a building contractor) and Margaret (a registered nurse; maiden name, Pritchard) Boone; married Shirley Foley, 1953; children: Cheryl Lynn, Linda Lee, Deborah Ann, Laura Gene. *Education:* Attended David Lipscomb College, one year, and North Texas State College, one year; Columbia University, B.S. (magna cum laude), 1958. *Religion:* Independent—"Church on the Way." *Home:* Beverly Hills, Calif. *Office:* 9255 Sunset Blvd., Los Angeles, Calif. 90060.

CAREER: First sang in public at local amateur shows, and went on to compete nationally on Ted Mack Amateur Hour and Arthur Godfrey Talent Scout Show. Signed to contract with Dot Records, 1954, while college student in Denton, Tex., and disc jockey and singer for radio station on side. After initial recordings, signed to film contract with 20th Century-Fox, 1956, and to television series by American Broadcasting Co. The weekly television program, "Pat Boone Chevy Showroom," was switched in 1959 to a series of specials. Has appeared in seven films since 1957, including "All Hands on Deck," 1961, "State Fair," 1962, and "The Main Attraction," 1963. Cooga Mooga, Inc., and Cooga Mooga Film Productions Corp., Beverly Hills, Calif., president. Northeastern Institute for Christian Education, member of board of directors. *Awards, honors:* Variety Clubs of America award, 1956, as "personality of the year"; U.S. Junior Chamber of Commerce award, 1958, as "one of ten outstanding young men"; Catholic Youth Organization Celebrity award for edifying influence on the youth of America in the field of entertainment; Brotherhood Award of National Association of Christians and Jews, 1961.

WRITINGS: *'Twixt Twelve and Twenty,* Prentice-Hall, 1958; *Between You, Me and the Gatepost,* Prentice-Hall, 1960; *The Real Christmas,* Fleming Revel, 1961; *A New Song* (autobiographical), Creation House, 1969; *Joy.* Series of monthly articles in *Ladies' Home Journal,* 1959.

SIDELIGHTS: A descendent of Daniel Boone, Pat Boone was born in Jacksonville, Florida in 1934 and is one of four children. Harmony was the natural trend between he and his brother Nick. Local amateur shows and a stint as the master of ceremonies for a highschool talent revue on radio eventually led to honors on the Ted Mack Amateur Hour and subsequently the Arthur Godfrey Talent Scout Show.

In the fall of 1954, Randy Wood, founder and president of Dot Records signed him to an exclusive contract. Six months later he went to Chicago to record, "Two Hearts, Two Kisses." This single, which was an immediate success, was followed by his first million seller, "Ain't That A Shame." Subsequent hits were "I Almost Lost My Mind," "Friendly Persuasion", "Don't Forbid Me", and a list of others.

At the time of his initial recording debut with "Two Hearts", he and his wife Shirley (daughter of radio and television recording artist, Red Foley) were residing in Denton, Texas, where he attended North Texas State College. He was also working at Fort Worth's WBAP-TV as a singer with a $44.50 weekly paycheck.

The Boones met while both were highschool students at David Lipscomb High School in Nashville. They began courting while both were active in chorus, dramatics and student council activities. Boone's popularity and excellent scholastics led to his election as student body president: a similar happening for Shirley, as she was elected secretary. Boone was, and is, an excellent scholar-athlete and was a four-letter man as well as captain of his baseball team. He was a cartoonist and reporter for his high school newspaper.

He and Shirley were married during his initial year at David Lipscomb College. Soon they relocated to Denton

PAT BOONE

where the following year the first of their four daughters was born. Although his success was meteoric, Boone's desire for learning was fulfilled in 1958 when he graduated Magna Cum Laude from Columbia University in speech and English. By this time the Boones were the proud parents to four girls. He considers his wife Shirley greatly responsible for encouraging him to reach this educational milestone which he still considers his greatest achievement. "My parents always stressed the importance of education to us. They often told me education is a great blessing, something that can never be lost or stolen."

In 1956, he signed a million dollar contract with 20th-Century Fox and starred in fifteen motion pictures which included "Bernadine," "April Love," "All Hands On Deck," "Mardi Gras," "Yellow Canary," and "Journey To The Center Of The Earth."

The same year, 1956, The American Broadcasting Co. signed him to his first television series, "The Pat Boone Chevy Showroom," produced by his TV production company, Cooga Mooga, Inc., making him the youngest performer on television with his own network show. On his subsequent NBC morning show, he played host to some of the top guest personalities in the industry. This half hour series was followed with a daily 90-minute syndicated segment for Filmways. Seen prime time in most major markets across the country, it too was in association with Cooga Mooga, Inc.

His acting credits are numerous; the most recent one being that of an embattled school teacher in the starring role of an "Owen Marshall" episode which aired in late 1973. Boone has also been a guest star in virtually every major variety show and musical special.

Another dimension to his career is his role as a writer. His first book *Twixt Twelve and Twenty,* a guide to teenagers, has sold more than 800,000 copies and all royalties have gone to the Northeastern Institute of Christian Education. *A New Song* has gone beyond the one-million mark and has been published in five different languages.

Following a tour of Japan, in which the distaff side of the Boone's was included, it was felt that a union of *all* the Boone's was not only very entertaining but would be extremely successful. In 1971, the Boone family recorded their first family album on the Word label. It was subsequently nominated for a Grammy. The Boone Family has continued to actively perform in the concert circuit. Boone likes to draw and take home movies, and is addicted to sports cars, steam baths, and steaks. His dislikes include his earlier records.

BOWEN, Catherine Drinker   1897-1973

PERSONAL: Born January 1, 1897, in Haverford, Pa.; daughter of Henry Sturgis and Aimee Ernesta (Beaux) Drinker; married Ezra Bowen, 1919; married second husband, T. McKean Downs, July 1, 1939 (deceased); children: (first marriage) Ezra, Catherine Drinker Bowen Prince. *Education:* Studied at Peabody Institute, Juilliard School of Music. *Home:* 260 Booth Lane, Haverford, Pa.

CAREER: Writer; lecturer. *Member:* Royal Society of Literature (fellow), American Philosophical Society (fellow), Phi Beta Kappa. *Awards, honors:* National Book Award in non-fiction, 1958, for *The Lion and the Throne;* Constance Lindsay Skinner Award from the Women's National Book Association, 1962; honorary Litt.D. from Dickinson College, University of Rochester, University of North Carolina, Russell Sage College, Temple University, Northeastern University.

WRITINGS: The Story of the Oak Tree, Chemical Publishing Co., 1924; *A History of Lehigh University,* Lehigh Alumni Bulletin, 1924; *Rufus Starbuck's Wife,* Putnam, 1932; *Friends and Fiddlers,* Little, Brown, 1935; (with Barbara von Meck) *Beloved Friend: The Story of Tchaikowsky and Nadejda von Meck* (Book-of-the-Month Club selection), Random House, 1937; *Free Artist: The Story of Anton and Nicholas Rubinstein,* Random House, 1939; *Yankee from Olympus: Justice Holmes and His Family* (Book-of-the-Month Club selection), Atlantic-Little, Brown, 1944, educational edition, Globe, 1956; *John Adams and the American Revolution* (Book-of-the-Month Club selection), Atlantic-Little, Brown, 1950; *The Lion and the Throne: The Life and Times of Sir Edward Coke* (Book-of-the-Month Club selection), Little, Brown, 1957;

Adventures of a Biographer, Little, Brown, 1959; *The Historian* (Bernard De Voto), Houghton, 1963; *Francis Bacon*, Little, Brown, 1963; *Miracle at Philadelphia: The Story of the Constitutional Convention, May to September, 1787* (Book-of-the-Month Club selection), Little, Brown, 1966. Booklets and published addresses include *The Writing of Biography*, Writer, 1951; *The Biographer Looks for News*, 1958, and *The Nature of the Artist*, 1961, both published by Scripps College Press.

SIDELIGHTS: "Whenever I do one of these books I'm always terrified of what the scholars are going to say. . . . I'm not a scholar at all you know. I've really no business messing around with this stuff." The continual debate between scholars and professional writers has fostered divergent opinions concerning the value of Mrs. Bowen's works. Henry Steele Commager, historian, said of *Yankee From Olympus*, a biography of Oliver Wendell Holmes, Jr.: "If Holmes had had his choice, we may well believe that it is rather by this portrait that he would prefer to be known. . . . It is a beautiful piece of workmanship, each piece fitted perfectly into the whole, no exaggeration, no straining for effect, not too much sentiment. Mrs. Bowen has not thought it essential to tell everything; something is left to the reader's imagination."

While she was working on the John Adams book, Mrs. Bowen attended a conference of historians, and, in *Adventurers of a Biographer*, she wrote of this confrontation with the "academicians": "From their platforms the scholars were forever taking shots at biography. 'The dangers of the

biographical approach,' they said. I knew what they meant, of course. Biography is written from a point of view; the writer likes his hero or dislikes him. Moreover, biography is filled with personal detail, those 'particulars' to which the historian does not 'descend' without apology. To the professional historian, biography has for centuries been tainted. . . . Bias, point of view, fury—are they then so dangerous and must they be ironed out of history, the hills flattened and the contours leveled? The professors talked about passion and point of view in history as a Calvinist talks about sin in the bedroom. There they sat, trying to get the heat out of history and here I sat, trying to get it in. There must surely be a balance between us somewhere, a place for us to meet.

"Biased history is of course the worst of sins. What I asked for, what I missed in academic history was not a bias toward events or nations but a point of view toward life, some hint that the writer belonged to the human race and had himself experienced passion, grief or disappointment. . . . There are ways to come at history. . . . Let us say the professors come at it from the northeast and I from the southwest. Either way will serve, provided the wind blows clean and the fog lifts."

Concerned with her romantic approach to history, she wrote to Bernard De Voto. He answered, in part: "The simplest truth you can ever write about our history will be charged and surcharged with romanticism, and if you are afraid of the word you had better start practicing seriously on your fiddle."

Mrs. Bowen's earlier musical aspirations, and the ability to play the "fiddle," resulted in her first three books which concerned either music or musicians. She enjoyed playing in string quartets and skiing and skating.

FOR MORE INFORMATION SEE: New Yorker, April 22, 1944; *Weekly Book Review*, April 23, 1944; *New Republic*, May 29, 1944; *Saturday Review*, June 17, 1950; *New York Times Book Review*, July 2, 1950, March 10, 1957; *New York Herald Tribune Book Review*, July 9, 1950; *Publishers' Weekly*, March 5, 1962, November 12, 1973; *Washington Post*, November 6, 1973; *Time*, November 12, 1973; *Newsweek*, November 12, 1973; *Variety*, November 14, 1973.

(Died November 1, 1973)

BRINDEL, June (Rachuy) 1919-

PERSONAL: Born June 5, 1919, on a farm near Little Rock, Iowa; daughter of Otto (a farmer) and Mina (Balster) Rachuy; married Bernard Brindel (a composer and teacher of music), 1939; children: Paul, Jill. *Education:* University of Chicago, B.A., 1945, M.A., 1958. *Politics:* "Radical reform." *Religion:* Humanist. *Home:* 2740 Lincoln Lane, Wilmette, Ill. 60091.

CAREER: Early work ranged from dime store clerk to secretary to a poet laureate, and included factory and office jobs and free-lance writing; Chicago City College, Wright Campus, Chicago, Ill., associate professor of English, 1958—. Teacher of creative drama and children's theater at National Music Camp, Interlochen, Mich., summers, 1958-67. *Member:* College English Association, National

CATHERINE DRINKER BOWEN

25

Council of Teachers of English, Phi Beta Kappa. *Awards, honors:* First prize for play, "Automation, King of Machines," Wilmette Children's Theater, 1971.

WRITINGS: "Automation, King of Machines," (children's play), first produced at National Music Camp, Interlochen, Mich., 1967; *Luap* (Junior Literary Guild selection), Bobbs, 1971. Collaborator with husband on songs and a recording for children. Contributor of poems and stories to *Carolina Quarterly, Perspective, Beloit Poetry Journal, Discourse,* and other literary magazines.

WORK IN PROGRESS: An adult novel; stories for adults and children; a collection of poems.

SIDELIGHTS: "Love travel, home and abroad. [Have] compulsion to verbalize experience, inability to stop writing. Find people-studying fascinating though sometimes horrifying and usually absurd. Kids are wisest."

"Look at him standing on his feet!" someone shouted. "How does he do it?" ■ (From *Luap* by June Rachuy Brindel. Illustrated by Jan Pyk.)

26

JUNE RACHUY BRINDEL

BROCK, Betty   1923-

PERSONAL: Born August 31, 1923, in Biltmore, N.C.; daughter of Aleck R. and Kathleen (Lipe) Carter; married Clarence C. Brock (a captain in the U.S. Navy), June 9, 1943; children: Leslie Elizabeth, Alison Carter. *Education:* University of North Carolina at Greensboro, student, 1941-42; George Washington University, Junior College Diploma, 1943. *Religion:* Episcopalian. *Home:* Potomac Ct., Alexandria, Va. 22314.

MEMBER: Children's Book Guild of Washington, D.C., Pi Beta Phi.

WRITINGS: No Flying in the House (juvenile), Harper, 1970; *The Shades,* Harper, 1971.

WORK IN PROGRESS: A fantasy.

SIDELIGHTS: "When my own children were almost grown, I realized that we shared a fondness for children's literature, especially fantasy. Writing had been a hobby since childhood, and though my first attempt to write a fantasy for children was unsuccessful, I enjoyed the experience so much I started *No Flying in the House.*

"The setting for *No Flying in the House* is an old villa on the water which we rented one year in Rhode Island. The setting for *The Shades* is imaginary, inspired by homes, circa 1850, which I visited in Newport, Rhode Island on a house tour. My own happy childhood in western North Carolina, growing up in a home where love of flowers and nature and belief in fairies were taken for granted, my fondness for New England where much of my adult life was spent, and my interest in art, antiques, gardens, and travel have influenced my writing."

FOR MORE INFORMATION SEE: New York Times Book Review, August 16, 1970, November 7, 1971; *Horn Book,* February, 1972.

BETTY BROCK

Gloria was waiting on Beatrice Cox's front steps when she and Annabel got off the school bus. ■ (From *No Flying in the House* by Betty Brock. Illustrated by Wallace Tripp.)

BROOKS, Lester 1924-

PERSONAL: Born November 8, 1924, in Des Moines, Iowa; son of Lester James (a regional manager for Prudential Insurance) and Dorothy (Boldrick) Brooks; married Patricia Kersten (a writer), September 10, 1950; children: James, Jonathan, Christopher. *Education:* University of Iowa, A.B., 1948; Columbia University, A.M., 1949; University of London, further graduate study, 1949. *Politics:* Democrat. *Home:* 43 Marshall Ridge Rd., New Canaan, Conn. 06840. *Agent:* Paul R. Reynolds, Inc., 599 Fifth Ave., New York, N.Y. 10017.

CAREER: National Urban League, New York, N.Y., assistant public relations director, 1950-51; U.S. Foreign Service, information officer in Manila, Philippine Islands, 1951-53; Chase Manhattan Bank, New York, N.Y., community relations director, 1958-64; since then writer specializing in Black and contemporary Japanese history. Art Originals Ltd., director. National Council on Philanthropy, vice-president, 1964; National Urban League, member of communication committee; Urban League of Southwestern Fairfield County, director. *Military service:* U.S. Army, 1943-46; served in Pacific theater.

MEMBER: Association for Asian Studies, Committee of Concerned Asian Scholars, Public Relations Society of America, National Association for the Advancement of Colored People, National Urban League, Museum of Black History, Connecticut Civil Liberties Union. *Awards, honors: Great Civilizations of Ancient Africa* was listed by *School Library Journal* as one of the best books of 1971.

WRITINGS: (Ghost-writer) Whitney M. Young, Jr., *To Be Equal,* McGraw, 1964; *Behind Japan's Surrender,* McGraw, 1968; (ghost-writer) Henry Steeger, *You Can Remake America,* Doubleday, 1970; *Great Civilizations of Ancient Africa* (ALA Notable Book), Four Winds, 1971; (with Guichard Parris) *Blacks in the City: A History of the Urban League,* Little, Brown, 1971; *Great American Autos* (juvenile), Scholastic Book Services, 1972; (with wife, Patricia K. Brooks) *How To Buy Property Abroad,* Doubleday, 1974.

WORK IN PROGRESS: Biographies of Marcus Garvey, Richard Wright, and Emperor Meiji, listed in order of expected completion.

LESTER BROOKS

28

BROWN, Marcia 1918-

PERSONAL: Born July 13, 1918, in Rochester, N.Y.; daughter of Clarence Edward (a minister) and Adelaide Elizabeth (Zimber) Brown. *Education:* Studied at Woodstock School of Painting, summer, 1938; New York College for Teachers (now State University of New York at Albany), B.A., 1940; also studied at New School for Social Research, Art Students League (New York, N.Y.), and Columbia University. *Residence:* West Redding, Conn.

CAREER: Artist and author of children's books. High school English and drama teacher in Cornwall, N.Y., 1940-43; New York Public Library, New York, N.Y., library assistant for rare book collection, 1943-48; University College of the West Indies, Jamaica, British West Indies, teacher of puppetry, 1953. Woodcuts have been exhibited at Brooklyn Museum, Peridot Gallery, Hacker Gallery, Library of Congress, Carnegie Institute, and Philadelphia Print Club. Work is part of permanent collections at Library of Congress, New York Public Library, and numerous private collections.

MEMBER: Authors League, Authors Guild, Art Students League (life member), Metropolitan Museum of Art. *Awards, honors:* Caldecott Medal for most distinguished American picture book, from Children's Services Division of American Library Association, 1955, for *Cinderella,* and 1962, for *Once a Mouse;* honor book award of Book World Spring Book Festival, 1969, for *How, Hippo!;* University of Southern Mississippi Medallion, 1972, for "her distinguished contribution to children's literature."

WRITINGS—All self-illustrated children's books published by Scribner, except as indicated: *The Little Carousel,* 1946; *Stone Soup* (Caldecott honor book), 1947; *Henry-Fisherman* (Caldecott honor book), 1949; *Dick Wittington and His Cat* (an adaptation; Caldecott honor book), 1950; *Skipper John's Cook* (Caldecott honor book), 1951; *The Flying Carpet* (an adaptation), 1956; *Felice,* 1958; *Peter Piper's Alphabet* (an adaptation), 1959; *Tamarindo!,* 1960; *Once a Mouse* (an adaptation; ALA Notable Book), 1961; *Backbone of the King,* (*Horn Book* Honor List), 1966; *The Neighbors,* 1967; *How Hippo!,* 1969; *The Bun* (an adaptation), Harcourt, 1972; *All Butterflies,* 1974.

Translator and illustrator: Charles Perrault, *Puss in Boots,* (Caldecott honor book), 1952; Charles Perrault, *Cinderella,* 1954.

Illustrator: Virginia Watson, *The Trail of Courage,* 1948; Hans Christian Andersen, *The Steadfast Tin Soldier* (Caldecott honor book; ALA Notable Book), translated by M. R. James, 1953; Philip Sherlock, *Anansi,* Crowell, 1954; Peter C. Asbjornsen and J. E. Moe, *The Three Billy Goats Gruff,* Harcourt, 1957; Hans Christian Andersen, *The Wild Swans* (ALA Notable Book), translated by James, 1963; Theophile Gautier, *Giselle,* translated by Violette Verdy, McGraw, 1970; Hans Christian Andersen, *The Snow Queen,* Scribner, 1972.

Filmstrip: *The Crystal Cavern,* Lyceum Productions, 1974.

SIDELIGHTS: Marcia Brown was born in Rochester, New York. Because her father was a minister, the family grew up in several towns. She liked Cooperstown especially because nearby was Otsego Lake with trails along its shores to Natty Bumppo's cave and other places made famous in the novels of James Fenimore Cooper.

"Every Christmas my sister and I received paints and crayons and large pads of drawing paper. Christmas morning would find us making paper dolls and painting pictures of sturdy red barns with angels or fairies hovering overhead. Sometimes my parents joined us, for drawing seemed most natural for the whole family to do. We all loved to read and listen to stories."

At thirteen, she decided to be one of three things—a doctor, an opera singer, or a painter. But for practical reasons she entered the State College for Teachers in Albany. She became interested in writing and every spring almost succumbed to the urge to run away and go to art school. For two summers, Judson Smith gave her scholarships to the Woodstock School of Painting.

After college came teaching English and dramatics. But there was still the urge to paint and write and illustrate books for children, so she came to New York to work in the New York Public Library and to paint and learn how to

MARCIA BROWN

Mice Nibbling. ■ (From *All Butterflies* by Marcia Brown. Illustrated by the author.)

make books. As a librarian she had valuable experience in storytelling; it led her to retell and illustrate a number of folk tales, always keeping in mind their possibilities for storytelling.

HOBBIES AND OTHER INTERESTS: Music, Ballet, reading, travel (Mexico, Virgin Islands, Europe, Near and Middle East, Denmark, Far East, Soviet Union), and "at present, a keen interest in nature photography."

FOR MORE INFORMATION SEE: Caldecott Medal Books: 1938-1957, edited by Miller and Field, Horn Book, 1957; *More Junior Authors,* edited by Muriel Fuller, H. W. Wilson, 1963; *Newbery & Caldecott Medal Books: 1956-1965,* edited by Lee Kingman, Horn Book, 1965; Diana Klemin, *The Art of Art for Children's Books,* Clarkson Potter, 1966; Lee Bennett Hopkins, *Books Are By People,* Citation, 1969; *Horn Book,* August, 1969, April, 1972, April, 1973, June, 1974; MacCann & Richard, *The Child's First Books,* H. W. Wilson, 1973; *Christian Science Monitor,* May 1, 1974.

BUCHWALD, Emilie 1935-

PERSONAL: Born September 6, 1935, in Vienna, Austria; daughter of Norbert Norton (a lawyer) and Marya (Knebel) Bix; married Henry Buchwald (a surgeon), June 6, 1954; children: Jane Nicole, Amy Elizabeth, Claire Gretchen, Dana Alexandra. *Education:* Barnard College, B.A. (magna cum laude), 1957; Columbia University, M.A., 1960; University of Minnesota, Ph.D., 1971. *Home:* 6808 Margaret's Lane, Edina, Minn. 55435.

CAREER: Worked summers during college as editorial assistant on New York edition of *TV Guide,* 1955, as guest fiction editor of *Mademoiselle,* 1956, and editorial secretary for *Sloane Hospital Magazine,* 1957; University of Minnesota, Minneapolis, instructor in English, 1960-68. *Member:* Modern Language Association of America, Women's Na-

Gildaen was that rarity among rabbits, an adventurer. ▪ (From *Gildaen, the Heroic Adventures of a Most Unusual Rabbit* by Emilie Buchwald. Illustrated by Barbara Flynn.)

tional Book Association, Phi Beta Kappa. *Awards, honors: Chicago Tribune* Children's Book Festival Award in middle age group, 1973, for *Gildaen.*

WRITINGS: Gildaen: The Heroic Adventures of a Most Unusual Rabbit, Harcourt, 1973. Short story included in *Prize Stories 1959: The O. Henry Awards,* poems in *Anthology of Magazine Verse,* 1958, and *When Women Look at Men,* 1961, and essay in *Studies in Criticism and Aesthetics,* 1968. Contributor to *Harper's, Ladies' Home Journal, Harper's Bazaar, Kenyon Review, American Quarterly,* and other periodicals.

WORK IN PROGRESS: A contemporary fantasy for children, completion expected in 1974.

SIDELIGHTS: "I began writing poetry as a child and I still believe that the techniques of poetry—metaphor, allusion, compression, attention to the texture of language—are basic to any good writing. My father was a marvelous story-teller, a man who loved to talk to others and exchange ideas, ask questions; his stories, his love of books, his interest in people and joy in living had a great deal to do with my interest in writing."

HOBBIES AND OTHER INTERESTS: Reading, playing the guitar, gardening, cooking, tennis, and most outdoor sports.

FOR MORE INFORMATION SEE: Publishers' Weekly, March 5, 1973.

EMILIE BUCHWALD

Was the Punch-and-Judy show the most wonderful wonder ever to come to Calico Row?
■ (From *Calico Row* by Lillian Budd. Illustrated by Leonard Vosburgh.)

BUDD, Lillian (Peterson) 1897-

PERSONAL: Born July 21, 1897, in Chicago, Ill.; daughter of Charles A. and Selma (Nelson) Peterson; married Fred H. Budd, 1918 (Navy officer, deceased); children: Richard Nelson. *Education:* Attended Chicago public schools. *Address:* 2535 Orella St., Santa Barbara, Calif. 93105.

CAREER: Western Electric Company, Hawthorne, Ill., secretary, 1915-18; U.S. Government, Selective Service System, Geneva, Ill., chief clerk, 1940-47; Campana Sales Company, Batavia, promotion manager, 1947-51. Writer and lecturer. American-Swedish Foundation, Philadelphia, Pa., member of Fredrika Bremer committee. *Military service:* U.S. Navy, 1918-20; became chief yeoman. *Member:* Midland Authors, Phi Gamma Nu, Friends of Literature, American Legion, Woman's Club (Geneva, Ill., past president), Sigma Kappa, Theta Sigma Phi. *Awards, honors:* Friends of Literature Fiction Award, 1959; Tree Towns Business and Professional Women's Club, "Woman of the year," 1967-68.

WRITINGS: April Snow, Lippincott, 1951; *Land of Strangers,* Lippincott, 1953; *April Harvest,* Duell, 1959; *The Pie Wagon* (picture book for children), Lothrop, 1960; *The Bell of Kamela* (historical novel for young people), Rand McNally, 1960; *Tekla's Easter* (for young people), Rand McNally, 1962; *The People on Long Ago Street* (picture book for children), Rand McNally, 1964; *One Heart, One Way* (novel for young adults), McKay, 1964; *Calico Row* (juvenile), A. Whitman, 1965; *Larry* (juvenile), McKay, 1966; *Full Moons* (Child Study Association book list), Rand McNally, 1971. Contributor to American, Swedish, and Norwegian magazines.

WORK IN PROGRESS: Her fifth novel; another book for children; history of Lombard, Illinois, for Bicentennial of U.S.

HOBBIES AND OTHER INTERESTS: Collecting antiques.

FOR MORE INFORMATION SEE: Illinois Libraries, June, 1965.

BURCHARDT, Nellie 1921-

PERSONAL: Born May 13, 1921, in Philadelphia, Pa.; daughter of Donald Lewis (a mechanical enigineer) and Marian Stewart (Harper) Kellogg; married Botho Burchardt (now a market researcher), May 23, 1948; children: Carol Joy, Wendy Ellen; Laurens (stepson). *Education:* Queens College, Flushing, N.Y., B.A., 1944; Yale University, M.A., 1946; Columbia University, graduate study in library science, 1954-55. *Politics:* Liberal. *Religion:* Unitarian Universalist. *Home:* 773 Manor Rd., Staten Island, New York, N.Y. 10314; summer: Judgment Ridge Rd:, Vershire, Vt. 05079.

CAREER: New York Public Library, New York, N.Y., trainee, 1954-55.

WRITING—Juveniles: *Project Cat,* Watts, 1966; *Reggie's No-Good Bird,* Watts, 1967; *A Surprise for Carlotta,* Watts, 1971; *What Are We Going to Do, Michael?,* Watts, 1973.

WORK IN PROGRESS: Another children's book.

SIDELIGHTS: "I wanted to write as long as I can remember, but the way I came to write the specific type of children's books that I do, was inspired by a friend of my younger daughter. When they were in the first grade together, they came in, slammed down their *Dick & Jane* readers on the kitchen table, and my daughter's friend exclaimed, 'Why doesn't someone write stories about children like *us*?' So *Project Cat* was born, very particularly about children like them and a real cat that they found in the Project where we live. My next book was inspired by the same daughter, who brought home a wounded blue jay one day. That was *Reggie's No-Good Bird.*

"I take a real incident, and then play around with it in my mind and invent characters who might get into such a situation. Sometimes the real incident that sets me off on a story is something that happened to my own children—sometimes it's something I've read in the newspaper, as in *What Are We Going to Do, Michael?* But always I take the background from places I've lived in myself, so it will feel real, and true-to-life.

LILLIAN BUDD

Last summer she would not have dared speak to those big boys for anything, but now she flung herself at the boy who had thrown the stone. "You leave my cat alone!" ▪ (From *Project Cat* by Nellie Burchardt. Illustrated by Fermin Rocker.)

"All my books have animals in them because animals fascinate me and because in the housing project where I've lived for over twenty years I feel that the lack of pets in the children's lives makes them miss a very important experience of learning to understand the needs of another creature. *A Surprise for Carlotta* was also based on a real animal—a duck—that one of my daughters watched grow in school. And the people in it were real, people I've known. And what I want to say in all these books is mainly that you can do something to get in charge of your own life—that you're not completely helpless even in the face of the apparently overwhelming problems of urban living."

FOR MORE INFORMATION SEE: Horn Book, October, 1971.

BURGWYN, Mebane H(oloman) 1914-

PERSONAL: Born December 10, 1914, in Rich Square, N.C.; daughter of Henry Dorsey and Pattie Vaughn (White) Holoman; married John Griffin Burgwyn (a farm owner), August 17, 1935; children: John Griffin, Jr., Josephine Mebane (Mrs. James D. Pratt), Henry Holoman, Stephen White. *Politics:* Democrat. *Religion:* Episcopalian. *Education:* University of North Carolina at Greensboro, A.B., 1935; East Carolina University, M.A., 1962. *Home:* Occoneechee Farms, Route I, Box 269, Jackson, N.C. 27845.

CAREER: Northampton County Schools, Jackson, N.C., director of guidance services, 1959-69. Member of executive committee, University of North Carolina board of trustees, 1955-71; member of board of trustees, East Carolina University, 1973—. Chairman of North Carolina Writer's Conference, 1962. *Member:* American Personnel and Guidance Association, National Education Association, North Carolina Personnel and Guidance Association (president, 1964), North Carolina Writers, Roanoke Chowan Group, Delta Kappa Gamma. *Awards, honors:* Juvenile Award of North Carolina Division of American Association of University Women for *Penny Rose,* 1954, and *The Crackajack Pony,* 1970; University of North Carolina at Greensboro Service Award, 1973.

WRITINGS—All for young people: *River Treasure,* Oxford University Press, 1948; *Lucky Mischief,* Oxford University Press, 1950; *Penny Rose,* Oxford University Press, 1952; *Moonflower,* Lippincott, 1954; *True Love for Jenny,*

He thought suddenly of Mama's words this morning when she told him how sometimes a thing wasn't cherished properly if it didn't belong to you. ▪ (From *The Crackajack Pony* by Mebane Holoman Burgwyn. Illustrated by Dale Payson.)

Something about the Author

Lippincott, 1956; *Hunter's Hideout,* Lippincott, 1959; *The Crackajack Pony,* Lippincott, 1969. Story included in collection, *Strange Things Happen.*

SIDELIGHTS: "Books for children have been a result of wanting to share experiences of farm living with those who do or do not know about such activities. Teen-age books reflect experiences with teen-agers and my interest in counseling young people. The *Crackajack Pony* was written out of my belief that the integration process which was taking place in the South and other sections created problems for the black child who had to face prejudice day after day. I wanted white children to know the trauma of that experience and I wanted the black child to know that he, too, had responsibility of living up to the best within himself in order to meet this challenge. Above all, I wanted to write a good story about a boy who wanted a pony more than anything in the world.

"Am interested in art. Have been studying acrylic painting under artist Barclay Sheaks."

FOR MORE INFORMATION SEE: Bernadette Hoyle, editor, *North Carolina Writers I Know,* Blair; Richard Walser, editor, *Picture Book of Tar Heel·Authors,* North Carolina State Department of Archives and History, 1960; *Book World,* Part II, November 9, 1969.

BURTON, Hester (Wood-Hill) 1913-

PERSONAL: Born December 6, 1913, in Beccles, Suffolk, England; daughter of Henry G. (a surgeon) and Amy (Crowfoot) Wood-Hill; married R. W. B. Burton (now a tutor-lecturer in classics at Oxford University), August 7, 1937; children: Catharine, Elizabeth, Janet. *Education:* Oxford University, honors degree in English literature, 1936. *Politics:* Liberal Party. *Home:* Mill House, Kidlington, Oxford, England.

CAREER: Part-time grammar school teacher; examiner in public examination. *Awards, honors:* Carnegie Medal, 1963, for *Time of Trial; Boston Globe–Horn Book* Award, 1971, for *Beyond the Weir Bridge.*

WRITINGS: Barbara Bodichon, John Murray, 1949; *Coleridge and the Wordsworths,* Oxford University Press, 1953; *Tennyson,* Oxford University Press, 1954; (editor) *Her First Ball* (short story collection), Oxford University Press, 1959; (editor) *A Book of Modern Short Stories,* Oxford University Press, 1959; *The Great Gale* (juvenile), Oxford University Press, 1960, published in America as *The Flood at Reedsmere,* World Publishing, 1961; *Castors Away* (juvenile), Oxford University Press, 1962, World Publishing, 1962; *Time of Trial* (juvenile), Oxford University Press, 1963, World Publishing, 1964; *No Beat of Drum* (juvenile), Oxford University Press, 1966, World Publishing, 1967; *In Spite of All Terror* (juvenile), Oxford University Press, 1968, World Publishing, 1969; *Otmoor for Ever!,* Hamish Hamilton, 1968; *Through the Fire,* Hamish Hamilton, 1969; *Thomas* (juvenile), Oxford University Press, 1969, published in America as *Beyond the Weir Bridge* (ALA Notable Book), Crowell, 1970; *The Henchmans at Home* (short stories), Oxford University Press, 1970, Crowell, 1972; *The Rebel* (ALA Notable Book), Oxford University Press, 1971, Crowell, 1972; *Riders of the Storm*

HESTER BURTON

(sequel to *The Rebel*), Oxford University Press, 1972, Crowell, 1973; *Kate Rider,* Oxford University Press, 1974. Assistant editor, *Oxford Junior Encyclopaedia, 1956-61.*

SIDELIGHTS: "I am interested in history and I love children: hence my historical novels for young people. My method is to find some fairly small episode in history which catches my imagination, such as a natural disaster, a battle, a siege, or a riot—find out all I can about it—and then plunge my imaginary young people into its toils and watch them struggle, usually very valiantly, for honor and survival. My favorite setting is England, because I love my native country; and my favorite period is the time of Nelson (1790-1805), partly because I come from East Anglia, which is 'Nelson country,' but mostly because England was fighting alone against an all-powerful European dictator (Napoleon) during that period, just as she was in 1940 against Hitler, so that I feel I understand the predicament of English people living in that earlier period. I have tried to describe the strange exaltation of living in England in 1940 in my story *In Spite of All Terror.*

"My very happy childhood in the little market town of Beccles and the beauty of the nearby Suffolk coast have given me the backgrounds of *The Great Gale, Castors Away!,* a part of *Time Of Trial* and the whole of *The Henchmans at Home.* The fact that my father was an unworldly and much-loved family physician has not only

given me many happy ideas for the pleasanter older characters in my books but has also persuaded me in book after book to describe the great humanity and high principles embodied in the Hippocratic Oath."

HOBBIES AND OTHER INTERESTS: Travel in France, Italy and Greece; theatre.

FOR MORE INFORMATION SEE: Roger Lancelyn Green, *Tellers of Tales,* Watts, 1965; Brian Doyle, *The Who's Who of Children's Literature,* Schocken, 1968; *Horn Book,* August, 1969, December, 1970, April, 1972, October, 1972, April, 1974, *Authors' Choice,* Crowell, 1971; *Third Book of Junior Authors,* edited by de Montreville and Hill, H. W. Wilson, 1972; *Saturday Review,* May 20, 1972; Haviland, *Children and Literature,* Scott, Foresman, 1973.

As he watched her sleep-walking over the tumbling water, he felt a terrible ache. ■ (From *Beyond the Weir Bridge* by Hester Burton. Illustrated by Victor Ambrus.)

BUTLER, Beverly (Kathleen) 1932-

PERSONAL: Born May 4, 1932, in Fond du Lac, Wis.; daughter of Leslie Willis and Muriel (Anderson) Butler. *Education:* Mount Mary College, B.A., 1954; Marquette University, M.A., 1961. *Religion:* Episcopalian. *Home:* 3019 North 90th St., Milwaukee, Wis. 53222.

CAREER: Mount Mary College, Milwaukee, Wis., teacher, 1962—. Lecturer at schools, libraries, clubs. *Member:* Allied Authors, Wisconsin Regional Writers Guild. *Awards, honors:* 17th Summer Literary Competition award, 1955, for *Song of the Voyageur;* Clara Ingram Judson Award, for *Light a Single Candle;* Johnson Foundation Award of Council for Wisconsin Writers, Award of Merit for distinguished service to history, State Historical Society of Wisconsin, both for *Feather in the Wind;* Woodrow Wilson fellowship, 1960-61.

WRITINGS: Song of the Voyageur, 1955, *Lion and the Otter,* 1957, *The Fur Lodge,* 1959, *The Silver Key,* 1961,

BEVERLY BUTLER

Light a Single Candle, 1962, *Feather in the Wind,* 1965, *Captive Thunder,* 1969, *The Wind and Me,* 1971, *Gift of Gold,* 1972 (all published by Dodd). Literary editor, *Dialogue.*

SIDELIGHTS: "Until I was fourteen I had always halfway intended to become an artist when I grew up, any kind of an artist as long as it was a great one. My fourteenth birthday brought the first sharp warnings of impending blindness, and my plans were drastically changed within a few months. No one had ever been able to read my handwriting easily when I could see, so the first thing I had to do before returning to school was learn to type papers for my teachers. I began by re-telling remembered stories on paper for typing practice. Soon I was improving on memory, adding details, and eventually branching out into stories completely of my own invention. It was an absorbing pastime, gave me plenty of typing practice, and when I discovered that my friends were eager to read each new installment of whatever story I was writing, the choice of writing as a career seemed as natural as though I had never considered any other.

"I had a sizeable stack of manuscripts by the time I finished high school, but I didn't encounter my first real writing teacher until I reached college. She was Sister Mary Hester of Mount Mary College, and under her encouragement and guidance I wrote *Song of the Voyageur.* The heroine was nineteen, the same age as I was at the time, and the story was as adult in scope as I was capable of then. When I later submitted it to Dodd, however, they accepted it as a juvenile, which taught me my first big lesson about writing for young people. What interested me at nineteen was of interest to other teens, too, and for the same reasons. My second big lesson came from the letters written by readers, which revealed that young readers are thoughtful, perceptive, and eager to be involved in a story. After that no one ever had to caution me not to write down to my audience. The challenge has always been to keep up with them.

"There is very little I can say about where I get the inspiration for my books, as there is really no single, complete answer. I am constantly gathering fragments of ideas from my reading, from places I visit, from conversations with friends, from various happenings I observe or take part in, and these fragments are stored away in the back of my mind. Often a new idea will somehow call forth an older one and the two match so well that they generate the beginnings of a story. Sometimes I carry around a picture of a character I'd like to write about but it isn't until I come across a special setting or some sort of unusual event that would be just right for this character that the story begins to bubble. Sometimes it is the event or the setting that is uppermost in my mind and has to wait for just the right characters to come together from the scrap bag of fragments in my mind.

"The reason I write for young people, however, is simple: I like it. I like the endless range and scope of material I can make use of in writing for them, I like the challenge of trying to produce a story good enough to keep the interest of such a discerning and choosy group of readers, and I like the readers themselves."

HOBBIES AND OTHER INTERESTS: Music, reading, travel, outdoor life, animals.

CADWALLADER, Sharon 1936-

PERSONAL: Surname is pronounced Cad-*wall*-a-der; born January 12, 1936, in Jamestown, N.D.; daughter of Herman Julius (an insurance agent) and Mildred A. (Hull) Wulfsberg; married Mervyn L. Cadwallader, July 4, 1959 (divorced); children: Leland Hull Cadwallader. *Education:* San Jose State College, A.B., 1958. *Home:* 174 12th Ave., Santa Cruz, Calif. 95060.

CAREER: One of founders of Whole Earth Restaurant on campus of University of California, Santa Cruz, an outgrowth of a student garden project dedicated to the restoration of man's kinship with his whole environment.

WRITINGS: (With Judi Ohr) *Whole Earth Cook Book,* Houghton, 1972; *In Celebration of Small Things,* Houghton, 1974; *Cooking Adventures for Kids,* Houghton, in press. Contributor to *Saturday Review.*

SIDELIGHTS: Spent five months in Mexico in 1973, where she collected recipes for Mexican soups and did some research with her brother on Miguel Hidalgo, a nineteenth-century revolutionary priest. Now working on television script of that project.

FOR MORE INFORMATION SEE: Horn Book, October, 1972.

The lack of imagination in our lunches has broken ground for thousands of prepared-hamburger havens. ▪ (From *Whole Earth Cook Book* by Sharon Cadwallader and Judi Ohr. Illustrated by Anita Walker Scott.)

CALDWELL, John C(ope) 1913-

PERSONAL: Born November 27, 1913, in Futsing, China; son of Harry Russell (a Methodist missionary) and Mary Belle (Cope) Caldwell; married Elsie I. Fletcher (now a writer and importer), May 27, 1949; children: John, Jr., Kendall Eidson, David F., William O., Karen Elizabeth. *Education:* Earlham College, student, 1931-32; Vanderbilt University, A.B., 1935; summer study at Cornell University, 1934, and University of Tennessee, 1939-41. *Religion:* Methodist. *Home and office:* 4526 Shy's Hill Rd., Nashville, Tenn. 37215.

CAREER: Tennessee Department of Conservation, Nashville, educational director, 1935-43; U.S. Office of War Information, writer in Washington, D.C., and China, 1943-45; U.S. Department of State, U.S. Information Service, assignments in China and Korea, 1945-50; free-lance writer and lecturer, 1950—, with periods on special assignment with U.S. Department of the Army, Christian Children's Fund of Richmond, Va., and Cordell Hull Foundation, Nashville, Tenn. For several years he conducted two tours each year to the Orient; formerly owned a travel agency, now consultant for a major travel agency. Member of board of directors, American Afro-Asian Educational Exchange, Inc., New York. *Member:* Society of American Travel Writers, Authors Guild of the Authors League of America, Outdoor Writers Association of America, Tennessee Ornithological Society, Nashville China Club.

WRITINGS: (With Harry R. Caldwell) *South China Birds,* H. M. Vanderburgh, 1931; (with J. L. Bailey and R. W. Watkins) *Our Land and Our Living,* Singer, 1941; (with Mark Gayn) *American Agent,* Holt, 1947; (with Lesley Frost) *The Korea Story,* Regnery, 1952; *China Coast Family,* Regnery, 1953 (published in England as *Our Friends the Tigers,* Hutchinson, 1954); *Still the Rice Grows Green:*

SHARON CADWALLADER

JOHN COPE CALDWELL

Asia in the Aftermath of Geneva and Panmunjom, Regnery, 1955; *Communism in Our World,* Day, 1956, revised edition, 1968; *Children of Calamity,* Day, 1957; *South of Tokyo,* Regnery, 1957; *Far East Travel Guide,* Day, 1959, revised edition, 1961; *South Asia Travel Guide,* Day, 1966; *Massage Girl, and Other Sketches of Thailand,* Day, 1968; *Orient Travel Guide,* Day, 1970.

"Let's Visit" Series, for ages nine to eleven: *Let's Visit Formosa, Island Home of Free China,* 1956, . . .*Southeast Asia, Hong Kong to Malaya,* 1957, revised edition, 1967, . . .*the Middle East,* 1958, revised edition, 1966, . . .*Middle Africa: East Africa, Central Africa,* 1958, . . .*Americans Overseas: The Story of Foreign Aid, the Voice of America, Military Assistance, Overseas Bases,* 1958, (with wife, Elsie F. Caldwell) . . .*Korea,* 1959, . . .*West Africa,* 1959, revised edition, 1969, . . .*China,* 1959, . . .*Japan,* 1959, . . .*the West Indies,* 1960, revised edition, 1963, . . .*India,* 1960, . . .*Indonesia,* 1960, . . .*Ceylon,* 1960, . . .*Pakistan,* 1960, . . .*the Philippines,* 1961, . . .*Argentina,* 1961, new edition, Burke, 1968, . . .*Brazil,* 1961, . . .*Venezuela,* 1962, . . .*Colombia,* 1962, . . .*Peru,* 1962, . . .*Chile,* 1963, . . .*the South Pacific: Fiji, Tonga, Tahiti,* 1963, . . .*Australia,* 1963, . . .*New Zealand,* 1963, . . .*Canada,* 1964, . . .*Central America,* 1964, . . .*Mexico,* 1965, (with Bernard Newman) . . .*France,* Burke, 1965, revised edition, Day, 1967, . . .*Vietnam,* 1966, (with Julian Popeseu) . . .*U.S.S.R.,* 1967, revised edition published as . . .*Russia,* 1968, . . .*Thailand,* 1967, (with Angus MacVicar) . . .*Scotland,* revised edition, 1967, . . .*Afghanistan,* 1968,

. . .*Malaysia,* 1968, (with Newman) . . .*South Africa,* 1968, . . .*Italy,* 1968, . . .*Turkey,* 1969, . . .*Micronesia, Guam, U.S.A.,* 1969, (with J. Popeseu) . . .*Yugoslavia,* 1969 (all published by Day except as indicated).

"World Neighbors" Series, with wife, Elsie F. Caldwell; for ages six to nine: *Our Neighbors in India,* 1960, . . .*in Japan,* 1960, . . .*in the Philippines,* 1961, . . .*in Korea,* 1961, . . .*in Africa,* 1961, . . .*in Peru,* 1962, . . .*in Brazil,* 1962, . . .*in Central America,* 1967, . . .*in Australia and New Zealand,* 1967, . . .*in Thailand,* 1968 (all published by Day).

Contributor to national magazines; has written syndicated newspaper column on travel.

SIDELIGHTS: Caldwell travels constantly, gathering material for new books and for updating the old. He has crossed the Pacific more than seventy times. A number of the books in the "Let's Visit" Series have also been published in England.

HOBBIES AND OTHER INTERESTS: Trout fishing, wild flower gardening.

CARRICK, Carol 1935-

PERSONAL: Born May 20, 1935, in Long Island, N.Y. daughter of Chauncey L. (a salesman) and Elsa (Schweizer) Hatfield; married Donald Carrick (an artist), March 26, 1965; children: Christopher, Paul. *Education:* Hofstra University, B.A., 1957. *Home address:* High St., Edgartown, Mass. 02539.

CAROL CARRICK

CAREER: Advertising artist.

WRITINGS—Books for children, all illustrated by husband, Donald Carrick: *The Old Barn,* Bobbs, 1966; *The Brook,* Macmillan, 1967; *Swamp Spring,* Macmillan, 1969; *The Pond,* Macmillan, 1970; *The Dirt Road,* Macmillan, 1970; *The Clearing in the Forest,* Dial, 1970; *The Dragon of Santa Lalia,* Bobbs, 1971; *The Sleep Out,* Seabury, 1973; *Beach Bird,* Dial, 1973; *Lost in the Storm,* Seabury, 1974.

FOR MORE INFORMATION SEE: Christian Science Monitor, November 2, 1967; *Times Literary Supplement,* April 16, 1970; *Horn Book,* February, 1971, June, 1973, October, 1973; *Christian Science Monitor,* May 2, 1973.

CARRICK, Donald 1929-

PERSONAL: Born April 7, 1929, in Dearborn, Mich.; son of Fay and Blanche (Soper) Carrick; married Carol Hatfield (a writer), March 26, 1965; children: Christopher, Paul. *Education:* Attended Colorado Springs Fine Art Center, 1948-49, Arts Student League, 1950, and Vienna Academy Fine Arts, 1953-54. *Home:* High St., Edgartown, Mass. 02539

CAREER: Artist. *Military service:* U.S. Army, 1950-51; became corporal. *Awards, honors:* Bank Street College of Education Irma Simonton Black Award, 1973; *Bear Mouse* was a Children's Book Showcase Title, 1974.

WRITINGS: The Tree (Child Study Association book list), Macmillan, 1971; *Drip Drop,* Macmillan, 1973.

Illustrator, all written by wife, Carol Carrick: *The Old Barn,* Bobbs, 1966; *The Brook,* Macmillan, 1967; *Swamp Spring,* Macmillan, 1969; *The Pond,* Macmillan, 1970; *The Dirt Road,* Macmillan, 1970; *The Clearing in the Forest,* Dial, 1970; *The Dragon of Santa Lalia,* Bobbs, 1971; *Beach Bird,* Dial, 1973; *The Sleep Out,* Seabury, 1973; *Lost in the Storm,* Seabury, 1974.

Illustrator: Robert Goldston, *The Civil War in Spain,* Bobbs, 1966; Goldston, *The Russian Revolution,* Bobbs, 1966; Goldston, *The Rise of Red China,* Bobbs, 1967; Goldston, *The Life and Death of Nazi Germany,* Bobbs, 1967; Goldston, *The Great Depression,* Bobbs, 1968; *London: The Civic Spirit,* Macmillan, 1969; *Barcelona: The Civic Stage,* Macmillan, 1969; Ernestine Byrd, *Tor: Wyoming Bighorn,* Scribner, 1969; *City in All Directions,* edited by Arnold Adoff, Macmillan, 1969; Goldston, *The Cuban Revolution,* Bobbs, 1970; *New York: Civic Exploitation,* Macmillan, 1970; *Suburbia: Civic Denial,* Macmillan, 1970; Lee McGiffin, *Yankee Doodle Dandies,* Dutton, 1970; Nancy Veglahn, *The Buffalo King,* Scribner, 1971; Uchida, *Journey to Topaz,* Scribner, 1971; Berniece Freschet, *Turtle Pond,* Scribner, 1971; Berniece Freschet, *Bear Mouse,* Scribner, 1973; Eleanor Schick, *Peter and Mr. Brandon,* Macmillan, 1973; David Budbill, *The Christmas Tree Farm,* Macmillan, 1974.

WORK IN PROGRESS: The Lobster Tale, The Deer in the Pasture, and *Grizzly Bear.*

SIDELIGHTS: Carrick lived and painted for several years in Spain.

LATROBE CARROLL,
drawn by Ruth Carroll

CARROLL, (Archer) Latrobe 1894-

PERSONAL: Born January 5, 1894, in Washington, D.C.; son of Archer Latrobe and Frances Hamilton (Gamble) Carroll; married Ruth Crombie Robinson, 1928. *Education:* Harvard University, A.B., 1918.

CAREER: The Century Co., New York, N.Y., editorial staff, 1919; Foreign Press Service, New York, N.Y., staff writer, 1920; *Liberty Magazine,* New York, N.Y., editorial staff, 1924-34; free-lance writer, 1934—. *Military service:* U.S. Army Engineer Corps, 1918. *Member:* Authors League of America, Friends of the Library (Asheville; second vice-president, 1960-63), Harvard Club of Western North Carolina. *Awards, honors:* Juvenile Award of American Association of University Women (North Carolina division), for *Peanut,* 1953, and *Digby the Only Dog,* 1955.

WRITINGS—Juveniles with Ruth Carroll: *Luck of the Roll and Go,* Macmillan, 1935; *Flight of the Silver Bird,* Messner, 1939; *Scuffles,* Walck, 1943; *School in the Sky,* Macmillan, 1945; *The Flying House,* Macmillan, 1946; *Pet Tale,* Walck, 1949; *Peanut,* Walck, 1951; *Salt and Pepper,* Walck, 1952; *Beanie,* Walck, 1953; *Tough Enough,* Walck, 1954; *Digby the Only Dog,* Walck, 1955; *Tough Enough's Trip,* Walck, 1956; *Tough Enough's Pony,* Walck, 1957; *Tough Enough and Sassy,* Walck, 1958; *Tough Enough's Indians,* Walck, 1960; *Runaway Pony, Runaway Dog,* Walck, 1963; *Danny and the Poi Pup,* Walck, 1965; *The Picnic Bear,* Walck, 1966; *Bumble Pup,* Walck, 1968; *The Christmas Kitten,* Walck, 1970; *The Managing Hen and the Floppy Hound,* Walck, 1972.

Tough Enough was very small, but he grew just a little every day. ■ (From *Tough Enough* by Latrobe Carroll. Illustrated by Ruth Carroll.)

Translator: Camille Flammarion, *Death and Its Mystery: At The Moment of Death,* Century, 1922; Camille Flammarion, *Death and Its Mystery: After Death,* Century, 1923.

SIDELIGHTS: "My main interests have shaped my work: a love of children, of travel, of animals and of putting words on paper.

"Ruth and I—Ruth is my artist-wife and collaborator on our books for children—have no children of our own. That has meant we had to borrow children and to seize every opportunity to meet and talk to them in schools and in the homes of their parents. We've given many dozen of illustrated talks—with Ruth drawing quick pictures—to thousands of children. Since most children have a refreshing habit of frankness, of coming right out with things, their questions and comments have helped us. Too, Ruth has had child-models posing for her in our studio; that gave her lots of chances to tell them stories and note the sort of plots and happenings that held them, kept them from wriggling. Both of us benefited from that.

"One thing, a big thing that has made our work so satisfying (to us) is that children like a straightforward plot with a beginning, a middle and an end: a problem, an all-out attempt to solve it, and at the end a success. In short, *new* human beings like *old* ways of plotting.

"As for travel, I've relished it ever since late babyhood. My mother, an eager cyclist, used to carry me in a basket attached to the handlebars of her bike—that is, she did so until I embarrassed her so often, she had to stop giving me rides. The trouble was, I was always so exhilarated by my journeys on wheels, I'd lift my voice loudly in song. People would smile or laugh or stare.

"But I had experienced the joys of going places; from then on, I was a rover—and, often, my roving was tied in with my interest in animals. In Denver, Colorado, where I went to elementary school, I had my own bike. My favorite ride was out to the city's zoo, where I'd made a friend of a certain wise old monkey; he and I had a profound rapport based on peanuts and popcorn. Whenever he chattered I chattered back at him, certain my monkey talk was improving, day by day.

"Too, there were pleasant encounters with prairie dogs and horned toads on dry plains near the city. There were summers spent with my mother and some of her friends in Rocky Mountains wilderness. There, during exploratory days, I sometimes caught exciting glimpses of lynxes and bears. At night, in our rented log cabin, I'd lie and listen to coyotes barking eerily and think how lucky they were to be wandering so free, without any school to have to sit still in, without any lessons they must learn. They'd never have to wonder what nine times seven was.

"But it was much later in my life, after Ruth and I teamed up on doing books for children, that both of us began to work animals we'd met on our travels, or kept as models in our studio, into our books. There was our haughty cat, Three Squares—we called her that because she insisted on three square meals a day—we used as a model for the valiant, bound-for-the-South-Pole puss in *Luck of the Roll and Go.* There was Stuffer, the small, pink, curly-tailed sow we had in our Greenwich Village home for a couple of weeks, serving as a model for various stories after Ruth had thoroughly sketched and photographed her and both of us had studied her. There was Mister Pokey, a turtle not much bigger than a silver dollar, who got into another book, *Flight of the Silver Bird*—as a pet of a fictional brother and sister in a plane flying across the Pacific. There were 'Wild' ponies (really not wild) we made friends with when we spent weeks on North Carolina's Outer Banks. From them we got pony pointers for books: *Tough Enough's Pony* and *Tough Enough and Sassy* and *Runaway Pony, Runaway Dog.* There were the black bears we saw in the Great Smoky Mountains; a bear hunt was a starting point for another story: *Beanie.*

"Our most difficult animal-model problem—it was really Ruth's dilemma—came when she had to draw the underside of a cow for a scene in another story of ours, *School in the Sky.* We found a fine, well-developed cow on a farm not very far from New York City—yes, but getting far enough under her on a wintry day with her standing on half-frozen mud—well . . . *The cow wasn't happy, either. So Ruth was lucky to get her milk pail's-eye view and finish her sketches without a hoofed kick coming her way.*

"Turning now to the problems and rewards of writing, I'm among those who get a large charge out of words going gloriously right: words written by giants of literature and, too, by authors not so gigantic in literary stature. For most writers, writing would be simpler if it didn't mean so much rewriting, even for masters of the craft. (Tolstoy rewrote *War and Peace* seven times; on the other hand, a less effulgent literary light, Frances Hodgson Burnett, told me she never made more than one draft of her fiction).

"Like so many people whose business is words, I'm a rewriting writer, usually making five or six drafts. Also, I side with those who say, 'Keep regular working hours, don't rely on inspiration.' Sometimes I sit down at my typewriter feeling no more inspired than a cold boiled potato. But usually, like so many slow starters, I find I can work into work.

"Certain authors I knew had words of advice for writers taking first steps on the long rough road toward successful authorship. Their words still carry weight: 'Apply the seat of the pants to the seat of the chair.'

"Switching from work habits to ideas, I don't think you can make a sharp distinction between themes for adult stories and themes for juveniles—though, of course, writers for children do work somewhat 'fenced off' even if certain fences have been falling. So often, a good theme has no age limits. The way you develop it results in either a book for children or one for adults. For instance, a good premise is 'great love defies even death.' With that in mind, you could write a fine dog story for children or, if you were a Shakespeare, you could write *Romeo and Juliet.*"

HOBBIES AND OTHER INTERESTS: Hiking, travel, and reading.

FOR MORE INFORMATION SEE: Tar Heel Writers I Know, Bernadette Hoyle, 1956; *Picturebook of Tar Heel Authors,* Richard Walser, 1960; *More Junior Authors,* edited by Muriel Fuller, H.W. Wilson, 1963.

DIANE CAVALLO

CAVALLO, Diana 1931-

PERSONAL: Born November 3, 1931, in Philadelphia, Pa.; daughter of Genuino and Josephine (Petrarca) Cavallo; married Henry Weinberg, 1954. *Education:* University of Pennsylvania, B.A., 1953; graduate study at New School for Social Research, 1956, 1958; Sarah Lawrence College, M.A., 1965.

CAREER: Philadelphia State Hospital, Philadelphia, Pa., psychiatric social worker, 1954-55; teacher in public schools, Philadelphia, Pa., and Clifton, N.J., and in private school in Brooklyn, N.Y., 1955-61; University of Pisa, Pisa, Italy, Fulbright fellow, 1961-63; Drexel Institute of Technology, Philadelphia, Pa., instructor in literature and creative writing, 1964; Queens College, New York, N.Y., lecturer in literature and creative writing, 1965-68; University of Pisa, Italy, lecturer in American literature, 1973. *Member:* P.E.N., Authors League, Phi Beta Kappa. *Awards, honors:* MacDowell Colony fellowship, 1960; *The Lower East Side* was a Children's Book Showcase Title, 1972.

WRITINGS: A Bridge of Leaves, Atheneum, 1961; *The Lower East Side: A Portrait in Time,* Crowell-Collier, 1971.

WORK IN PROGRESS: The Escapements; The Piano Teacher, for Simon & Schuster; short stories.

SIDELIGHTS: "I enjoy combining writing and teaching and divide my time between New York City and Florence, Italy. By so doing, I have stimulation on the one hand and meditation on the other, and thus find these places and these professions ideal complements to one another."

FOR MORE INFORMATION SEE: New York Times Book Review, November 21, 1971.

CERF, Bennett (Alfred) 1898-1971

PERSONAL: Born May 25, 1898, in New York, N.Y.; son of Gustave (a lithographer) and Fredericka (Wise) Cerf; married Sylvia Sidney, 1935 (divorced); married Phyllis Fraser (an editor), 1940; children: (second marriage) Christopher Bennett, Jonathan Fraser. *Education:* Columbia University, A.B., 1919; Columbia School of Journalism, Litt.B., 1920. *Home:* 132 East 62nd St., New York, N.Y.; Orchard Rd., Mt. Kisco, N.Y. *Office:* 457 Madison Ave., New York, N.Y. 10022.

CAREER: New York Herald Tribune, reporter, and New York Stock Exchange, clerk, 1921-23; Boni and Liveright (publishers), New York, N.Y., vice-president, 1923-25; Modern Library, Inc. (publishers), New York, N.Y., founder and president, 1925-71; Random House, Inc. (publishers), New York; N.Y., founder with Donald S. Klopfer, and president, 1927-66, chairman of the board,1966-71; Bantam Books, New York, N.Y., director, 1945-71. Panelist on "What's My Line," Columbia Broadcasting System, 1952-67; Peabody Awards Committee, member, 1950-71, chairman, 1955-71; member of board of directors, Metro-Goldwyn-Mayer, Inc., and Alfred A. Knopf, Inc. *Military Service:* Served in Officers Training Corp, 1918. *Member:* Pi Lambda Phi, Phi Beta Kappa, Phi Delta Epsilon; Dutch Treat, Overseas Press Club, Century Country Club (all New York). *Awards, honors:* New York Philanthropic League, Distinguished Service Award, 1964.

*WRITINGS—*Editor: (With Van H. Cartmell) *Sixteen Famous American Plays,* Garden City, 1941; (with Cartmell) *Sixteen Famous British Plays,* Garden City, 1942; (with Cartmell) *Thirty Famous One-Act Plays,* Modern Library, 1943; *Shake Well Before Using: A New Collection of Impressions and Anecdotes Mostly Humorous,* Simon &

BENNETT CERF

Schuster, 1948; *Laughter, Incorporated: The Cream of the Recent Crop of Stories and Anecdotes, Harvested, Assorted and Prepared for Market,* Garden City, 1950; *Good for a Laugh: A New Collection of Humorous Tidbits and Anecdotes from Aardvark to Zythum,* Hanover House, 1952; (with John Angus Burrell) *An Anthology of Famous American Stories,* Modern Library, 1953; *An Encyclopedia of Modern American Humor,* Doubleday, 1954; *Vest Pocket Book for All Occasions,* Random, 1956; *The Laugh's on Me,* Doubleday, 1959; *Bennett Cerf's Bumper Crop of Anecdotes and Stories, Mostly Humorous, About the Famous and Near Famous,* Garden City, 1959.

Book of Laughs, Random, 1959; *Out on a Limerick: A Collection of over 300 of the World's Best Printable Limericks, Assembled, Revised, Dry-Cleaned, and Annotated by*

What is the best way
to keep a skunk from smelling? ∎
(From *More Riddles* by Bennett Cerf
Illustrated by Roy McKie.)

Mister Cerf, Harper, 1960; *Book of Riddles,* Beginner Books, 1960; *More Riddles,* Beginner Books, 1961; *Four Contemporary American Plays,* Vintage, 1961; *Six American Plays for Today,* Modern Library, 1961; *Riddle-De-Dee: 458, Count Them, 458 Riddles Old and New for Children from 12 to 112,* Random, 1962; *Houseful of Laughter,* Random, 1963; (with Leonora Hornblow) *Bennett Cerf's Take Along Treasury,* Doubleday, 1963; *Book of Animal Riddles,* Beginner Books, 1964; *Bennett Cerf's Little Riddle Book,* Random, 1964; *Laugh Day,* Doubleday, 1965; *Treasury of Atrocious Puns,* Harper, 1968; *The Sound of Laughter,* Doubleday, 1970. (For complete list of books see *Contemporary Authors,* Volume 19-20.) Wrote daily feature, "Try and Stop Me," for King Features Syndicate. Contributed to *This Week* Magazine and *Saturday Review.*

SIDELIGHTS: Random House began when Mr. Cerf and Mr. Klopfer purchased 109 Modern Library titles from the publishing firm of Boni & Liveright. This venture made literary classics easily available to the U.S. public. With the formation of the publishing firm, Cerf immediately sought the current literary giants. He signed Eugene O'Neill and Robinson Jeffers and then sailed to Europe to see James Joyce about the publication of *Ulysses* in the U.S. Upon his return, his copy of the book was promptly seized at customs and with an attorney, Morris Ernst, Cerf took the case to court. The historic decision by Judge John Woolsey

was not only a victory for Cerf; it also proved to be a landmark in the struggle against censorship.

"Every publisher," said Cerf, "thinks of himself as an idealist, although the idealism is in the back of his head." Cerf tried to fulfill his idealistic responsibility "by publishing poetry, belles-lettres, the first novels you know won't sell a copy. We do two or three of those a year." Nevertheless he conceded that "it's awfully hard to turn down a book that's going to make money. If I thought nobody else was going to publish it, it wouldn't matter. But the thought that if I don't, somebody else will—I can't stand that."

Cerf spent a good deal of his time coddling his authors. One of his temperamental clients was Sinclair Lewis. Once, when Lewis spent the night at Cerf's apartment, "Bill Faulkner called up and said he was in town," commented Cerf. "I told Lewis and asked him, could Bill come over? Lewis said, 'Certainly not. This is my night!' Then at 9:30, Lewis went to bed. At 10:30, he shouted downstairs, 'Bennett!' I answered him, and he said, 'I just wanted to see if you sneaked out to see Faulkner'."

FOR MORE INFORMATION SEE: New York Times, December 7, 1965; *Time,* December 16, 1966; *Publishers' Weekly,* September 6, 1971.

(Died August 27, 1971)

Hold its nose.

BILL CHARMATZ

CHARMATZ, Bill 1925-

PERSONAL: Surname is pronounced Charm-ats; born November 15, 1925, in New York, N.Y.; son of Morris and Beckie Charmatz; married Marianne Charmatz, November 14, 1959; children: Katrina. *Education:* Attended Industrial Arts High School, New York, Academie de la Grande Chaumiere, Paris, 1950-52. *Home:* 45 West 68th St., New York, N.Y. 10023, and Rifton, N.Y. 12471.

CAREER: Author, illustrator. *Military service:* U.S. Navy, 1944-46.

WRITINGS—Self-illustrated juveniles: *The Little Duster,* Macmillan, 1967; *The Cat's Whiskers,* Macmillan, 1969; *Endeerments,* Ballantine, 1971.

He had very long whiskers and did useful things with them.
■ (From *The Cat's Whiskers* by Bill Charmatz. Illustrated by the author.)

CHEW, Ruth
(Ruth Silver)

PERSONAL: Born April 8, 1920, in Minneapolis, Minn.; daughter of Arthur Percy (a writer) and Pauline (Foucar) Chew; married Aaron B. Z. Silver (a lawyer), April 18, 1948; children: David, Eve (Mrs. Hugh Hamilton Sprunt, Jr.), George, Anne, Helen. *Education:* Corcoran School of Art, student, 1936-40. *Religion:* None. *Home:* 305 East Fifth St., Brooklyn, N.Y. 11218.

CAREER: Artist for *Washington Post,* Washington, D.C., 1942-43, Grey Advertising Agency, New York, N.Y., 1944-46, and Kresge-Newark Department Store, Newark, N.J., 1946-48.

WRITINGS—All self-illustrated books for children: *The Wednesday Witch,* Scholastic Book Services, 1969, Holiday House, 1972; *Baked Beans for Breakfast,* Scholastic Book Services, 1970, published as *The Secret Summer,* 1974; *No Such Thing as a Witch,* Scholastic Book Services, 1971; *Magic in the Park,* Scholastic Book Services, 1972; *What the Witch Left,* Scholastic Book Services and Hastings House, 1973; *The Hidden Cave,* Scholastic Book Services, 1973; *The Witch's Buttons,* Scholastic Book Services, 1974; *The Secret Tree House,* Scholastic Book Services, 1974.

RUTH CHEW

Illustrator: Carol Morse, *Three Cheers for Polly*, Doubleday, 1967; E. W. Hildick, *The Questers*, Hawthorn, 1970; Val Abbott, *Mystery of the Ghost Bell*, Dodd, 1971.

WORK IN PROGRESS: A Witch in the House.

SIDELIGHTS: "Although my education was as an artist I have always been interested in writing. After leaving school I worked as a fashion artist in Washington, Baltimore, Newark, and New York. This was interrupted by the deluge of diapers when my five children were small. When I tried to return to advertising art, I found that my work was out of date. I worked my way into children's book illustration and started writing in order to have something to illustrate. To my chagrin I found that I was considered a better writer than an artist. As a result I went back to school in 1973, studying at the Art Students' League with John Groth and Robert Shore.

Soon the vacuum cleaner was high in the air. From the ground it looked like a strange kite. ■ (From *The Wednesday Witch* by Ruth Chew. Illustrated by the author.)

"When my children were small I told them stories to stop them crying or to induce them to eat. I confess to being an imitator of E. Nesbit. I speak pigeon French and have travelled extensively. I collect, identify, and consume wild mushrooms."

FOR MORE INFORMATION SEE: New York Times Book Review, October 29, 1972.

CHILDRESS, Alice 1920-

PERSONAL: Surname is pronounced *Chill*-dress; born in 1920, in Charleston, S.C.; married Nathan Woodard (a musician and film editor); children: Jean (Mrs. Richard Lee). *Education:* Attended Radcliffe Institute for Independent Study. *Home:* 800 Riverside Dr., New York, N.Y. 10032. *Agent:* Flora Roberts, Inc., 116 East 59th St., New York, N.Y.

CAREER: Actress, writer, and lecturer; director of American Negro Theatre, New York, N.Y., for twelve years. *Member:* Dramatists Guild, Actors Equity, New Dramatists, Harlem Writers Guild, Radcliffe Club (New York). *Awards, honors: Village Voice*, Obie Award for best original Off-Broadway play, 1956, for "Trouble in Mind"; National Book Award nomination, 1974, for *A Hero Ain't Nothin' But a Sandwich.*

WRITINGS: Like One of the Family: Conversations from a Domestic's Life, Independence Press, 1956; *Wine in the Wilderness* (play), Dramatists Play Service, 1970; *Mojo [and] String* (two one-act plays), Dramatists Play Service, 1971; (editor) *Black Scenes: Collection of Scenes from Plays Written by Black People about Black Experience*, Doubleday, 1971, paperback edition published as *Black Scenes*, 1971; *A Hero Ain't Nothin' But a Sandwich* (juvenile), Coward, 1973.

Everybody always waitin to see where I'm comin from. I don't feel like before skag and don't feel skagged . . . feel old and beat, feelin jumpy and scared. I don't know what I'm scared of. I don't like bein scared-a nothin. My mama didn't have no chickens, you know. ■ (From *A Hero Ain't Nothin' but a Sandwich* by Alice Childress. Jacket design by David Brown.)

Unpublished plays: "Trouble in Mind," produced Off-Broadway, 1955-56; "Wedding Band," first produced at University of Michigan, 1966, produced Off-Broadway at Public Theatre, 1972.

Also author of "Gold through the Trees."

WORK IN PROGRESS: A Short Walk, a novel; "African Garden," a musical, with husband, Nathan Woodard.

SIDELIGHTS: Wine in the Wilderness was produced for television by Channel WGBH, Boston, in 1969; "Wedding Band" was produced on national television in 1974.

HOBBIES AND OTHER INTERESTS: Traveling.

CHITTUM, Ida   1918-

PERSONAL: Born April 6, 1918, in Canton, Ohio; daughter of Harry A. (a farmer) and Ida (Klingaman) Hoover; married James R. Chittum (a tool designer), August 26, 1936; children: Rosalind (Mrs. Thomas Lawrence), James H., Thomas W., Edith Irene, Samme R. *Education:* Attended school through eighth grade in Illinois and Missouri. *Residence:* Findlay, Ill. 62534. *Agent:* Ruth Cantor, 156 Fifth Ave., New York, N.Y. 10010.

CAREER: Writer of books for children. *Member:* National League of American Pen Women, Friends of Libraries, American Legion Auxiliary. *Awards, honors:* Lewis Carroll Shelf award of University of Wisconsin for *Farmer Hoo and the Baboons.*

WRITINGS—children's books: *Farmer Hoo and the Baboons,* Delacorte, 1971; *The Hermit Boy,* Delacorte, 1972; *Clabber Biscuits,* Steck, 1973; *A Nutty Business,* Putnam, 1973; *The Empty Grave,* American Educational Publications, 1974; *The Princess Pella,* Rand, in press; *The Secrets of Madam Renee,* Hearld, in press. Contributor of short stories and articles to magazines.

WORK IN PROGRESS: Clem Amounts to Something, for Delacorte.

SIDELIGHTS: "I write in a light-hearted fashion much as I live. I enjoy telling of wild and funny adventures which happen to everyone. I wish to see people smile more, and see the humorous side of life. I hope to write with a warmth which will encourage children to read. And to leave any group I talk to with the thought, our goal in life should not be to out-do the other fellow but to make the most of our God-given talents. Be as the heroes in my stories, don't give up and don't give in."

HOBBIES AND OTHER INTERESTS: Trees, birds, and all living things; collecting books, especially old ones.

FOR MORE INFORMATION SEE: Horn Book, June, 1971.

IDA CHITTUM

As the sun set, they stood proudly on the highest knob—Farmer Flint, Madam Flint, and little Glory Ann Flint, hand in hand, looking forward to many prosperous and nutty years ahead. ■ (From *A Nutty Business* by Ida Chittum. Illustrated by Stephen Gammell.)

CLARK, Virginia
See GRAY, Patricia

CLARKE, Clorinda   1917-

PERSONAL: Born March 4, 1917, in Utica, N.Y.; daughter of T. Wood (a physician and historian) and Clorinda (Tracy) Clarke. *Education:* Manhattanville College, B.A., 1938; Oxford University, graduate study, 1938-39; Columbia University, M.A., 1943. *Religion:* Roman Catholic. *Home:* 38 Gramercy Park, New York, N.Y. 10010. *Office:* New York Life Insurance Co., 51 Madison Ave., New York, N.Y. 10010.

CAREER: U.S. Army, Security and Intelligence Division, Governors Island, N.Y., employee, 1942-45; St. Peter's Church, New York, N.Y., editor, 1946-50; New York Life Insurance Co., New York, N.Y., managing editor of *Nylic Review,* 1950—. Convent of the Sacred Heart, New York, N.Y., lecturer, 1958-65. *Member:* New York State Historical Society, New York Historical Society, Kappa Gamma Pi, Manhattanville Club of New York.

WRITINGS—Youth books: *The American Revolution, 1775-1783,* Longmans, Green (London), 1964, published in United States as *The American Revolution: A British View,* McGraw, 1967; (contributor) *Tales of Life and Legend*

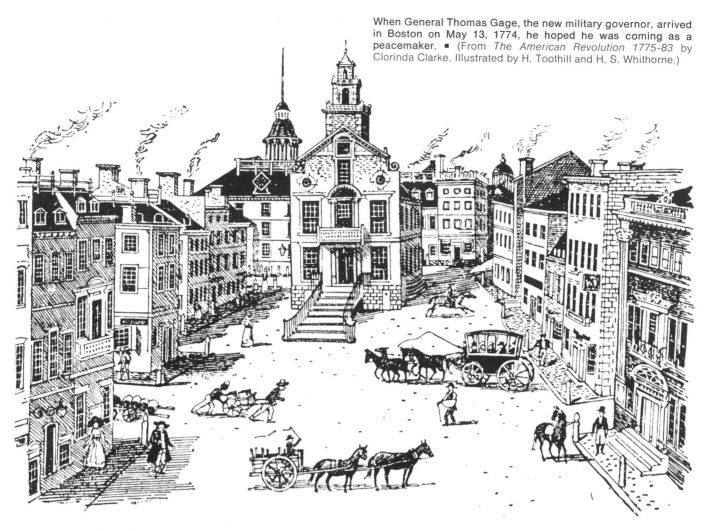

When General Thomas Gage, the new military governor, arrived in Boston on May 13, 1774, he hoped he was coming as a peacemaker. ■ (From *The American Revolution 1775-83* by Clorinda Clarke. Illustrated by H. Toothill and H. S. Whithorne.)

("Ballad of Helmer's Run"), Ginn, 1965; *The Young American Republic,* Longmans, Green, 1969; (contributor) *Time for Discovery* ("The Fate of the Loyalists"), Scott, Foresman, 1971. Member of editorial staff, *Manhattanville Alumnae Magazine,* 1960-65. Book reviewer, *Sign Magazine* and *Catholic World,* 1950-60.

WORK IN PROGRESS: A book on colonial New York, for Longman Group Ltd.; a book on Washington's spies in New York City during the Revolution.

SIDELIGHTS: "I began telling and writing stories when I was about six, and wrote my first novel when I was twelve. During my boarding school and college years I wrote, produced, directed and acted in many plays.

"Most of my jobs have involved writing and editing—though I needed shorthand to get started in business journalism. From 1950-60 book reviewing was the only way I could get into print.

"About thirteen years ago while I was visiting my old college at Oxford University in England, a former tutor asked me to write a book about the American Revolution for the British elementary schools. This book was followed by one on Washington and Jefferson. I am now writing about colonial New York.

"A writer has many problems. One is to find a subject that is interesting both to him and a publisher. It's a lonely and often financially undependable work, so it's wise to have a paying job, as I do.

"I depended on standard histories and biographies for the train of historical events, and use contemporary diaries, newspapers and letters for my quotations and characterizations. I do my research in the New York public libraries and most of my writing on weekends, although I try to do a little research or re-writing every day."

CLEVIN, Joergen 1920-

PERSONAL: Surname is pronounced Cle-*vin;* born April 24, 1920 in Copenhagen, Denmark; son of Peter and Ellen (Larsen) Petersen; married Gudrun Bondgaard, June 27, 1945; children; Helle, Janne, Lotte (all daughters). *Education:* Training College for Teachers, Copenhagen, graduate, 1941. *Religion:* Protestant. *Home:* Marielystvej 14, Copenhagen, Denmark.

CAREER: Teacher at a municipal school in Frederiksberg, Denmark, 1943—, and at Training College for Teachers, Copenhagen, Denmark, 1947—. Producer of more than

"Did you have a nice day at school?" Johnny asks. ■ From *Pete's First Day at School* by Jörgen Clevin. Illustrated by the author.)

50

JOERGEN CLEVIN

CAREER: Artist and illustrator. *Military service:* U.S. Army, 1958-60. *Member:* American Institute of Graphic Arts, Society of Illustrators. *Awards, honors:* Named Artist of the Year by Artists Guild of New York, 1965; various awards for books from American Institute of Graphic Arts, 1965-72; *Winter's Eve* and *Mr. Corbett's Ghost* appeared on *New York Times* list of best-illustrated books of the year; Gold Medal of Society of Illustrators for *Beowulf,* 1969, and *The Pigeon Man,* 1972, and in "institutional categories," 1974; Art Director's Club, gold medal, 1974, for magazine illustrations. Other medals in national drawing competitions.

ILLUSTRATOR: George Sanderlin, *First Around the World,* Harper, 1964; George Sanderlin, *Eastward to India,* Harper, 1965; Madeleine Polland, *The White Twilight,* Holt, 1965; Robert P. Smith, *Nothingatall, Nothingatall, Nothingatall,* Harper, 1965; Julia Cunningham, *Viollet,* Pantheon, 1966; Carl Withers, adapter, *The Tale of the Black Cat,* Holt, 1966; Phyllis LaFarge, *The Gumdrop Necklace,* Knopf, 1967; Leon Garfield, *Mr. Corbett's Ghost,* Pantheon, 1968; Carl Withers, adapter, *The Wild Ducks and the Goose,* Holt, 1968; Robert Nye, *Beowulf* (retold), Hill & Wang, 1968; Natalia M. Belting, *Winter's Eve* (poem), Holt, 1969; Florence Melman White, *Your Friend, the Tree,* Knopf, 1969; Jeane-Pierre Abraham, *The Pigeon Man,* Quist, 1972; Susan Cooper, *The Dark is Rising* (Newbery Honor Book), Atheneum, 1973; Ted Hughes, *The Tiger Bones,* Viking, 1973; *The Forgotten Society,* Dover, 1974.

seven hundred television programs for children, 1952—; also has conducted his own weekly television program for children, 1967—. *Member:* Danish Authors' Association, Danish Council of Educational Toys.

WRITINGS—Self-illustrated books for children: *Rasmus,* Gyldendal, 1945; *Historien om Brille,* Gyldendal, 1946; *Rasmus faar Besoeg,* Gyldendal, 1948; *Mads og Mikkel,* Gyldendal, 1966; *Jakob og Joakim,* Gyldendal, 1966, translation published as *Pete's First Day at School,* Random House, 1973; *Nicki,* Gyldendal, 1966; *Nikkolajsen,* Gyldendal, 1967; *Clevins legebog,* Samleren, 1968; *Kom og Se,* Gyldendal, 1969; *Kom og se Mere,* Gyldendal, 1970; *Jakob og Joakims redningskorps,* Gyldendal, 1971; *Kom og laer,* Gyldendal, 1971. Has written and illustrated more than thirty other books for children, including six editions of playbooks, 1963-70, hobby books, school texts, and drawing books.

WORK IN PROGRESS: Two books for children.

FOR MORE INFORMATION SEE: Times Literary Supplement, June 26, 1969; *Top of the News,* January, 1973.

COBER, Alan E(dwin) 1935-

PERSONAL: Born May 18, 1935, in New York, N.Y.; married Ellen Ross, 1961; children: Leslie (daughter), Peter. *Education:* Studied at University of Vermont, 1952-54, and School of Visual Arts, 1954-56. *Home:* Croton Dam Rd., Ossining, N.Y. 10562.

ALAN E. COBER by Alan E. Cober

HOBBIES AND OTHER INTERESTS: Collecting antique toys and folk art sculpture; has a well-known collection of Black Americana including carvings, slave documents, books, toys, advertising.

FOR MORE INFORMATION SEE: Print, December, 1963, May-June, 1973; *American Artist,* May-June, 1966, April, 1972.

COCAGNAC, A(ugustin) M(aurice-Jean) 1924-
(J.M. Warbler)

PERSONAL: Born June 20, 1924, in Tarbes, Haut Pyrenees, France; son of Joseph and Clemence (Rebeille) Cocagnac. *Education:* Received license in theology from the Dominican Fathers. *Home and office:* 222 rue du Faubourg, Saint-Honore, Paris 8e, France. *Office:* Le Periscope, 33 rue du Rocher, Paris 8e, France.

CAREER: Roman Catholic priest; Editions du Cerf, Paris, France, director of *Art Sacre* (periodical), 1954—, and director of children's bible series, 1970; Le Periscope, Paris, France, director, 1970—. *Member:* Societe des Auteurs, Compositeurs et Editeurs de Musique, Societe Asiatique.

WRITINGS: Le Jugement dernier dans l'art, Editions du Cerf, 1958; *Pour comprendre ma messe* (youth book), Editions du Cerf, 1965, translation by William Barrow published as *When I Go to Mass,* Macmillan, 1965; *L'Ancienne alliance,* Editions du Cerf, 1966; (with Rosemary Haughton) *Bible for Young Christians: The New Testament,* Macmillan, 1967; *La Nouvelle alliance,* Editions du Cerf, 1967; (with Rosemary Haughton) *Bible for Young Christians: The Old Testament,* Macmillan, 1967; *The Three Trees of the Samurai,* (Child Study Association Book list), Harlan Quist, 1970. Editor of collection, "Les Albums de l'arc-en-ciel," Editions du Cerf, published in England as "Dove Books," under pseudonym J.M. Warbler, by Chapman. Has done recordings of Bible songs in French.

COLLINS, David   1940-

PERSONAL: Born February 29, 1940, in Marshalltown, Iowa; son of Raymond A. (an educator) and Mary Elizabeth (Brecht) Collins. *Education:* Western Illinois University, B.S., 1962, M.S., 1966. *Politics:* Democrat. *Religion:* Roman Catholic. *Home:* 3724 15th Ave., Moline, Ill. 61265.

CAREER: Teacher of English at Woodrow Wilson Junior High School in Moline, Illinois, 1962—. *Member:* National Education Association (life member), Illinois Education Association, Moline Education Association, Illinois Parent Teacher Association (life member), Illinois State Historical Society (life member), Blackhawk Division Teachers of English (past president), Western Illinois University Alumni Control Board, Authors Guild, Society of Children's Book Writers, Children's Reading Roundtable, Writers' Studio (past president), Quad City Writers Club, American Amateur Press Association, Friends of the Moline Public Library (past president), River Bend Writers League, Kappa Delta Pi, Delta Sigma Phi, Sigma Tau Delta. *Awards, honors:* Writer's Digest Short Story Award winner in 1967; Writers' Studio "Writer of the Year Award" for 1970; Bobbs-Merrill Grant-in-Aid for juvenile writing in 1971; Judson College writing awards in 1971; Quad City Writers Club "Writer of the Year Award," 1972; Western Illinois University Achievement Award, 1973.

WRITINGS—Juvenile: Kim Soo and His Tortoise, Lion Press, 1970; *Great American Nurses,* Messner, 1971; *Walt Disney's Surprise Christmas Present,* Broadman, 1971; *Linda Richards, First Trained Nurse in America,* Garrard, 1973; *Harry S. Truman: Man of Independence,* Garrard, in press. Contributor to *Plays, The Instructor, Child Life, Venture, Guide, Hearthstone, Modern People, Vista,* and other periodicals.

WORK IN PROGRESS: Harry S. Truman, Man Of Independence for Garrard; picture books.

SIDELIGHTS: "I grew up in a world of books and readers. My father had an insatiable reading appetite for mysteries; my mother favored Gothics and biographies; my older brother was always surrounded by history and sports

DAVID R. COLLINS

One day, as Kim Soo helped lift a fishing net from the water, he saw that his father was sad.
■ (From *Kim Soo and His Tortoise* by David Collins. Illustrated by Alix Cohen.)

books. Our house could easily have been mistaken for a branch of our city's public library. I quickly joined the reading ranks of my family.

"Reading soon led to an interest in writing. I enjoyed working on staffs of the newspaper and yearbook while I was in school. I was lucky enough to receive much encouragement from my teachers. While in college, I spent every spare minute in the newspaper office.

"When I began teaching English, I found my own personal writing time greatly reduced—I was busy working with my students on their own writing skills. In fact, it was a student who got me started writing again. I had given a class of freshmen students an assignment—each student was to provide a short piece of historical fiction based on research done in our school library. 'That's too hard!' one boy protested. 'Not so,' I countered. 'It should be fun.' The boy was unconvinced. 'Then why don't you join the fun?' he challenged. 'Okay, I will!' I answered, setting the noble example. Well, I did the assignment—and discovered my rebellious young friend was right. It *was* hard. But once I'd finished my own assignment, I thought I should find out if it had any value to an audience. Happily, it was accepted by a magazine and I started seriously writing for publication.

"Why do I write for younger readers? The answer is simple. Young readers are curious, their minds open and flexible. They want to enjoy new reading adventures. Providing such adventures is an exciting task, but one that pays countless rewards. The fan mail—those letters, often carefully printed in pencil on big lined paper that say 'I liked your book' or 'You write good.' The youngsters who surround you after you've given a library story hour and say 'I wish I could write like you' or 'Gee, you're a nice man.' Those rewards are the greatest!"

HOBBIES AND OTHER INTERESTS: "Lecturing, reading (naturally!), tennis, bridge, people."

"We get up at five o'clock in the morning," Florence wrote home. "We have only ten minutes for each meal. The food is very plain. We only have bread and tea and vegetables." ■ (From *Florence Nightingale* by Anne Colver. Illustrated by Gerald McCann.)

COLVER, Anne 1908-
(Polly Anne Graff, Colver Harris)

PERSONAL: Born June 20, 1908, in Cleveland, Ohio; daughter of William Byron (a newspaper editor) and Pauline (Simmons) Colver; married Markham Harris, May 16, 1929 (divorced, 1942); married S. Stewart Graff (a lawyer, businessman, and writer), March 3, 1945; children: (first marriage) Jeremy Markham; (second marriage) Kate Stewart (Mrs. Stephen L. Danielski). *Education:* Attended Pine Manor Junior College, 1926-27; Whitman College, A.B., 1931. *Politics:* Democratic-Independent. *Religion:* Episcopalian. *Home:* Irvington, N.Y. *Agent:* McIntosh & Otis, Inc., 18 East 41st St., New York, N.Y. 10017.

CAREER: Writer. Member of board, Westchester County Society for Prevention of Cruelty to Children, 1956-66; member of library board, Irvington, N.Y., 1962-65; alumni trustee, Pine Manor Junior College, 1966-69.

WRITINGS—All juveniles, except as noted: *Listen for the Voices: A Novel of Concord* (adult fiction), Farrar & Rinehart, 1939; *Theodosia, Daughter of Aaron Burr* (historical novel), Farrar & Rinehart, 1941, revised edition, Holt, 1962; *Mr. Lincoln's Wife* (adult fiction), Farrar & Rinehart, 1943; *Shamrock Cargo: A Story of the Irish Potato Famine*, Winston, 1952; *Yankee Doodle Painter*, Knopf, 1955; *Old Bet*, Knopf, 1957; *Borrowed Treasure*, Knopf, 1958; *Secret Castle*, Knopf, 1960; *Lucky Four*, Duell, Sloan & Pearce, 1960; *Abraham Lincoln: For the People*, Garrard, 1960; *Nobody's Birthday*, Knopf, 1961; *Florence Nightingale: War Nurse*, Garrard, 1961; *Thomas Jefferson, Author of Independence*, Garrard, 1963; *Bread-and-Butter Indian*, Holt, 1964; *Louisa May Alcott*, Garrard, 1969; *Bread-and-Butter Journey*, Holt, 1970.

With husband, Stewart Graff; all juveniles: *Squanto: Indian Adventurer*, Garrard, 1965; *Helen Keller: Toward the Light*, Garrard, 1965; *The Wayfarer's Tree*, Dutton, 1973.

Under pseudonym Colver Harris; all adult fiction: *Hide and Go Seek*, Minton, Balch, 1933; *Going to St. Ives*, Macrae Smith, 1936; *Murder in Amber*, Hillman-Curl, 1938.

HOBBIES AND OTHER INTERESTS: Gardening, cooking, reading.

CORDELL, Alexander
See GRABER, Alexander

COSKEY, Evelyn 1932-

PERSONAL: Surname is pronounced Ka-skee; born November 16, 1932, in Jersey City, N.J.; daughter of Charles E. and Clara (Peters) Coskey. *Education:* Warren Wilson College, A.A., 1958; Berea College, B.A., 1960; University of Kentucky, M.S. in L.S., 1963. *Religion:* Presbyterian. *Home:* 1040 Beech Ave., Charleston, W.Va. 25302. *Office:* Kanawha County Public Library, 123 Capitol St., Charleston, W.Va. 25301.

CAREER: Kanawha County Public Library, Charleston, W.Va., extension librarian, 1964—. Member of advisory board of Public Library-Adult Basic Education Program operating out of Morehead State University. *Member:* West Virginia Arts and Crafts Guild, Mountain State Cat Club.

WRITINGS: Easter Eggs for Everyone, Abingdon, 1973. Former book review columnist, *Charleston Sunday Gazette-Mail.* Contributor to *Library Journal* and *Library Trends.*

WORK IN PROGRESS: A Christmas handicraft book, for Abingdon, 1976; research on World War II, with emphasis on Poland, and on Methodist history, the latter in connection with a projected biography of an uncle, once general superintendent of the Polish Methodist Church.

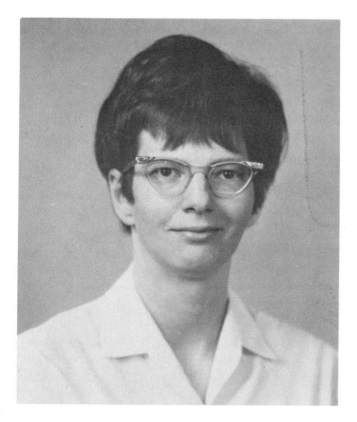

EVELYN COSKEY

SIDELIGHTS: "My first book was done for a rather odd reason. A school nurse in New Jersey saw things in me that others failed to see and kept saying that she wanted to see me publish a book before she died. She was getting old, had already gone blind, and time was running out. So I knew the subject had to be one about which I knew something, one which was badly needed in libraries, and non-competitive with with too many other books. So I chose Easter Eggs. The school nurse is one of the two women to whom the book is dedicated. She knew it was to be published. Unfortunately, it came out in January, 1973, and she died, at the age of 95, the previous June. She was Mary Davis Fee."

Evelyn Coskey has always been interested in crafts of all kinds, once ran a small wooden Christmas tree ornament business and used the proceeds to help finance a visit to relatives in Poland in 1969. Since then she has made three more trips to Poland. She lives with two Siamese cats, Juliette ("who positively loathes typewriters") and Jennifer.

FOR MORE INFORMATION SEE: Publishers' Weekly, February 19, 1973; *New York Times Book Review,* April 15, 1973; *Horn Book,* June, 1973.

CRAYDER, Dorothy 1906-

PERSONAL: Born September 12, 1906, in New York, N.Y.; daughter of Harris (a manufacturer) and Sarah (Kinsberg) Crayder; married Robert Newman (a writer), October 30, 1936; children: Hila (Mrs. Gerald Feil). *Education:* New York University, student, 1924-27; also studied journalism at Columbia University, 1923. *Home and office:* 7 School Street, Stonington, Conn. 06378. *Agent:* Harold Ober Assoicates, Inc., 40 East 49th St., New York, N.Y. 10017.

The conversation was going along nicely with everyone agreeing that life aboard a transatlantic liner was great, that last night's movie was a stinker, that the food was great, and so was this pool, when without warning the conversation took a terrible turn. ■ (From *She, The Adventuress* by Dorothy Crayder. Illustrated by Velma Ilsley.)

DOROTHY CRAYDER

CAREER: Has worked as secretary, salesgirl, manager of an art gallery, and model. *Member:* Authors Guild. *Awards, honors:* Book World's Children's Spring Book Festival Award, 1973, for *She, the Adventuress.*

WRITINGS: (With Helen McCully) *The Christmas Pony,* Bobbs, 1967; *The Pluperfect of Love,* Atheneum, 1971; *She, the Adventuress* (Junior Literary Guild selection), Atheneum, 1973; *She and the Dubious Three,* Atheneum, 1974. Also author of short stories and radio and television plays.

WORK IN PROGRESS: Other fiction, and a possible biography for children.

SIDELIGHTS: "I was born in New York City and was mistakenly labeled a delicate child by a consensus of pediatricians and hypochondriacal relatives. Because of that bizarre diagnosis I was privately tutored until I was ten years old, was allowed to go to school only part time when I did go, spent a bewildering year at a convent, and then four years at a private school for young ladies where the myth of my delicate health excused me from Latin. That pleased me no end then, but I have since very much regretted it. Somehow I slipped through New York University and some courses at the Columbia School of Journalism. This education has left me with huge blank spaces and a lifelong terror of playing parlor games that expose one's ignorance of geography and history.

"The summers of this 'delicate' childhood were spent in the Adirondacks, New Hampshire, and on Long Island—swimming, playing tennis, riding, and walking. Walking remains a passion.

"I have always wanted to write. Indeed, when I was fifteen years old I actually persuaded the editor of a country newspaper that I could furnish him with a weekly column about the doings at the neighboring country clubs. I believe we both thought my sources were better than they were. I lasted two weeks. It was a long time before I wrote professionally again. In between, I was a saleslady, a secretary, a model, the manager of an art gallery, a wife, and a mother.

"I am married to Robert Newman, the writer. We have one daughter, Hila Feil. And we are all currently writing for children, which makes us rather like the Flying Wallendas."

FOR MORE INFORMATION SEE: Horn Book, October, 1973.

CUNNINGHAM, E. V.
See FAST, Howard

DAHL, Borghild   1890-

PERSONAL: Born February 5, 1890, in Minneapolis, Minn.; daughter of Peder M. and Ingeborg (Haugseth) Dahl. *Education:* University of Minnesota, A.B., 1912; Columbia University, M.A., 1923; University of Oslo, Norsk Akademiker, 1924. *Politics:* Republican. *Religion:* Lutheran. *Home:* 1909 Amsterdam Ave., New York, N.Y. 10032.

CAREER: High schools in South Dakota, North Dakota, and Minnesota, teacher, principal, 1912-22; Augustana College, Sioux Falls, S.D., professor of literature and journalism, 1926-39. Lecturer and radio book reviewer. *Member:* Delta Phi Lambda, Kappa Delta. *Awards, honors:* Medal of St. Olaf, presented by the King of Norway, for promoting good relations between Norway and the United States; World Who's Who of Women diploma, 1973.

WRITINGS: Glimpses of Norway, privately printed, 1935; *I Wanted to See,* Macmillan, 1944; *Karen,* Random House, 1947; *Homecoming,* Dutton, 1953; *The Daughter,* Dutton, 1956; *The Cloud Shoes,* Dutton, 1958; *Stowaway to America,* Dutton, 1959; *A Minnetonka Summer,* Dutton, 1960; *Under This Roof,* Dutton, 1961; *Finding My Way,* Dutton, 1962; *This Precious Year,* Dutton, 1964; *Good News,* Dutton, 1966; *Rikk of the Rendal Clan,* Dutton, 1968; *My Window on America,* Dutton, 1970. "Marit," originally written in English, translated into Norwegian, ran as a serial in a Norwegian weekly newspaper, *Decorah Posten,* 1945-46. Contributor of stories and poetry to magazines and newspapers.

SIDELIGHTS: Miss Dahl's experience as the daughter of Norweigian parents in the Midwest provides background for much of her writing. Her first story was published when she was twelve in the *Minneapolis Journal Junior.* After a losing battle to save her eyesight she continues to write with what her publishers call "a singleness of purpose which she had never experienced before." Miss Dahl told the *New York Times* that she writes her stories on a typewriter and mails them to the author, Marchette Chute. Miss Chute and Miss Dahl then discuss the stories on the telephone.

"Every person who writes draws on his own life or his environment or what others tell him or what he reads. However indirect these may be, they still reflect some phase of his own living. Even such matter as scientific treatises are a result of the time he has spent in order to prepare himself for his enterprise.

"Generally speaking the following catagories comprise most sources of subject matter for most authors. Personal biographical writing lies closest to him. Then he uses his environment or his observation of what has been going on around him, or he may make use of things told him by word of mouth from others. His own imagination often stands him in good stead. And, of course, the wider his reading, the greater is his wealth from books. I have made use of all these sources.

"Four of my books are autobiographical. *Glimpses of Norway* was written as a result of my studies in Norway. I attended the University of Oslo; heard discussions in the Norwegian national parliament called the Stortin; spent whole days in city and country schools, high schools as well as those housing the lower grades; witnessed the best performances at the theaters, concerts, and other cultural activities; and was in the presence of the King. I wrote a series of articles which were published in *Aften Posten* newspapers, and these I translated from the Norwegian and included them in my book.

Rikk could hardly believe his eyes. Spinster Great-aunt Aasve was smiling at him. ■ (From *Rikk of the Rendal Clan* by Borghild Dahl. Illustrated by Ib Ohlsson.)

"*I Wanted to See* and *Finding My Way* tell of the difficulty with my eyes, which finally ended in total blindness. These were written at the urgent advice of both my eye surgeon, Dr. W. L. Benedict of the Mayo Clinic, and my literary critic, Marchette Chute. And finally the two books I have written for younger children, *Rikk of the Rendal Clan* and *The Cloud Shoes* are pure and simply a product of my imagination.

"Four of my books reflect the influence of my environment—my life among Norwegian Americans. *Homecoming* tells of the struggles of a family directly from Norway that settled and continued to Americanize itself in the city of Minneapolis, Minnesota. *This Precious Year* was made possible by the thirteen years I spent teaching at Augustana College in Sioux Falls, South Dakota. It had been founded by sturdy Norwegian pioneers of that state, and my students were children of these pioneers. The drought which took place during my stay there was especially lucrative in portraying the great fortitude of these people.

"And *Under This Roof* came out of the years I spent in Twin Valley, Minnesota, among early settlers, just at the time there was the turnover from the horse and buggy stage to the coming of the first Model-T Fords. In fact, the first ride I ever had in an automobile took place in one of these the first week I started my teaching career there.

"One other book of mine reflects my environment, *Good News*. But this came as a result of my living in a highly integrated apartment house in New York City. Most of my neighbors were Negroes, and my life among them taught me so much about how well people of different ethnic backgrounds can get along together, that I felt impelled to let people get the benefit of my findings.

"Two of my books were written because of what two people told me by word of mouth, *The Daughter* and *Karen*. A woman who came to South Dakota in the early seventies described to me how the prairies were converted

BORGHILD DAHL

into two fine popuated states in our Union. This one, South Dakota. The title is *Karen*. As far back as I can remember, my mother used to tell me about her childhood and youth in her native country of Norway. I was so intrigued by her graphic accounts of the estate on which she grew up and the customs of her people that my greatest wish as a little girl was to have the privilege of seeing the places she described. *The Daughter* contains much of what she told me.

"And finally one book was made possible from things which I read. In 1925, the one-hundredth anniversary of the first successful colony of Norwegians at Kendall, New York, was celebrated by proud sons and daughters of their native land in all parts of the United States. I was so intrigued by the tales of how this colony was founded that I decided to write a novel with this event as its background. It was called *Stowaway to America*.

"I have been most fortunate in having lived for more than eighty years, and so on the anniversary of this event, my publishers, E. P. Dutton, published as a gift to me and my friends, a paperback, *My Window on America*. It is a history of the events which have taken place during my life, from 1890 up to 1970. It is a long span of years. From a time when only oil lamps were used, no refrigerators, no automobiles, no airplanes, and a host of other modern things which we take for granted now, but which were not even imagined during my youth. I especially remember two expressions which were often heard in those days: 'I could no more do that than fly' and 'one might as well tell that as to say one might reach the moon.' Both these impossible pronouncements and many more have come to pass.

FOR MORE INFORMATION SEE: New York Times, May 13, 1966; *Third Book of Junior Authors*, edited by de Montreville and Hill, H. W. Wilson, 1972.

DANIELS, Guy 1919-

PERSONAL: Born May 11, 1919, in Gilmore City, Iowa; son of Guy Emmett (a gentleman farmer) and Gretchen (Van Alstine) Daniels; married Margaret Holbrook (now a teacher), November 14, 1943; married second wife, Anne McCrea, January 13, 1963; married third wife, Vernell Groom, December 2, 1967; children: (first marriage) Brooke (Mrs. Donald Hinrichsen); (second marriage) Matthew; (third marriage) Guy III. *Education:* University of Iowa, B.A., 1941, graduate student, 1941-42. *Home and office:* 416 East 65th St., New York, N.Y. 10021. *Agent:* Gunther Stuhlmann, 65 Irving Pl., New York, N.Y. 10003.

CAREER: Trans-World Airlines, International Division, chief language instructor at Training School, Reading, Pa., and Newark, Del., 1946-47; U.S. Government, Washington, D.C., "petty bureaucrat," 1947-52; full-time writer and translator, 1952—. *Military service:* U.S. Navy, 1942-45; became lieutenant junior grade; received combat star. *Member:* P.E.N., Phi Beta Kappa.

WRITINGS: Poems and Translations, Inferno Press, 1959; *Progress, U.S.A.* (novel), Macmillan, 1968.

Translations: Erich Auerbach, *An Introduction to Romance Languages and Literature*, Putnam, 1961; Stendhal, *Racine and Shakespeare*, Crowell-Collier, 1962; *A Lermontov Reader*, Macmillan, 1965; *Fifteen Fables of Krylov* (juvenile), Macmillan, 1965; *Ivan the Fool, and Other Tales of Leo Tolstoy* (juvenile), Macmillan, 1966; *The Tsar's Riddles* (juvenile), McGraw, 1967; Nikolai Leskov, *The Wild Beast* (juvenile), Funk, 1968; *The Complete Plays of Vladimir Mayakovsky*, Washington Square, 1968;

And off he went toward the enemy, scrunched down on his old nag's mane. ■ (From *Foma the Terrible* by Guy Daniels. Illustrated by Imero Gobbato.) ⸼

Mikhalkov, *Let's Fight, and Other Russian Fables* (juvenile), Pantheon, 1968; *The Falcon under the Hat: Favorite Russian Merry Tales and Fairy Tales* (juvenile), Funk, 1969.

Russian Comic Fiction, New American Library, 1970; Ivan Bunin, *Velga* (juvenile), S. G. Phillips, 1970; Mayakovsky, *Timothy's Horse* (juvenile), Pantheon, 1970; *Foma the Terrible* (juvenile), Delacorte, 1970; Andre Castelot, *Napoleon*, Harper, 1971; Yevgeny Riabchikov, *Russians in Space*, Doubleday, 1971; Chekhov, *The Wolf and the Mutt* (juvenile), McGraw-Hill, 1971; *The Peasant's Pea Patch* (juvenile), Delacorte, 1971; Colette Portal, *The Beauty of Birth* (juvenile), Pantheon, 1971; *Azmun and the Old Man of the Sea* (juvenile), McGraw-Hill, in press; Pierre Louys, *Dialogues of the Courtisans*, Cercle des Editions Limitees, in press; Balzac, *The Unknown Masterpiece*, Cercle des Editions Limitees, in press.

Contributor of original poetry, fiction, and articles to anthologies and periodicals, including *New Republic, Nation, New Directions, Kenyon Review,* and *Beloit Poetry Journal;* translations of poetry, fiction, and essays have also appeared in anthologies, *New Republic, Playboy, Vogue,* and elsewhere. Associate editor, *Trace* (magazine), 1956-58; member of advisory board, *Soviet Studies in Literature.*

WORK IN PROGRESS: Translating a series of French classics for the Cercle des Editions Limitees.

SIDELIGHTS: "Rather deeply involved in 'classical' (i.e., largely nineteenth-century) Russian authors, especially the poets. Am getting mired down in this vast bog to the detriment of my poetry (abandoned) and fiction (lately resumed with a vengeance)." In addition to translating ability in Russian and French, Daniels has some competence in Spanish and Italian.

DARBY, Ray(mond) K. 1912-

PERSONAL: Born March 9, 1912, in Edmonton, Alberta, Canada; son of Charles Edgar (a salesman) and Julala M. (Hopkins) Darby; married Patricia Paulsen, October 26, 1954; children: Glen, Jessica, Grant, Raymond Jr.; stepchildren: Edward, Rebecca. *Education:* Attended Kelvin Technical High School, Winnipeg, Canada. *Politics:* Republican. *Religion:* Episcopalian. *Home:* 2527 Hereford Rd., Lake Sherwood, Thousand Oaks, Calif. 91360. *Agent:* August Lenniger Literary Agency, Fifth Avenue, New York, N.Y.

CAREER: Full-time professional writer. Has been employed at periods as motion picture writer for Walt Disney Productions and the U.S. Air Force, and as both writer and director for U.S. Navy. Free lances concurrently and between employed periods. *Member:* American Society of Composers, Authors and Publishers, Conejo Valley Historical Society (Board of Directors), Lake Sherwood Property Owners Association (Board of Directors), Honorary Member, Eugene Field Society. *Awards, honors:* Columbus "Chris" Award for film "The U.S. Air Force in Southeast Asia", 1968; film "The Chuting Stars" represented U.S. military films at Versailles and Edinburgh film

RAY DARBY (right)
with members of the Navy's "Chuting Stars"

festivals, 1963; Christopher Award for Disney film series, 1957.

WRITINGS: Oomah, Contemporary Publishers, 1946; *Peter Smith and the Bugs* and *Peter Smith and the Sky People*, School Aids and Textbook Publishing Co, 1944; *The Space Age Sport, Sky Diving*, (Junior Literary Guild selection), Julian Messner, 1964; *Your Career in Physical Therapy*, (Junior Literary Guild selection), Julian Messner, 1968; *Conquering the Deep Sea Frontier*, (Junior Literary Guild selection), David McKay, 1972. Author of about 100 motion picture documentaries. Contributor to *Reader's Digest, This Week, True, Cavalier, Gook Housekeeping, Coronet,* and other magazines.

WORK IN PROGRESS: Books for backward readers.

SIDELIGHTS: "Decided on a writing career at the age of sixteen, but worked hard at it for six years before making a major sale. Got started in radio. Sold first ½ hour commercially sponsored drama for $5, then boosted pay to $750 per script or better. Wrote for Canadian, U.S. and Australian networks, also heard in Belgium, France and Italy. Progressed to TV, then magazines, finally to combination of books and movies, which I like best. "Material comes from (1) experience, and (2) imagination. My belief . . . if you let your mind hang open, the ideas will fall in. Long experience in meeting deadlines has taught me to be able to write anywhere, anytime. As a father of six children, I particularly enjoy writing for young people. Another belief . . . anyone with a maximum of desire and even a minimum of talent can learn to write successfully, but it may take a long time and a great deal of consistent effort."

HOBBIES AND OTHER INTERESTS: Travel, fishing, golf.

One of the favorite methods of shooting free fall pictures—with the camera mounted on the photographer's forearm. ■ (From *The Space Age Sport* by Ray Darby. Photograph by U.S. Navy.)

DeGERING, Etta (Fowler) 1898-

PERSONAL: Born January 7, 1898, in Arcadia, Neb.; daughter of Charles Henry (rancher) and Beryl (Brown) Fowler; married Claud DeGering (educator), July 22, 1917; children; Harvey, Trudy-Anne (Mrs. Dean R. Johnson). *Education:* Walla Walla College, student, four years. *Home:* 2945 16th St., Boulder, Colo.

CAREER: Elementary teacher, British Columbia, Canada; instructor in French and English, Battleford, Sask., Canada, 1917-30; editor of Braille reprint magazine, *The Children's Friend*, Braille Foundation for the Blind, Lincoln, Nebr. 1950-60; and now writer. *Awards, honors:* Thomas Alva Edison Mass Media book award for *Seeing Fingers, the Story of Louis Braille,* (juvenile) 1962; Colorado Top-hand Award for juvenile non-fiction, *Gallaudet, Friend of the Deaf,* 1965; honorary certificates: *Two Thousand Women of Achievement,* 1971, *The World Who's Who of Women,* 1973, Cambridge, England, as a biographee.

WRITINGS: Seeing Fingers, the Story of Louis Braille (Junior Literary Guild Selection), McKay, 1962; *Gallaudet, Friend of the Deaf,* McKay, 1964; *Christopher Jones, Captain of the Mayflower,* McKay, 1965; *Wilderness Wife, the Story of Rebecca Bryan Boone,* McKay, 1966; *My Bible Friends* (set of ten picture books), Review and Herald, 1963-1968. Former contributor to *Wee Wisdom, Humpty Dumpty, Scholastic Magazines,* and others.

WORK IN PROGRESS: Who Was McGuffey?, young adult; *William Brewster, Fugitive for Freedom* (three chapters to completion); *Once Upon a Bible Time,* (set of seven pre-school Bible story books) the first book now at press, Review and Herald.

SIDELIGHTS: "I like to write the kind of history not taught in schools, telling rather the story of someone who lived it. The best writing hours for me are early morning (often 4 AM) to noon. Afternoons, I hardly know a common from a proper noun. On completing the basic research, my husband and I drive (we drive over Daniel Boone's Wilderness Trail) or fly to the locale where the story took place. There we search musty records, seek out descendants, and try to absorb the background of sights, sound, smells . . . I like to write Bible stories, agreeing with an eightyear-old fan, 'Bible stories are the best stories.'

As I brailled stories for blind readers (though sighted, I read and write Braille) my desire to know the French boy who perfected the six-dot system grew with each story. I wrote the headmaster of the Paris School for the Blind who rewarded me (in French, of course) with undreamed of information and pictures. Out of this grew *Seeing Fingers.* Emil Weiss's cover lithographs are as authentic as the text—the bust of Braille which may be seen in the Paris School for the Blind, the house with pump, Braille's birthplace in Coupvray, the church where the boy Braille spent many hours with Abbe Palluy. The hands in the lower lefthand corner are those of twelve-year-old blind Karen of Chicago reading her Braille magazine.

"When the old "Pensy" train missed connections with the Denver Zephyr in Chicago, it did me a rare service. Forced to wait over, I visited the Newberry Library, and there found the information on Chris Jones originally researched by the Historian of Harwich where the captain grew up. Having long carried a flag for the Mayflower Captain who not only furnished the ship but gave his life helping to establish America's first permanent colony, I canceled my reservation, phoned home for money, and stayed in Chi-

He walked on and on, thinking over what he had just heard: eighty-four deaf in Connecticut, four hundred in New England, a thousand in America! No schools! No education for them! ■ (From *Gallaudet: Friend of the Deaf* by Etta DeGering. Illustrated by Emil Weiss.)

ETTA DeGERING

CAREER: Self-employed writer. Reads and judges novels for publishers in English, French, German, Dutch, Flemish, South African. *Member:* Academy of Arts and Letters (Holland). *Awards, honors:* Literature Prize of Holland, 1947, for *And the Field is the World.*

WRITINGS: *Nikkernik, Nakkernak and Nokkernok,* Scribner, 1942; *The level Land,* Scribner, 1943; *And the Field is the World,* Scribner, 1945; *Picture Story of Holland,* Reynal and Hitchcock, 1946; *Sand for the Sandmen,* Scribner, 1946; *Return to the Level Land,* Scribner, 1947; *The Tree and The Vine,* Querido, 1960, Lyle Stuart, 1963; *By Marvelous Agreement,* Knopf, 1960; *Between Home and Horizon,* Knopf, 1962; *The House on Charlton Street,* Scribner, 1962; *A Summer's Secret,* McKay, 1963; *The Khirligig of Time* (Crimm Club Selection), Doubleday, 1964; (editor) *An Anthology of Contemporary American Short Stories,* Polak & Van Gennep, 1965.

WORK IN PROGRESS: Juveniles for Scribner.

SIDELIGHTS: Dola de Jong was born in Arnhem, Holland. Growing up, she had two hobbies—writing and dancing—and when she graduated from high school she

cago to begin *Christopher Jones.* When completed, the manuscript crossed the Atlantic to Oxford, England, where the old ships' language was so courteously checked by none other than the Captain of Mayflower II.

"Looking over the heads of my grandsons at the dramatic portrayal of Daniel Boone, I became indignant at the gap between fact and fiction. Examples: A copy of a letter in my files, written by Daniel's youngest son, reads,'My father always wore a hat; he hated coonskin caps.' Rebecca had raven-black hair. Why in this day of wigs should she be portrayed a blond? Israel was but a wee chap, not big brother to teenage Jemima . . . I resolved to write the true story of the Boones, and since old Daniel had had so much glory, decided to tell it from Rebecca's view point. Please don't let your librarian put *Wilderness Wife* on the fiction shelf."

FOR MORE INFORMATION SEE: *The Boulder Camera,* January 30, 1963; *Denver Post,* February 7, 1963; *Rocky Mountain News,* March 21, 1963; *Horn Book,* February, 1964.

de JONG, Dola

PERSONAL: Born in Arnhem, Holland; daughter of S. L. and Lotte (Benjamin) de Jong; children: Ian. *Education* Educated in Holland and England. *Home:* 400 Central Park West, Apt. 18L, New York, N.Y. 10025. *Agent:* Robert Mills, 20 East 53rd St., New York, N.Y.

The flags were flying in the wind (it was cold all right), the music was real skating music, and the people laughed and talked and had lots of fun. ■ (From *The Level Land* by Dola de Jong. Illustrated by Peter Spier.)

DOLA DE JONG

in New York, Rome, Munich, and Paris, 1950-57; Central Office of Information, London, England, radio producer, 1958-60; free-lance writer in New York, N.Y., 1961-66; *Interplay,* New York, N.Y., special projects editor, 1967-69; *Horizon,* New York, N.Y., articles editor, 1970—. *Military service:* U.S. Naval Reserve, active duty, 1944-46, 1950-51. *Member:* Authors League of America, P.E.N., Coffee House, and Holland Society (all New York). *Awards, honors:* Shared with co-author M. J. Furland the Cannes Film Festival Award for best scenerio, 1949, for "Lost Boundaries."

WRITINGS: Universal History of the World, Western Publishing, Volume V· *The East in the Middle Ages,* 1964, Volume XIII; *Imperialism and World War I,* 1964; *Meet Theodore Roosevelt* (juvenile), Random House, 1967; *Meet Andrew Jackson* (juvenile), Random House, 1967; *The Adventures of Lewis and Clark* (juvenile), Random House, 1968; (translator into French and author of comments) *Rimes de la Mere Oie* (translation accompanied by original English Mother Goose rhymes), Little, Brown, 1971.

Contributor of poems to *Harper's , Atlantic, New Yorker,* and other magazines.

FOR MORE INFORMATION SEE: New York Times Book Review, June 16, 1967; *Publishers' Weekly,* December 13, 1971.

soon made good use of both of them. She went to work for a newspaper in Amsterdam and then she had a chance to dance in the Royal Ballet. She managed to combine her careers of dancing and writing very well, for at eighteen had her first juvenile novel published.

In 1940, just before Hitler invaded Holland, Dola de Jong escaped to North Africa. The following year she went to the United States and in 1946 she became an American citizen. Now she lives in New York City with her young son Ivan and is busy at work with her novels, literary essays, book reviewing, and various other interests.

de Kay, Ormonde, Jr. 1923-

PERSONAL: Born December 17, 1923, in New York, N.Y.; son of Ormonde and Margaret (McClure) de Kay; married Barbara Scott, January 20, 1967; children: Thomas. *Education:* Choate School, student, 1937-41; Harvard University, A.B., 1947. *Politics:* Democrat. *Home:* 1225 Park Ave., New York, N.Y. 10028. *Agent:* Julian Bach, Jr., 3 East 48th St., New York, N.Y. 10017. *Office: Horizon,* 1221 Avenue of the Americas, New York, N.Y. 10020.

CAREER: Louis de Rochemont Associates, inc., New York, N.Y., screen writer, 1948-49; free-lance screenwriter

He taught him how to live alone in wild country. And he taught him a lot about Indians. ■ From *The Adventures of Lewis and Clark* by Ormonde de Kay, Jr. Illustrated by John Powers Severin.)

Something about the Author

DELAUNE, (Jewel) Lynn (de Grummond)

PERSONAL: Born in Canterville, La.; daughter of Will White (engineer) and Lena (Young) de Grummond; married Richard K. Delaune (lieutenant colonel, U.S. Army), March 1, 1952; children: Richard K., Jr., Linden Marjorie, Jonathan Ernest. *Education:* Louisiana State University, B.A., M.A. *Home:* 316 Burns Lane, Williamsburg, Va. 23185.

CAREER: Army and Navy Publishing Co., Baton Rouge, La., layout artist, one year; Louisiana State University, Baton Rouge, graduate assistant in history, two years, acquisitions department of library, two years, circulation librarian, one year; Special Services (civilian personnel working for U.S. Army), Sendai, Japan, area librarian, two years; College of William and Mary, Williamsburg, Va., lecturer, 1966-70, assistant professor, 1971—.

WRITINGS: Giraffes Can Be a Trouble, Dutton, 1955; (with Lena Young de Grummond) *Jeff Davis, Confederate Boy,* Bobbs, 1960; (with Lena Young de Grummond) *Jeb Stuart,* Lippincott, 1962; (with Lena Young de Grummond) *Babe Didrikson,* Bobbs, 1963; (with Lena Young de Grummond) *Jean Piccard, Balloon Boy,* Bobbs. Contributor to *World Book Yearbook.*

WORK IN PROGRESS: Editing a group of Civil War letters; further collaboration with mother on biographies.

SIDELIGHTS: "I probably have always wanted to write because I have always loved to read. I was especially fortunate in my choice of a mother, having chosen one who loved books and who loved sharing them with her children, something I have tried to do, too. She made books important and fun! Right now, when my duties as wife, mother, homemaker, teacher (it's supposed to be part-time, but often gets to be rather full-time-ish instead), needlework designers and 'manufacturer' (my husband and I have a small business hand-silkscreen-printing crewel embroidery kits for several commercial outlets) seem to leave me little time for either reading or writing, I often find myself stirring something on the stove with one hand and holding an open book with the other.

"The writing has been harder to fit in, but I have one or two things started and hope to be able to make myself push ahead with them one of these days. The requirements of each day seem so numerous that I usually feel I'm doing fairly well just to take care of things-that-absolutely-must-be-done without even touching the category of things-it-would-be-nice-to-do! I thoroughly enjoy painting (not the walls and doors kind, though I often do that too), handwork of any variety, and gardening. Our busy household consists of not only my husband, myself, our two sons, and daughter, but two dogs, one cat, two gerbils, four turtles, and (outside of the household) a horse."

Ms. Delaune writes in collaboration with her mother, Lena Young de Grummond. She does much of the actual writing while her mother concentrates on research. She spent two years in Japan, studied flower arranging, Japanese painting, and dancing.

De WAARD, E(lliott) John   1935-

PERSONAL: Born March 30, 1935, in Sault Ste Marie, Mich.; son of Otto (a game biologist with Michigan Department of Conservation) and Elma (Elliott) De Waard; married Nancy Jean Wisner (a teacher and writer), June 21, 1958; children: Eric, Edward. *Education:* Adrian College, B.S., 1957; Michigan State University, M.S., 1962; Ohio State University, further graduate study, 1962-63. *Home:* 201 Creekside Dr., Palo Alto, Calif. 94306. *Office:* Addison-Wesley Publishing Co., Menlo Park, Calif.

CAREER: High school teacher of science in Napoleon, Mich., 1958-62; American Education Publications, Middletown, Conn., editor of *Current Science,* 1963-66; Silver Burdett Co., Morristown, N.J., senior editor of science textbooks, 1966-70; Addison-Wesley Publishing Co., Menlo Park, Calif., senior editor and associate publisher-science, 1970-74, executive science editor, 1974—. Special lecturer at Wesleyan University, Middletown, Conn., 1963-66. *Member:* National Science Teachers Association (life member), National Association of Biology Teachers, American Institute of Biological Sciences, National Association of Physics Teachers, School Science and Mathematics Association, American Forestry Association, New York Academy of Science.

WRITINGS: What Insect Is That? American Education Publications, 1964; *Plants and Animals in the Air,* Doubleday, 1969; *The Shape of Living Things,* Doubleday, 1969; *The Color of Life* (Junior Literary Guild selection), Doubleday, 1971; *The Metric System,* Addison-Wesley, 1974. Author with wife, Nancy DeWaard, of three study guides, *The Doubleday Companion to Through the Microscope, The Doubleday Companion to Man and Insects,* and *The Doubleday Companion to Man Probes the Universe,* all 1967. Wrote more than one hundred short feature stories for *Current Science,* 1963-66.

WORK IN PROGRESS: Two more juvenile science books.

HOBBIES AND OTHER INTERESTS: Little League manager, piloting sailplane, woodworking, electronics, hunting, fishing, photography.

FOR MORE INFORMATION SEE: Library Journal, May 15, 1969; *Christian Science Monitor,* October 30, 1969.

DEWEY, Ariane   1937-
(Ariane Aruego)

PERSONAL: Born August 17, 1937, in Chicago, Ill.; daughter of Charles S., Jr. and Marjorie G. (Graff) Dewey; married Jose E. Aruego, Jr. (an author and illustrator), 1961 (divorced, 1973); children: Juan. *Education:* Sarah Lawrence College, B.A., 1959; studied art (woodcuts) with Antonio Frasconi. *Residence:* New York, N.Y.

CAREER: Harcourt, Brace & World, Inc., New York, N.Y., researcher and art editor for children's textbooks, 1964-65; free-lance illustrator and other work on children's books, 1969—. Member of board, Experiments in Interactive Arts, New York, 1973; performer, "Artists in Process

Herman liked to help.

Thank you, Herman.

ARIANE DEWEY

Improvisational Dance Group,'' 1973-74. *Awards, honors:* American Institute of Graphic Arts, Children's Book Show, 1971/72, selected *A Crocodiles Tale;* Society of Illustrators citation of merit for *Milton the Early Riser* and a Children's Book Council poster; *The Chick and the Duckling* and *A Crocodiles Tale* were Children's Book Showcase Titles, 1973; Brooklyn Art Books for children citation, 1974, for *Milton the Early Riser.*

WRITINGS: (Author and illustrator with Jose Aruego, under name Ariane Aruego) *A Crocodile's Tale,* Scribner, 1972.

Illustrator with Jose Aruego, under name Ariane Aruego: Vladimir G. Suteyev, *The Chick and the Duckling,* translation by Mirra Ginsburg, Macmillan, 1972; Richard Kraus, *Milton the Early Riser,* Windmill Books, 1972.

Illustrator with Jose Aruego, under name Ariane Dewey: Natalie Savage Carlson, *Marie Louise and Christophe,* Scribner, 1974; Robert Kraus, *Herman the Helper,* Windmill Books, 1974; V. Suteyev, *Mushroom in the Rain,* adapted and translated by Mirra Ginsburg, Macmillan, 1974.

DINES, (Harry) Glen   1925-

PERSONAL: Born November 19, 1925, in Casper, Wyo.; son of Harry G. and Caroline (Maltby) Dines; married Ruth Goldberg, February, 1954; children: Lisa, Woody. *Education:* Attended University of Washington, Seattle, and Art Center School, Los Angeles, Calif.; Sacramento State College, B.A. and M.A., 1957. *Home:* Fairfax, Calif.

CAREER: Before becoming full-time writer and illustrator worked at variety of jobs, including apple picker, handicraft instructor in Young Men's Christian Association camp on Santa Catalina Island, high school teacher, and department store layout artist. *Military service:* U.S. Army, Eighth Army Special Services, Tokyo, Japan, staff artist on Pacific edition *Stars and Stripes,* World War II; became sergeant.

WRITINGS: (With Raymond Price) *Dog Soldiers: The Famous Warrior Society of the Cheyenne Indians,* Macmillan, 1961; *End 'o Steel: Man and Rails Across a Wilderness,* Macmillan, 1963.

Author and illustrator: *The Useful Dragon of Sam Ling Toy,* Macmillan, 1956; *The Mysterious Machine,* Macmillan, 1957; *A Tiger in the Cherry Tree,* Macmillan, 1958; *Pitidoe, the Color Maker,* Macmillan, 1959; *The Fabulous Flying Bicycle,* Macmillan, 1960; *Overland Stage: The Story of the Famous Overland Stagecoaches of the 1860's,* Macmillan, 1961; *Long Knife: The Story of the Fighting U.S. Cavalry of the 1860 Frontier,* Macmillan, 1961; *Bull Wagon: Strong Wheels for Rugged Men–The Frontier Freighters,* Macmillan, 1963; *Indian Pony: The Tough, Hardy Little Horse of the Far-Roving Red Man,* Macmillan, 1963; *Crazy Horse,* Putnam, 1966; *Gilly and the Whicharoo,* Lothrop, 1968; *Golden Cities, Golden Ships,* McGraw, 1968; *Kit Carson's Black Deed and Other True Stories from Marin's Lively Past,* Academy Press, 1968; *Sir Cecil and the Bad Blue Beast,* S. G. Phillips, 1970; *Sun, Sand, and Steel: Costumes and Equipment of the Spanish-Mexican Southwest,* Putnam, 1972.

66

Illustrator: Richard Watkins, *Milliken's Ark,* Thomas Nelson, 1956; Patricia Miles Martin, *The Bony Pony,* Putnam, 1965; Patricia Miles Martin, *Daniel Boone,* Putnam, 1965; Don Berry, *Mountain Men: The Trappers of the Great Fur-Trading Sea,* Macmillan, 1966; Carl P. Russell, *Fire-arms, Traps and Tools of the Mountain Men,* Knopf, 1967.

WORK IN PROGRESS: John Muir, for Putnam; cartooning (single panel gag type) and planning and/or doing graphics for exhibits for the U.S. National Park Service.

SIDELIGHTS: "I'm primarily an artist. . .a visual person. My writing, even for the older readers where illustrations are perhaps not so important, seem to be based on visual concepts. Especially when the plot calls for mood or a specific location, I find myself picturing the scene in my mind's eye, then writing a description of that mental image. This may not be unique except that the characters and plot seem to develop from a visual concept or kind of mental image trigger rather than a word orientation. But, of course, the main trouble with expressing this particular idea is that I can't draw it. In fact, since it doesn't even come from the kind of visual trigger I'm trying to describe. . .I guess I'd better quit!''

HOBBIES AND OTHER INTERESTS: Camping and hiking, especially in wilderness areas; skin diving, tennis, good books, and people.

GLEN DINES

The noisiest thing in the village was the lumpity, battered old goat cart of Gilly Goodwill, the rag boy. ■ (From *Gilly and the Whicharoo* by Glen Dines. Illustrated by the author.)

Di VALENTIN, Maria (Messuri) 1911-

PERSONAL: Born October 29, 1911, in New York, N.Y.; daughter of Philip Alexander (an importer) and Anna (Castaldi) Messuri; married Louis Di Valentin (an artist), April 20, 1940; children: Val. *Education:* College of New Rochelle, A.B., 1933; Catholic University, L.L.B., 1939, graduate student, 1940-42; George Washington University, graduate study, summer, 1938.

MEMBER: American Society of International Law, American Foreign Law Association, Societe de Legislation Comparee, Washington Foreign Law Society, Parent-Teacher Association of Edgemont High School (chairman, 1962-63). *Awards, honors:* Honorable mention for sculpture, Westchester Arts and Crafts Guild Exhibition, 1950.

WRITINGS: A Child's Day, Bruce, 1959; *Little Beaver,* Rand McNally, 1963; *Sculpture for Beginners,* Sterling, 1965; *Color in Oil Painting,* Sterling, 1965: *Everyday Pleasures of Sculpture,* Heinemann, 1965; *Practical Encyclopedia of Crafts,* Sterling, 1970; *Sculpturing in Wood,* Sterling, 1971; *Getting Started in Leathercraft,* Macmillan, 1972. Poetry included in anthologies, *Testament of Faith,* first and second series, 1942, *American Voice,* 1942, *New American Poetry,* 1945 (all published by Harbinger House, except where otherwise noted). Contributor of poetry to *Washington Star* and *Junior Messenger.*

SIDELIGHTS: "My first inspiration to write children's books and poetry, was my son. I spent many hours reading to him and teaching him to read. I found he absorbed everything presented to him which led me to the conclusion that we underestimate very young children and talk down to them, condescend, patronize. Soon we had depleted the resources of our library and I decided to try writing amusing, informatively accurate poetry about ants, bees, beavers, and about the stars and wind; and finally on more imaginative and abstract subject matter.

"Writing requires deep interest and desire—generosity with time and a subtle and sustained enthusiasm (and thorough research and persistence when necessary). An idea or stimulus may occur at anytime, anywhere: while watching a colony of ants, a bee buzzing a flower, a cloud racing across the sky, the wind upstagi   a   ch of jonquils; a remark, a phrase—anything may activate a reaction to be stirred, to observe, to feel.

"To sit and write and re-write may seem a lonely task but it has an aura of love and an environment of accomplishment, of achievement—an end in itself after the beautiful struggle.

"A child should be made aware of the world around him: the colors—the textures, shapes and sizes—to help the sense of observation, of truly 'seeing.' He should be exposed to as many experiences as possible, to travel, different customs, museums, art galleries, concerts, languages, to interior and exterior environments. The humanities are the most important and should become part of a child's life from the very beginning: to develop and enrich to the fullest his innate potential to make of him a whole and universal being."

Painting and sculpture exhibited at Arts Club, Washington Artists, and Arts and Crafts Guild. Speaks French and Italian.

DOANE, Pelagie 1906-1966

PERSONAL: Born April 11, 1906, in Palmyra, N.J.; daughter of Warren F(inney) and Pelagie (Plasschaert) Doane; married Warren E. Hoffner, March 26, 1934 (deceased). *Education:* Moore Institute, student, 1924-28. *Home and office:* 1513 Hamilton Rd., Belmar, N.J.

CAREER: Writer and illustrator of children's books, who went to New York to free-lance in 1928, and started her career in greeting card work. Designer of book jackets, and of covers and illustrations for children's magazines. Illustrator of more than seventy books, 1931-66, including all of her own.

WRITINGS: A Small Child's Bible, Oxford University Press, 1944; *One Rainy Night,* Walck, 1946; *A Book of Nature,* Oxford University Press, 1952; *The Boy Jesus,* Oxford University Press, 1953; *Bible Children,* Lippincott, 1954; *The First Day,* Lippincott, 1956; *The Big Trip,* Walck, 1958; *The Story of Moses,* Lippincott, 1958; *St. Francis,* Walck, 1960; *God Made the World,* Lippincott, 1960; *Understanding Kim,* Lippincott, 1962; *Animals in the Bible,* Golden Press, 1963; *The Twenty-Third Psalm,* Lippincott, 1963; *Wings of the Morning,* Walck, 1967.

Editor: *Brother, Baby and I,* Grosset, 1947; *A Small Child's Book of Verse,* Oxford University Press, 1948; *Poems of Praise,* Lippincott, 1955; *Littlest Ones,* Oxford University Press, 1956.

(Died December 9, 1966)

DORIAN, Marguerite

PERSONAL: Born in Bucharest, Rumania; came to United States, 1952; married Hugo Taussig. *Education:* Attended University of Bucharest and the Sorbonne, University of Paris; Brown University, M.Sc. *Residence:* Providence, R.I.

CAREER: Lived in Paris, France, for several years. Writer and illustrator. *Member:* Sigma Xi. *Awards, honors:* Fellowship to Bread Loaf Writers' Conference, 1965; associate scholar, Radcliffe Institute for Independent Study, 1966-68.

WRITINGS: Ierbar (poems), Forum (Bucharest), 1946; *Le roi qui ne pouvait pas eternuer* (juvenile), Flammarion (Paris), 1954; (self-illustrated) *When the Snow Is Blue* (juvenile), Lothrop, 1960; (self-illustrated) *The Alligator's Toothache* (juvenile), Lothrop, 1965; *A Ride on the Milky Way* (novel), Crown, 1967. Contributor of short fiction to the *New Yorker.*

FOR MORE INFORMATION SEE: Saturday Review, April 29, 1967; *National Review,* June 27, 1967.

DORMAN, Michael 1932-

PERSONAL: Born October 9, 1932, in New York, N.Y.; son of Arthur A. (an auctioneer) and Hortense (Lowy) Dorman; married Jeanne O'Brien, June 25, 1955; children: Pamela Grace, Patricia Alice. *Education:* New York University, B.S. in Journalism, 1953; University of Houston, graduate study, 1954-55. *Politics:* Democrat. *Religion:* Presbyterian. *Home:* 7 Lauren Ave. South, Dix Hills,

MICHAEL DORMAN

N.Y. *Agent:* McIntosh & Otis, Inc., 18 East 41st St., New York, N.Y. 10017.

CAREER: Reporter or department editor for Associated Press, Albany, N.Y., 1953, *Houston Press,* Houston, Tex., 1953-58, *Newsday,* Garden City, N.Y., 1959-64; Democratic Party, speech writer, 1964-65. Free-lance writer on political and civil rights topics. *Member:* American Newspaper Guild, Authors League, Liebling Group (chairman), Kappa Tau Alpha. *Awards, honors:* First prize in news story competition, Houston Press Club, for coverage of the Louisiana hurricane, 1957.

WRITINGS: We Shall Overcome, Delacorte, 1964; *The Secret Service Story,* Delacorte, 1967; *The Second Man,* Delacorte, 1968; *King of the Courtroom,* Delacorte, 1969; *Under Twenty-one* (ALA Notable Book), Delacorte, 1970; *Payoff,* David McKay, 1972; *The Making of a Slum,* Delacorte, 1972; *Confrontation: Politics and Protest,* Delacorte, 1974.

WORK IN PROGRESS: A book on political witch-hunts for expected publication by Delacorte in hard cover and Dell in paperback.

SIDELIGHTS: "As a former investigative reporter for newspapers, now writing nonfiction books and magazine articles full-time, I try to pursue my research with far more penetrating investigative work than was ever possible for newspapers. Much of my work concerns political topics. I have interviewed the last four Presidents and Vice Presidents of the United States. At the same time, I have also spent a good deal of time interviewing such assorted characters as some of the country's leading Mafia bosses, other criminals, federal agents, defense and prosecuting attorneys.

"What I cherish most about my career as a freelance writer is my freedom to pursue the subjects that interest me most. I go where I want, when I want, and am answerable only to myself. Of course, I must find a market for my wares and must produce acceptable copy for my publishers. But, within those limits, I am my own boss. I find myself a stern taskmaster. I write every day of the year, even when traveling on research projects. Often, I research one book while writing another. Some people ask how I can divide my interests that way. My reply is that, for someone who started in the newspaper business at the age of seventeen and often wrote as many as fifteen or twenty news stories a day, it is no problem at all.

"I find that one of the most valuable attributes a writer can have is a genuine curiosity about people. Every individual has at least one story worth telling in him. If a writer is alert and has the patience to listen to the people he meets, he runs across all sorts of unexpected, interesting yarns. Also, this curiosity can be an important research tool. Even if you have no inte i n of writing anything about a certain person's life, your genuine concern about him as an individual may lead him to provide you with information you need.

"I keep an extensive 'morgue' in my study, containing thousands upon thousands of clippings, notes, pamphlets and the like. Although my passion for clipping newspapers and magazines is the subject of constant teasing from my wife and two daughters, I have found the practice invaluable. It saves enormous amounts of time that would otherwise be spent on research in libraries and newspaper offices."

DOWDEN, Anne Ophelia (Todd) 1907-
(Anne Ophelia Todd)

PERSONAL: Born September 17, 1907, in Denver, Colo.; daughter of James Campbell (head of department of clinical pathology at University of Colorado) and Edith (Brownfield) Todd; married Raymond Baxter Dowden (head of art department at Cooper Union School of Art and Architecture, now retired), April 1, 1934. *Education:* University of Colorado, student, 1925-26; Carnegie Institute of Technology, B.A., 1930; additional study at Art Students League of New York and Beaux Arts Institute of Design, New York, N.Y. *Religion:* Protestant. *Home:* 205 West 15th St., New York, N.Y. 10011.

CAREER: Pratt Institute, Brooklyn, N.Y., instructor in drawing, 1930-33; Manhattanville College, Purchase, N.Y., head of art department, 1932-53; free-lance textile designer, 1935-55; botanical illustrator, 1950—. Paintings, textiles, and botanical water colors have been exhibited at Carnegie Institute, Whitney Museum, Metropolitan Museum of Art, Newark Museum, Silvermine Artists Guild, Cooper Union Museum, Brooklyn Botanic Garden, and Hunt Botanical Library. *Awards, honors:* Fellow of Tiffany Foundation, 1929, 1930, 1932; *Wild Green Things in the City* was a Children's Book Showcase Title, 1973.

People who may be trying desperately to keep a shrub alive or make a houseplant bloom in the adverse conditions of the city seldom stop to think that the success of the uncared-for wild things is almost miraculous. ■ (From *Wild Green Things in the City* by Anne Ophelia Dowden. Illustrated by the author.)

70

WRITINGS: (Under name Anne Ophelia Todd) *CUAS 8,* Cooper Union Art School, 1961; (under name Anne Ophelia Dowden) *Look at a Flower* (ALA Notable Book), Crowell, 1963; *The Secret Life of the Flowers,* Odyssey, 1964; (with Richard Thomson) *Roses,* Odyssey, 1965; *Wild Green Things in the City: A Book of Weeds,* Crowell, 1972; *Trees,* Crowell, in press. Botanical illustrations published in four issues of *Life,* 1952-57, in *House Beautiful, Audubon Magazine,* and in *Natural History.*

Illustrator: Hal Borland, *Plants of Christmas,* Golden Press, 1969; Jessica Kerr, *Shakespeare's Flowers,* Crowell, 1969; Louis Untermeyer, *Roses,* Golden Press, 1970; Louis Untermeyer, *Plants of the Bible,* Golden Press, 1970.

SIDELIGHTS: "I was born in Denver, but grew up in the then-small college town of Boulder, Colorado; and my childhood was spent in the foothills of the Rockies, wandering over grassy mesas, scrambling up rocks in mountain canyons, and living as close to nature as my playtime would allow. Two major influences shaped my early interests, one at home, the other close by. My father, who was head of the Department of Pathology in the University of Colorado Medical School, not only gave me an insight into scientific matters, but also encouraged my wish to be an artist. Affiliation with the University gave us access to libraries and museum collections, but above all it afforded us a stimulating association with scholars, especially our neighbor and friend T. D. A. Cockerell the noted zoologist. He and his biologist wife were patient tutors, always ready for the kind of questions inquisitive children ask. 'What bug is this?'—'what flower?'—'what bird?' Mrs. Cockerell be-

came my biology teacher in high school and Dr. Cockerell my zoology professor in college, but I never did get around to the study of botany.

"As a small child, with the Cockerells' encouragement and help, I collected and drew any living thing that came my way—especially insects. My sister and I spent hours feeding spiders and ant-lions, watching caterpillars turn into chrysalids, and investigating crawling things in general—a preoccupation which our parents, fortunately, did not consider peculiar. They hoped it was an indication of a scientific bent. However, I was determined to become an artist and, even with this beginning, never even thought of being a nature artist.

"The first opportunity for professional work came, when at the age of 16, I made a number of microscopic drawings for my father's book, *Clinical Diagnosis by Laboratory Methods.* Some of these are still included in the current thirteenth edition of the book.

"After a year at the University of Colorado, I went east to study painting and illustration. Graduating at the height of the Depression, but intent on illustrating books, I went where the book market was—New York City. This was a precarious move, as I found out when I began to make the rounds of the publishers; and to earn a living, I took the first job that came my way—teaching drawing at Pratt Institute in Brooklyn—even though teaching was the last thing I wanted to do. At the same time I continued to study, in a painting class at the Art Students League and a mural atelier at the Beaux Arts Institute of Design. Though defi-

ANNE OPHELIA DOWDEN

nitely not a muralist, I did however work with a group that designed and executed a mural for the Chicago World's Fair. This association turned out to be so congenial that we dubbed ourselves, somewhat grandiloquently, the American Design Group; and with no experience, started designing wallpapers and drapery fabrics. The venture succeeded very well, and for fifteen years we sold steadily to the high-style market.

"But far less of my time went into designing than into teaching, and, in spite of my original antipathy, I found that pedagogy suited me very well. I moved from Pratt to Manhattanville College, where, you might say, I was the founding mother of the Art Department. I served as its chairman for more than twenty years and taught everything from beginning drawing to history of architecture.

"In all these years of textiles and teaching, the scientific study of plants and insects played no part. But since drapery fabrics have always used flowers as a dominating motif, I often sketched plants for the purposes of design; and nature still provided me with a very satisfying hobby. One of the advantages of teaching is the long free summers it offers. During our vacations, my husband and I drove all over the United States, painting, observing whereever we went.

"It was during the war years, when we went to help a Michigan friend tend his thousand-acre farm, that I was able to get close to plants again. Very often, while my husband conscientiously hoed the carrots and spinach, I squatted in the fields looking closely at some ordinary weed. In those summers at the Starr Commonwealth for Boys, where the school motto was 'There is no such thing as a bad boy,' I began to think '—or a bad weed.'

"A sabbatical from Manhattanville provided the time for making a sizeable number of fully documented paintings of edible wild plants, for which I hoped to find a publisher. I envisioned them in portfolio form, but no one was interested in such plush and expensive projects during the war years. Eventually *Life* magazine used nine of these paintings, and then several other picture stories for *Life* followed. At last I was introduced to botanical illustration. Combining my hobby with my profession in this way was so satisfactory that I resigned from my teaching, gave up textile design, and concentrated entirely on flower painting. (I have never found any demand for insect painting.)

"My convictions have led to the development of what is probably the world's slowest working method. Literal and detailed research paintings nearly always precede any finished illustration. Working from living plants, I make drawings as slowly or as rapidly as the fragile nature of the specimen will permit. Later I can re-paint these plants in the arrangement demanded by a particular project, making whatever changes are necessary in position of parts or pattern of dark and light. My research paintings, now numbering several hundred, are useful references for future projects, especially when someone wants a violet or a wild rose in the middle of the winter. For this reason, I never part with any original research plates.

"This stubborn insistence on working from living plants makes life difficult for a city-bound artist. But the country is not that far away, and trips out of New York often end with the bathtub full of floating flowers, there to be kept fresh until I can preserve them permanently on paper. Plants not available in areas close to New York must be shipped by special air-mail, which is often a problem of logistics and timing. Even specimens from the easily accessible botanic gardens involve careful timing and planning, and every large project requires extensive long-range organization.

"In January and February I list the species needed for the following summer's work, checking their blooming dates and the places where they will be available. If the plants do not grow in the New York botanic gardens, or in nearby New Jersey or Connecticut, inquiries must go out to collectors all over the country. At this point I have to rely on the good will and cooperation of my friends, and no one is immune from my urgent requests for specimens. Often I must have plants grown from seed, and in these cases the Brooklyn Botanic Garden and a very special friend in Connecticut have been most helpful; but I then have to arrange to be in the right place at the right time when the blooms are ready. Synchronizing my schedule with that of nature and my friends requires a lot of phone calls and voluminous correspondence; the file of letters in preparation for a book is often bulkier than the manuscript itself.

DUCORNET, Erica 1943-

PERSONAL: Born April 19, 1943, in Canton, N.Y.; daughter of Gerard and Muriel DeGre; married Guy Ducornet (painter and poet); children: Jean-Yves. *Education:* Bard College, B.A., 1962. *Home:* "Le Bout du Monde," Le Puy Notre Dame, 49260 Montreuil Bellay, France.

CAREER: Writer and painter. Began a puppet theatre for children, 1972.

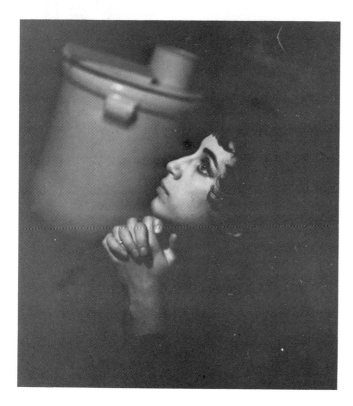

ERICA DUCORNET

WRITINGS: (Illustrator) Mme. Leprince de Beaumont, *Beauty and the Beast* (translated from the French by P. H. Muir), Knopf, 1968; (self-illustrated) *The Blue Bird* (adaptation of Mme. D'Aulnoy's old French tale), Knopf, 1970; (illustrated by husband, Guy Ducornet) *Shazira Shazam and the Devil* (Junior Literary Guild Selection), Prentice-Hall, 1970; (illustrator) *Jack Spratt Cook Book,* Doubleday, 1965; *From the Star Chamber* (poetry and short fiction for adults), Fiddlehead Press, 1974; (illustrator) Susan Musgrave, *Gullband Thought Measles was a Happy Ending,* L. L. Douglas, 1974; (contributor) *The Stonewall Anthology,* University of Iowa Press, 1974. Contributor of short stories and poetry to *The Canadian Fiction Magazine,* Prism International, Phases, Arsenal, Oasis, Soror Elementales, Radical America, *and* Brumes Blondes.

Also illustrated two books of poetry by Guy Ducornet both published in France: *Silex de L'avenir* and *Trophees en Selle.*

WORK IN PROGRESS: A book of short stories for young readers; several books of poetry for children; short stories; three books in preparation for adults.

SIDELIGHTS: "Kids are my favorite people, that is the FREE ones who haven't had the MAGIC BEANS rooted out of them yet, by parents or schools who demand that they 'behave like young adults.' Or had their MAGIC BEANS dried out and shriveled up by that hateful watchdog called the boobtoob, our carniverous domestic soul policeman, the DREAM robber, the 'LET'S PRETEND' robber, the YOU and ME eater. It spends most of its time telling the kids how and what to play (how and what to BE!)—that play means playing war and a whole plasti-

world barbie bag of consummerism—all that HATEFUL nonsense that has NOTHING to do with REAL LIFE. By REAL LIFE I mean CREATIVE life. Kids, people—as MYTH MAKERS, STORY TELLERS vs THE PLASTI-GOOP HOT DOG EATERS.

"Kids need books and not piggychoochoo stories either! Good books feed the imagination, demand ACTIVE DISCOVERY. All kids from the start have all those magic beans tucked inside their hearts and heads ready to grow into all sorts of gorgeous tropical flowers. They are all DANCERS until some nut tells them that their bodies are ugly and all PAINTERS until mother screams one time too many 'GET THAT HORRIBLE MESS OFF MY NICE NEW SPANISH MOOD ANTIQUE PLASTIC TABLE!' and all MUSIC MAKERS AND POETS AND DREAMERS AND LOVERS AND MAGICIANS. They need BOOKS and AIR and FORESTS and BOOKS and MEADOWS and BOOKS and healthy fish swimming in happy water, flocks and flocks of birds in skies free from smog and—that REAL WORLD FULL OF STARS AND FLOWERS AND BOOKS MADE WITH LOVE!

"I write for kids because I love to tell stories to kids—then I see all those magic beans POPPING ALL OVER THE PLACE! And almost always some madhatter remark, or a question up to its mustache in good sense or a burst of wild laughter sends me spinning to the typewriter! And It's FUN, I'm at play and I have a good time and I hope they do too. 'Cause that's the only way to keep those MAGIC BEANS POPPING.''

Shazira Shazam and the Devil has been put to music by Canadian composer, Benjamin McPeek, and is performed throughout Canada by the Canadian Brass.

DUNNAHOO, Terry 1927-

PERSONAL: Born December 8, 1927, in Fall River, Mass.; daughter of Joseph Alfred (a mill worker) and Emma (Dolbec) Janson; married Thomas William Dunnahoo (president of Thunderbird Films), September 18, 1954; children: Kim, Sean, Kelly. *Education:* Attended parochial schools in Massachusetts. *Politics:* "I vote for the man—or the woman." *Religion:* Roman Catholic. *Home:* 4061 Tropico Way, Los Angeles, Calif. 90065. *Agent:* Evelyn Singer Agency, P. O. Box 163, Briarcliff Manor, N.Y. 10510.

CAREER: Writer. Has worked in a civilian capacity for U. S. Navy on Guam. *Member:* International P.E.N. (member of board of director of Los Angeles chapter), California Writer's Guild (board of directors), Southern California Council on Literature for Children and Young People, Society of Children's Book Writers.

WRITINGS: Emily Dunning, Reilly & Lee, 1970; *Nellie Bly,* (Child Study Association book list), Reilly & Lee, 1970; *Annie Sullivan* (Child Study Association book list), Reilly & Lee, 1970; *Before the Supreme Court* (the story of Belva Ann Lockwood), Houghton, 1974.

TERRY DUNNAHOO

WORK IN PROGRESS: A book about Ellen Richards; a book about a Mexican-American girl who joins the Explorer Scouts to work with the Los Angeles Police Department.

SIDELIGHTS: "Most authors say they've been voracious readers all their lives. I can't make that statement. When I was a child there were few books in our home. There was no money to buy any, the closest library was miles away, and my nun teachers never encouraged me to read anything but the limited number of school books assigned by the church bishops and pastors.

"I probably would have become a reader when I entered high school—there was a modest library—but I had no free time. I had to work after school and, at times worked at three jobs simultaneously so I could stay in high school. I worked in restaurants, movie theatres. I did baby sitting. I even made gas tanks for airplanes.

"One summer I took a job in a 'sweat shop' where hundreds of girls ran sewing machines in temperatures that often reached one hundred and ten degrees. As I ran the material through my machine, I vowed that after I finished high school I would never touch a sewing machine again. And I haven't.

"Despite my work schedule, I graduated at the head of my class. However, for financial reasons, there was no chance of my going to college so I continued to work at any job I could get until the owner of a business school let me attend her classes in return for work in her office. When I finished

the courses, she got me a job in a title attorney's office. For the first time since I was a small child I was working only eight hours a day and not attending school. From that moment I was seldom without a book.

"I worked in the law office a year. Then the limited opportunities in my home town convinced me to make a move. It was not a small one. I signed an eighteen month contract for a civilian job with the Navy Department nine thousand miles from home on the island of Guam in the south Pacific. For eighteen months I searched land records and established rightful ownership to property taken by the government after World War II. When I returned to the United States, I married an Air Force man I had met on the island.

"After an assignment in Riverside, California where our first child was born, the Air Force sent us back to Guam. Friends and relatives complimented me on my letters home. They said they were interesting and exciting. Several people suggested I write professionally. I thought they were being kind. I had no training in creative writing and I had no desire to write.

"But several years later when tragedy struck our family I stopped to take inventory of my life. I found I had existed during most of the years instead of living them. I decided to direct my life so I could accomplish something, be somebody.

Christmas is for children. And they're children for so little time." ■ (From *Before the Supreme Court* by Terry Dunnahoo. Illustrated by Bea Holmes.)

Something about the Author

"But, although I had worked at many jobs, I found I was expert at none. What could I do that would give meaning to my life? I decided to listen to all those relatives and friends and become a writer. And, to my surprise, I did. With no background in creative writing, I wrote *Nellie Bly* in six weeks and sold it. Then I wrote *Annie Sullivan* in six weeks and sold that. The same thing happened with *Emily Dunning*. What had begun as something to do became my life. Now, I can't imagine doing anything else. I give talks in schools throughout the Los Angeles area about writing. I enjoy the students and I enjoy my readers' fan letters. I answer all of them personally because I feel if I can get one child to read one book he wouldn't have read ordinarily, then I've led him one step closer to success.

"This year I did my first fiction book which is about a runaway Mexican-American girl named Espie Sanchez who eventually joins the Explorer Scouts to work with the police. In order to get the authentic background, I attended the police academy for eight weeks and went to hundreds of Explorer meetings. The experience has made me a more understanding parent and a more sensitive writer. Fictitious Espie has become as important to me as my own children and I'll do a sequel.

"For those of you who are curious about authors and their writing habits, I'll give you a closing sentence that's certain to bring me piles of letters. I wrote *Annie Sullivan* in the bathroom. Why? A letter to me will bring you the answer. Happy reading!"

EARLE, Olive L(ydia)

PERSONAL: Born in London, England; daughter of E. J. Vavasour (an importer) and Elizabeth (Bedbrook) Earle; married Sydney Hannon, January 16, 1920 (deceased); married Harry R. Daugherty (an artist), September 12, 1934 (deceased). *Education:* Attended a private school in England and National Academy of Design, New York, N.Y. *Politics:* Liberal. *Religion:* Unitarian Universalist. *Residence:* Staten Island, N.Y.

CAREER: Writer and illustrator of nature books for children; illustrator on nature subjects for encyclopedias. Work has been exhibited in group shows at American Museum of Natural History, Brooklyn Museum, Los Angeles Museum, and elsewhere.

WRITINGS—Self-illustrated: *State Birds and Flowers,* 1951, *Thunder Wings,* 1951, *Birds and Their Nests,* 1952, *Robins in the Garden,* 1953, *Paws, Hoofs, and Flippers,*

These horny callus pads act as shock absorbers, hitting the ground when the camel suddenly drops to a kneeling position to rest. . . . All his movements are accompanied by much squealing, grunting, and grumbling. ■ (From *Camels and Llamas* by Olive L. Earle. Illustrated by the author.)

1954, *The Octopus,* 1955, *Mice at Home and Afield,* 1957, *Crickets,* 1956, *White Patch, a City Sparrow,* 1958, *Pigs, Tame and Wild,* 1959, *State Trees,* 1960, revised, 1973, *Camels and Llamas,* 1961, *Birds of the Crow Family,* 1962, *Squirrels in the Garden,* 1963, *Strange Lizards,* 1964, *Birds and Their Beaks,* 1965, *Strange Companions in Nature,* 1965, *The Strangler Fig and Other Strange Plants,* 1967, *Strange Fishes of the Sea,* 1968, *Praying Mantis,* 1969, *Rose Family,* 1970, *Peas, Beans and Licorice,* 1971, *Pond and Marsh Plants,* 1972, *Scavengers,* 1973 (all published by Morrow). Contributor of illustrations and articles to nature magazines.

WORK IN PROGRESS: Another nature book.

SIDELIGHTS: "I garden like crazy. The other aspects of my life I do not consider of public interest."

FOR MORE INFORMATION SEE: More Junior Authors, edited by Muriel Fuller, H. W. Wilson, 1963.

EDWARDS, Julie
See ANDREWS, Julie

EDWARDS, Sally (Cary) 1929-

PERSONAL: Born July 28, 1929, in Spartanburg, S.C.; daughter of Frank Bee and Cary (Lindsay) Edwards. *Education:* Converse College, B.A., 1950; graduate study at Columbia University, New York University, and New School for Social Research. *Home:* 3 Grey Ct., Spartanburg, S.C. 29302. *Agent:* Carolyn Willyoung Stagg, Lester Lewis Associates, 15 East 48th St., New York, N.Y. 10017.

WRITINGS: South Carolina, Coward, 1968; *The Man Who Said No,* Coward, 1970; *When the World's on Fire,* Coward, 1972; *Isaac and Snow,* Coward, 1973. Short stories published in *Ladies' Home Journal, Redbook,* and *Carleton Miscellany.*

Annie ran faster than she had ever run. And then she was running on air. She was lifted up, as free as a laughing gull, floating up, up to the sky. ■ (From *When the World's on Fire* by Sally Edwards. Illustrated by Richard Lebenson.)

SIDELIGHTS: "I write to teach myself things I should have been taught as a child. I write children's books based on historical fact. Even *Isaac and Snow,* the story of a contemporary teen-ager who saves the life of a white dolphin, is based on fact.

"Secondly, today's children are going to be in just the shape I'm in at my age if somebody doesn't tell them things they ought to know. It is appalling to know that today's children think the pilgrims drank frozen orange juice and ate cornflakes on the MAYFLOWER. It is equally appalling to see them looking at a quill pen and asking where the ink comes from. An inkwell or a bottle of ink is simply beyond their ken."

FOR MORE INFORMATION SEE: Horn Book, April, 1974.

ELLIS, Ella Thorp 1928-

PERSONAL: Born July 14, 1928, in Los Angeles, Calif.; daughter of William Dunham (a film writer) and Marion (Yates) Thorp; married Leo Ellis (an economist), 1949; children: Steven, David, Patrick. *Education:* Continued education after marriage, studying at eight colleges and universities before receiving B.A. from University of California, Los Angeles, 1966; presently enrolled in M.A. program at San Francisco State University. *Politics:* Democrat. *Religion:* Episcopalian. *Home:* 1438 Grizzly Peak, Berkeley, Calif. 94708. *Agent:* Patricia Myrer, McIntosh & Otis, Inc., 18 East 41st St., New York, N.Y. 10017.

CAREER: Writer and part-time teacher of creative writing. *Awards, honors: Roam the Wild Country* was an American Library Association Honor Book, 1967.

WRITINGS—Books for teens: *Roam the Wild Country,* Atheneum, 1967; *Riptide,* Atheneum, 1969; *Celebrate the Morning* (Junior Literary Guild selection), Atheneum, 1972; *Where the Road Ends,* Atheneum, 1974.

WORK IN PROGRESS: Two books, a fantasy set on the planet of Hallelujah and the other set in Argentina during the 1860's.

SIDELIGHTS: "I have always been a vagabond. My father was a free-lance writer and during the Depression I lived up and down the coast of California: in a commune on the beach; with the only doctor in a small town; in South Berkeley; in San Francisco's Richmond District; and in Washington, D.C., with an uncle who is a painter. I had the chance to know different kinds of people well. But every summer I returned to Oceano, California, the small town where my mother lived and where *Riptide* and *Celebrate the Morning* take place. This is home."

ELLA THORP ELLIS

76

Martin could barely make out his uncle and Alonso through the dust cloud in which they rode. He could barely hear the crack of their whips above the sound of the hoofbeats. ■ (From *Roam the Wild Country* by Ella Thorp Ellis. Illustrated by Bret Schlesinger.)

"When I was seventeen, I contracted tuberculosis and spent the next three years reading, watching, and waiting. I try to bring to my books the capacity for precise observation that I learned during those years, so that my readers will be able to read my descriptions of the places I have been and feel that they have been there, too.

"In 1949 I married Lee Ellis, an electrical engineer working in construction. The first five years of our marriage we moved a dozen times, following construction jobs. When our three sons started school, we developed a home base—Berkeley, California—and leave only a year or two at a time. We went to Argentina for two years, and *Roam the Wild Country* grew out of summers on a horse ranch there. Another time we spent a year in a beach town similar to my home, and *Riptide* started. Whenever we lived in a town that had one, I went to college. Eight colleges and universities later I graduated in English literature from UCLA. This educational meandering made headaches for the people who had to evaluate my credits but I could savor each course and often share them with growing sons.

"Like most people, I have always wanted to write, to share adventure and insight with a reader. I began to write poems and stories. Now I have long enough time stretches to write novels, and sons who are good critics. *Celebrate the Morning* grew from three stories about my life with my 'mother. One of these stories, 'David,' appeared in *Mademoiselle* two years ago. The main problem was finding a quiet place to work and my husband solved this by getting me a small house trailer which we park about a mile from our house.

"What I like to do when not writing is visit with friends and family, read, listen to music, attend plays, and travel. I try to be outdoors as much as possible. We are a family of gardeners but the more aware of ecology I become the more difficult it gets to choose between the flowers and the weeds."

FOR MORE INFORMATION SEE: Young Readers' Review, December, 1967; *Book World,* January 28, 1968, November 9, 1969; *Christian Science Monitor,* November 6, 1969; *New York Times Book Review,* November 9, 1969; *Horn Book,* December, 1972, August, 1974.

ELLIS, Mel(vin Richard) 1912-

PERSONAL: Born February 21, 1912, in Beaver Dam, Wis.; son of Fay Nathan (a businessman) and Paula (Hinkes) Ellis; married Gwendolyn; children: Sharon, Suzanne, Deborah, Dianne, Mary. *Education:* University of Notre Dame, B.A. in Journalism. *Religion:* Catholic. *Home:* On-Little-Lakes, Big Bend, Wis. 53103. *Agent:* Larry Sternig, 2407 North 44th St., Milwaukee, Wis.

CAREER: Newspaperman in Sheboygan, Wis., and Rockford, Ill., 1935-40; *Milwaukee Journal,* Milwaukee, Wis., outdoors editor, 1947-63; *Field and Stream,* New York, N.Y., associate editor, 1958-69; Associated Press weekly syndicated column, "The Good Earth Crusade," 1971—. *Military service:* U.S. Air Force; became technical sergeant; received Legion of Merit, Distinguished Flying Cross, and five Air Medals. *Awards, honors:* Gordon MacQuarrie Award for conservation writing, 1961; Dorothy Canfield Fisher award, 1972, and Sequoyah award, 1974, for *Flight of the White Wolf;* five time winner for "book of the year" award of the Wisconsin Council of Writers; Audubon award, 1973.

WRITINGS: Good Fishing, Milwaukee Journal, 1956; *Notes from Little Lakes,* Milwaukee Journal, 1963; *Sad Song of the Coyote,* Holt, 1967; *Run, Rainey, Run,* Holt, 1967; *Softly Roars the Lion,* Holt, 1968; *Ironhead,* Holt, 1968; *Wild Goose, Brother Goose,* Holt, 1969; *The Wild Runners,* Holt, 1969; *Ghost Dog of Killicut,* Four Winds, 1969; *Flight of the White Wolf,* Holt, 1970; *When Lightening Strikes,* Four Winds, 1970; *Caribou Crossing,* Holt,

"We lifted the two nets and took a couple of boxes of chubs." ■ (From *Ghost Dog of Killicut* by Mel Ellis. Illustrated by Dick Amundsen.)

1971; *This Mysterious River*, Holt, 1972; *Hurry-Up Harry Hanson*, Four Winds, 1972; *Peg Leg Pete*, Holt, 1973; *No Man for Murder*, Holt, 1973; *Sidewalk Indian*, Holt, 1974; *Sermons in Stones*, Holt, 1974. Contributor of articles and fiction to some thirty magazines.

SIDELIGHTS: Ellis was born on a farm, the son of a part-time trapper and market hunter. He has traveled all the states and South, Central and North America as a rod and gun editor. His home is on a southern Wisconsin animal and bird sanctuary, with trees and thousands of wild flowers native to the region. A health buff, Ellis is a daily runner of three "torturous miles."

FOR MORE INFORMATION SEE: Horn Book, August, 1972, February, 1974.

ELLSBERG, Edward 1891-

PERSONAL: Born November 21, 1891, in New Haven, Conn.; son of Joseph and Edna (Lavine) Ellsberg; married Lucy Knowlton Buck, 1918; children: Mary Phillips (Mrs. Goldwin S. Pollard). *Education:* U.S. Naval Academy, B.Sc., 1914; Massachusetts Institute of Technology, M.Sc., 1920; University of Colorado, Eng.D., 1929. *Home:*

. . . there suddenly reared up from the sea the vast tail of the harpooned monster. Full forty feet above the surface it soared, flinging both the larboard oars up into the air like straws in the wind, leaving the boat helpless to row away. ■ (From *"I Have Just Begun to Fight"* by Commander Edward Ellsberg. Illustrated by Gerald Foster.)

Windswept, Southwest Harbor, Me. 04679. *Agent:* Marie Rodell.

CAREER: U.S. Navy, midshipman, 1910-14, regular officer, 1914-26, winning promotion to commander by special act of Congress for work on raising two sunken U.S. submarines; Tide Water Oil Co., New York, N.Y., chief engineer, 1926-35; self-employed consulting engineer, New York, N.Y., 1935-41; U.S. Navy, 1941-51, serving as salvage officer in the Red Sea and western Mediterranean areas and participating in Normandy Invasion, 1944; retired from Navy as rear admiral. *Member:* P.E.N., Society of American Historians, Society of American Military Engineers, U.S. Naval Institute, American Petroleum Institute, American Polar Society, Army and Navy Club (Washington, D.C.), Explorers Club and Army and Navy Club (New York), Causeway Club (Southwest Harbor, Me.), Northeast Harbor Fleet (Maine), Ends of the Earth Club, Pot and Kettle (Bar Harbor). *Awards, honors:* Military: Distinguished Service Medal for raising S-51 from bottom of the sea, 1926; Legion of Merit (twice); commander, Order of the British Empire. Academic: Sc.D., Bowdoin College, 1952; L.H.D., University of Maine, 1955.

WRITINGS: On the Bottom, Dodd, 1929; *Thirty Fathoms Deep* (juvenile), Dodd, 1930; *Pigboats,* Dodd, 1931; *S-54,* Dodd, 1932; *Submerged,* Hurst, 1932; *Hell Below* (motion picture version of *Pigboats*), Grosset, 1933; *Ocean Gold* (juvenile), Dodd, 1935; *Spanish Ingots* (juvenile), Dodd, 1936 (reissued as *Submarine Treasure,* Dodd, 1953); *Hell on Ice,* Dodd, 1938; *Men Under the Sea,* Dodd, 1939; *Treasure Below* (juvenile), Dodd, 1940; *Captain Paul,* Dodd, 1942; *"I Have Just Begun to Fight!"* (juvenile), Dodd, 1942; *Under the Red Sea Sun,* Dodd, 1946; *No Banners, No Bugles,* Dodd, 1949; *Cruise of the Jeannette* (juvenile), Dodd, 1949; *Passport for Jennifer,* Dodd, 1952; *Mid Watch,* Dodd, 1954; *The Far Shore,* Dodd, 1960. Author of numerous magazine articles and serials in popular magazines, such as *Saturday Evening Post,* and in technical journals.

SIDELIGHTS: "I received my inspiration for writing about the sea from the extreme dissimilarity of my boyhood surroundings (I grew up in Colorado) with anything remotely resembling the oceans or even water. I could look only at the nearby Rocky Mountains or try to go swimming in the adjacent Platte River. (Since the Platte is a mile wide and an inch deep, as a boy I had to lie on my stomach in the Platte and then turn over on my back if I wished to get wet all over.) Consequently you will understand, I yearned for a look at an actual ocean of water rather than at the mountains.

"Somewhat later, when I saw a chance to go to the Naval Academy at Annapolis, I seized it with avidity. And following that, chance threw me into diving and salvage in the Navy, both in war and in peace. Since grammar school I had always had an urge to write and the romance of searching for lost treasures turned my mind from buried and sunken treasures to writing for boys. What Robert Louis Stevenson had so superbly done with pirates, I wanted to do for divers. The only difference in our situations being that I knew divers while Stevenson never saw a pirate in his life. And thus from the depths of the sea came *Thirty Fathoms Deep* and its three treasure hunting sequels, ending with *Treasure Below*.

"For a little boy trying (not too successfully) to get himself wet all over in the Platte River, by the time I had finished struggling with the enormous tides washing the Normandy Beachhead, I had pretty thoroughly managed to get myself completely saturated in the sea—enough anyway to write about it feelingly."

FOR MORE INFORMATION SEE: New York Herald Tribune Book Review, October 16, 1949, October 12, 1952; *Junior Book of Authors,* edited by Kunitz and Haycraft, H. W. Wilson, 1951; Frederick Wagner, *Famous Underwater Adventurers,* Dodd, 1962.

ERICSON, Walter
See FAST, Howard

ESTES, Eleanor   1906-

PERSONAL: Born May 9, 1906, in West Haven, Conn.; daughter of Louis and Caroline (Gewecke) Rosenfeld; married Rice Estes, December 8, 1932; children: Helena. *Education:* Pratt Institute Library School, 1931-32. *Politics:* Democrat. *Religion:* Episcopalian. *Home:* 175 Steuben St., Brooklyn, N.Y.

CAREER: Free Public Library, New Haven, Conn., children's librarian, 1924-31; New York Public Library, chil-

ELEANOR ESTES

Instead of living in the briers and the brambles, the caves and the heaths, instead of flying around on her broomstick wherever she wanted, chanting runes, doing abracadabras, . . . this Old Witch had to go and live on the top of an awful, high, lonely hill. ■ (From The *Witch Family* by Eleanor Estes. Illustrated by Edward Ardizzone.)

dren's librarian, 1932-40; now full-time writer. *Member:* P.E.N., Author's Guild. *Awards, honors:* Herald-Tribune Spring Book Festival Award, 1951, Newbery Medal for distinguished contribution to children's literature, 1952, both for *Ginger Pye.*

WRITINGS: The Moffats, 1941, *The Middle Moffat,* 1942, *Rufus M.,* 1943, *The Sun and The Wind and Mr. Todd,* 1943, *The Hundred Dresses,* 1944, *The Echoing Green,* Macmillan, 1947, *The Sleeping Giant,* 1948, *Ginger Pye,* 1951, *A Little Oven,* 1955, *Pinky Pye,* 1958, *The Witch Family,* 1960, *The Alley,* 1964, *Miranda the Great,* 1967, *The Tunnel of Hugsy Goode,* 1972, *The Coat-Hanger Christmas Tree,* Atheneum, 1973 (all published by Harcourt, unless otherwise noted). Has also contributed to magazines.

SIDELIGHTS: Eleanor Estes remembers West Haven, Connecticut, as the perfect town to grow up in, and she has used it as the setting for many of her books. "The town had everything a child could want, great vacant fields with daisies and clover and buttercups and an occasional peaceful cow. There were marvelous trees to climb, fishing and clamming in the summertime, ice and snow and sliding down hills in the wintertime.

"My first four years at school were spent in the small wooden school that is the scene for a chapter in *The Moffats.* The remaining years were spent in a pretty ivy-covered brick school. In one of those classrooms the hero dog of *Ginger Pye,* the book which won the Newbery Medal, appeared in the window with a pencil in his mouth, earning the nickname of 'intellectual dog.'

"I like to feel that I am holding up a mirror and I hope that what is reflected in it is a true image of childhood. I feel that the impressions I have gathered through the years must be woven into a structure of the imagination—a book written purely for the enjoyment and entertainment of children. I like to make children laugh or cry, to be moved in some way. I am grateful to the children everywhere who have looked in my mirror and have liked what they have seen."

FOR MORE INFORMATION SEE: Junior Book of Authors, edited by Kunitz and Haycraft, H. W. Wilson, 1951; *Newbery Medal Books: 1922-1955,* edited by Miller and Field, Horn Book, 1955; Eleanor Cameron, *The Green and Burning Tree,* Atlantic-Little, Brown, 1969; Elinor W. Field, *Horn Book Reflections,* Horn Book, 1969; Selma G. Lanes, *Down the Rabbit Hole,* Atheneum, 1971; John Rowe Townsend, *A Sense of Story,* Lippincott, 1971; *Horn Book,* April, 1972; *Junior Literary Guild Catalogue,* September, 1973; *Cricket,* February, 1974; Lee Bennett Hopkins, *More Books By More People,* Citation Press, 1974.

FAST, Howard (Melvin) 1914-
(E. V. Cunningham, Walter Ericson)

PERSONAL: Born November 11, 1914, in New York, N.Y.; son of Barney and Ida (Miller) Fast; married Betty Cohen, June 6, 1937; children: Rachel, Jonathan. *Education:* Attended George Washington High School, New York, N.Y., and National Academy of Design. *Agent:* Paul R. Reynolds & Son, 599 Fifth Ave., New York, N.Y. 10017.

CAREER: Worked at several odd jobs and as a page in the New York Public Library before having his first novel published in 1932, at eighteen. Writer, in a variety of forms, since. A public lecturer who has appeared often on radio and television, he has been active politically at several periods, and once ran for Congress on the American Labor Party ticket. During World War II he was on the overseas staff of the Office of War Information, 1942-44, with a special Signal Corps unit and then war correspondent in the China-Burma-India Theater, 1944-45; worked as a foreign correspondent for *Esquire* and *Coronet* during 1945. *Awards, honors:* Breadloaf Literary Award, 1937; Schomburg Award for Race Relations, 1944; Newspaper Guild award, 1947; Jewish Book Council of America annual award, 1947; Stalin International Peace Prize, of the U.S.S.R., 1954; Screen-writers Annual Award, 1960; Secondary Education Board annual book award, 1962.

WRITINGS: Two Valleys, Dial Press, 1933; *Strange Yesterday,* Dodd, 1934; *Place in the City,* Harcourt, 1937; *Conceived in Liberty: A Novel of Valley Forge,* Simon & Schuster, 1939; *Last Frontier,* Duell, Sloan & Pearce, 1941; *The Romance of a People,* Hebrew Publishing Co., 1941; *Lord Baden-Powell of the Boy Scouts,* Messner, 1941; *Haym Salomon, Son of Liberty,* Messner, 1941; *The Unvanquished,* Duell, 1942; *The Tall Hunter,* Harper, 1942; (with Bette Fast) *The Picture-Book History of the Jews,* Hebrew Publishing Co., 1942; *Goethals and the Panama Canal,* Messner, 1942; *Citizen Tom Paine,* Duell, 1943; *The Incredible Tito,* Magazine House, 1944; *Freedom Road,* Duell, 1944; *Patrick Henry and the Frigate's Keel* (collection), Duell, 1945; *The American, A*

HOWARD FAST

Middle Western Legend (Literary Guild selection), Duell, 1946; *The Children,* Duell, 1947; *Clarkton* (novel), Duell, 1947; *Tito and His People,* Contemporary Publishers, 1948; *My Glorious Brothers,* Little, 1948; *Departure and Other Stories,* Little, 1949.

The Proud and the Free, Little, 1950; *Literature and Reality,* International Publishers, 1950; *Spartacus,* privately printed, 1951, Citadel Press, 1952; *Peekskill, USA: A Personal Experience,* Civil Rights Congress, 1951; *Tony and the Wonderful Door,* Blue Heron, 1952; *The Passion of Sacco and Vanzetti: A New England Legend,* Blue Heron, 1953; *Silas Timberman,* Blue Heron, 1954; *The Last Supper, and Other Stories,* Blue Heron, 1955; *The Story of Lola Gregg,* Blue Heron, 1956; *The Naked God: The Writer and the Communist Party,* Praeger, 1957; *Moses, Prince of Egypt,* Crown, 1958; *The Winston Affair,* Crown, 1959; *The Howard Fast Reader,* Crown, 1960; *April Morning,* Crown, 1961; *Power,* Doubleday, 1962; *Agrippa's Daughter,* Doubleday, 1964; *The Hill* (a screenplay), Doubleday, 1964; *Torquemada,* Doubleday, 1966; *The Hunter and the Trap,* 1967; *The Jews,* 1968; *The General Zapped an Angel,* 1970; *The Crossing,* 1971; *The Hessian* (ALA Notable Book), Morrow, 1972.

The gladiator doesn't like to fight. He fights because you give him a weapon and take off his chains. And when he has that weapon in his hand, he dreams that he is free—and that is what he wants, to have the weapon in his hand and dream that he is free. ■ (From the movie "*Spartacus*," © 1960 by Universal Pictures Company, Inc.)

Plays: *Thirty Pieces of Silver*, Bodley Head, 1954; *General Washington and the Water Witch*, Bodley Head, 1956; "The Crossing," and "Annabelle."

Editor: *The Selected Works of Tom Paine*, Modern Library, 1946; *Best Short Stories of Theodore Dreiser*, World Publishing, 1947.

Under pseudonym E. V. Cunningham: *Sylvia*, 1960, *Phyllis*, 1962, *Alice*, 1963, *Shirley*, 1963, *Lydia*, 1964, *Penelope*, 1965, *Helen*, 1966, *Margie*, Morrow, 1966, *Sally*, Morrow, 1967, *Samantha*, 1968, *Cynthia*, 1969, *The Assassin Who Gave Up His Gun*, 1970, *Millie*, 1972 (all published by Doubleday except where otherwise noted).

Under pseudonym Walter Ericson: *Fallen Angel*, Little, 1951.

SIDELIGHTS: "I am always delighted when any book of mine is read widely by young people. Books—especially fiction—are for the young; when they are good, they open a thousand doors, they shape lives and answer questions, they widen horizons, they offer hope for the heart and food for the soul. And since the young are the continuity of life, only books they will read will endure."

Fast holds that he has never developed a biographical turn of mind, adding, "I am too close to the incidents of my life to be able to separate the important from the unimportant. In a book called *Peekskill, USA*, I told how I was thrown into a situation where I was instrumental in saving the lives of many people. That was probably the most important act of my life, but would not rate so in this kind of an index. In the years since my first novel was published I have lectured, preached, exhorted, and agitated on platform, in classroom, on radio and television more times than I care to recall."

In an interview with Roy Newquist, Fast said that "*April Morning* is as good a book as I have ever written, as nearly perfect a book as I could hope to write." Fast told Newquist that "there are few writers in today's America who write literate and intelligent work that can be read for pleasure." Fast believes that the writer, as an artist, owes nothing to his material or his public: "His only obligation is to truth."

The film, "Mirage," released in 1965, was based on a story by Fast, written under the pseudonym Walter Ericson; *Spartacus* was filmed by Universal in 1960; *Freedom Road* has been optioned by Harold D. Cohen; nine other books have been filmed.

Cunningham knew that if you let a prisoner stand at the door and wait when he was brought in, never looking at him, it would increase his sense of guilt. ■ (From *Haym Salomon* by Howard Fast. Illustrated by Eric M. Simon.)

HOBBIES AND OTHER INTERESTS: "My home, my family, the theater, the film, and the proper study of ancient history. And the follies of mankind."

FOR MORE INFORMATION SEE: Spectator, April 3, 1959; *Nation,* May 30, 1959; *New Statesman,* August 8, 1959; *New York Times Book Review,* July 14, 1963; *New York Herald Tribune Books,* July 21, 1963; Roy Newquist, *Counterpoint,* Rand McNally, 1964; *Horn Book,* June, 1973.

FAULHABER, Martha   1926-

PERSONAL: Born September 6, 1926, in Dayton, Ohio; daughter of Harry Francis (an engineer) and Hildegarde (Elsbernd) Finke; married Robert W. Faulhaber (a professor), June 19, 1950; children: Roberta, Peter, Christina, Elizabeth. *Education:* St. Mary's College, Notre Dame, Ind., B.A., 1948; Chicago Musical College, M.Mus., 1950; Ecole Normale de Musique, Paris, further study, 1950-52. *Home:* 5653 South Harper, Chicago, Ill. 60637.

CAREER: University of Chicago, Chicago, Ill., teacher in Orthogenic School, 1955-56. Former private teacher of piano; accompanist for Chicago Children's Choir; pianist with Trio Musicale, 1969-71.

WRITINGS: (With John Hawkinson) *Music and Instruments for Children to Make,* Albert Whitman, 1969; (with Hawkinson) *Rhythms, Music, and Instruments to Make,* Albert Whitman, 1970; (with Janet Underhill) *Invent Your Own,* Albert Whitman, 1974.

SIDELIGHTS: "When my children were young, I was, as a musician, especially interested in introducing them to music. I worked with other young children of their ages at the same time. Out of this experience grew my ideas about *the* books. John Hawkinson, my co-author, was also interested in developing books for children where they could learn about art and nature and other experiences for themselves through reading. He asked me to collaborate with him to write a book about music. Our joint aim was to develop books where children through their own experiments, could learn about music. Now I am still working with children and using many of these ideas."

FOR MORE INFORMATION SEE: Horn Book, December, 1969.

MARTHA FAULHABER

You can have a rhythm band with your friends using your rhythm instruments. Take turns being the conductor. ■ (From *Music and Instruments for Children to Make* by John Hawkinson and Martha Faulhaber. Illustrated by John Hawkinson.)

FECHER, Constance 1911-
(Constance Heaven)

PERSONAL: Born August 6, 1911, in London, England; daughter of Michael Joseph and Caroline (Rand) Fecher; married William Heaven (a theatrical director), May 11, 1939 (died, 1958). *Education:* Attended convent school in Woodford Green, England, 1920-28; King's College, University of London, B.A. (honors), 1932; London College of Music, Licentiate, 1931. *Politics:* Liberal. *Religion:* Roman Catholic. *Home:* Tudor Green, 37 Teddington Park Rd., Teddington TW11 8NB, Middlesex, England. *Agent:* Carl Routledge, Charles Lovell Ltd., 176 Wardour St., London W.1, England.

CAREER: Actress, 1938-64; began writing in early 1960's; tutor in seventeenth-century history and literature and in creative writing at City Literary Institute, London, 1967—. With her husband operated a little theater at Henley-on-Thames, 1939; played with companies touring throughout England during World War II; after her husband was released from Royal Air Force they ran their own theatrical companies until his death in 1958; still gives occasional stage recitals of verse and prose. *Awards, honors:* Romantic Novelists Association Prize for best romantic historical novel, 1972, for *The House of Kuragin.*

WRITINGS—Children's books: *Venture for a Crown,* Farrar, Straus, 1968; *Heir to Pendarrow,* Farrar, Straus, 1969; *Bright Star* (biography of Ellen Terry), Farrar, Straus, 1970; *The Link Boys,* Farrar, Straus, 1971; *The Last Elizabethan: A Portrait of Sir Walter Raleigh,* Farrar, Straus, 1972; *The Leopard Dagger* (Junior Literary Guild selection), Farrar, Straus, 1973.

Adult novels: Trilogy consisting of *Queen's Delight,* 1966, *Traitor's Son,* 1967, and *King's Legacy,* 1967, R. Hale; *Player Queen,* R. Hale, 1968; *Lion of Trevarrock,* R. Hale, 1969; *The Night of the Wolf,* R. Hale, 1971; (under name Constance Heaven) *The House of Kuragin,* Coward, 1972; (under name Constance Heaven) *The Astrov Legacy,* Coward, 1973; (under name Constance Heaven) *Castle of Eagles,* Coward, 1974.

WORK IN PROGRESS: Place of Stones, a novel set during the Napoleonic War in France, for Heinemann; research into Scottish life for a novel set in the Highlands during 1770-75.

SIDELIGHTS: "Writing has now taken over from the theatre...but my interest in theatre remains and finds expression in many of my books, viz. *The Leopard Dagger* which

CONSTANCE FECHER

is set in the Elizabethan Globe Theatre with Dick Burbage and Will Shakespeare playing a part."

Her other fascination is with history, particularly Elizabethan, and both her adult and children's books have historical themes. The trilogy that began with *Queen's Delight* is on Sir Walter Raleigh's family and descendents.

FOR MORE INFORMATION SEE: Horn Book, October, 1969, April, 1971, June, 1971, June, 1972, June, 1973; *Junior Literary Guild Catalogue,* March, 1973.

. . . the next instant it was a pandemonium of rolling glass balls, of sliding, slithering animals, of men cursing, women shrieking, and children screaming. ■ (From *The Link Boys* by Constance Fecher. Illustrated by Richard Cuffari.)

FENNER, Carol (Elizabeth) 1929-

PERSONAL: Born September 30, 1929, in New York, N.Y.; daughter of Andrew J. and Esther (Rowe) Fenner; married Jiles B. Williams (major, U.S.A.F., ret.). *Home:* 190 Rebecca Rd., Battle Creek, Mich. 49015.

CAREER: Illustrator, writer, publicist. *Awards, honors:* Christopher Award, 1973, for *Gorilla, Gorilla.*

WRITINGS: Tigers in the Cellar (juvenile), Harcourt, 1963; *Christmas Tree on the Mountain,* Harcourt, 1966; *Lagalag, the Wanderer,* Harcourt, 1968; *Gorilla, Gorilla* (ALA Notable Book), Random House, 1973.

WORK IN PROGRESS: The Skates of Uncle Richard, Phyllis' Dream, Tales from the Unicorn.

SIDELIGHTS: "I remember this clearly. I was six years old. I sat in a field of grass and sun and dandelions and decided to become a poet. I wrote a poem. It was loyally typed up by my mother. Years later, looking through a crumbly old scrapbook of my father's, I came across this first poem, 'The Dandelion' ,which had been printed in a newspaper loyally submitted by my father.

"I don't remember when I began to draw. It seems as if I have always done it. I have no formal training in either writing or drawing, but I've read a lot and looked a lot.

"I was born in the autumn of 1929 in Almond, New York, county of Alleghany. The town sports a population of about 750 people. Parts of my childhood were spent in Brooklyn and rural Connecticut.

"At age eleven, I was writing, producing and directing such unreknowned works as 'The Modern Version of Romeo and Juliet, A Comedy' and 'The Mystery of the Arabian Dagger.' These highly attended performances were held in the basement. To this day, my business sense, which failed to prompt me to charge admission then, has remained underdeveloped. I understand that this is not an adult attitude. I do my best to remedy it. Also, about this time I began writing a novel. As I remember, it was an interesting and original conception. . . .unlike a perfectly dreadful bunch of plays I wrote, which were watery combinations of Nancy Drewish characters in very weepy situations, fraught with mystery and suspense.

"I am the eldest of five children. I am fortunate to have a magic aunt, Phyllis Fenner, who, whenever we could capture her, told us unforgettable fairy tales drenched with her own excitement and pleasure. She also provided me with every wonderful children's book in print. She was for me when I was a child, a treat the way ice cream is, and I still find her delicious. She has been a delightful and unpretentious influence."

HOBBIES AND OTHER INTERESTS: Horses, tennis, swimming, cooking, gardening.

FOR MORE INFORMATION SEE: Christian Science Monitor, May 2, 1973; *New York Times Book Review,* May 27, 1973; *Horn Book,* June 6, 1973.

He was born, wet and tiny and gray, one wet and gray morning. ■ (From *Gorilla Gorilla* by Carol Fenner. Illustrated by Symeon Shimin.)

CAROL FENNER

FENTON, Edward 1917-

PERSONAL: Born July 7, 1917, in New York, N.Y.; son of Henry Clemence and Fannie (Golden) Fenton; married Sophia Harvati (now a psychologist and educator), March 23, 1963. *Education:* Attended Amherst College. *Home:* 24 Evrou St., Athens 610, Greece.

CAREER: Metropolitan Museum of Art, New York, N.Y., staff member in department of prints, 1950-55; self-employed writer, formerly in New York State, currently in Athens, Greece. *Awards, honors:* Mystery Writers of America "Edgar" for best juvenile of year in its field, for *The Phantom of Walkaway Hill,* 1961; Mildred L. Batchelder Award, 1969, for *Wildcat Under Glass,* 1974, for *Petros' War.*

WRITINGS: Soldiers and Strangers (poems), Macmillan, 1944; *The Double Darkness* (novel), Doubleday, 1947; *Anne of the Thousand Days,* New American Library, 1970; *The Mystery of the Mad Millionairess,* Curtis, 1973.

Juveniles: *Us and the Duchess,* 1947, *Aleko's Island,* 1948, *Hidden Trapezes,* 1950; *Nine Lives,* Pantheon, 1952, *The Golden Doors,* 1957, *Once Upon a Saturday,* 1958; *Fierce John,* 1959, *The Nine Questions,* 1959, *Phantom of Walkaway Hill,* 1961, *An Island for a Pelican,* 1963, *The Riddle of the Red Whale,* 1966, *The Big Yellow Balloon,* 1967, *A Matter of Miracles,* Holt, 1967, *Penny Candy,* Holt, 1970, *Duffy's Rocks,* Dutton, 1974 (all published by Doubleday, except as noted).

Translator: Alki Zei, *Wildcat Under Glass,* Holt, 1968; Alki Zei, *Petros' War,* Dutton, 1972.

WORK IN PROGRESS: A juvenile with a Greek background.

SIDELIGHTS: "For the moment I'm living in Athens, with my Greek wife. Have lived and worked in Italy and Greece chiefly. Have been translated into French, Italian, German, Dutch, Polish, Greek, Spanish. When asked why I write for children, I can only reply that it's because certain books turn out that way."

Fenton has definite ideas as to what children require in a book. "Children hunger for plot. The recognition of this desire for a story is another way of saying that they require form. Subconsciously they recognize that the function of art is to wrest shape out of chaos. They abhor chaos—unless, of course, they are creating it themselves. They are absolutely logical, and impossible to deceive. They know when the Emperor is wearing no more than his underdrawers. Even when engrossed in fantasy, they demand of the story that it be based on almost geometric logic and that it advance with the inevitableness of an equation."

FOR MORE INFORMATION SEE: New York Times Book Review, August 6, 1967; *Book World,* September 10, 1967, November 5, 1967; *Young Reader's Review,* October, 1967; *Horn Book,* June, 1968, June, 1974; *The Writer,* April, 1969; *Saturday Review,* May 10, 1969; *Library Journal,* July, 1970; *Third Book of Junior Authors,* edited by de Montreville and Hill, H. W. Wilson, 1972; *Top of the News,* June, 1974.

EDWARD FENTON

FERBER, Edna   1887-1968

PERSONAL: Born August 15, 1887, in Kalamazoo, Mich.; daughter of Jacob Charles (Hungarian-born small businessman) and Julia (Newmann) Ferber. *Education:* Graduated from Ryan High School, Appleton, Wis. *Address:* c/o Doubleday & Co., Inc., 277 Park Ave., New York, N.Y. 10017.

CAREER: Novelist, short story writer, playwright. At seventeen, began working as a full-time reporter for *Appleton Daily Crescent*, Appleton, Wis.; later worked as a writer and reporter for *Milwaukee Journal*. *Wartime activity:* During World War II, served in civilian capacity as war correspondent for U.S. Army Air Forces. *Member:* National Institute of Arts and Letters, Authors League of America, Authors Guild, Dramatists Guild. *Awards, honors:* Pulitzer Prize for Fiction, 1924, for *So Big;* Litt. D., Columbia University and Adelphi College.

WRITINGS—Novels: *Dawn O'Hara, the Girl Who Laughed,* Stokes, 1911; *Fanny Herself,* Stokes, 1917; *The Girls,* Doubleday, 1921; *So Big,* Doubleday, 1924; *Show Boat,* Doubleday, 1926; *Cimarron,* Doubleday, 1930, revised edition, Grosset, 1942, new edition by Frederick H. Law, Globe, 1954; *American Beauty,* Doubleday, 1931; *Come and Get It,* Doubleday, 1935; *Nobody's In Town,* (two novellas, including "Trees Die at the Top"), Doubleday, 1938; *Saratoga Trunk,* Doubleday, 1941; *Great Son,* Doubleday, 1945; *Giant,* Doubleday, 1952; *Ice Palace,* Doubleday, 1958.

Short stories: *Buttered Side Down,* Stokes, 1912; *Roast Beef, Medium: The Business Adventures of Emma Mc-*

Chesney, Stokes, 1913; *Personality Plus: Some Experiences of Emma McChesney and Her Son, Jock,* Stokes, 1914; *Emma McChesney & Co.,* Stokes, 1915; *Cheerful, by Request,* Doubleday, 1918; *Half Portions,* Doubleday, 1920; *Gigolo,* Doubleday, 1922; "Old Man Minick," 1924 (see Omnibus volumes, below); *Mother Knows Best: A Fiction Book,* Doubleday, 1927; *They Brought Their Women,* Doubleday, 1933; *No Room at the Inn,* Doubleday, 1941; *One Basket,* Simon & Shuster, 1947.

Plays: (With George V. Hobart) *Our Mrs. McChesney* (first produced in New York at Lyceum Theater, October 19, 1905), 1917; (with Newman Levy) *$1200 a Year,* Doubleday, 1920; (with George S. Kaufman) "Minick" (dramatization of her short story, "Old Man Minick"; first produced in New York at Booth Theater, September 24, 1924), 1924 (see Omnibus volumes, below); *The Eldest: A Drama of American Life,* Appleton, 1925; (with Kaufman) "The Royal Family," first produced in New York at Selwyn Theater, December 28, 1927, produced as television play, 1954; (with Kaufman) "Dinner at Eight," first produced on Broadway at Music Box Theater, October 22, 1932; (with Kaufman) *Stage Door* (first produced on Broadway at Music Box Theater, October 22, 1936), Doubleday, 1936; (with Kaufman) *The Land Is Bright* (first produced on Broadway at Music Box Theater, October 28, 1941), Doubleday, 1941; (with Kaufman) *Bravo!* (first produced in New York at Lyceum Theater, November 11, 1948), Dramatists Play Service, 1949.

EDNA FERBER

The Haymarket buyers did not want to purchase its vegetables from Selina DeJong. It wasn't used to buying from women, but to selling to them. . . . It was not unkindness that prompted them, but a certain shyness, a fear of the unaccustomed. ■ (From the movie "So Big," copyright 1953 by Warner Bros. Pictures, Inc.)

Others: (Author of filmscript) "A Gay Old Dog," Pathe Exchange, 1919; (contributor) *My Story That I Like Best,* International Magazine Co., 1924; (with Kaufman, author of filmscript) "Welcome Home," Paramount, 1925; *A Peculiar Treasure* (autobiography), Doubleday, 1939; *A Kind of Magic* (autobiography; sequel to *A Peculiar Treasure),* Doubleday, 1963.

Omnibus volumes: *Old Man Minick* [and] *Minick* (the story and the play; the latter with Kaufman), Doubleday, 1924; *Show Boat, So Big,* [*and*] *Cimarron: Three Living Novels of American Life,* Doubleday, 1962.

WORK IN PROGRESS: At the time of her death, Ferber was collecting material for a book on American Indians but, according to *Variety,* "it is not believed that anything was actually written."

SIDELIGHTS: Edna Ferber loved America and all of her stories in many ways depict a passing American way of life.

Along with her great love for America, Edna Ferber greatly admired the characters she portrayed. These characters, drawn from the Midwestern lower middle and middle classes, exemplify the American ideal for her. (She always found the conversation of a truck driver more vigorous and stimulating than the conversation of a Cadillac owner.)

Miss Ferber wrote about the United States for four decades. Even though her father, a Hungarian Jew, was an unsuccessful storekeeper and she was forced to work instead of attending college where she wanted to study drama. Her enthusiasm made her books especially enjoyable reading for young people. She gave us a fragment of life important to her. Her "sentimentality" was typical of an era we may never see again. William Allen White believes that "the historian will find no better picture of America in the first three decades of this century than Edna Ferber has drawn."

Critics of the twenties and thirties did not hesitate to call

88

Ranches are full of life and death and birth. . . . A couple of hundred thousand of any living thing and you're likely to see some pretty fundamental stuff going on. ▪ (From the movie "*Giant,*" copyright 1956 by Warner Bros. Pictures Distributing Corp.)

She was attempting to produce the effect of being a woman of the world, a connoisseur of food, a *femme fatale.* . . . That choice section of New Orleans which was engaged in the rite of Sunday breakfast . . . stared, whispered, engaged in facial gymnastics that ranged all the way from looking down their noses to raising their eyebrows. ▪ (From the movie "*Saratoga Trunk,*" copyright 1945 by Warner Bros. Pictures Distributing Corp.)

Every member of the *Cotton Blossom* troupe must be able to sing, dance, play some musical instrument, or give a monologue. . . . Here were warmth, enchantment, laughter, music. It was Anodyne. It was Lethe. It was Escape. It was the Theatre. ■ (From the movie *"Showboat,"* copyright 1951 by Loew's Inc. A Metro-Goldwyn-Mayer Picture.)

"Supper and wine . . . and first thing you know it's five thousand dollars, no matter how skimpy. . . . The way things are now, it gets into the papers . . . and next thing you know they've got it around it really was a big expensive party." ■ (From the movie *"Come and Get It,"* later released as *"Roaring Timber,"* copyright 1936 by Samuel Goldwyn.)

Something about the Author

"Around [Alaska] you can live to be a hundred, easy, unless you're shot, or your plane cracks up on you, or a bear sees you first." ■ (From the movie "Ice Palace," copyright © 1959 by Warner Bros. Pictures Distributing Corp.)

her the greatest American woman novelist of her day. *So Big,* Pulitzer Prize-winning novel of 1924, is the story of Selina Peake Dejong who is left penniless when her gambler father dies of a bullet wound. "Selina's victory in the novel is Ferber's extended homily on the gospel of rugged individualism," W. T. Stuckey concludes. She continued writing with the "escapist" technique in *Showboat,* living in James Adams' Floating Theater for two months to get the right atmosphere; in 1924, she dramatized her own personal doubts in *Cimarron* (she had been fired by a new city editor after working on the paper for a year and a half). Her eleventh novel, *Giant,* was, according to the author, "not only a story of Texas today but, I hope, Texas tomorrow." Oddly, her latest novel, *Ice Palace,* which concerns Alaska "was given much credit for the admission of the territory," notes William Rutledge III.

In later years, Ferber often helped young writers and used her leisure time for travel (in her youth, she wrote more than 1,000 words a day, 350 days a year). Her own philosophy will undoubtedly continue to help the talented young writers in whom she was so interested: "Life," she said, "can't ever really defeat a writer who is in love with writing, for life itself is a writer's lover until death—fascinating, cruel, lavish, warm, cold, treacherous, constant; the more varied the moods the richer the experience."

The following films were based on her work: "Our Mrs. McChesney," Metro, 1918; "No Woman Knows" (based on *Fanny Herself*), Universal, 1921; "Classified" (based on her short story of the same title), Corinne Griffith Productions, 1925; "Gigolo," Cinema Corporation of America, 1926; "Mother Knows Best," Fox, 1928; "The Home Girl" (based on a short story), Paramount, 1928; "Show Boat," Universal, 1929, remade by Universal, 1936, and M-G-M, 1951; "The Royal Family of Broadway" (based on the play "The Royal Family," by Ferber and Kaufman), Paramount, 1930; "Cimarron," RKO, 1931, remade by M-G-M, 1960; "The Expert" (based on her short story, "Old Man Minick"), Warner Bros., 1932; "So Big," Warner Bros., 1932, remade by Warner Bros., 1953; "Dinner at Eight" (based on play written with Kaufman), M-G-M, 1933; "Come and Get It," United Artists, 1936; "Stage Door," RKO, 1937; "No Place to Go" (based on the play, "Minick," by Ferber and Kaufman), Warner Bros., 1939; "Saratoga Trunk," Warner Bros., 1945; "Giant," Warner Bros., 1956; "Ice Palace," Warner Bros., 1960.

Show Boat was adapted for the stage and was first produced in New York at Ziegfeld Theater, December 27, 1927. *Saratoga Trunk* was adapted for a musical, "Saratoga," with a libretto by Harold Arlen; it was first produced on Broadway at Winter Garden Theater, December 7, 1959.

FOR MORE INFORMATION SEE— Articles: *Atlantic*, November, 1912, December 1941; *Literary Review*, October 28, 1922, August 21, 1926; *Springfield Republican*, March 2, 1924; *New York Times (Book Review)*, August 22, 1926, April 17, 1927, March 23, 1930, May 14, 1933, April 17, 1968; *New York World*, March 20, 1930; *Nation*, April 23, 1930; *New Republic*, April 30, 1930; *Saturday Review*, October 17, 1931, September 27, 1952, March 29, 1958; *Atlantic Bookshelf*, December, 1931; *New Yorker*, February 4, 1939; *Literary Journal*, November 1, 1941; *United States Quarterly Booklist*, September, 1947; *Dial*, November 20, 1950; *Christian Science Monitor*, March 27, 1958; *Chicago Sunday Tribune Book Review*, March 30, 1958; *London Times*, April 17, 1968; *Variety*, April 24, 1968; *Publishers' Weekly*, April 29, 1968.

Books: R. Dickinson, *Edna Ferber*, Doubleday, 1925; *Junior Book of Authors*, edited by Kunitz and Haycraft, H. W. Wilson, 1934; Robert Van Gelder, *Writers and Writing*, Scribner, 1946; W. Tasker Witham, *Panorama of American Literature*, Doubleday, 1947; John Cournos and Sybil Norton (pseudonym of H.S.N.K. Cournos), *Famous American Modern Novelists*, Dodd, 1952; Loring Holmes Dodd, *Celebrities at Our Hearthside*, Dresser, 1959.

(Died April 16, 1968)

GEORGE S. FICHTER

FICHTER, George S. 1922-

PERSONAL: Born September 17, 1922, in Reily, Ohio; married Nadine K. Warner, February 10, 1945; children: Susan Kay, Thomas Matt, Jane Ann. *Education:* Miami University, Oxford, Ohio, B.A., 1947; North Carolina State College, M.Sc., 1948; postgraduate study at University of North Carolina. *Address:* P.O. Box 1368, Homestead, Fla. 33030.

CAREER: Miami University, Oxford, Ohio, instructor in zoology, 1948-50; editor, *Fisherman* (magazine), 1950-56; Sport Fishing Institute, Washington, D.C., assistant executive vice-president, 1956; Western Publishing Company, Fla., editor of Golden Guides, 1963-67, director of Golden Guides, 1967-68; writer and editor of natural history books, primarily for young people, 1957—. *Member:* Sigma Xi, Phi Kappa Phi.

WRITINGS: (Co-author) *Good Fishing*, Harper, 1958; *Fishes and How They Live*, Golden Press, 1959; *Reptiles and Their Way of Life*, Golden Press, 1960; *Flying Animals*, Golden Press, 1960; (managing editor and contributor) *Golden Encyclopedia of Natural History*, Golden Press, 1962; *Fishes*, Golden Press, 1963; *Snakes*, Golden Press, 1964; (managing editor) *Insects*, Golden Press, 1965; (co-author) *Fishing*, Golden Press, 1965; *Rocks*, Golden Press, 1966; *Insect Pests*, Golden Press, 1966; *Rocks*, Golden Press, 1966; *Animal Kingdom*, Golden Press, 1968; *Snakes and Other Reptiles*, Golden Press, 1968; *Airborne Animals*, Golden Press, 1969; *Exploring Biology*, Golden Press, 1970; *Exploring with a Microscope*, Golden Press, 1970; *Your World, Your Survival* (Junior Literary Guild selection), Abelard, 1970; *Birds of Florida*, Seemann, 1971;

Earth and Ecology, Golden Press, 1972; *The World of Animals*, Golden Press, 1972; (co-author) *Bicycling*, Golden Press, 1972; *Cats*, Golden Press, 1973; (co-author) *Ecology*, Golden Press, 1973; *The Florida Cookbook*, Seemann, 1973; *Fishes of the World*, Vineyard, in press; *Vegetables of the World*, Golden Press, in press; *Fruits of the World*, Golden Press, in press; *Fishes of Florida*, Seemann, in press; *Reptiles and Amphibians*, Golden Press, in press; *Insects*, Golden Press, in press; *The Human Body*, Golden Press, in press; *Underwater Farming*, Golden Press, in press; *Exploring the Oceans*, Golden Press, in press. Contributor of several hundred articles to *Reader's Digest*, *Coronet*, *Pageant*, *Science Digest*, and other magazines.

FLITNER, David P(erkins) 1949-

PERSONAL: Born January 3, 1949, in Boston, Mass.; son of David Perkins (employed in engineering) and Mariam (Merrill) Flitner; married Emilie Munyan (accounting-sales office employee), December 15, 1973; children: Lisa Marie. *Education:* University of Cincinnati, student, 1967-71, M.A., 1974; Tufts University, graduate study, 1974—; University of Maine in Portland, B.A., 1972. *Politics:* Democrat. *Religion:* Protestant. *Home:* 26 Shipman Rd., Andover, Mass. 01810.

WRITINGS: *Those People in Washington*, Childrens Press, 1973. Has written and recorded songs.

WORK IN PROGRESS: A political analysis of the effectiveness of presidential commissions, tentatively titled *A Passing of Comets: The Case for Presidential Commissions*.

Some time before the election the political parties have meetings called conventions. ■ (From *Those People in Washington* by David Flitner. Illustrated by William Neebe.)

DAVID P. FLITNER

SIDELIGHTS: "I was motivated to write *Those People in Washington* primarily by the interest of my younger sister in my studies and my activities in the New Hampshire primary in 1972. I have two basic desires for the book: one, that it inform and bring some order out of the chaos of names, places and events that young children hear about; two, and most importantly, that it possibly help spark interest at a formative age in public affairs—which have a direct and increasing bearing on the lives of the readers. An ancillary possibility for the book has been its suggested use by those for whom English is a newly acquired language in grasping some of the basics of American government.

"Many people urged that I give more attention in the book to how the governmental structure has been abused. While I agree that the abuse is deep I felt that my job was to present the picture as it is supposed to be; abuse may then be self-evident to young observers.

"The book I have just finished on Presidential commissions grew from research done as an undergraduate and the belief that there might be some value in defining the contributions those groups could make to solving some of the nation's most pressing problems.

"The bulk of my writing, however, has never been submitted for publication and consists of poems and songs. For a number of years, while in high school and undergraduate college I performed in rock groups. Music, aside from politics, is the pursuit most meaningful to me. While not performing at this time, I still write and record my songs.

"Vocationally, I hope to teach international relations as well as American government at the college level. Later, if the opportunity presents itself, I hope very much to serve in some elective office."

Flitner has been to Europe twice and Great Britain and Morocco. He has some competence in Spanish.

FRAZIER, Neta Lohnes

PERSONAL: Pronounced "Nita Lowness"; born in Owosso, Mich.; daughter of Emory Edward and Jennie (Osborn) Lohnes; married Earl Cooper Frazier (teacher, now deceased); children: Lesley (Mrs. Perry Thompson), Philip E., Richard B. Education: Whitman College, B.A. Home and office: West 2340 First Ave., Spokane, Wash. 99204.

CAREER: Waitsburg (Washington) High School, teacher; Spokane Valley Herald, Opportunity, Wash., assistant editor, editor; professional writer, 1947—. Member: Spokane Penwomen (past president, vice-president), American Association of University Women (president, Spokane branch, 1951-53), Theta Sigma Phi, Kappa Kappa Gamma, Delta Kappa Gamma, Phi Beta Kappa, Pacific Northwest Writers' Conference, Women's National Book Association. Awards, honors: Named one of seven outstanding Kappa Kappa Gamma alumnae, 1960.

WRITINGS: By-Line Dennie, Crowell, 1947; My Love is a Gypsy, 1952; Little Rhody, McKay, 1953; Somebody Special, McKay, 1954; Secret Friend, Longmans, 1956; Young Bill Fargo, Longmans, 1956; Rawhide Johnny, McKay, 1957; Magic Ring, McKay, 1959; Something of My Own, McKay, 1960; (contributor) Grandma Moses Storybook, Random, 1961; One Long Picnic, McKay, 1962; Five Roads to the Pacific, McKay, 1964; The General's Boots, McKay, 1965; Eastern Washington State Historical Society: The First Half-Century (monograph), Eastern Washington State Historical Society, 1966; Sacajawea: The Girl Nobody Knows, Crowell, 1967; Stout-Hearted Seven, Harcourt, 1973.

WORK IN PROGRESS: Fiction and nonfiction about the early West.

SIDELIGHTS: "I think I have been writing since I was a child. When about eight or nine years old, I made my first attempt but found, to my dismay, that writing was hard work, so I gave it up. At intervals through my school and college years I tried my hand at short stories but did nothing of value until I had some experience of living to write about.

"Several of my books have come from personal experience but a series I love concerns pioneer life in Michigan and my grandmother, whose name was Rhoda Rebecca Sperry. Things she had told me formed the basis of the series, *Little Rhody, Somebody Special,* and *Secret Friend.*

NETA LOHNES FRAZIER

"I was born and grew up in Owosso, Michigan, but when I was about fifteen years old, my father brought our family west to Spokane, Washington, where I have lived much of the time since. At Whitman College, Walla Walla, Washington, I became interested in the history of the early West and at least half of my fourteen books are based on historical events.

"Book ideas come from various sources. Once I was interviewing an elderly neighbor who could remember crossing the plains in a covered wagon when he was a small boy. I said, 'That must have been a terrible experience.' He smiled a little and said, 'I guess it was, for the grown folks, but for us kids it was just *one long picnic.*' Those three words became the title of one of my most popular books.

"I had a college friend whose grandfather had built the first railroad in the state of Washington. From her I got the idea of 'Rawhide Johnny.' Another family I know well still live on the homestead their family has owned for more than one hundred years. The double log cabin on this ranch, and the story of its building, formed the basis of *The General's Boots.*

"My book, *Stout-Hearted Seven,* began when I met an old friend whom I had not seen since we were in college together and learned that she was the granddaughter of Cath-

erine Sager, member of a famous family of children orphaned on the Oregon Trail in 1844. What she told me and the vast amount of letters, clippings, scrapbooks, etc., started me off on a research project that led to this book.

"So it goes. If one is a professional writer, one has an antenna out at all times for ideas. At any moment, one may jump out at you so you must be ready to grab it as it goes by."

Four of her books have been Junior Literary Guild selections.

FOR MORE INFORMATION SEE: Spokane Daily Chronicle, April 5, 1962, September 28, 1973.

FRIEDMAN, Estelle (Ehrenwald) 1920-

PERSONAL: Born January, 1920, in Nashville, Tenn.; daughter of Alfred S. (merchant) and Marie (Weil) Ehrenwald; married Jack E. Friedman (investment salesman), June 23, 1941; children: Julie, Katherine. *Education:* Vassar College, student, 1937-38; Vanderbilt University, B.A., 1941. *Home:* 4633 Tara Dr., Nashville, Tenn. 37215.

CAREER: Gallup & Robinson, Nashville, Tenn., supervisor, public opinion surveys, 1957-59. *Member:* Phi Beta Kappa. *Awards, honors:* Junior book award, Boys Clubs of America, 1959, for *Digging Into Yesterday.*

WRITINGS: Digging Into Yesterday, 1958, *Man in the Making,* 1960, *Boy Who Lived in a Cave,* 1960, *Ben Franklin,* 1961 (all published by Putman).

WORK IN PROGRESS: A controlled vocabulary book concerning ancient Egypt.

SIDELIGHTS: "At the time I wrote my first book, *Digging Into Yesterday,* there were no books available for young people about archaeology. Now, of course, there are many. But at that time, I wanted young readers to be able to share my interest in a fascinating and romantic subject."

HOBBIES AND OTHER INTERESTS: Anthropology and archaeology. Has traveled to archaeological sites of Mayan civilization, such as Chichen-Itza and Uxmal, Mexico, Tikal, Guatemala, and Copan, Honduras. *Digging Into Yesterday* has been published in England and Egypt.

FRIIS, Babbis
See FRIIS-BAASTAD, Babbis

FRIIS-BAASTAD, Babbis (Ellinor) 1921-1970
(Babbis Friis Baastad, Eleanor Babbis, Babbis Friis)

PERSONAL: Name pronounced "Freeze *Baw*-stahd"; born August 27, 1921, in Bergen, Norway; daughter of Carl H. and Edel J. (Moenness) Blauenfeldt; married Kaare Friis-Baastad (an airline operations manager), June 17, 1942; children: Anne (Mrs. Arvid Henriksen), Winnie,

BABBIS FRIIS-BAASTAD

Beth, Wilhelm. *Education:* Attended Oslo University, 1941-42, received degree, 1948. *Home:* Trosterudveien, Oslo 3, Norway. *Agent:* American Literary Exchange, 325 East 53rd St., New York, N.Y. 10022.

CAREER: Had to leave school during the war; subsequently lived as a refugee in Sweden. Writer and housewife. *Member:* Norwegian Association of Writers for Young People (member of board). *Awards, honors:* Damm Prize, 1959, for *Aeresord,* and 1962, for *Kjersti;* H. C. Andersen prize, 1964; Ministry of Education, 2nd prize, 1960, 3rd prize, 1963, 1st prize for *Ikke ta Bamse,* 1965; Damm prize, 1968, for *Wanted! A Horse!;* has won prizes for radio plays.

WRITINGS: (Under the name Eleanor Babbis) *Aeresord,* N. W. Damm, 1959 (published in America as *Word of Honour,* Clarke, Irwin, 1960); *Hvorfor det?,* N. W. Damm, 1960; *Tulutta og Makronelle,* N. W. Damm, 1960; *Kjertsi,* N. W. Damm, 1962 (published in America under name Babbis Friis Baastad as *Kristy's Courage,* Harcourt, 1965); *Ikke to Bamse,* N. W. Damm, 1964 (published in America as *Don't Take Teddy,* Scribner, 1967); *Du na vakne, Tor* (title means "Wake up, Tor"), N. W. Damm, 1967; *Hest pa onskelisten,* N. W. Damm, 1968 (published in America as *Wanted! A Horse!,* Harcourt, 1972); *Hest i sentrum,* N. W. Damm, 1969. Has written scripts and serials for radio and TV.

SIDELIGHTS: "Being surrounded by doctors, both in family and neighbourhood, has pressed the handicapped child's problem on me and made me feel it a vocation to write so that others too can understand some more about it."

FOR MORE INFORMATION SEE: Horn Book, August, 1972; *Third Book of Junior Authors,* edited by de Montreville and Hill, H. W. Wilson, 1972.

(Died January 11, 1970)

She must have walked the wrong way after all. . . . The soles of her feet were burning, and the sneakers squeezed her toes together so that they felt clammy and unpleasant. ■ (From *Kristy's Courage* by Babbis Friis. Illustrated by Charles Geer.)

The bird looked tired and sleepy but the boy knew she was very happy to be home. ■ (From *The Boy and the Bird* by Tamao Fujita. Illustrated by Chiyo Ono.)

TAMAO FUJITA

FUJITA, Tamao 1905-

PERSONAL: Born November 11, 1905, in Tokyo, Japan; son of Akira (a history professor) and Ayako (Wada) Fujita; married Yuri Goto, March 2, 1934; children: Atsuko (Mrs. Iwase Kaiichiro), Shigeru, Sakiko (Mrs. Atsushi Ideno). *Education:* Waseda University, student, 1924-30. *Home:* 2-49 Sakuradai, Nerima-ku, Tokyo, Japan.

CAREER: Chuo-Koron-Sha, Tokyo, Japan, chief editor and director, 1933-70. Welfare Ministry, member of board of directors of Children's Welfare Committee. *Member:* Japan Pen Club (member of board of directors, 1969), Juvenile Literature Association of Japan (member of board of directors).

WRITINGS: Bokuwa kaizoku (title means "I Am a Pirate"), Froebel Kan, 1965; *Uta no naka no Nihango* (title means "Japanese Language in Songs") Asahi Shimbun, 1965; *Kenchan Asobimasho* (title means "Let up Play Kenchan"), Kodan Sha, 1966; *Ojiisan no Violin* (title means "The Old Man and His Violin"), Shiko-Sha, 1969; *Maigo no Ohmu* (title means "The Missing Parrott"), Shiko-Sha, 1970, translation by Tiyoko Tucker published in the United States as *The Boy and the Bird,* John Day, 1971. Contributor to *World Encyclopedia for Children* and *World's Masterpieces for Children.*

WORK IN PROGRESS: A novel for young readers about the death of a father; a study of the Japanese language; a historical study of children's songs.

FOR MORE INFORMATION SEE: Horn Book, June, 1972.

FUNK, Thompson 1911-
(Tom Funk)

PERSONAL: Born July 18, 1911, in Brooklyn, N.Y.; son of Merton Layton (a physician) and Marion Anna (Thompson) Funk; married Edna Eicke (an artist, whose work includes *New Yorker* covers), December 23, 1943; children: Susan Deborah (Mrs. Robert Colburn), Victoria Greenwood, Peter. *Education:* Amherst College, B.A., 1933; studied at Art Students' League, New York, 1933-34, and Beaux-Arts Institute of Design, New York, 1934-35. *Religion:* Protestant. *Home and studio:* 7 Lincoln St., Westport, Conn. 06880. *Agent:* (Children's book art) Helen Wohlberg, Inc., 331 East 50th St., New York, N.Y. 10022.

CAREER: Lord & Taylor, New York, N.Y., display decorator, 1935-36; display designer, New York, N.Y., 1937-40; free-lance artist and illustrator using name Tom Funk, 1940—. Book, magazine, and advertising illustrator; designer of Christmas cards and Amherst New Year's cards.

WRITINGS—Under name Tom Funk: (Self-illustrated) *I Read Signs* (juvenile), Holiday House, 1962.

TOM FUNK

98

"I read signs,"
Says Peter Malone.
"I know how to read them
By myself alone."
(From *I Read Signs* by Tom Funk. Illustrated by the author.)

Illustrator under name Tom Funk—Juvenile books: Ruth Crawford Seeger, *Let's Build a Railroad*, Aladdin Books, 1954; Rachel Learnard, *Mrs. Roo and the Bunnies* (verse), Houghton, 1953; *Spaniel in the Lion's Den*, Hyperion Press, 1950; Leslie Waller, *Weather*, Holt, 1959; Margaret C. Farquhar, *Lights*, Holt, 1960; Harry Milgrom, *Adventures With a String*, Dutton, 1965; *New Math*, Birk & Co., 1965; Edith Battles, *The Terrible Trick or Treat* (Junior Literary Guild selection), Addison-Wesley, 1970; Charlotte Herman, *String Bean*, O'Hara, 1972; Edith Battles, *The Terrible Terrier* (Junior Literary Guild selection), Addison-Wesley, 1972; Harry Milgrom, *Adventures With a Cardboard Tube* (Junior Literary Guild selection), Dutton, 1973; Edith Battles, *Eddie Couldn't Find the Elephants*, Whitman, 1974.

Illustrator—other books: A. C. Moore, *How to Clean Everything*, Simon & Schuster, 1957; Arnold & White, *Food*, Holiday House, 1959; Arnold & White, *Homes*, Holiday House, 1960; Arnold & White, *Money*, Holiday House, 1962; Gregor, *Short History of Science*, Macmillan, 1963; Gregor, *Short History of the Universe*, Macmillan, 1964; Roma Gans, *Fact and Fiction about Phonics*, Bobbs, 1964; *The Presidency in Conflict*, Collier, 1965; Andries De Groot, *Feasts for All Seasons*, McCall's, 1966; Craig Claiborne, *Craig Claiborne's Kitchen Primer*, Knopf, 1969; Julia Dannenbaum, *Creative Cooking School*, McCall's, 1971; Floss and Stan Dworkin, *Bake Your Own Bread: And Be Healthier*, Holt, 1972; Kenneth Lo, *Chinese Vegetarian Cookbook*, Simon & Schuster, 1974.

Designer of "Playing in the Playstreet," a Headstart kit with mural, five books, and a book of push-out: an environment kit for primary grades with mural posters, die-cuts, and books, and other textbooks. Illustrations have appeared in *New Yorker* (profiles), 1957—, frequently in *Gourmet, House & Garden, Life, Fortune, Woman's Day, Harper's,* and *Cue,* and less regularly in other magazines. Member of staff, *Dramatists Guild Quarterly.*

SIDELIGHTS: "My grandfather and great-uncle founded Funk & Wagnalls Co. and an uncle, Charles E. Funk, was head lexicographer. After he retired he wrote three books on word derivations, which I illustrated."

HOBBIES AND OTHER INTERESTS: Photography, playing guitar and banjo, swimming, yoga, folk dancing.

FUNK, Tom
See FUNK, Thompson

GARTHWAITE, Marion H(ook)   1893-

PERSONAL: Born December 17, 1893, in Oakland, Calif.; daughter of William P. and Sarah Lloyd (McAllis) Hook; married Edwin Lowell Garthwaite, October 7, 1917 (deceased); children: Edwin Lowell, Jr., Jean Gordon Garthwaite Maddox. *Education:* University of California, A.B., 1916. *Religion:* Episcopalian. *Home:* 3358 Moraga Blvd., Lafayette, Calif. 94549.

CAREER: Madera County, Calif., children's librarian, 1944-51; San Mateo County, Calif., children's librarian, 1952-61; University of the Pacific, Stockton, Calif., lecturer on children's literature and storytelling, 1953-65; free-lance writer, lecturer, University of San Francisco, Calif., 1968-72. *Member:* American Association of University Women. *Awards, honors:* Julia Ellsworth Ford Award and Commonwealth Award, both for *Tomas and the Red Headed Angel.*

MARION H. GARTHWAITE

Mariano dug his cruel, inch-long spur into Swift as the Wind's soft side. The horse had never felt spurs. ■ (From *Tomas and the Red-Headed Angel* by Marion Garthwaite. Illustrated by Lorence F. Bjorklund.)

WRITINGS: *Tomas and the Red Headed Angel,* Messner, 1950; *Shaken Days,* Messner, 1952; *You Just Never Know,* Messner, 1955; *Coarse Gold Gulch,* Doubleday, 1956; *Bright Particular Star,* Messner, 1958; *Mystery of Skull Cap Island,* Doubleday, 1959; *Mario,* Doubleday, 1960; *Holdup on Bootjack Hill,* Doubleday, 1961; *Locked Crowns,* Doubleday, 1963; *Twelfth Night,* Doubleday, 1965. Contributor of articles on children's reading to professional journals, *Horn Book,* and of short stories to *American Girl, Story Parade, Jack and Jill.*

WORK IN PROGRESS: An adult book.

SIDELIGHTS: "The last few years I have been more interested and concerned with storytelling and lecturing in schools throughout California. When it became too difficult for me to drive over to the University of San Francisco for my class in 'storytelling and curriculum enrichment,' it was arranged for me to teach it in my own home in Lafayette across the Bay. It was a delightful class of teachers and librarians in the field. They came from all over the Bay area, arriving with pans and plates and boxes of cookies and huge pots of tea and coffee all disappeared during the fifteen minute break at five o'clock.

"I tell stories in school all over the state, was one of a five-man team to teach storytelling at a 'Storytelling Institute' at Ashland for the College of Southern Oregon. I still go to the Santa Barbara County Schools for their author-go-round and to Monterey and Santa Cruz Counties."

FOR MORE INFORMATION SEE: Elinor W. Field, *Horn Book Reflections,* Horn Book, 1969.

GEIS, Darlene (Stern)
(Ralph Kelly, Jane London; Peter Stevens, a joint pseudonym)

PERSONAL: Born April 8th in Chicago, Ill.; daughter of Oscar D. and Anne (Preaskil) Stern; married Bernard Geis, 1940; children: Peter, Stephen. *Education:* Attended Connecticut College for Women, 1934-36; Northwestern University, B.S., 1938; Columbia University, extension courses, 1946-59. *Home:* 1385 York Ave., New York, N.Y. 10021.

CAREER: Sherman Dresses, Chicago, designer, 1939-40; Harry N. Abrams, Inc., art book publishers, New York, N.Y., writer, editor, 1959, assistant to Harry N. Abrams, 1970—; Columbia Record Club, Panorama Travel Program, New York, N.Y., writer, editor, 1959—. *Awards, honors:* Junior Book Award, Boy's Clubs of America, for *Dinosaurs and Other Prehistoric Animals,* 1960.

WRITINGS: The Little Train That Won a Medal, Random, 1947; *Design for Ann,* Crowell, 1949; *The Mystery of the Thirteenth Floor,* Winston, 1953; *The Singing Baby Book,* Winston, 1955; *The Speedy Little Taxi,* Winston, 1955; (under pseudonym Ralph Kelly) *The Little Circus Train That Led a Parade,* Winston, 1955; (under pseudonym Jane London) *The Musical Toy Parade,* Winston, 1955; (with Bernard Geis, under joint pseudonym Peter Stevens) *The Noisy Baby Animals,* Winston, 1955; (adapter) Johanna Spyri, *The Children's Christmas Carol,* Prentice-Hall, 1957; (author of commentary) Harold Jacobs, *Camera Around the World,* A. S. Barnes, 1958; (adapter) Jules Verne, *20,000 Leagues Under the Sea,* Grossett, 1958; *Dinosaurs and Other Prehistoric Animals,* Grossett, 1959; *The How and Why Book of Dinosaurs,* Grosset, 1960; (with Dione N. M. W. Lucas) *The Gourmet*

As the braves huddled together, feeling very small in that empty land, a blazing zigzag of lightning ripped the sky. There was a clap of thunder that shook the earth. ■ (From *Dinosaurs and Other Prehistoric Animals* by Darlene Geis. Illustrated by R. F. Peterson.)

DARLENE GEIS

Cooking School Cookbook, Bernard Geis, 1964; (editor) Vincent Price, *A Treasury of Great Recipes,* Ampersand Press, 1965.

Author and editor—"Let's Travel" Series (all republished by Children's Press from the original "Panorama Color-slide" Series produced by Columbia Record Club): *Let's Travel in England,* 1964, . . .*France,* 1964, . . .*Greece,* 1964, . . .*Hong Kong,* 1964, . . .*Italy,* 1964, . . .*the Soviet Union,* 1964, . . .*Spain,* 1964, . . .*Switzerland,* 1964, . . .*China,* 1965, . . .*Hawaii,* 1965, . . .*the Holy Land,* 1965, . . .*India,* 1965, . . .*Japan,* 1965, . . .*Mexico,* 1965, . . .*the South Seas,* 1965, . . .*the Philippines,* 1965. Also edited *Let's Travel in Ghana,* and *Let's Travel in Holland,* by Theodore Irwin, both for Children's Press. Contributor to *Pageant, Good Housekeeping, Family Circle.*

GENTLEMAN, David (William)   1930-

PERSONAL: Born March 11, 1930, in England; son of Tom (an artist) and Winifred Gentleman; married Susan Evans: children: Fenella Jane, Sarah, Amelia. *Education:* Studied at St. Albans School of Art, 1947-48, and Royal College of Art, London, 1950-53. *Home and studio:* 25 Gloucester Cr., Regents Park, London N.W. 1, England.

CAREER: Royal College of Art, London, England, instructor in School of Graphic Design, 1953-55; free-lance designer, illustrator, photographer, wood engraver, and painter, including book illustrations and jackets, wallpapers, murals, posters, series of British postage stamps, display, and packaging. Watercolor paintings have been exhibited at Royal Academy, and he has had several exhibitions at Mercury Gallery and Curwen Gallery, London.

WRITINGS—Self-illustrated children's books: *Fenella in Spain,* 1967, *Fenella in the South of France,* 1967, *Fenella in Greece,* 1967, *Fenella in Ireland,* 1967, *Design in Miniature,* Studio Vista, 1972, (all published in Canada by Clarke, Irwin, and in England by J. Cape, except where noted).

Illustrator: Andre L. Simon, *What about Wine?,* Newman Neame, 1953; Patience Gray and Primrose Boyd, *Plats du Jour,* Penguin, 1957; *Italian Journey* (language learning booklet), British Broadcasting Corp., 1958; John Pudney, *Bristol Fashion,* Putnam, 1960; Charles Dickens, *The Magic Fishbone,* Bodley Head, 1960, Dufour, 1965; Frank R. Stockton, *The Griffin and the Minor Canon,* Bodley Head, 1960, Dufour, 1965; Elizabeth Kendall, *House into Home,* Dent, 1962; J. Wyss, *Swiss Family Robinson,* Limited Editions Club of New York, 1963; L. Notstein, *Hill Towns of Italy,* Hutchinson, 1963; G. Grigson, *The Shell Book of Roads,* Rainbird, 1964; John Clare, *The Shepherd's Calendar,* Oxford University Press, 1964; J. L. Styan, *The Dramatic Experience,* Cambridge University Press, 1965; John Hornby, *Gypsies,* Oliver & Boyd, 1965; *Poems of John Keats,* Limited Editions Club of New York, 1966; G. Ewart Evans, *Pattern Under the Plough,* Faber, 1966; R. Wilson, *Poems to Compare,* Macmillan (London), 1966; Rudyard Kipling, *The Jungle Book,* Limited Editions Club of New York, 1967; Edmund Blunden, *Midnight Skaters,* Bodley Head, 1967; J. P. Moreau, *The Departed Village,* Oxford University Press, 1968; *Collected Poems*

of Wordsworth, Bodley Head, 1969; G. Ewart Evans, *Where Beards Way All,* Faber, 1970; *St. George and the Dragon,* Atheneum, 1973; *Tales of the Pujab,* Bodley Head, 1973. A portfolio of drawings, "Bridges on the Backs," was published in 1961.

WORK IN PROGRESS: Set of dinner plates for Wedgewood.

GEORGIOU, Constantine   1927-

PERSONAL: Born April 2, 1927, in Calcutta, India; son of Anthony (an industrialist) and Harichlia (Dangas) Georgiou. *Education:* Early education in India and other countries; Columbia Union College, B.A., 1952; University of Maryland, M.Ed., 1954; New York University, Ed.D., 1964. *Home:* 1 Washington Square Village, New York, N.Y. 10012.

CAREER: New York University, New York, N.Y., professor of children's literature, 1961—. Author of books for children. *Member:* National Council of Teachers of English, American Association of University Professors, American Library Association, Kappa Delta Pi.

WRITINGS: Wait and See, Harvey, 1962; *The Little Red Hen and the Gingerbread Boy,* American Book Co., 1963; *Ham the Astrochimp,* American Book Co., 1963; *The Elephant's Funny Way,* American Book Co., 1963; *The Monkey and the Alligator: Who Was the Strongest?,* American Book Co., 1963; *Whitey and Whiskers,* Harvey, 1964;

CONSTANTINE GEORGIOU

102

The branches of the old apple tree swished and swayed in the darkness. ■ (From *The Nest* by Constantine Georgiou. Illustrated by Bethany Tudor.)

Escape From Moscow, American Book Co., 1964; *The Clock,* Harvey, 1967; *Prosperpina,* Harvey, 1968; *Children and Their Literature,* Prentice-Hall, 1969; *Rani, Queen of the Jungle,* Prentice-Hall, 1970; *The Nest,* Harvey, 1972.

WORK IN PROGRESS: "The Heritage Series."

SIDELIGHTS: Started seeing the world in early childhood, accompanying parents (of Greek descent) to various countries where his father had business interests. Visits Greece often, "especially since I enjoy the classical heritage."

HOBBIES AND OTHER INTERESTS: Music, Byzantine art.

GILLETT, Mary (Bledsoe)

PERSONAL: Born in Jefferson, N.C.; daughter of John Tyrell (a farmer) and Sara Jane (Tulbert) Bledsoe; married Rupert Gillett (an editorial writer), October 5, 1926; children: John Bledsoe, Jane (Mrs. Louis Estes). *Education:* University of Texas, B.A., 1920. *Politics:* Republican. *Religion:* Episcopalian. *Home:* 1939 Providence Rd., Charlotte, N.C. 28211. *Agent:* Lenninger Literary Agency, 11 West 42nd St., New York, N.Y. 10026.

CAREER: San Antonio Express, San Antonio, Tex., reporter, 1920-21; Library of Congress, Washington, D.C., cataloguer, 1921-22; *Richmond News Leader,* Richmond, Va., feature writer, 1922-24; Chesapeake & Ohio Railroad, publicity staff member, 1924-26; Ayer & Gillette (advertising), Charlotte, N.C., vice-president and head copywriter, 1953-63. Member of board, Charlotte Symphony Orchestra, 1953, and Charlotte Nature Museum, 1959-62.

AWARDS, HONORS: American Association of University Women's Award in Juvenile literature (North Carolina Division), 1969, for *Bugles at the Border.*

WRITINGS: (Editor) *Read Aloud Stories* (juvenile anthology); (editor) *Child Life Reader* (juvenile anthology), Rand McNally; *Shadows Slant North* (adult novel), Lothrop, 1937; *Bugles at the Border* (juvenile novel), Blair, 1968.

WORK IN PROGRESS: Story of Catawbas; another boys' book.

GIOVANOPOULOS, Paul (Arthur) 1939-

PERSONAL: Born November 12, 1939, in Kastoria, Greece; came to United States, 1954, naturalized, 1961; son of Athanasios T. (a furrier) and Maria (Benjou) Giovanopoulos. *Education:* Studied at New York University, 1958-59, and School of Visual Arts, New York, 1959-61. *Home and office:* 73 Vermilyea Ave., New York, NY. 10034.

CAREER: Artist and illustrator; teacher of art at School of Visual Arts, New York, N.Y., 1969, and Parsons School

PAUL GIOVANOPOULOS

(From *The Real Tin Flower* by Aliki Barnstone. Illustrated by Paul Giovanopoulos.)

of Design, New York, 1970-73. Has had one-man show shows at Lacarda Gallery, New York; 1965, 1967, 1968; exhibitor in XXII American Drawing Biennial at Norfolk Museum, 1967 (entry chosen for Smithsonian traveling exhibition), National Academy of Design, 1966, Philadelphia Academy of Fine Arts, Corcoran Gallery, Baltimore Museum, and other museums and galleries.

AWARDS, HONORS: Gold Medal of Society of Illustrators, 1961; John Armstrong Chaloner Foundation fellowship to work and study abroad, 1964-65; *The Real Tin Flower* was judged by *New York Times* as one of ten best illustrated children's books of 1968 and *Free as a Frog* as one of ten best illustrated of 1969; nine awards from Art Directors Club of Miami as illustrator for Storer Broadcasting Corp. extended series.

ILLUSTRATOR: Paula Fox, *How Many Miles to Babylon?,* David White, 1967; Margaret Chase Smith and H. P. Jeffers, *Gallant Women,* McGraw, 1968; Aliki Barnstone, *The Real Tin Flower: Poems About the World at Nine,* Crowell-Collier, 1968; Leigh Dean, *The Looking-*

Down Game, Funk, 1968; Elizabeth J. Hodges, *Free as a Frog,* Addison-Wesley, 1969; Elizabeth Jane Coatsworth, *George and Red,* Macmillan, 1969; Freda Linde, *Toto and the Aardvark,* Doubleday, 1969; Leigh Dean, *Rufus Gideon Grant,* Scribner, 1970. Illustrations have appeared in *Playboy, New York Magazine, Ladies' Home Journal, Seventeen, Redbook, Fortune, Intellectual Digest,* and *New York Times.*

GLOVACH, Linda 1947-

PERSONAL: Surname is pronounced *Glo*-vack; born June 24, 1947, in Rockville Centre, N.Y.; daughter of John Maurice (a maintenance engineer) and Elvira (Martone) Glovach, *Education:* Studied at Farmingdale University, 1965-66, Art Students League of New York, 1966-68, and California Art Center College of Design, 1969. *Politics:* Liberal. *Home and office:* 16 Saxon Ave., Apt 21, Bayshore, Long Island, N.Y. 11706.

CAREER: Free-lance artist. Has worked as a secretary and a hostess at Disneyland, Calif. Speaker in grade schools in Brentwood, N.Y. and local Long Island libraries and schools. *Member:* Catholic Society for Welfare of Animals, Society for Animal Rights, Defenders of Wildlife, Library Club of Bayshore. *Awards, honors:* Art Students League of New York award for book illustration, 1970.

WRITINGS—Children's books, all self-illustrated: *Hey, Wait for Me! I'm Amelia,* Prentice-Hall, 1971; *The Cat and the Collector,* Prentice-Hall, 1972; *The Little Witch's Black Magic Cookbook,* Prentice-Hall, 1972; *The Little Witch's Black Magic Book of Disguises,* (Junior Literary Guild selection), Prentice-Hall, 1973; *The Little Witch's Game Book,* Prentice-Hall, 1974; *The Rabbitt and the Rainmaker,* Prentice Hall, 1974; *The Witch's Black Magic Christmas Book,* Prentice-Hall, 1974.

WORK IN PROGRESS: A book of ten spooky stories for young people; a picture book tentatively titled, *Heads or Tails.*

SIDELIGHTS: "I was an only child of working parents and at the age of four I was left in the care of an elderly lady who drank beer hidden in the pantry and then fell asleep. So until my parents came home I was left alone with my imagination (which was wild) and the elderly lady's cat, Shirley, who I used to tell fantastic stories to.

"Since I can remember I have been writing stories about the simple every day things I see around me. It starts with an eerie or uncanny or uncommon feeling about a particular person or place and I cannot rest until I have my say either in words, pictures or both.

"I write early in the morning (4:00 a.m.), or late at night, draw or illustrate during the day and worry about it in

That night the cat seemed restless. He did not eat. He kept watching the man and the plump little bird. ■ (From *The Cat and the Collector* by Linda Glovach. Illustrated by the author.)

LINDA GLOVACH

between. I find storybook characters wherever I go. I just came back from New Orleans. There I met a wonderful cat in Pirate's Alley. Her master is blind so she's kind of a 'seeing eye' cat. Who knows, it might be the start of another book.''

Linda Glovach sent her first horror story to Twentieth-Century Fox at age eleven.

HOBBIES AND OTHER INTERESTS: Travel.

FOR MORE INFORMATION .SEE: Junior Literary Guild Catalogue, September, 1973.

GOTTLIEB, Gerald   1923-

PERSONAL: Born August 12, 1923, in New York, N.Y.; son of Harold J. (an engineer) and Jeanette (Beck) Gottlieb; married Robin Grossman (a writer), November 29, 1952. Education: City College of New York, B.S., 1948; Columbia University, M.S. in Library Science, 1973. Home: 210 East 68th St., New York, N.Y. 10021. Agent: Harold Ober Associates Inc., 40 East 49th St., New York, N.Y. 10017.

CAREER: Funk & Wagnalls Co., New York, N.Y., editor, 1948-50; Alfred A. Knopf, Inc., New York, N.Y., editor, 1950-54; Random House, Inc., New York, N.Y., editor, 1954-57; free-lance writer, consultant to publishers, rewrite man and ghost writer for publishers, 1957—. Military service: U.S. Army Air Forces, 1943-45; navigator; became first lieutenant; awarded Air Medal with five oak leaf clusters and Presidential Citation. Awards, honors: First Bread Loaf Writers Conference fellowship in juvenile literature, 1957, for The Adventures of Ulysses; Jewish National Book Award, 1970, for The Story of Masada.

WRITINGS: The Adventures of Ulysses, Random, 1959; . The First Book of France, Watts, 1959; The First Book of the Mediterranean, Watts, 1960; Wonders of Africa, Simon and Schuster, 1961; Wonders of Asia, Golden Press, 1962; The Story of Masada (retold for young readers from Yigael Yadin's Masada), Random House, 1969.

FOR MORE INFORMATION SEE: Horn Book, August, 1969.

GRABER, Alexander
(Alexander Cordell)

PERSONAL: Born September 9, 1914, in Colombo, Ceylon; son of Frank Alfred (an English soldier) and Amelia (Young) Graber; married Rosina Wells, 1937; children: Georgina Elizabeth. Education: By Private tutors, at Marist Brothers' College, and at a technical institute. Politics: Active Socialist. Religion: Church of England. Home: "Fair Country," Waen Wen, Bangor, Wales.

CAREER: Civil surveyor, Wales, 1936-39, 1945—. Began writing in 1950. Military service: Royal Army, sapper, 1932-36; Royal Engineers, 1939-45, became major. Member: Cardiff Writers' Circle (vice president).

WRITINGS: A Thought of Honour, Museum Press, 1954; Rape of the Fair Country, Doubleday, 1959; Robe of Honour, Doubleday, 1961; Race of the Tiger, Doubleday, 1963; The Sinews of Love, Doubleday, 1965; The Bright Cantonese, Simon & Schuster, 1967; Song of the Earth, Simon & Schuster, 1969; The Fire People, Simon & Schuster, 1971; The White Cockade (Child Study Association Book list), Viking, 1971; Witches Sabbath, Viking, 1971; The Healing Blade, Viking, 1971; The Traitor Within, Nelson, 1972; If you Believe in Soldiers, Doubleday, 1973; The Dream and the Destiny (adult), Doubleday, 1974. Contributes poems, short stories, and serials to various magazines.

ALEXANDER GRABER

SIDELIGHTS: "My books are mainly about the past because I believe fervently that the future is shaped by the past; that we today enjoy freedom because of the sacrifices made by the old people. Britain, for instance, is now reaping the whirlwind of her brutality in Ireland: this dates from the era of Cromwell to the days of the comparatively recent Black and Tans. Edward Kennedy's attitude I believe to be perfectly right and justified. Hence the trilogy on the truth of the 1798 Irish Rebellion, for children (*The White Cockade, Witches Sabbath, The Healing Blade*).

"I try, too, to build political bridges by showing how the other side of the world, particularly China, lives and breathes. My children's book, *The Traitor Within*, is about a little Chinese boy, his mother and sister, living in a commune near Canton—a contemporary story. I applaud your government's attempt to draw closer to China in the interests of world peace. Only the children can do this in the new generations.

"I travel extensively for material—in 1966 I was in Peking—researching for the story of the Chinese epic, *The Dream and the Destiny*. Research often takes me two years, the writing of the actual book barely six months. (I do not write more than two hours at a time, and then at white heat—furiously, and it exhausts me.) I slept rough in Ireland in winter to recapture, for children, the famine cold of those who, in desperation, ran to America, their promised land. I ate, in four days, only half a loaf of bread and drank only water, to recapture the heady swims of hunger, and expressed it in my story of Pittsburgh steel—*Race of the Tiger.*

"I like fast cars and movement—incessant travel and people; this is why I lecture a great deal here. I have no politics save that of the compassion and regret for human suffering, and I belong to, and follow the precepts of no political party.

"I write in quick bursts, some times at night when the Welsh mountains sleep. When on research I visit the old people in their homes and listen to the old stories, never speaking unless absolutely necessary: age and experience enchants me—nothing but age can give wisdom, and I love the old. I hate cruelty of any kind, and oppression; the children can build us a new world, if we open the doors to their ambitions and desires; if we, the adults, build the bridges over which they can pass to new lands and new understandings.

"I write to *expose* the cruelties of the past, to build a sort of miner's Farewell Rock upon which we can build a new and glorious future, not only for mankind but for the animals, too. I see the world as a bright meteor of hope and greening and in the young there is a new and urgent call to brotherhood and sisterhood—but the young must know and understand the errors of the past, the greeds that have controlled and divided us. It is the world's children who will build up that which my generation and those before me have destroyed."

HOBBIES AND OTHER INTERESTS: Anti-blood sport movements.

GRAFF, Polly Anne
See COLVER, Anne

"It's fun to watch them find their sea legs . . . Both the cats love to watch the water when it runs along the gunwales. They sit absolutely still as if they are waiting to pounce on a mouse or something." ■ (From the movie *"The Dove,"* © 1974 by St. George Productions, Inc.)

GRAHAM, Robin Lee 1949-

PERSONAL: Born March 5, 1949, in Santa Ana, Calif.; son of Lyle G. (a realtor) and Norma (Tisdel) Graham; married Patricia K. Ratterree, June 4, 1968; children: Quimby Anna. *Education:* Stanford University, student for one quarter. *Religion:* Christian. *Home:* Kalispell, Mont. 59901.

CAREER: At the age of 16 set out from California in a 24-foot sloop and sailed solo around the world, 1965-70; after completing the 33,000-mile odyssey he settled in Montana where he has been building log cabins and farming. Member of board of directors, Flathead Innerfaith Fellowship.

WRITINGS: (With Derek T. L. Gill) *Dove* (account of his voyage; ALA Notable Book), Harper, 1972; (with Gill) *The Boy Who Sailed Around the World Alone* (juvenile adaptation of *Dove*), Western Publishing, 1973. Contributor to *Christian Life, Woman's World,* and *Campus Life.*

WORK IN PROGRESS: A book on the adventures of Graham and his wife in Montana and their spiritual discoveries.

SIDELIGHTS: "Since Christianity has had such a tremendous influence upon our lives and given us direction and power to lead fulfilled lives, we naturally devote a lot of our time to the things of God and rejoice in the knowledge that He has a wonderful plan for our lives. He has manifest Himself to us in miraculous ways and is the Lord and Master of our lives."

Graham's adventure at sea was made into a film produced by Gregory Peck, 1974. A lesser benefit of his voyage was the title Maverick of the Year and the gift of a Ford Maverick.

HOBBIES AND OTHER INTERESTS: Playing the violin, mountain climbing, and snow camping.

ROBIN LEE GRAHAM, with wife and daughter

GRANT, Eva 1907-

PERSONAL: Born November 23, 1907, in New York, N.Y.; daughter of Harry (owner of a women's clothing store) and Minnie (Cohen) Cohen; married Reuben Grant, February 5, 1927; children: Arleen (Mrs. Bud Natelson), Judith (Mrs. Kenneth Goldman). *Education:* After her children were married took writing and other courses at New York University, Bank Street College of Education, and New School for Social Research. *Religion:* Jewish. *Home:* 255 Kingsland Ter., South Orange, N.J. 07079. *Agent:* Ruth Cantor, 156 Fifth Ave., New York, N.Y. 10010.

AWARDS, HONORS: First prize for narrative poem, "A Bit of Cheese," Cooper Hill Writer's Conference, 1972; Newark College of Engineering Author Award, 1974, for *A Cow for Jaya.*

WRITINGS: Timothy Slept On, Whitman Publishing, 1964; *Cecil Kitten,* Whitman Publishing, 1968; *A Cow for Jaya* (Junior Literary Guild selection), Coward, 1973; *The Apple of His Eye,* Scholastic Magazine Press, in press. Poems published in *Let's Read More Stories* (anthology), and *Instructor,* and short stories in *Highlights for Children, Young World, Humpty-Dumpty's Magazine, Scholastic Magazines,* and church publications. *Series of kindergarten stories for David C. Cook publications.*

WORK IN PROGRESS: A book to be illustrated with eight dolls created by Suzanne Gibson of the National Institute of American Doll Artists; the dolls are called Kalico Kids.

. . . what compelled me at the age of sixteen to take a twenty-four-foot sailboat out of San Pedro harbor (it flanks Long Beach) and to tell my family and friends, "going around the world." ▪ (From *Dove* by Robin Lee Graham with Derek L. T. Gill. Photograph by L. Graham.)

SIDELIGHTS: "I realize there has always been controversy over whether a writer is born or becomes one through hard work and perseverance. Examining my own experience, I lean to the premise that if writing is in you, it will somehow out.

"My parents, who were the owners of a ladies' clothing store, would have been happy to see me become a salesgirl. Unfortunately, my Sagittarian birthday handed me truth and bluntness as my salient characteristics, not conducive to a good relationship with say, a size 20 trying to stuff herself into a 14.

"So my mother and father were happy to excuse me from working in the store. I did better with my job in a law office, but marriage ended that career. In 1927, if you were a working woman, you were 'taking away a job from a man who needs it.' So for the next twenty years I spent all my time raising my two little girls and doing a minimum of housework. When I see a young mother today, doing most of her own housework, and doing a darn good job of it, raising a brood, holding down full time outside work, I marvel.

"I wonder. Why didn't I know I was a writer all those years ago? Nobody seemed to expect anything more from me than to be a good wife and mother. Then I lost part of that job. My girls married. I couldn't mother my husband. He wouldn't stand for that. So I had to look around for something to do with my extra energy.

"I applied to Steven's Institute of Technology in Hoboken for tests and was told unequivocally that I was a writer! 'I'll be looking for your name in magazines,' my counselor told me. Since I was already forty-eight years old at this time, I felt I had not a moment to lose! I rushed out and bought a typewriter, took a writing course, and sat down to write.

"Of course, the inevitable happened. The moment I told myself that I was trying to write for publication, chaos ensued! I, who had always been the one to volunteer in school for a writing job, who was the prolific author of articles to the complaint department in newspapers, diaries, letters, laundry lists—I found I did not have one word to say! What did I want to write about, I asked myself. I ruled out sex and violence, westerns and mysteries, psychological novels, or any kind of novels for that matter.

"It might seem that I arrived at children's stories by elimination. Not so. It was my teacher at Columbia High School night school who told me that I had the simplicity and directness to write for children. First, however, I would have to try to put myself into the child's skin—into the child's world. This made sense to me. Because I have always, even in my adult years been an inveterate reader of children's authors—Robert Louis Stevenson, Rudyard Kipling, Luisa May Alcott, Rumer Godden, Eleanor Farjeon—I loved them all. And it came naturally to me to pick up armfuls of children's books and begin reading to learn how to write, rather than just for enjoyment.

"My six grandchildren, who arrived one after the other, besides being a world of fun for me, were also inspirations for many of my stories and poems. The children loved my stories, although Jon, the youngest, didn't want me to 'tell' him a story. He preferred to have me 'read' him one out of a book—with pictures. I didn't blame him. I too, wanted to see pictures with my stories. My greatest thrill is to see one of my made-up children pictured lovingly and colorfully in a book or magazine. I suppose that is why I don't even try for a longer book, but stick mostly to the picture-book field.

"My paternal grandfather, Aaron Cohen, was a revered Rabbi. I used to love the smell of his library, and would climb on a chair to handle his books, although, since they were in Hebrew, I couldn't read a word. Grandfather Aaron wore a long, snowy white beard. When I visited him, he would shake hands with me, and when I took my hand away, there would be a nickel in it. Mama would protest that he was spoiling me. But Grandpa would pat my head and say, 'Why should the child love me—for my long, white beard?' If Grandpa only knew, I loved him, not for his beard, and for the nickel, but because he understood the heart of a child.

"My six grandchildren, Steven, David, Richard, Andrea, Carol and Jon have been a strong influence in my work. I have used the characteristics of one or another at many points in my stories. As the children grew older, so did my characters."

FOR MORE INFORMATION SEE: News Record of Maplewood and South Orange, April 18, 1963.

EVA GRANT

He was proud to walk beside such a beautiful cow. ■ (From *A Cow for Jaya* by Eva Grant. Illustrated by Michael Hampshire.)

GRAY, Patricia (Clark)
(Patsey Gray, Virginia Clark)

PERSONAL: Born in San Mateo, Calif.; daughter of Charles (a copper mine owner and operator) and Celia (Tobin) Clark; married Gerald Gray (a surgeon), February 17, 1934; children: Gerald Clark, Celia (Mrs. Jon Cum-

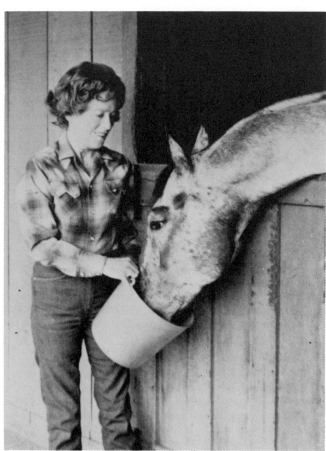

PATRICIA GRAY

mings), Alice (Mrs. Louis Coelho), Tim. *Education:* Attended Sacred Heart Convent High School in Menlo Park, Calif. *Home:* Ten Acre Ranch, Walnut Creek, Calif. 94595. *Agent:* Curtis Brown, Ltd., 60 East 56th St., New York, N.Y. 10022.

CAREER: Breeds and shows horses. Author.

WRITINGS—All under name Patsey Gray, except where otherwise noted: *Heads Up,* Coward, 1956; *The Doggone Roan,* Coward, 1957; *4-H Filly,* Coward, 1958; *Galloping Gold,* Coward, 1958; *Challenger,* Coward, 1959; (under pseudonym Virginia Clark) *The Mysterious Buckskin,* Macmillian, 1960; *Diving Horse,* Coward, 1960; *Horse in Her Heart,* Coward, 1960; *Loco, The Bronc,* Coward, 1961; *The Horse Trap,* Coward, 1962; *Show Ring Rogue,* Coward, 1963; *Star Bright,* Norton, 1964; *Star Lost,* Norton, 1965; *Jumping Jack,* Norton, 1965; *Horsepower,* Norton, 1966; *Norah's Ark,* Norton, 1966; *Lucky Star,* Norton, 1967; *Blue Ribbon Summer,* Norton, 1968; *Star, the Sea Horse,* Norton, 1968; *The Flag is Up,* Nelson, 1970.

Contributor of 32 short stories to various magazines.

WORK IN PROGRESS: A how-to book on showing horses, titled *Show and Tell.*

SIDELIGHTS: "I do most of my writing in my camper, on the road with horses. First draft is longhand. In *Show and Tell,* my husband took most of the photographs here on the ranch (which now includes thirty-three acres). It is greatly autobiographical, being instructions in the kind of showing I am presently doing—the western trail horse."

GRAY, Patsey
See GRAY, Patricia

GRAYLAND, V. Merle
See GRAYLAND, Valerie

GRAYLAND, Valerie (Merle Spanner)
(Lee Belvedere, V. Merle Grayland,
Valerie Subond)

PERSONAL: Born in Thames, New Zealand; daughter of Jens Koeford (a farmer) and Eva (Howe) Spanner; married Eugene Charles Grayland (a journalist), November 13, 1948. *Education:* Attended Seddon Memorial Technical College, Auckland, New Zealand. *Religion:* Anglican. *Home:* 129 Canal Rd., Avondale. *Postal Address:* P.O. Box 689, Auckland, New Zealand.

CAREER: Free-lance writer of mystery novels and books for children, 1948—. *Member:* P.E.N., Mystery Writers of America.

I picked up the two biggest snails to race on the path. But they wouldn't play. One went the wrong way. One hid in his shell and wouldn't come out. ■ (From *Early One Morning* by Valerie Grayland. Illustrated by Marjorie Cooper.)

WRITINGS—Mystery novels under name V. Merle Grayland: *The Dead Men of Eden*, R. Hale, 1962; *Night of the Reaper*, R. Hale, 1963; *The Grave-Digger's Apprentice*, R. Hale, 1964; *Jest of Darkness*, R. Hale, 1965.

Novels under pseudonym Lee Belvedere: *Farewell to a Valley*, Bouregy, 1971; *Meet a Dark Stranger*, Bouregy, 1971; *Thunder Beach*, Bouregy, 1972; *Fringe of Heaven*, Bouregy, 1972; *The Smiling House*, Bouregy, 1973; *Return to Moon Bay*, Bouregy, 1973.

Children's books under name Valerie Grayland: *The First Strawberry*, Colenso Press, 1954; *John and Hoani*, Blackie & Son, 1962; *Early One Morning*, Rand McNally, 1963; *Baby Sister*, Rand McNally, 1964. Children's stories anthologized in *White Robin Story-Book*, Longacre Press, 1960, and *Lucky Dip*, edited by Barbara Ker Wilson, Angus & Robertson, 1970.

Novels under pseudonym Valerie Subond: *The Heights of Havenrest* (gothic mystery), Beagle Books, 1972; *The House over Hell Valley*, Beagle Books, 1974.

Non-fiction, with husband, Eugene C. Grayland: *Coromandel Coast*, A. H. & A. W. Reed, 1965, revised edition, 1968; *Historic Coromandel*, A. H. & A. W. Reed, 1969; *Tarawera*, Hodder & Stoughton, 1971. Contributor of articles and short stories to magazines in Australia and New Zealand. Joint editor, *Hearing News*.

WORK IN PROGRESS: A juvenile, *Mystery at Golden Sands;* a gothic mystery, *House at Haunted Inlet* under pseudonym Valerie Subond; a novel, *Necklace of Islands*, under pseudonym Lee Belvedere.

SIDELIGHTS: "I started writing when I was seven, maybe because I was an only child and rather lonely. My father died when I was so young I have no memories of him. I remember what I wanted more than anything else

VALERIE GRAYLAND

112

when I was a child was a brother. Maybe this is why so many of the main characters in my stories are boys.

"I like beaches, particularly exploring them when the tide is out. Gardening is another interest for I love growing things and I'm fond of animals. I have two Siamese cats, brothers from the same litter, and they are great company when I'm writing. They sit on my desk and occasionally talk in their loud Siamese voices. My husband and I write travel books and love seeing our country and meeting people.

"I always write in longhand first as I find it hard to type and think out a story at the same time. I write because I feel I have to and like writing for children as I like so many of the things they like. I suppose I write for people like myself whatever their age, for writing is a way of sharing things and a way of talking to people you don't know and will never see.

"I am keener on fiction than factual writing and think fiction is not shown sufficient emphasis for children. Gaining factual information has value but understanding people is important and fiction can help us to do this. Almost everyone has favorite characters in books that are as real as their friends. A lot of happiness and knowledge has been gained through knowing these paper people."

Ms. Grayland created a Maori detective, Hoani Mata, for her mystery novels. She has given her children's book manuscripts to the Southern Mississippi University Library for a special collection, and, with her husband, runs a private press as a hobby.

GREAVES, Margaret 1914-

PERSONAL: Born June 13, 1914, in Birmingham, England; daughter of Joseph William (a clergyman) and Jessie May (Greenup) Greaves. *Education:* Attended Alice Ottley School, Worcester, England; St. Hugh's College, Oxford, B.A. (first class honors), 1936, B.Litt., 1938, M.A., 1947. *Politics:* None. *Religion:* Church of England. *Home:* Castle House, Winchcombe, near Cheltenham, Gloucestershire, England.

CAREER: Teacher of English at Lincoln High School for Girls, 1938-40, and Prior School, Shrewsbury, 1940-41; head of English at Pate's Grammar School for Girls, Cheltenham; St. Mary's College, Cheltenham, England, lecturer in English, 1946-61, principal lecturer in English and head of department, 1961-70, now retired. *Military service:* Women's Land Army. *Member:* English Association, School Library Association.

WRITINGS: The Blazon of Honour (studies in English Renaissance literature), Methuen, 1964; *Regency Patron: Sir George Beaumont,* Methuen, 1966; *Your Turn Next,* Methuen, 1966; *One World and Another* (for juniors), Methuen, 1967; *Gallery* (stories for juniors), Methuen, 1968; (compiler) *Scrap-Box: Poems for Grown-ups to Share with Children,* Methuen, 1969; *Gallimaufry* (for juniors), Methuen, 1971; *The Dagger and the Bird* (children's novel), Methuen, 1972; *The Grandmother Stone* (a novel), Methuen, 1972; *The Gryphen Quest,* Methuen, 1974. Contributor of reviews to *Renaissance Quarterly.*

MARGARET GREAVES

WORK IN PROGRESS: Seventeenth-century biography; children's stories; English for primary schools.

SIDELIGHTS: "I have made up stories ever since my childhood, but never thought of publication until my own students needed an introduction to certain ideas about literature and art not easily available to them elsewhere. For them also I first wrote a series of English books for juniors, consisting of original stories and anthologized poems, because I believe that children can learn more from imaginative literature than from text-books. I enjoyed writing the stories for these books so much that I have gone on to write full-length novels, sometimes for juniors and sometimes for near adults.

"My ideas spring from an interest in human relationships and a deep love of the countryside in which I have always lived, and from a heritage of folk-lore and history. My books often grow from a single image that comes to me quite unexpectedly—an ancient statue seen at a church gate in the Channel Islands, or a mental picture of the desolation of a changeling in a human household; and I recognize the image as the germ of a story that may become clear to me if I wait quietly and patiently. It is as if the story is there already and only waiting to be discovered.

"I enjoy writing for young people, but in the next year or so I shall probably be working on novels that will concern mature readers as well."

Charles ate hardly anything at all, for he was reading the cereal box. ■ (From *The Bears Who Stayed Indoors* by Susanna Gretz. Illustrated by the author.)

GRETZ, Susanna 1937-

PERSONAL: Born September 27, 1937, in New York, N.Y.; daughter of George G. (a lawyer) and Helen (White) Tennant; married Guenter Gretz (an industrial designer), 1966. *Education:* Smith College, B.A., 1959. *Home:* 6 Frankfurt 90, Damaschke-Anger 51, West Germany.

CAREER: Writer and illustrator.

WRITINGS: (Illustrator) Helen Cresswell, *Rug Is a Bear*, Benn, 1968; (illustrator) Helen Cresswell, *Rug Plays Tricks*, Benn, 1968; (illustrator) *Rug Plays Ball*, Benn, 1968; (illustrator) *Rug and a Picnic*, Benn, 1968; (author and illustrator) *Teddybears 1 to 10*, Follett, 1969; (author and illustrator) *The Bears Who Stayed Indoors*, Follett, 1970; (author and illustrator) *The Bears Who Went to the Seaside*, Follett, 1972; (illustrator) *Rillsby-Rill*, O'Hara, 1972; (illustrator) *The Book of Kalila and Dinna*, Societe Nationale des Editions (Algeria), 1973; (author and illustrator) *Teddy Bears ABC*, Benn, 1974.

FOR MORE INFORMATION SEE: Horn Book, February, 1970, August, 1971, April, 1974.

GROHSKOPF, Bernice

PERSONAL: Born September 22, in Troy, N.Y.; married Herbert Grohskopf (a chemical engineer), September 2, 1952; children: Peggy. *Education:* Columbia University, B.S., 1948, M.A., 1954; New York University, graduate studies, 1960-65. *Home:* 73 Buckingham Rd., Upper Montclair, N.J. 07043.

CAREER: Worked for Columbia University Press, 1946-48, Dell Publishing Co., 1948-50, later free-lance writer for Dell. *Member:* Author's Guild, American Association of University Women. *Awards, honors: Seeds of Time* appeared on the American Library Association's list of Notable Children's Books for 1963; New Jersey Association of Teachers of English Author Award, 1970, for *The Treasure of Sutton Hoo.*

WRITINGS: Seeds of Time (introduction to Shakespeare for young readers), Atheneum, 1963; *From Age to Age*, Atheneum, 1968; *The Treasure of Sutton Hoo*, Atheneum, 1970; *Shadow in the Sun*, Atheneum, in press. Contributor of short stories to *Folio, Phylon.*

WORK IN PROGRESS: A novel for young adults; a book on 15th-century England; short fiction.

SIDELIGHTS: "I can remember the exact moment when, at the age of eight, having written my first poem, I decided I wanted to be a writer. Despite the years of obstacles and diversions, early trials were interspersed with enough triumphs to keep me going. Fortunately, during my adolescent years I had the much needed encouragement from an aunt who had faith in my writing ability, but without that necessary support, I might have given up. Young people need someone who believes in them.

"I took my Bachelor's and Master's degrees in English literature at Columbia University, then returned to graduate school after the birth of my child and spent five years fulfilling all requirements for the Ph.D. I am happy to say I'm now a Ph.D. drop-out.

"Among some of my varied jobs: taught fourth and fifth grade in a rural school in Mississippi; worked for Columbia University Press while completing my Bachelor's degree, after which I worked as an editor at Dell Publishing Company.

"I love to write, both fiction and non-fiction, and feel a sense of mission about the latter because I want to share

A horse and a man
Is more than one,
And yet not many.
　—*The Taming of the Shrew* ∎ (From *Seeds of Time* by Bernice Grohskopf. Illustrated by Kelly Oechsli.)

with others some of the joys of English literature that scholars clutch to themselves. My first book, *Seeds of Time,* is a compilation of short, separate, readable, passages from Shakespeare, meant to introduce young children to the varied world of Shakespeare, so that later on, when

BERNICE GROHSKOPF

they begin to read his work, they will come upon familiar passages. I wrote *From Age to Age* to make up a deficiency I had felt when in college, searching for a *readable* book on early English literature and history, and finding either brief, inadequate sections in anthologies, or formidable and unreadable works by scholars. I tried in that book to present some of our earliest English writing, along with some background on the way of life during that period. It was a happy moment for me when I saw my book on the open shelves in the main reference room of the New York Public Library on Fifth Avenue.

"The idea for *The Treasure of Sutton Hoo* emerged as I was doing research for the above book and became fascinated by the true, buried-treasure tale. I found little available in the United States about this exciting archaeological dig, and so I travelled to England, visited the site, studied the treasure in the British Museum, and talked with the archaeologist who was in charge of the dig, before writing my book.

"I had just finished work on a short story (later published in *Woman's Day*, July '73; also *Homes and Gardens*, April '74) and had begun work on another book on medieval England, when my daughter gave me a box of bond paper for Christmas. She was eleven years old then and I told her I would use the paper to write a book for her. The result, *Shadow in the Sun.*

"Once again I am working on the book on medieval England, but I interrupt work once in a while to work on fiction, long (another novel for young adults) and short. I enjoy the contrast between writing fiction and non-fiction, although I find it difficult to work on both at the same time. For me, the creative process is one of continual growth, learning, and renewal. When I'm not writing, I'm reading or studying, since the research books I write require considerable study. This leaves no time for hobbies or handwork, but there are so many things that interest me, so many things I'd like to learn, that I could easily fill the day. At the moment, on my day off, I study French at the French Institute in New York City one morning a week, and then in the afternoon I work at the Morgan Library or at the New York Public Library. My husband and I enjoy going to concerts and museums, and we love to travel. Since I spend most of my day at my desk, working until four when my daughter comes home from school, it's a full, busy life. That's why I have an annual New Year's resolution: not to waste a minute of my time on trivia, especially on idle conversations, one of the things I most dislike, along with snobbery, arrogance, and dishonesty."

FOR MORE INFORMATION SEE: Montclair Times, May 16, 1963.

GUGLIOTTA, Bobette   1918-

PERSONAL: Surname is pronounced Gu-*lyot*-ta; born November 8, 1918, in Chicago, Ill.; daughter of Irving M. (a music composer) and Aline (Waite) Bibo; married Guy Frank Gugliotta (a military officer and marine engineer), June 2, 1940; children: Guy Bibo (reporter for United Press International). *Education:* Studied creative writing at Stanford University, University of Southern California, and

BOBETTE GUGLIOTTA

University of California, Los Angeles. *Home:* 25351 Moody Rd., Los Altos Hills, Calif. 94022. *Agent:* Henriette Neatrour, Curtis Brown Ltd., 60 East 56th St., New York, N.Y. 10022.

CAREER: Foothill International League, Los Altos Hills, Calif., founder and first chairman, 1962-65; Young Women's Christian Association (YWCA), Honolulu, Hawaii, master of ceremonies on beach club radio program, 1965-66; Recording for the Blind, Palo Alto, Calif., reader and auxiliary member, 1969—. Founded University of Hawaii foreign student program, 1965-66.

WRITINGS: Nolle Smith: Cowboy, Engineer, Statesman (Child Study Association book list), Dodd, 1971; *Katzimo: Mysterious Mesa,* Dodd, 1974. Contributor to *Good Housekeeping, Woman, Virginia Quarterly Review,* and other periodicals and newspapers.

WORK IN PROGRESS: A book on Ecuador in 1853.

SIDELIGHTS: "The inception of my books, so far, has been a personal contact that stimulated my interest to the point of wanting to write a story. *Nolle Smith* was the result of a long friendship with the now 85-year-old subject of the book who is still hale and hearty in Honolulu. *Katzimo: Mysterious Mesa* was the result of meeting Carl

Bibo, the boy hero of half Jewish, half Acoma Indian parentage, and becoming intrigued with the unique quality of the first summer he spent with his mother's tribe at age thirteen, in New Mexico.

"The present work in progress, still untitled, is the result of having lived for several years in Quito, Ecuador and maintaining many contacts with Ecuadorian friends. I am endlessly fascinated by the many blood strains that make up the 'average' American and hope to project the universality of this commingling in the past, present and future of the United States."

Ms. Gugliotta wrote her first story at age eleven for Walt Disney.

FOR MORE INFORMATION SEE: Los Altos Town Crier, December 29, 1971; Palo Alto Times, January 11, 1972.

GUILLOT, Rene   1900-1969

PERSONAL: Born January 24, 1900, in Courcoury, Charente-Maritime, France; son of Arsene and Marie-Louise (Drouard) Guillot; married Gisele Mervaud (a writer); children: Jean Marie (son; also a writer). Education: Studied at College de Saintes and University of Bordeaux; Sorbonne, University of Paris, Licence es-sciences mathematiques, 1922. Home: 76 Avenue de Paris, Vincennes, Seine, France. Agent: Hachette-Larousse.

CAREER: Began writing in Africa, where he went as a schoolteacher, 1923; teacher of mathematics in French West Africa, principally in Dakar, 1923-50; professor of mathematics at Lycee Condorcet, Paris, 1950-60; retired from teaching, 1960, continuing to write at his home in the Paris suburbs. Military service: Fought with American forces as artilleryman, 1943-46; took part in campaigns in northern France and Germany; became lieutenant; received Legion d'honneur, Croix de Guerre, and Bronze Star (United States).

MEMBER: Societe des Gens de Lettres (Society of Men of Letters), Societe des auteurs dramatiques (Society of Dramatic Authors), Societe des ecrivains combattants (Society of Ex-Service Writers), Societe des ecrivains de le mer et de l'outre mer (Society of Writers of the Sea).

AWARDS, HONORS: Grand Prix du roman d'aventures, 1946, for Les Equipages de Peter Hill; Prix Jeunesse, 1950, for Sama, prince des elephants; Belgian Prix M. Proumen for juvenile literature, 1953, for L'Extraordinaire aventure de Michel Santanrea; Jugendbuchpries, 1956, for German edition of Sirga, la lionne; Prix Enfance du Monde, 1958, for Grichka et son ours; the American edition was an American Library Association Notable Book and received a Boys' Clubs of America Junior Book Award, 1961; Hans Christian Andersen International Children's Book Medal, 1964, for his complete works (as a distinguished contribution to international literature for young people); two other books, La Petite infante and Encyclopedie Larousse des enfants, were cited for excellence by the French Academy.

WRITINGS—Titles prior to 1948 are adult books, those since 1948 primarily for young people: Histoire d'un blanc qui s'etait fait negre (novel), 1932; (compiler) Contes d'-Afrique, published as special issue of Bulletin de l'-Enseignement de l'A.O.F., [Goree, West Africa], 1933; Ras el Gua, poste du Sud (novel), [Casablanca], 1936; Vent de norois (novel), [Casablanca], 1938.

Contes de la magie rousse, Viale (Dakar), 1941; Loaga, Viale, 1941; Visages de sable, Viale, 1944; Contes de la brousse fauve, Arthaud, 1945; Les Equipages de Peter Hill (novel), Librairie des Champs-Elysees, 1946; La Grande renaude, Arthaud, 1946; Atonement in the Sun, Staples Press, 1947; Maraouna du Bambassou (first novel for young people), Editions de l'Amitie, 1948, published under same title as a French reader, Oxford University Press, 1956, translation by Brian Rhys published as The White Shadow, Oxford University Press, 1959, translation by Gwen Marsh published as Beyond the Bambassu, Harrap, 1961; Chasses de brousse: Savanes et sortileges (on hunting in Africa), Librairie des Champs-Elysees, 1948; Au Pays des betes sauvages, Editions de l'Amitie, 1948.

Les Compagnons de la fortune, Editions de l'Amitie, 1950, translation by Geoffrey Trease published as Companions of Fortune, Oxford University Press, 1952; Sama, prince des elephants, 1950, translation by Gwen Marsh published as Sama, Oxford University Press, 1952, Criterion, 1961; Sirga, la lionne, Magnard, 1951, translation by Gwen Marsh published as Sirga, Queen of the African Bush, Oxford University Press, 1953, Criterion, 1959; Ouoro le chimpanze, Magnard, 1951, translation by Gwen Marsh

RENE GUILLOT

published as *Oworo*, Oxford University Press, 1954; *L'-Extraordinaire aventure de Michel Santanrea*, Editions de l'Amitie, 1951, translation by Norman Dale published as *The Winds of Chance*, Oxford University Press, 1955, Criterion, 1958; *Betes sauvages, mes amies* (on animal habits and behavior), Magnard, 1952; *L'Aventure de Buscambille*, Magnard, 1952; *Trois bonds dans le jungle*, Magnard, 1952; *Les Cavaliers du vent*, Magnard, 1953, translation by George H. Bell published as *Riders of the Wind*, Methuen, 1960, Rand McNally, 1961, reissued in French as *Aux Quatre vents d'Afrique*, Delagrave, 1962; *Le Petite infante*, 1953; *Plein nord*, Magnard, 1953, translation by published as *A Boy and Five Huskies*, Pantheon, 1957; *Contes des mille et une betes*, Magnard, 1953; *La Legende des licornes*, Magnard, 1953, translation by Christopher Hampton published as *The Fantastic Brother*, Methuen, 1961, Rand McNally, 1963; *Luc la baleine, corsaire du roi*, Delagrave, 1953, translation by Geoffrey Trease published as *The King's Corsair*, Oxford University Press, 1954; *The 397th White Elephant* (first published as "Le 397ieme elephant blanc" in *Trois bonds dans la jungle* [supra, 1952], translation by Gwen Marsh, Oxford University Press, 1954, Criterion, 1957; *Le Chevalier aux loups*, Magnard, 1954; *Shrimp, le corsaire*, Magnard, 1954, translation by Norman Dale published as *The Sea Rover*, Oxford University Press, 1956; *De Dague et d'epee*, Editions Magnard, 1955; *Au Royaume de la bete*, Delagrave, 1955, translation by Gwen Marsh published as *The Animal Kingdom*, Oxford University Press, 1957; *Kpo la panthere*, Magnard, 1955, translation by Gwen Marsh published as *Kpo, the Leopard*, Oxford University Press, 1955; *Tam-Tam de Kotokro*, Presses de la Cite, 1956, translation by Brian Rhys published as *Tom-Toms in Kotokro*, Criterion, 1957; *La Biche noire*, Magnard, 1956; *Encyclopedie Larousse des enfants*, Larousse, 1956, translation and adaptation by Maurice Michael published in England as *The New Encyclopedia for the Younger Generation*, Spring House, 1958, and in America as *The Illustrated Encyclopedia: Based on an Encyclopedia of the Famous Librairie Larousse*, Grosset, 1959, also adapted by Michael for two-volume *Learn About People* and *Learn About the World*, Golden Pleasure Books, 1962; *Les Elephants de Sargabal*, Editions Delagrave, 1956, translation by Gwen Marsh published as *The Elephants of Sargabal*, Oxford University Press, 1956, Criterion, 1957; *Prince de la jungle*, Hachette, 1956, translation by Brian Rhys published as *Prince of the Jungle*, Oxford University Press, 1958, Criterion, 1959; *Le Clan des betes sauvages*, Hachette, 1956, translation by John Marshall published as *Mokokambo, the Lost Land*, Criterion, 1961; *Bleu de cobalt*, Librairie des Champs-Elysees, 1957; *Grichka et son ours*, Hachette, 1958, translation by Gwen Marsh published as *Grishka and the Bear*, Oxford University Press, 1959, Criterion, 1960; *Le Chef au masque d'or*, Hachette, 1958, translation by John Marshall published as *Mountain With a Secret*, Van Nostrand, 1963; *La Grande terre des elephants*, Editions Magnard, 1958, translation by Richard Graves published as *Elephant Road*, Bodley Head, 1959, Criterion, 1960; *Le Jour bleu*, 1958, translation by Gwen Marsh published as *The Blue Day*, Bodley Head, 1958, Abelard, 1959; *Le Moulin de Nicolette*, translation by Gwen Marsh published as *Nicolette and the Mill*, Bodley Head, 1960, Abelard, 1961; *Crin-Blanc* (based on Albert Lamorisse's film of the same name), Hachette, 1959, translation by Gwen Marsh published as *The Wild White Stallion*, F. Watts, 1961, abridged edition edited by J. R. Watson, F. Watts, 1963; *Anne et le roi des chats*, Hachette,

1959, translation by John Marshall published as *The King of the Cats*, Collins, 1962, Lothrop, 1963.

Il Etait mille et une fois. . .; Des Contes et des histoires pour nos enfants, Magnard, 1960; *Le Grande aventure des machines*, Larousse, 1960, translation published as *Man's Adventure With Machines: The Story of the Mechanical Age and How It Came About*, Odhams, 1961; *Grichka et les loups*, Hachette, 1960, translation by Joyce Emerson published as *Grichka and the Wolves*, Van Nostrand, 1965 (published in England as *Grichka and Brother Bear*, University of London Press, 1965), translation and abridgement by Christina Holyoak published as *Pascal and the Lioness*, McGraw, 1965; *Trois filles et un secret*, Hachette, 1960, translation by Joan Selby-Lowndes published as *Three Girls and a Secret*, Harrap, 1961, F. Watts, 1963; *Le Maitre des elephants*, Magnard, 1960, translation by Barbara Seccombe published in England as *Master of the Elephants*, Oxford University Press, 1961, and in America as *Fofana*, Criterion, 1962; *Tipiti, le rouge-gorge*, Larousse, 1962, translation by Gwen Marsh published as *Tipiti, the Robin*, Bodley Head, 1962; *Marjolaine et le troubadour*, Hachette, 1961, translation by Anne Carter published as *The Troubadour*, Collins, 1965, McGraw, 1967; *Deux garcons pour un cheval*, Hachette, 1961; *Mon premier atlas: Voyage autour de monde*, Larousse, 1961, translation published as *Our Colorful World and Its Peoples*, Odhams,

Every day the boy went off in his little boat to comb the marshes, but he was out of luck: he never saw [the white stallion]. ■ (From *The White Stallion* by Rene Guillot. Illustrated by Jean Reschofsky.)

1963; *L'Etranger du port*, Hachette, 1961, translation by Gwen Marsh published as *The Stranger from the Sea*, F. Watts, 1967; (editor) *My First English-French Dictionary/Mon premier dictionnaire anglais-francais*, Golden Pleasure Books, 1962; *La Marque de Grichka*, Hachette, 1962; *Le Voyage en ballon* (based on Albert Lamorisse's film of the same name), Hachette, 1962, translation by Anne Carter published as *Balloon Journey*, Collins, 1964, Clark McCutcheon, 1966; *La Planete ignoree*, Hachette, 1963; *L'Espace*, Hachette, 1963, translation published as *Astronomy*, Whitman Publishing, 1963; *Fonabio et le lion*, Hachette, 1963, adaptation edited by Margaret Ledesert published in French under same title, Harrap, 1966, translation by Sarah Chokla Gross published as *Fonabio and the Lion*, F. Watts, 1966; *Rex et Mistigri*, Larousse, 1963, translation by Gwen Marsh published as *Rex and Mistigri*, Bodley Head, 1963; *Petite histoire d'un petit chien*, Hachette, 1964, translation by Joan Selby-Lowndes published as *Little Dog Lost*, Harrap, 1968, revised English translation by Selby-Lowndes published under same title, Lothrop, 1970; *Grichka et les turbans jaunes*, Hachette, 1964; *The Children of the Wind* (selections from four of Guillot's books), compiled and translated by Gwen Marsh, Oxford University Press, 1964, published in America as *African Folk Tales*, F. Watts, 1965; *Red Kid de l'Arizona*, Hachette, 1953; *Le Grand Marc et les aigles noirs*, Hachette, 1965; *Six destins en etoile*, Magnard, 1965; *Un Chateau en Espagne*, Hachette, 1966, translation by Dorothy Ward published as *Castle in Spain*, Brockhampton Press, 1970; *Chansons de brousse* (poems), Messeiller, 1966; *Le Maison de l'oiseau*, Delagrave, 1966, translation by Gwen Marsh published as *The Castle of the Crested Bird*, F. Watts, 1968; *La Brousse et la bete*, Delagrave, 1966; *Fode Koro et les hommes-pantheres*, Hachette, 1966, translation by Joan Selby-Lowndes published as *Fodai and the Leopard-Men*, Harrap, 1969, Funk, 1970; *King of the Reindeer and Other Animal Stories*, adapted from John Orpen's translations, Odhams, 1967; *Un Roman de Renart*, Delagrave, 1967; *La Belle au bois dore*, Hachette, 1967; *Le Champion D'-Olympic*, Hachette, 1965, translation by Anne Carter published as *The Champion of Olympia*, Reilly & Lee, 1968; *L'Equipage du grand Marc*, Hachette, 1968; *La Nuit de contrebandiers*, Hachette, 1968?; *Cinq coleres de fauves*, O D E G E, 1968; *Great Horse Stories*, adapted by Mollie Chappell, Lion Press, 1969; *Tireli, roi des rossignols*, Hachette, 1969.

Un Petit chien va dans la lune, Hachette, 1970; *Cinq tours de magiciens*, O D E G E, 1970; *Images et mots*, Larousse, 1970; *Tales of the Wild*, adapted by Mollie Chappell, Collins, 1971; *Le Chevalier Sans Visage*, Hachette, 1973; *L'Extra-ordinaire Aventure du Messue Renart*, Delagrave, 1973.

Also has written detective stories and radio scripts.

FOR MORE INFORMATION SEE: Muriel Fuller, editor, *More Junior Authors*, H. W. Wilson, 1963; *Young Readers' Review*, October, 1966; Brian Doyle, *Who's Who of Children's Literature*, Schocken, 1968; *Books and Bookman*, November, 1969, May, 1970; *Library Journal*, July, 1970, September, 1970.

(Died March 28, 1969)

MARYLIN HAFNER

HAFNER, Marylin   1925-

PERSONAL: Born December 14, 1925, in Brooklyn, N.Y.; daughter of Mark (an artist) and Frances (Cisin) Hafner; married Harvey B. Cushman, June 9, 1950; married second husband, Rudolf G. de Reyna, (a painter and writer), August 17, 1970; children: (first marriage) Abigail Cushman, Jennifer Cushman, Amanda Cushman. *Education:* Pratt Institute, B.Sc., 1947; New School for Social Research, further study, 1948-50; also studied at School of Visual Arts, Silvermine School of Art, and then at Slade School, London, England, 1965-66. *Politics:* Democrat. *Religion:* Unitarian Universalist. *Home:* 98 Woodland Rd., New Canaan, Conn. 06840.

CAREER: Artist, illustrator, and designer; art director of *McCall's*, New York, N.Y., 1950-54; art instructor, Famous Schools Inc., Westport, Conn., 1968-70. Has taught art to children, designed advertising materials and fabrics, and worked in graphics. *Member:* Society of Illustrators, Westport Artists Guild, Silvermine Guild of Artists. *Awards, honors:* New York Herald Tribune Children's Spring Book Festival Award, 1949, shared with author of *Bonnie Bess: The Weathervane Horse*.

ILLUSTRATOR: Alvin Tresselt, *Bonnie Bess: The Weathervane Horse*, Lothrop, 1949; Hal Dareff, *Fun with ABC and 1-2-3*, Parents' Magazine Press, 1965; Mabel Watts, *The Story of Zachary Zween*, Parents' Magazine

Press, 1967; Marguerite Staunton, *That's What* (poems), Random House, 1968; Charlotte Reynolds and Barbara Parker, *Poetry Please,* Random House, 1968; Eleanor Felder, *X Marks the Spot* (Junior Literary Guild selection), Coward, 1971; Lou A. Gaeddert, *Too Many Girls,* Coward, 1972; Sally Cartwright, *Water Is West,* Coward, 1973; Sally Cartwright, *Sunlight,* Coward, in press. Her illustrations have appeared in *Good Housekeeping, Humpty Dumpty's Magazine,* and other periodicals.

SIDELIGHTS: "I lived in London for two years and worked on *Zachary Zween* while there—using the surrounding neighborhood (Chelsea) for inspiration in my drawings. My most important influences in my work are Saul Steinberg, Ronald Searle, Andre Francois, John Birmingham. I do not apply a 'formula' to illustration (using the same style or technique for every book)—but instead let the author's concept and general attitude decide what 'look' the book should have. I try to use the limitations of budget and color, etc. as a challenge to create a unity between words and pictures. My feeling about picture books is that the pictures can add another dimension without overpowering the author's intention."

HOBBIES AND OTHER INTERESTS: Cooking, antiques, travel, gardening, music.

HALL, Adele 1910-

PERSONAL: Born October 2, 1910, in Philadelphia, Pa.; daughter of Henry and Mary Ellen (Greenwood) Hall; married Frank A. Schwickerath, Jr. (jeweler), October 16, 1937. *Education:* Glassboro State College, student, 1929-31. *Home:* 5511 Winchester Ave., Ventnor, N.J. 08406. *Agent:* Lenniger Literary Agency, 437 Fifth Ave., New York, N.Y. 10016.

CAREER: Public schools, Atlantic City, N.J., elementary teacher, 1931-41; Friends' School, Atlantic City, N.J., teacher of literature and composition, 1962-73. Florence Crittenton Home, Atlantic City, N.J., secretary, 1958-60, member of board of directors, 1956—. Miss America Pageant, member of hostess committee, 1940—. *Member:* Antique Collectors Club of Atlantic City (president, 1959-61), League of South Jersey Artists, Atlantic County Humane Society, Auxiliary to Absecon Island Power Squadron. *Awards, honors:* Citation for *Seashore Summer* from New Jersey Teachers of English, 1962; New Jersey Tercentenary Committee, citation for historic writings, 1964.

WRITINGS: Beauty Queen, Messner, 1957; *Seashore Summer,* Harper, 1962. Contributor to teen-age magazines.

WORK IN PROGRESS: Teen-age novel.

SIDELIGHTS: "Basically, I guess my books grew out of my affection for Atlantic City where I lived most of my life, although *Beauty Queen* was the idea of my agent, Edith Margolis. Until then, I had written only short stories.

"For a number of years I had been a member of the hostess committee of the Miss America Pageant (which means exactly what the name implies—acting as hostess to contestants) and I thought there was an interesting short story in my experiences. But writing a book instead proved much more rewarding for me and presented a more complete picture of the Pageant for the reader. Originally we had called the book *Miss America,* but at that time the Miss America Pageant held a copyright to that title so we had to substitute *Beauty Queen.* But it was about the Pageant and, despite the years that have passed since its publication, most of the information in the book remains relevant.

"Girls who write to me invariably ask if the heroine was a contestant I chaperoned, but the answer is the one most authors give about their characters: she is a composite of several.

"*Seashore Summer* was inspired by a research paper I was asked to do about early Atlantic City. I felt that the charm and delight of that early resort life should be recorded for young people, particularly those who live or visit there today.

"When I returned to teaching, I didn't have the time to spend on another novel, for that is a very lengthy project and I happen to be a morning worker. I go to the typewriter the way a person goes to the office, shop, or wherever he labors. And on a regular schedule. I find writing is only one part inspiration and the rest plain old-fashioned discipline."

HOBBIES AND OTHER INTERESTS: Collects antiques for use in her home. Enjoys oil and water color painting, boating and puppeteering.

ADELE HALL

MALCOLM HALL

HALL, Malcolm   1945-

PERSONAL: Born June 6, 1945, in Chicago, Ill.; son of David B. (a physicist) and Jane (also a physicist; maiden name, Hamilton) Hall; married Mary J. Reneski (a teacher), June 6, 1971. *Education:* Pomona College, B.A., 1967. *Home:* 6300 Keystone St., Philadelphia, Pa. 19135.

CAREER: "Let it be enough to say that I have been a furniture mover, weather man, car junker, advertising writer, handyman-carpenter, thief, bookstore clerk, and editor"; Media Systems, Inc., Moorestown, N.J., editor, 1973—.

WRITINGS: Headlines (Junior Literary Guild selection), Coward, 1973. Writer of more than thirty filmstrips.

WORK IN PROGRESS: The Electric Book, for publication by Coward.

SIDELIGHTS: "I grew up in Los Alamos, New Mexico, where both my parents were employed as physicists. The environment was a bit strange. The town itself is located on a 7000-foot mesa in a spur of the Sangre de Cristo Mountains. During the war years and the early to middle fifties, access was restricted to those with government clearance. (Children twelve and over were required to wear badges upon entering or leaving the town. I was deeply disappointed when this regulation was rescinded shortly before my twelfth birthday.)

"I have a resulting love and horror of things technical and scientific. I have no great desire to exploit or examine my ambivalence in what I write, but find the subject usually manages to surface in one way or another.

"Except for the accidental facet of my boyhood town, my life and personal philosophy is quite ordinary, and even, at times, boring."

FOR MORE INFORMATION SEE: Junior Literary Guild Catalogue, August, 1973; *New York Times Book Review,* November 4, 1973.

HALL, Rosalys Haskell   1914-

PERSONAL: Born March 27, 1914, in New York, N.Y.; daughter of Henry Marion (an author) and Alice Louise (Haskell) Hall. *Education:* Studied at Ecole Sevigne, Paris, France, at New Jersey College for Women (now Douglass College), and at Ethical Culture Normal Training School; special courses at Columbia University and New York University. *Politics:* Republican. *Religion:* Dutch Reformed. *Office:* David McKay Co., Inc., 750 Third Ave., New York, N.Y. 10017.

CAREER: Sutton Beekman School, New York, N.Y., former kindergarten and French teacher; Doubleday Book shop, New York, N.Y., seller of children's books, 1938-44; Longmans, Green & Co. (now merged with David McKay Co., Inc., under McKay name), New York, N.Y., editor in children's book department, 1944—. Free-lance editor for other publishers. *Member:* Roger Williams Family Association, Audubon Society of Rhode Island, Junior Writers Forum (New York), Newport Historical Society, Redwood Library (Newport, R.I.).

WRITINGS: Animals to Africa, Holiday House, 1939; *Out of Provincetown,* Farrar & Rinehart, 1941; *The Merry Miller,* Oxford University Press, 1952; *No Ducks for Dinner,* Oxford University Press, 1953; *Baker's Man,* Lippincott, 1954; *The Tailor's Trick,* Lippincott, 1955; *Bertie and Eddie,* Oxford University Press, 1956; *Green as Spring,* Longmans, Green, 1957; *Seven for Saint Nicholas,* Lippin-

Carrying a whirling paper star, they would sing a simple song about the three kings as they made their way from house to house, collecting some of the good cheer from the tables of kindly folk. This is the story of three such kings. ■ (From *The Three Beggar Kings* by Rosalys Haskell Hall. Illustrated by Kurt Werth.)

cott, 1958; (with sister, Julia Hall) *Animal Hide and Seek,* Lothrop, 1958; *Young Fancy,* Longmans, Green, 1960; *The Dog's Boy,* Lothrop, 1962; *Miranda's Dragon,* McGraw, 1968; *The Bright and Shining Breadboard,* Lothrop, 1969.

WORK IN PROGRESS: A biography of Roger Williams; a sequel to *Seven for Saint Nicholas.*

HOBBIES AND OTHER INTERESTS: Tennis, swimming, gardening, cats, and nature walks.

FOR MORE INFORMATION SEE: More Junior Authors, edited by Muriel Fuller, H. W. Wilson, 1963; *Young Readers' Review,* December, 1968; *Library Journal,* March 15, 1970.

HARRIS, Colver
See COLVER, Anne

HAYES, Will

PERSONAL: Born in New York, N.Y.; married Barbara Griffin, December 31, 1941; children: William II, Douglas Russell, Laird Harding, Rand Tilton. *Education:* Rutgers University, B.S.; Columbia University, M.A., Ph.D.; Duke University, M.Ed. *Religion:* Presbyterian. *Home:* Hope Ranch, Santa Barbara, Calif.

WILL HAYES

In most harbors in the United States, there is a Coast Guard rescue boat ready to speed to boats in trouble. ■ (From *Good Times on Boats* by Will Hayes. Illustrated by Henry Luhrs.)

CAREER: Public schools, Bridgewater, N.J., principal; University of California, Santa Barbara, assistant professor and dean of men, 1945—. Visiting professor, University of Oregon, Eugene, 1948, University of Nebraska, Lincoln, 1949, University of Wyoming, Laramie, 1950, University of Maine, Orono, 1953, University of Redlands, Redlands, Calif., 1954, Punahou School, Hawaii, 1960—. Consultant in education to Korea for Department of Defense, 1950. Foreman, Santa Barbara County Grand Jury; Santa Barbara Public Library, president, board of trustees; California Aeronautics Advisory Committee, chairman; Beechcraft Summer Flying Camp, director; Quarterback and Receiver Camp, director. *Military service:* U.S. Navy, in World War II, became lieutenant (junior grade); U.S. Army, 1949-52, became major. *Member:* American Association for the United Nations (president), Mensa, Rotary Club (president), Channel City Club, The Navy League, The Dissenters. *Awards, honors:* Recipient of "Bold Journey," "High Road," and "Expedition" television awards; Templeton Prize, 1960; Federal Aviation Agency's Certificate of Merit for contributions to aviation.

WRITINGS: Norman and the Nursery School, Platt, 1949; *Biggest Pine Tree,* Melmont, 1957; *Biggest Pig,* Melmont, 1958; *Biggest Salmon,* Melmont, 1961; *Good Times on Boats,* Childrens, 1963. Contributor to *New Yorker, Coronet, The Rotarian,* and to numerous professional journals. Contributing editor, *Flite Handbook;* educational consultant, *World Almanac.*

WORK IN PROGRESS: Handbook of Ballooning.

FOR MORE INFORMATION SEE: Wilton Weekly, Wilton, Conn., December 7, 1941.

HEADY, Eleanor B(utler) 1917-

PERSONAL: Surname rhymes with "ready"; born March 13, 1917, in Bliss, Idaho; daughter of Arthur Harrison and Effie (Carrico) Butler; married Harold F. Heady (a professor of ecology), June 12, 1940; children: Carol Marie (Mrs. Don De Maria), Kent Arthur. *Education:* University of Idaho, B.A., 1939. *Politics:* Liberal Republican. *Religion:* Congregationalist. *Home and office:* 1864 Capistrano

Ave., Berkeley, Calif. 94707. *Agent:* Marilyn Marlow, Curtis Brown Ltd., 60 East 56th St., New York, N.Y. 10022.

CAREER: Has worked as a high school English teacher, radio announcer, and script writer. Member of board of directors, Concerned Berkeley Citizens. *Member:* League of American Penwomen, California Writers' Club (president, 1972-74), Berkeley City Club.

WRITINGS—Juvenile: *Jambo, Sungura,* Norton, 1965; *When the Stones Were Soft: East African Fireside Tales,* Funk, 1968; *Coat of the Earth,* Norton, 1968; *Brave Johnny O'Hare,* Parents' Magazine Press, 1969; *Tales of the Nimipoo,* World Publishing, 1970; (with Harold F. Heady) *High Meadow,* Grosset, 1970; *Safiri the Singer,* Follett, 1972; *The Soil That Feeds Us,* Parents' Magazine Press, 1972; *Sage Smoke,* Follett, 1973; *Dolls You Can Make,* Lothrop, 1974; *Traveling Plants,* Parents' Magazine Press, in press. Contributor to *Ranger Rick's Nature Magazine, Cricket,* and *Highlights for Children.*

WORK IN PROGRESS: With Harold F. Heady, *Range and Wildlife Management in the Tropics,* for Longman's Green.

FOR MORE INFORMATION SEE: New York Times Book Review, May 5, 1965; *Saturday Review,* September 21, 1968.

HEAL, Edith 1903-
(Edith Heal Berrien; pseudonyms: Eileen Page, Margaret Powers)

PERSONAL: Born August 23, 1903; daughter of Charles Frederick and Eva (Page) Heal; married Gil Meynier (writer), 1930 (divorced, 1944); married Stephen Berrien, November 22, 1944; children: step-daughter, Leigh (Mrs. Procter Smith, Jr.). *Education:* University of Chicago, Ph.B., 1925; Columbia University, M.A., 1957. *Home:* 130 Orient Way, Rutherford, N.J. 07070. *Agent:* McIntosh & Otis, 18 East 41st St., New York, N.Y. *Office:* English Department, Fairleigh Dickinson University, Rutherford, N.J. 07070.

1944; *The Golden Bowl,* Lothrop, 1947; *Teen Age Manual,* Simon & Schuster, 1948; *First Book of America,* Watts, 1952; *Tim Trains his Terrier,* Whitman, 1952; *The Shadow Boxers* (novel), Scribner, 1956; (with William Carlos Williams) *I Wanted to Write a Poem,* Beacon, 1958; *The Young Executive's Wife* (non-fiction), Dodd, 1958; *What Happened to Jenny,* Atheneum, 1962; (under name of Edith Heal Berrien) *Visual Thinking in Advertising* (work book), Holt, Rinehart & Winston, 1963; *Careers,* Messner, 1966. Short stories and articles in magazines, including *Mademoiselle, Vogue, Atlantic.*

WORK IN PROGRESS: A novel, *August Is the Month of Vacations for Psychiatrists,* working title.

SIDELIGHTS: "I always had a hard time deciding which to be—a writer or an Olympic champion. Now that I am too old to be an Olympic champion, I am happy to be a writer. But I shall always be proud of the scar on my knee where I once scraped the high diving board.

"Besides the scar there is a small bump on the middle finger of my right hand. It is a writer's bump. For when I wasn't swimming or playing field hockey, I was lost in the enchanting world of books. My family called me 'Blue Stocking.'

"A Blue Stocking is a person who hides behind the covers of a book and forgets when it is lunch time. A Blue Stocking is absent-minded. I remember when I put the loaf of bread down the clothes chute instead of in the bread box. I came down to earth when I heard the bread thudding its way down to the basement! For years I had a wonderful time living other people's stories, until the day came when it was time for me to write.

"Until then, fortunately, there was another side of life because a writer must live outside the world of books. I went to school in Oak Park, Illinois, where Ernest Hemingway went—only four years ahead of me. We had a wise athletic director who taught us how to lose as well as win. And most important of all, we learned there is a time for work as well as for play. And that there can be just as much excitement in a classroom as on the hockey field. And of course I found that true when I attended the University of Chicago, and later at Columbia University where I got my Master's Degree.

"I am still writing many years after college graduation, and I find the typewriter good exercise as well as productive. I have written some thirty books, counting anthologies and re-edited classics. I shall keep on dividing my time between the typewriter and the golf links."

HEAVEN, Constance
See FECHER, Constance

HILTON, Irene (Pothus) 1912-

PERSONAL: Born July 4, 1912, in London, England; daughter of Edward and Florence (Sloman) Pothus; married Brian Joseph Hilton (a physician), 1941; children: Diana, Marion. *Education:* Attended schools and colleges in London, England. *Home:* 646 The Alameda, Berkeley, Calif. 94707.

EDITH HEAL

CAREER: Marshall Field and Co., Chicago, Ill., copywriter, 1927-29; Sears Roebuck and Co., Chicago, Ill., copywriter, 1932-35; *Tucson Daily Citizen,* Tucson, Ariz., copywriter, 1935-40; University of Arizona, Tucson, testing assistant, psychology department, 1941-43; Conde Nast Publications, New York, N.Y., copywriter, promotion department, copy chief, 1944-53; Fairleigh Dickinson University, Rutherford, N.J., assistant professor, English department, specialist in advertising, 1953—. *Member:* American Association of University Professors, Quadrangler Club, Women's Metropolitan Golf Association (board), Upper Montclair Country Club.

WRITINGS: Robin Hood, Rand McNally, 1928; *The Topaz Seal,* Laidlaw Brothers, 1928; *Siegfried, How the World Began,* Rockwell, 1930; *How the World is Changing,* Rockwell, 1931; (as Margaret Powers) *World of Insects,* Rockwell, 1931; (as Eileen Page) *Hound of Culain,* Rockwell, 1931; *Mr. Pink and the House on the Roof,* Messner 1941; (with Louis E. Asher) *Send No Money* (adult non-fiction), Abrams, 1942.

Dogie Boy, Whitman, 1943; *This Very Sun* (novel), Crown,

CAREER: Art teacher in London, England, 1933-46. Girl Scouts of America, troop chairman in Berkeley, Calif., 1957-63. *Member:* National Society of Art Masters (England), Royal Art Society (Sydney, Australia), California Writers Club.

WRITINGS: *Bluey From Down Under,* Westminster, 1962; *Bluey's Runaway Kangaroo,* Westminster, 1963; *Enemy in the Sky,* Westminster, 1964; *Chilling Escape,* Leswing Press, 1967.

WORK IN PROGRESS: *The Stumble Street Secret.*

SIDELIGHTS: "The kind of writing I like to do most is realistic fiction. Into these stories go real life adventures I have experienced or heard about. Across the pages, in heavy disguise, real people and animals parade.

"When we lived in Sydney, Australia, our family frequently visited the Taronga Park Zoo. There, one day, we helped feed two motherless baby kangaroos. They lived in a sack, blanket-pinned and suspended on the back wall of their enclosure. Their lady keeper told us the sack imitated the warmth and closeness of their mother's pouch, without which the little animals would surely die. It was just a short step on the typewriter from orphan twins in the zoo to Hoppit, Bluey's prize in the television contest (*Bluey's Runaway Kangaroo*).

"In a more serious vein, *Enemy in the Sky* is based on real life happenings during the London Blitz. The incident where the bomb dropped with such disastrous effect on the Foskett family, actually happened to a young neighbor of ours, a school girl. Unlike Bob Foskett in the story, she

In a flash, boys, girls, and teachers were flat on their stomachs on the platform. Books and satchels were tossed anywhere as hands flew up to protect heads and necks. ■ (From *Enemy in the Sky* by Irene Hilton. Illustrated by John Gretzer.)

had no brothers or sisters, and had to struggle on alone until her father came home from the front on compassionate leave.

"Although my stories are based on real life I check all my facts meticulously. In my files lie long questionnaires and discussions on the exact spelling of a place called Dee Why, on the meaning of yam sticks and whether the Australian jacaranda flower is blue as I described it or purple, like its South American counterpart.

"Just a few words in an old copy of the *Times* of London forced me to scrap a whole chapter in *Enemy in the Sky.* Instead of the glorious thunderstorm and torrential rain I seemed to remember on that particular day, the *Times* said we were suffering from the worst drought in sixty years!

"Laughing with the imaginary characters, peeping into their homes and sometimes suffering with them are stepping stones towards complete understanding and final acceptance. The more that children identify with children of other times and other countries the more tolerant they will become as adults."

IRENE P. HILTON

Ms. Hilton has made tapes of her three books for Pacifica Foundation. She and her husband left England after the war and made their home in Australia for three years before coming to the United States. She has exhibited her paintings in all three countries.

FOR MORE INFORMATION SEE: Berkeley Gazette, May 4, 1962; *Oakland Tribune,* July 9, 1962; *San Francisco Examiner,* May 14, 1963.

HIRSH, Marilyn 1944-

PERSONAL: Born January 1, 1944, in Chicago, Ill.; daughter of Eugene (a meat-market owner) and Rose (Warshell) Hirsh; married James Harris, November 18, 1973. *Education:* Began art study as child at Art Institute of Chicago's Junior School; Carnegie-Mellon University, B.F.A., 1965; New York University, Institute of Fine Arts, M.A., 1974. *Religion:* Jewish. *Home:* 1580 Third Ave., Apt. 6, New York, N.Y. 10028. *Agent:* Florence Alexander, 50 East 42nd St., New York, N.Y. 10016.

CAREER: Peace Corps volunteer teaching English and art in Nasik, India, 1965-67; writer and illustrator for Children's Book Trust, New Delhi, India, 1967; writer and illustrator of children's books, New York, N.Y., 1968—. Part-time teacher of art.

WRITINGS—Author and illustrator: *The Elephants and the Mice: A Panchatantra Story,* Children's Book Trust [New Delhi], 1967, American edition (Junior Literary Guild selection), World Publishing, 1970; *Where Is Yonkela?,* Crown, 1969; *The Pink Suit* (Child Study Association book list), Crown, 1970; (with Maya Narayan) *Leela and the Watermelon,* Crown, 1971; *How the World Got Its Color,* Crown, 1972; *George and the Goblins,* Crown, 1972; *Ben Goes Into Business,* Holiday House, 1973.

Illustrator: Florence Adams, *Mush Eggs,* Putnam, 1973.

WORK IN PROGRESS: Illustrating an anthropology book, *The Polynesians Knew Joseph Levine and Tillie S. Pine,* for McGraw; *Could Anything Be Worse?,* a Yiddish folktale, retold and illustrated; illustrating a poem on Jean La Fitte by Carl Carmer, for Harvey House.

SIDELIGHTS: "India is a second home to me and my career in children's books also began there." She is studying towards a master's degree in the art history of India, taking Sanskrit, and hopes to continue on for a Ph.D.

FOR MORE INFORMATION SEE: Christian Science Monitor, November 6, 1969; *Library Journal,* October 15, 1970; *Horn Book,* June, 1971; *Washington Post* (Children's Book World), November 5, 1972; *Publishers' Weekly,* April 30, 1973.

Working by moonlight, the goblins made a secret potion while George stood in the distance. "How strange," he thought.
■ (From *George and the Goblins* by Marilyn Hirsh. Illustrated by the author.)

MARILYN HIRSH

HOBART, Lois (Elaine)

PERSONAL: Born August 9, in Minneapolis, Minn.; daughter of Evan Llewellyn (an insurance manager) and Alveda Irene (Gjertsen) Hobart; married Harold Black (a painter, enamelist, horseman), November 17, 1950; children: Anthony Hobart. *Education:* University of Minnesota, B.A., M.A., B.S. *Home:* Huertas 19 A, San Miguel de Allende, Guanajuato, Mexico. *Agent:* James Brown Associates, 22 East 60th St., New York, N.Y.

CAREER: Esquire, Chicago, Ill., associate editor, 1943-45; Conde Nast Publications, New York, N.Y., associate editor, 1945-53. Photographer, whose work has been exhibited in shows and appeared in *Life, Glamour, New York Times, This Week, Parents, U.S. Camera,* other magazines and newspapers.

WRITINGS—Under name Lois Hobart: *Katie and Her Camera,* Messner, 1955; *A Palette for Ingrid,* Messner, 1956; *Laurie, Physical Therapist,* Messner, 1958; *Strangers Among Us,* Funk, 1958; *Elaine Forrest, Visiting Nurse,* Messner, 1959; *Patriot's Lady* (Life of Sarah Jay), Funk, 1960; *Behind the Walls,* Funk, 1961; *Mexican Mural* (with own photographs), Harcourt, 1963; *What is a Whispery Secret?,* Parents Magazine Press, 1968. Writings also in-

clude play, "The Emissary," short shorts for Universal Publishers, 1963; short scripts for Canadian Broadcasting Corp.; script for documentary for On Film, Inc.; columnist for *The News* of Mexico City, 1964, *Mexico City Times,* 1965-66; articles for *Childcraft, Compact, Parents, Humpty Dumpty, Arizona Highways, Mexico this Month, Mexican World, Intercambio, Chronicle of the Horse;* book reviews in *New York Times.*

SIDELIGHTS: "My first memory, at four, was learning to read, and my first idea of a vocation, almost from then on, was writing. In grade school I wrote a couple of stories about dogs and another about D'Artagnan, but I never took a course in creative writing at college, though I majored in English. Writing papers in college was always a pleasure rather than a duty, and my M.A. thesis on autobiographies was well received. Most writers nowadays probably have a somewhat similar background, of early involvement in the *idea* of writing. And I suppose that for most writers hardly a phase of their lives is complete without some commitment to a written expression of it. The most revealing document I know about writers is Anais Nin's series of diaries.

"After a year of teaching I worked for *Esquire* in Chicago and two years later I worked for *Glamour Magazine,* part of Condé Nast Publishing Co. After ten years of editing, and not long after the birth of my son, I tried free-lancing. Photography became a part of my working life, and I can remember that a week devoted to completing a story based on the idea of using blurred action to form a pattern (as in people leaving a train or subway, or the motion of a horse, or the action of parading) was perhaps the most exciting creative experience of my life. This story was used in *Life* in 1949.

"It was the suggestion of an agent that since I had worked and written so much about vocational fields, I might try doing what is called a vocational novel. I had a very interesting interview on the subject of doing a book on a photographer with Gertrude Rosenblum and Lee Hoffman of Julian Messner. They were very encouraging and assured me they would give me a contract as soon as I gave them an outline and a couple of chapters. But it took me three months to think of an outline and approach. I kept wondering whether I could really write a whole book, but I soon learned it was mainly a matter of sitting at the desk at regular intervals and working on it faithfully.

"My first book was extremely well reviewed and singled out as one of the outstanding juveniles for adolescents of the year. For a while I was doing about one a year, a series for Julian Messner, later novels for girls and a biography of Sally Livingston Jay for Funk & Wagnalls. I was commissioned to do a book on Mexico by one firm and had some disagreeable relations with the editor, the first to attempt to rewrite a book of mine. So the book was published as originally written by Harcourt, Brace & World. I later had an amusing encounter with a woman who was doing the same assignment and was so annoyed by the editor that she refused to work with her and was assigned someone else. My most recent book was one for small children called What is a Whispery Secret? and has just come out in the form of record-film-strip combination.

"I greatly enjoy doing non-fiction in a way that adheres closely to documented history but in a lively fictional way.

Biography and autobiography have long been of interest to me and I find it challenging to soak myself in whatever material of the period, the person and the milieu I can find to develop a sense of the personality of the subject.

"When I came to Mexico fourteen years ago I was intrigued by the woman known as La Malinche, interpreter and mistress of Cortés during the Conquest of Mexico and mother of his son. She is commonly considered a traitor. I began a novel about her two years ago after doing considerable research, which included Nahuatl sources and the Indian version of her life, but half way along discovered (a not uncommon hazard for writers) that another person had just published a novel on the subject. At my husband's suggestion I decided to make it into a play, particularly since I had done one before about Sally Jay and liked the medium so much.

"Certain aspects of writing are seldom commented on, and one of them is this frequent encounter with the subject under treatment by other authors—evidently at times certain subjects are in the air and intrigue many people at the same time. Another aspect is the difficulty of choosing names for characters in fiction to reflect not only a certain function in a novel or short story but names representative of an environment, country and period. Still another is the importance of maintaining a certain objectivity about a subject which appeals to the writer's sympathy and empathy.

"A writer's work is very apt to reflect much of his personal preoccupations and predilections. For instance, it occurred to me one day that every book of mine has something about chess in it. And most have something about horses and dogs, more recently also about cats. (Our household includes at the moment three collies and three cats, three horses and a ram.) The ram will be next to make his appearance, no doubt. Also because of my husband's dedication to horsemanship after a long career in art, designing and building exhibitions, these areas too enter my work. And my son Tony naturally increases my interest in the problems and concerns of young people today. It would be nice to think that grandchildren will eventually exert an influence too. . ."

Resident of San Miguel de Allende since 1958; speaks Spanish, has reading knowledge of French.

HOBBIES AND OTHER INTERESTS: Chess, tennis, horseback riding, bowling.

HOGROGIAN, Nonny 1932-

PERSONAL: Surname pronounced Ha-*GROH*-gee-an; born May 7, 1932, in New York, N.Y.; daughter of Henry Mugerditch and Rachel (Ansoorian) Hogrogian; married David Kherdian (a poet), March 17, 1971. *Education:* Hunter College (now Hunter College of the City University of New York), B.A., 1953; graduate study, New School for Social Research, 1957. *Home:* East Chatham, New York 12060.

CAREER: Designer and art buyer for William Morrow & Co., New York, N.Y.; illustrator for Thomas Y. Crowell Co., Holt, Rinehart & Winston, and Charles Scribner's Sons, all New York; illustrator and writer of children's books. *Member:* P.E.N. *Awards, honors:* Caldecott Award, 1966, for *Always Room for One More,* and, 1972, for *One Fine Day.*

WRITINGS—All children's books; all self-illustrated: *One Fine Day,* (ALA Notable Book), Macmillan, 1971; *Apples,* Macmillan, 1972; *Billy Goat and His Well-Fed Friends,* Harper, 1972; *The Hermit & Harry & Me,* Little, Brown, 1972; *Rooster Brother,* Macmillan, 1974.

Illustrator: Nicolete Meredith, *King of the Kerry Fair,* Crowell, 1960; Leclaire G. Alger, *Gaelic Ghosts,* Holt, 1963; Alger, *Ghosts Go Hunting,* Holt, 1965; Aileen L. Fisher, *Arbor Day,* Crowell, 1965; Alger, *Always Room for One More,* Holt, 1965; Robert Burns, *Hand in Hand We'll Go: Ten Poems,* Crowell, 1965; William Shakespeare, *Poems,* Crowell, 1966; Virginia A. Tashjian, *Once There Was and Was Not,* Little, Brown, 1966; Mary O'Neill, *The White Palace,* Crowell, 1966; Julie Whitney, *Bears Are Sleeping,* Scribner, 1967; Beatrice S. De Regniers, *The Day Everybody Cried,* Viking, 1967; Isaac Bashevis Singer, *The Fearsome Inn,* Scribner, 1967; *The Renowned History of Little Red Riding-Hood,* Crowell, 1967; *The Thirteen Days of Yule,* Crowell, 1968; Christian Morgenstern, *The Three Sparrows and Other Nursery Rhymes,* Scribner, 1968; *The Story of Prince Ivan, the Firebird, and the Gray Wolf,* Scribner, 1968; Theodore Fontane, *Sir Ribbeck of Ribbeck of Havelland,* Macmillan, 1969; Virginia Hamil-

NONNY HOGROGIAN

Then he went back to the bakery and picked up the goose and left a note on the door. ■ (From *Rooster Brother* by Nonny Hogrogian. Illustrated by the author.)

ton, *The Time-Ago Tales of Jahdu,* Macmillan, 1969; Esther Hautzig, *In School Learning in Four Languages,* Macmillan, 1969; Virginia Haviland, *Favorite Fairy Tales Told in Greece,* Little, Brown, 1970; James Stephens, *Deirdre* (*Horn Book* honor list), Macmillan, 1970; *Vasilisa the Beautiful* (ALA Notable Book), Macmillan, 1970; Rachel Hogrogian, *The Armenian Cookbook,* Atheneum, 1971; Jacob Ludwig Karl Grimm, *About Wisemen and Simpletons* (*Horn Book* honor list), Macmillan, 1971; Cheli Duran Ryan, *Paz,* Macmillan, 1971; Virginia Tashjian, *Three Apples Fell from Heaven,* Little, Brown, 1971; Barbara Schiller, *The Kitchen Knight,* Holt, 1972; *One I Love, Two I Love & Other Loving Mother Goose Rhymes,* Dutton, 1972; David Kherdian, *Looking over Hills,* Giligia, 1972; *Visions of America by the Poets of Our Time,* edited by David Kherdian, Macmillan, 1973.

WORK IN PROGRESS: The Contest, an Armenian folk tale.

HOBBIES AND OTHER INTERESTS: Good music, particularly Vivaldi and Bach.

FOR MORE INFORMATION SEE: American Artist, October, 1966; *Horn Book,* August, 1966, April, 1972, August, 1972; Lee Bennett Hopkins, *Books Are By People,* Citation Press, 1969; *New York Times Book Review,* September 19, 1970, May 7, 1972; *Christian Science Monitor,* November 11, 1971; *Graphis 155,* Volume 27, 1971/72; *Third Book of Junior Authors,* edited by de Montreville and Hill, H. W. Wilson, 1972; *Publishers' Weekly,* February 7, 1972; *Top of the News,* April, 1972; *Washington Post* "Children's Book World," November 5, 1972; MacCann and Richard, *The Child's First Books,* H. W. Wilson, 1973.

HOKE, John (Lindsay) 1925-

PERSONAL: Born June 26, 1925, in Pittsburgh, Pa.; son of John (an editor) and Helen Hoke (a writer and editor; surname now Watts); married Sylvia Hyde, June 25, 1950; children: Franklin, Bonnie, Edward, Larry. *Education:* Antioch College, B.A., 1950. *Home:* 5421 Waneta Rd., Washington, D.C. 20016. *Office:* Division of Urban and Environmental Activities, National Capital Parks, National Park Service, Washington, D.C. 20242.

JOHN HOKE

CAREER: American Automobile Association, Washington, D.C., technician in motion picture production and photographic laboratory, 1950-57; International Cooperation Administration, communications media officer in Paramaribo, Surinam (Netherlands Guiana), 1957-61; self-employed as writer and inventor, 1961-62; Agency for International Development, Communications Resources Division, Washington, D.C., development officer, 1962-63; Atlantic Research Corp., Alexandria, Va., engineer, 1963-66; U.S. Department of Interior, Washington, D.C., writer-editor, Division of Nationwide Planning, 1966-67, program liaison specialist, Division of Environmental Conservation, 1967-70; National Park Service, Division of Urban Park Programs, 1970-72, National Capital Parks, 1972—. Designer of Hoke Electric Vehicle, a solar powered boat, and small power sources for remote field operation of electrical equipment, including one for archaeological field use by National Geographic Society; helped develop field incubator to transport eggs of whooping cranes and other endangered species. Photographer and producer of documentary films. *Awards, honors:* Meritorious Service Award of U.S. Department of Interior for conversion of Bolviar Pond into wetlands ecosystem.

WRITINGS—Juvenile books, except as indicated: *The First Book of Snakes,* Watts, 1952; *The First Book of Photography,* Watts, 1957, wholly revised edition, 1965; *Music Boxes: Their Lure and Lore* (adult), Hawthorn, 1957; *The First Book of the Jungle,* Watts, 1963; *The First Book of the Guianas,* Watts, 1964; *The First Book of Solar Energy,* Watts, 1968; *Turtles and Their Care,* Watts, 1970; *Ecology: The Environment, Its Mechanisms, and Man,* Watts, 1971;

. . . the black *toucan,* with his enormous banana-shaped yellow bill. ■ (From *The First Book of the Jungle* by John Hoke. Illustrated by Russell Peterson.)

Terrariums, Watts, 1972; *Aquariums,* Watts, in press. Author and illustrator of book-length article on the three-toed sloth for *National Geographic;* contributor to government publications and popular and technical periodicals, including *Popular Science, Ranger Rick, Popular Mechanics, National Geographic Society School Bulletin,* and *Aquarium.*

SIDELIGHTS: Hoke's interest in electric power sources antedates the surge of concern about environment. While in Surinam he designed and fabricated a collapsible lightweight watercraft that could operate on a noiseless electric drive in vegetation-choked waterways. Shortly after that he began working on a simple low-cost electric vehicle for urban use, one that could be built "from items already on the shelf" to operate without fouling the air. He took several months leave in 1966 to develope the version he finally settled on, logged 1,600 miles in test drives around Washington, and assisted in the Senate hearings on electric vehicles. Television viewers saw his car and other selected electric prototypes on the "Today" show, March 14, 1967.

In 1969 Hoke worked with the U.S. Fish and Wildlife Service to develop a case for transporting the eggs of the periled whooping crane from Canadian nesting areas to Maryland for artificial incubation under controlled conditions. He also has designed miniature environments for classroom use, devised a simplified system of classification of tropical vegetation, and designed or modified photographic devices. A licensed diver, he served as watch director on the Tektite II program in the Virgin Islands.

FOR MORE INFORMATION SEE: *New Republic,* August 13, 1966; *Life,* October 21, 1966; *Library Journal,* September 15, 1970.

Elisabeth stood on her tiptoes and spread sunflower seed and cracked corn over the feeder. Then she called, "All right, birds, come and get it!" ▪ (From *Elisabeth the Bird Watcher* by Felice Holman. Illustrated by Erik Blegvad.)

HOLMAN, Felice   1919-

PERSONAL: Born October 24, 1919, in New York, N.Y.; daughter of Jac C. (an engineering consultant) and Celia (an artist; maiden name, Hotchner) Holman; married Herbert Valen, April 13, 1941; children: Nanine Elisabeth. *Education:* Syracuse University, B.A., 1941. *Home:* 158 Hillspoint Rd., Westport, Conn.

WRITINGS: *Elisabeth, The Birdwatcher,* Macmillan, 1963; *Elisabeth, The Treasure Hunter,* Macmillan, 1964; *Silently, The Cat and Miss Theodosia,* Macmillan, 1965; *Victoria's Castle,* Norton, 1966; *Elisabeth and the Marsh Mystery,* Macmillan, 1966; *Professor Diggin's Dragons,* Macmillan, 1966; *The Witch on the Corner,* Norton, 1966; *The Cricket Winter,* Norton, 1967; *The Blackmail Machine,* Macmillan, 1968; *A Year to Grow,* Norton, 1968; *At the Top of My Voice: Other Poems,* Norton, 1969; *The Holiday Rat and the Utmost Mouse,* Grosset, 1969; *Solomon's Search,* Grosset, 1970; *The Future of Hooper Toote,* Scribners, 1972; *I Hear You Smiling and Other Poems,* Scribner, 1973; *The Escape of the Giant Hogstalk,* Scribner, 1974; *Slake's Limbo,* Scribner, 1974.

SIDELIGHTS: "When people ask why or how I happened to write for young people, I sometimes give a sort of flip answer because I am not really sure. It must have been a combination of things. I know I didn't sit down and say 'Now I am going to write a story for young people.' I had always been writing *something* from the time I was a child and I just kept on writing. Since I like to talk with young people and I like to hear what they have to say, it is only natural that I would like them to hear what I have to say, too. One of the ways to have people listen to you is to write.

"I have a lot of respect for the intelligence of young readers and I don't write to them in different ways than I would speak with them. Since young people are going to be the grown up people very soon, I think they are probably the most important people around. It gives me a lot of satisfaction to be talking to the most important people around—the people who are going to help fix up a lot of the things we know are wrong.

"My books are sometimes spin-offs from real experiences. *The Witch on the Corner* lived on my corner. I took it over from there. I knew a man like Professor Diggins. And sometimes ideas can come from newspaper stories as in *The Holiday Rat and the Utmost Mouse.* And then sometimes they just seem to come out of my head like daydreams that settle themselves onto pages of a book. Sometimes it's fun and sometimes it's hard work. But there is always the good thought that at the end of the fun or work there will be a book."

FOR MORE INFORMATION SEE: *Saturday Review,* May 20, 1972; *Horn Book,* February, 1974.

FELICE HOLMAN

HOUGHTON, Eric 1930-

PERSONAL: Born January 4, 1930, in Yorkshire, England; son of Alfred William (hydraulic engineer) and Mary Elizabeth (Meffen) Houghton; married Cecile Wolffe (a teacher), June 4, 1954; children: Ian, Jill. *Education:* Sheffield City Training College, certificate in education, 1952. *Home:* 42 Collier Rd., Hastings, Sussex, England.

CAREER: Junior school history teacher in London, England, 1952-64, in Hastings, Sussex, England, 1965—. Writer of children's books. *Military service:* Royal Air Force, 1948-50. *Member:* National Union of Teachers, Society of Authors, Playwrights and Composers. *Awards, honors: The White Wall* named one of "Books of the Year" in 1962 by the American Child Study Association, and *They Marched with Spartacus* similarly chosen in 1963; Boys' Clubs of America Junior Book Award, 1963, for *They Marched with Spartacus.*

WRITINGS: The White Wall, McGraw, 1962; *They Marched With Spartacus,* McGraw, 1963; *Summer Silver,* Oliver & Boyd, 1963 (published in America as *Mystery of the Old Field,* McGraw, 1964); *Boy Beyond the Mist,* Whiting & Wheaton, 1966; *The Mouse and the Magician,* Lippincott, 1970; *A Giant Can Do Anything,* Deutsch, 1975.

WORK IN PROGRESS: Two picture storybooks, *The Amazing Feat of King Caboodle* and *The King Who Loved Yellow.*

SIDELIGHTS: "I try to write the kind of books I would have enjoyed as a boy. So I aim at plenty of action and excitement, tempered with suspense and humor. In fact as time goes on, I am inclined to give more and more importance to the need for humor in children's stories. I believe now that showing the lighter and happier side of life is absolutely essential to a good children's story. (Surprisingly it is far easier to write a story about crime or fear or other evil forces than it is to show goodness and happiness. . . . Perhaps this is because we are all afraid of roughly the same things, but the things that make us laugh are more personal and therefore more varied).

"As a result of this conviction, my later stories have turned towards humor as the main ingredient—humor sometimes of the slapstick variety (*The King Who Loved Yellow*), or the satirical kind (*The Amazing Feat of King Caboodle*), or the more subtle, tongue-in-cheek sort, such as *The Mouse and the Magician.*

"Once I am convinced that an initial idea is strong enough to carry a whole story, I make a fairly simple outline of the course of the plot. Then I begin to type; initially I am not capable of doing more than three hours a day, but this increases when the basic spade-work is completed.

The mouse watched hungrily. Behind him the wind roared in the trees. A snowflake landed on his tail, making it freeze. ■ (From *The Mouse and the Magician* by Eric Houghton. Illustrated by Faith Jaques.)

Something about the Author

point out discrepancies between text and drawing (sometimes it has been easier to alter the text than the drawing!) The artists have nearly always cooperated with my tentative suggestions as to dress and physique and backgrounds, etc. The result of this painstaking cooperation is that at least 75% of the artwork in my books reflects exactly what the words intended—not only in the pictorial sense but also as regards atmosphere and style.

"On the personal side, my main hobby is playing chess: I am a member of the famous Hastings Chess Club. I also like to swim a lot, mainly in the covered pool at the foot of my garden."

FOR MORE INFORMATION SEE: Times Literary Supplement. May 25, 1967; *New Statesman,* May 26, 1967.

HUME, Lotta Carswell

PERSONAL: Married Edward Hicks Hume (a doctor). *Home:* White Sands, 7450 Olivetas Ave., LaJolla, Calif.

WRITINGS: Songs Along the Way, privately printed by Yale University Press; *Drama at the Doctor's Gate,* Yale-in-China Association, 1961; *Favorite Children's Stories from China and Tibet,* Tuttle, 1962.

ERIC HOUGHTON

"I re-write my stories three times. The first typing adds real-life dimensions to the plot-synopsis; the second typing is to high-light those aspects discovered to require emphasis for the sake of clarity, and to dovetail in any new ideas found to be necessary. The third typing is the final copy, when I make all details consistent, polish the style and condense the narrative as much as possible.

"I have been lucky with the illustrators for all my books, on two counts. Firstly, I have always been given an element of choice as to which artist I would prefer. And secondly my publishers have allowed me to get the art-work before the book is made up; this has given me the chance to

LOTTA CARSWELL HUME

The moon was full and golden and the night as bright as noon. As the boy walked aimlessly along, he kept his eyes fastened on the big friendly moon above. All of a sudden, he saw a tiny golden boat come floating down on a moonbeam. ■ (From *Favorite Children's Stories from China and Tibet* by Lotta Carswell Hume. Illustrated by Lo Koon-chiu.)

SIDELIGHTS: Ms. Hume was a longtime former resident of China, with special interest in collecting and publishing Chinese legends as a cultural bond between American and Chinese children.

"Our little house in the center of the great walled city of Changsha was surrounded by high walls and every day the voices from the narrow, crowded bustling street came to us over those walls.

"Gradually these voices began to tell us something of our Chinese neighbors and the fascinating life all about us. As we learned to know our neighbors over the walls better, the city came to be a Story-Book-World, with spirits cavorting up and down the streets—good spirits by day, bad spirits by night—and we were very glad that our house was built with a twisting and turning entrance to keep those bad spirits from rushing inside to catch us.

"It was a Story-Book-World where lightning was the eye of the god looking for evil-doers, and where spirit winds moaned as they flew over the top of our house.

"A Story-Book-World indeed, where we had only to step through the great Moon Gate to reach the Land of Once-Upon-a-Time, where we could hear the stories of Magic Pancakes and Fairy Boats, and could listen to the little animals and big animals telling their wonderful stories; for of course in the Land of Once-Upon-a-Time, all the animals can talk."

Something about the Author

HUNTER, Hilda   1921-

PERSONAL: Born May 11, 1921, in Liverpool, England; daughter of Frederick Newton (an engineer) and Elizabeth (Billington) Hunter. *Education:* London College of Music, A.L.C.M., 1945. *Religion:* Roman Catholic. *Home:* 44 Argyle St. S., Birkenhead L41 9BX, Cheshire, England. *Agent:* Norah Smaridge, 11 Godfrey Rd., Upper Montclair, N.J. 07043.

CAREER: Free lance writer. Pianist, appearing as soloist and accompanist at charity concerts and with local bands. *Member:* Society of Authors, Liverpool Writers Club (chairman, 1972-73).

WRITINGS: *Growing Up With Music,* Hewitt House, 1970; (with Norah Smaridge) *The Teen-Agers Guide to Collecting Practically Anything* (Junior Literary Guild selection), Dodd, 1972; (with Norah Smaridge) *The Teenagers Guide to Hobbies for Here and Now,* Dodd, 1974. Contributor of articles on American, British, and continental silver and other subjects to *Antique Dealer, Apollo, Times* (London), trade and religious periodicals, and other journals and newspapers. Former columnist in antiques magazine, identifying silver articles and their marks.

WORK IN PROGRESS: A teen-age hobby guide.

SIDELIGHTS: "I have an extensive library of nonfiction: art, antiques, music, travel, psychology, religion, history of food, cookery books, local history, and biography—subjects connected with my writing projects.

"Apart from collecting books and antiques, I hunt for items with a musical association. Ever since I was a handbell ringer in a kindergarten band, I have been fascinated by bells, and I like playing with a group. I enjoy all kinds of music: church, folk, opera, classical and jazz. I am keenly interested in music therapy. I come from a music-loving family. Apart from the piano and violin, there was always some kind of musical instrument appearing in my home unexpectedly, such as an organ, a zither and a mandolin. Added to these were kitchen band instruments we made ourselves for fun.

"In my teens I was a pharmaceutical student. I still try my hand at dispensing, if it is only making my own cosmetics. I have never lost interest in the history of medicine, materia medica, herbal lore, or drug jars and pharmacy equipment.

"I am a regular visitor to museums and art galleries, and historic houses. On my travels, I love visiting 'off-beat' places for copy: factories, Sevres porcelain, Paris; craft centers like the Lacemakers' Corner in Bruges, Belgium. Vacations spent with my co-author, Norah Smaridge, have been the inspiration for some of our books and articles."

FOR MORE INFORMATION SEE: *Junior Literary Guild Catalog,* September, 1972.

HILDA HUNTER

HYDE, Wayne F(rederick)   1922-

PERSONAL: Born July 31, 1922, in Clintonville, Wis.; son of Roger Welcome and Lydia (Goerlitz) Hyde; married Marilyn C. Freyer, October 26, 1946; children: Jeffrey David, Lisa Beth, Abby Jane. *Education:* College and Conservatory of Music of Cincinnati, B.F.A, Radio Education, 1949. *Agent:* Paul R. Reynolds & Son, 599 Fifth Ave., New York, N.Y. 10017. *Office:* Voice of America, 330 Independence Ave., S.W., Washington, D.C.

CAREER: Before college, sang with dance bands throughout the United States; formed nineteen-piece dance band in New York, 1942; held various jobs in radio and television, from writing commercial copy to radio and television acting; now writes, mainly children's books, and works as news correspondent for Voice of America. *Military service:* U.S. Army, paratroops, 1943-47; became sergeant; received Silver Star, Purple Heart with cluster, and Presidential Unit Citation. *Member:* American Federation of Television and Radio Artists, Writers Guild.

WRITINGS: *What Does a Parachutist Do?* Dodd, 1960; *What Does a Diver Do?* Dodd, 1961; *What Does A Secret Service Agent Do?,* Dodd, 1962; *What Does a Cowboy Do?,* Dodd, 1963; *What Does a Forest Ranger Do?,* Dodd, 1964; *The Men behind the Astronauts,* Dodd, 1965. Contributor of short stories and articles to national magazines.

SIDELIGHTS: "How did I come to write my books for children? I was a paratrooper in World War Two—which gives you some indication of how old I am—and I realized there was very little written about parachuting, how it's done and why, how it feels to jump from an airplane in flight. My first book was about that subject.

"The second, *What Does a Diver Do?,* was a little more difficult, since I knew absolutely nothing about diving. I lived in Washington, D.C. at the time—and our capital city is the best city in the world to do research on ANY subject.

Also, the U.S. Navy Diving School is located there. The people there were most helpful, even to putting me into a deep sea suit and letting me go down into one of their practice tanks. (The Navy also serves wonderful coffee.)

"As a reporter for the Voice of America in Washington, I had many occasions to attend press conferences held by our Presidents, and I was always aware of the presence of Secret Service agents. I was most impressed with their work, their attitude concerning their important job, their appearance, their intelligence. I thought a book about these men would be of interest. Again, I had excellent cooperation from the people involved, and it led to *What Does a Secret Service Agent Do?*

"The book about the cowboy was the result of a thirteen-week series I did for the Voice of America, titled *The American Cowboy–Past and Present*. I researched him back to his beginnings up to today. I also spent a week on a working cattle ranch in Texas, actually working as a cowboy. I may have been the only reporter ever to cover a cattle roundup on horseback with a tape recorder hung around my neck. It was all so interesting that I decided to write a book on the subject of the cowboy.

"*What Does a Forest Ranger Do?* practically wrote itself. On a Monday morning I visited the Forestry Service of the Department of Agriculture in Washington. I talked to two

The so-called "ten-gallon hat" will not hold ten gallons of water, or even one gallon. But many an old-time cowboy has shown a youngster how to bend the brim upward and use the upper surface of it for a drinking cup. ■ (From *What Does a Cowboy Do?* by Wayne Hyde.)

forest rangers, gathered all the literature I could, selected the photographs I needed. By one o'clock that same afternoon I was writing the book, and I was writing the finished manuscript as I typed each page. By Thursday afternoon it was done and in the mail to Dodd, Mead & Company.

"The final book, *The Men Behind The Astronauts,* was also written as a result of my work as a reporter with the Voice of America. I had covered several of the manned space flights in the "Mercury" and "Gemini" series, reporting from both Cape Canaveral (later to become Cape Kennedy) and from the Manned Space Center in Houston, Texas. The interest, of course, was predominantly upon the astronauts themselves, but I had talked to and observed so many of the men behind the scenes on the space flights that I thought they, too, should get some publicity. Also, the National Aeronautics and Space Agency (NASA) is located directly across the street from the Voice of America in Washington. It was simply a matter of crossing the street, gathering photos from the people I had come to know so well, and then putting together the story from the material I had gathered while reporting all the manned flights. I wrote *The Men Behind The Astronauts* at my desk at the Voice of America (during office hours, and when ever I had some spare time), and again I wrote the finished manuscript as I typed the original pages.

"If that sounds unusual, I like to think that if I can write this way it must be only because I know I am trying for the finished product as it is being typed. Therefore, I'll try harder—and my typing will be neater, too.

WAYNE F. HYDE

"I love to write. I find it relaxing and hard work at the same time. I also have come to know what anyone who has ever seriously tried to write knows: Writing is one of the loneliest occupations in the world. You talk to no one, don't answer your telephone. You miss meals, simply because they are interruptions to writing. And you may sit half the night pounding away at your typewriter, thinking every single word is a perfect *jewel*. After some sleep and a new perspective, you read your night-time labors in the five-hundred-watt daylight, and quite often you wonder how you could have written such *terrible* stuff.

"As a reporter, my business is writing—and has been for going on twenty-six years. I was part of a reporting team that won a national radio news award in 1959, and I suppose I've been trying to do as well ever since. And I *haven't* done as well. It is a matter of opportunity, and of having a certain type of story break at a certain time, of being the person *there* at the time. Mostly, I think, it's a matter of INTEREST. Reporters are curious, aggressive, probably egocentric to some degree. All of these traits help them. But if the reporter does not have the INTEREST, the other three qualities might as well be turned toward the study of becoming a baseball umpire or something. I happen to like baseball umpires, however.

"I have often thought of—and suggested—doing a book about a reporter and his work. But the truth of the matter is that reporters are not generally liked by many people. This does not bother me in the least. I may not be able to write a book about my work, but I love my work, have for years, and always will."

HOBBIES AND OTHER INTERESTS: Judo, golf, collecting jazz records.

HYLANDER, Clarence J(ohn)   1897-1964

PERSONAL: Born November 24, 1897, in Waterbury, Conn.; son of John C. (a factory worker) and Augusta (Persson) Hylander; married Doris Dann Leopold, November 10, 1922; children: Robert John, Betty Jeanne Hylander Menges. *Education:* Yale University, B.A., 1920, M.A., 1922, Ph.D., 1925. *Politics:* Republican. *Religion:* Protestant. *Home and office:* Seely Rd., Bar Harbor, Me.

CAREER: Science teacher in private and public secondary schools, 1920-29; science writer in California, 1929-30, 1933; American International College, Springfield, Mass., professor of biology and geology, 1930-32; Colgate University, Hamilton, N.Y., chairman of botany department, 1933-43; Macmillan Co., New York, N.Y., science editor, college department, 1945-48; U.S. Army Chemical Corps, Medical Department, chief of Technical Information Division, 1949-50, 1952. Bowdoin College, Brunswick, Me., visiting professor of biology; Pomona College, Claremont, Calif., visiting professor of botony, 1964. American Institute of Biological Sciences, Washington, D.C., executive secretary. Consultant to Northeastern Research Foundation, Brunswick, Me., and to Grolier Society, New York, N.Y. *Military service:* U.S. Naval Reserve, 1943-45; served in Naval Aviation: became lieutenant senior grade. *Member:* American Academy of Arts and Sciences, Phi Beta Kappa, Sigma Xi.

WRITINGS: The World of Plant Life, Macmillan, 1939; (with O. B. Stanley) *College Botany,* Macmillan, 1945; *The Macmillan Wildflower Book,* Macmillan, 1954; *The Wild Life Community,* Houghton, 1965; *American Scientists,* Macmillan, 1968, abridged edition, 1968.

"Out of Doors Series": *Out of Doors in Autumn,* and similarly titled books for the other three seasons, Macmillan, 1942-43, revised editions, 1948-50.

"Young Naturalist Series": *Sea and Shore, Trees and Trails, Animals in Armour, Insects on Parade, Animals in Fur, Flowers of Field and Forest, Feathers in Flight, Fishes and Their Ways,* Macmillan, 1940-64.

(Died October 8, 1964)

HYMAN, Trina Schart   1939-

PERSONAL: Born April 8, 1939, in Philadelphia, Pa.; daughter of Albert H. and Margaret Doris (Bruck) Schart; married Harris Hyman (a mathematician and engineer), 1959 (divorced, 1968); children: Katrin. *Education:* Studied at Philadelphia Museum College of Art, 1956-59, Boston Museum School of the Arts, 1959-60, and Konstfackskolan (Swedish State Art School), Stockholm, 1960-61. *Politics:* "Royalist." *Religion:* "Druid." *Home:* Brick Hill Rd., Lyme, N.H. 03768.

CAREER: Artist and illustrator; art director of *Cricket* (magazine), LaSalle, Ill., 1972—.

WRITINGS—Author and illustrator: *How Six Found Christmas,* Little, Brown, 1969.

Illustrator: Hertha Von Gebhardt, *Toffe och den lilla Bilen,* Raben & Sjogren, 1961; *Riddles Riddles from A to Z,* Western, 1963; *Bow Wow! Meow!,* Western, 1963; Sandol S. Warburg, *Curl Up Small,* Houghton, 1964; Eileen O'-Faolain, *Children of the Salmon,* Little, Brown, 1965; *All Kinds of Signs,* Western, 1965; Ruth Sawyer, *Joy to the World: Christmas Legends* (*Horn Book* honor list), Little, Brown, 1966; Joyce Varney, *The Magic Maker,* Bobbs,

TRINA SCHART HYMAN

TRINA SCHART HYMAN
by Trina Schart Hyman

1966; Virginia Haviland, *Favorite Fairy Tales Told in Czechoslovakia* (retold), Little, Brown, 1966; Edna Butler Trickey, *Billy Finds Out,* United Church Press, 1966; Jacob D. Townsend, *The Five Trials of the Pansy Bed,* Houghton, 1967; Elizabeth Johnson, *Stuck with Luck,* Little, Brown, 1967; Josephine Poole, *Moon Eyes,* Little, Brown, 1967; John T. Moore, *Cinnamon Seed,* Houghton, 1967; Paul Tripp, *The Little Red Flower,* Doubleday, 1968; Eve Merriam, *Epaminondas* (retold), Follett, 1968; Joyce Varney, *The Half-Time Gypsy,* Bobbs, 1968; Elizabeth Johnson, *All in Free,* Little, Brown, 1968; Tom McGowen, *Dragon Stew,* Follett, 1969; Susan Meyers, *The Cabin on the Fjord,* Doubleday, 1969; Peter Hunter Blair, *The Coming of Pout,* Little, Brown, 1969; Clyde R. Bulla, *The Moon Singer,* Crowell, 1969; Ruth Nichols, *A Walk Out of the World,* Harcourt, 1969; Claudia Paley, *Benjamin the True,* Little, Brown, 1969.

Paul Tripp, *The Vi-Daylin Book of Minnie the Mump,* Ross Laboratories, 1970; Donald J. Sobol, *Greta the Strong,* Follett, 1970; Blanche Luria Serwer, *Let's Steal the Moon: Jewish Tales, Ancient and Recent* (retold), Little, 1970; Maureen McIlwraith, under name Mollie Hunter, *The Walking Stones: A Story of Suspense,* Harper, 1970; Tom McGowen, *Sir Machinery,* Follett, 1970; Phyllis Krasilovsky, *The Shy Little Girl,* Houghton, 1970; Ellin Greene, *The Pumpkin Giant,* Lothrop, 1970; Wylly Folk St. John, *The Ghost Next Door,* Harper, 1971; Osmond Molarsky, *The Bigger They Come,* Walck, 1971; Osmond Molarsky, *Take It or Leave It,* Walck, 1971; Carolyn Meyer, *The Bread Book: All About Bread and How to Make It,* Harcourt, 1971; Elizabeth Johnson, *Break a Magic Circle,* Little, Brown, 1971; Ellin Green, *Princess*

Rosetta and the Popcorn Man (from *The Pot of Gold* by Mary E. Wilkins; retold), Lothrop, 1971; Eleanor Cameron, *A Room Made of Windows,* Atlantic-Little, Brown, 1971; *Who Says So?,* Lothrop, 1972; Dori White, *Sarah and Katie,* Harper, 1972; Jan Wahl, *Magic Heart,* Seabury, 1972; Phyllis Krasilovsky, *The Popular Girls Club,* Simon & Schuster, 1972; Howard Pyle, *King Stork* (story first published in Pyle's collection, *The Wonder Clock*), Little, Brown, 1973; Phyllis La Farge, *Joanna Runs Away,* Holt, 1973; Ellin Greene, *Clever Crooks,* Lothrop, 1973; *Listen, Children, Listen* (anthology by Myra Cohn Livingston), Harcourt, 1973; Carol Ryrie Brink, *The Bad Times of Irma Baumlein,* Macmillan, 1973; Elizabeth Coatsworth, *The Wanderers,* Four Winds Press, 1973; Carol Ryrie Brink, *Caddie Woodlawn* (newly illustrated), Macmillan, 1973; Eleanor G. Vance, *The Everything Book,* Western, 1974; *Greedy Mariani,* Atheneum, 1974; *Figgie Hobbin,* Walker & Co., 1974; *You've Come a Long Way, Sybil McIntosh,* Philip J. O'Hara Co., 1974. Also illustrator of "Many Many" school textbooks and, readers.

WORK IN PROGRESS: Picture books and anthologies of folk tales.

SIDELIGHTS: "I have been illustrating books for children for fifteen years, because I love to draw, and I love stories, and I love kids. I live on a small farm in northern New Hampshire with my daughter, a friend, two dogs, nine cats, twenty-two sheep and twelve chickens. I take occa-

Christmas is not only
where you find it; it's
what you make of it.
TSH 1969

And lo! It was Christmas! ■ (From *How Six Found Christmas* by Trina Schart Hyman. Illustrated by the author.)

sional trips to England and Scandinavia (I speak Swedish, and lived in Stockholm for two years), but mostly I stay home and work. My favorite illustrators are Howard Pyle, Arthur Rackham and Jon Bauer, all of whom have probably influenced my work somewhat.''

The house on Trina Schart Hyman's farm is two-hundred-years-old and overlooks the Connecticut River. Besides raising animals, she likes to hike, canoe, and bicycle.

FOR MORE INFORMATION SEE: Horn Book, December, 1969, August, 1973.

HYMES, Lucia M(anley) 1907-

PERSONAL: Born February 6, 1907, in Marietta, Ohio; daughter of Joseph (college professor) and Florence (Lane) Manley; married James L. Hymes, Jr. (professor of education, University of Maryland), August 20, 1938; children: Lucia Lane, James L. III, Jo Ann. *Education:* Marietta College, B.A., 1927; Simmons College, B.S., 1928; Columbia University, M.A., 1936. *Residence:* Carmel, Calif.

CAREER: Teachers College, Columbia University, New York, N.Y., research assistant, Child Development Institute, 1934-36.

WRITINGS: (With James L. Hymes, Jr.) *Hooray for Chocolate,* W. R. Scott, 1960; (with J. L. Hymes, Jr.) *Oodles of Noodles,* (Junior Literary Guild selection), W. R. Scott, 1964.

"Maybe you should have a dog, Andy. Will you take care of him all by yourself?" ■ (From *Andy and Mr. Wagner* by Gina Bell. Illustrated by George Wilde.)

IANNONE, Jeanne (Koppel)
(Gina Bell, Gina Bell-Zano)

PERSONAL: Born April 1, in Philadelphia, Pa.; daughter of Walter I. (painter) and Mae (Tannenholz) Koppel; married James V. Balzano (a contractor), November 19, 1930 (died); married second husband, surname Iannone. *Education:* Brooklyn College, B.Lit. *Politics:* Democrat. *Home:* 441 Ocean Ave., Brooklyn, N.Y. 11226.

CAREER: Onetime librarian's assistant, social reporter for *Brooklyn Times,* employee of correspondence department of Abraham & Straus Department Store, all Brooklyn, N.Y., and writer of advice column for children, *Children's Playmate.*

WRITINGS—Under pseudonym Gina Bell: *Andy and Mr. Wagner,* Abingdon, 1957; *Wanted: A Brother,* Abingdon, 1959; *Good for Nothing,* Abingdon, 1961; *Three Boys and a Dog,* Abingdon, 1963; *Who Wants Willy Wells?,* Abingdon, 1965; *The Wee Moose,* Parents Magazine Press, 1965; *Presents for Johnny Jerome,* Ginn, 1966; *What Makes Siggy Smart?,* Abingdon, 1967. Contributor of about 485 stories and poems to *Humpty-Dumpty, Child Life, Instructor, Highlights for Children,* and other juvenile magazines, and of adult stories to *B'nai B'rith, Sunshine,* and others.

SIDELIGHTS: "When I was very young I used to think that people who wrote books all had long beards and wore long black suits. I never thought these people could be young or be women or even mothers. I know better now.

I love noodles. Give me oodles. ■ (From *Oodle's of Noodles* by Lucia and James L. Hymes, Jr. Illustrated by Leonard Kessler.)

"Writers are just like any other people, your mother or your father, only instead of working at a hard job, they have the wonderful chance to write stories for young people like you.

"And where do we get our ideas? From you, of course, from the things you do and the things you say, the things you like and the things you don't like, your animal friends and the places you live. I have four grandchildren (two girls and two boys) and the things they do and say, give me so many things to write about. The most wonderful thing in my life is that children read my stories and so many of them have written to tell me they like them.

"I love children, any age, any size, any color and all animals except snakes or any crawly ones. I live near the water, and boating and swimming and listening to the waves are some of my favorite things.

"Even though I am all grown up (grandmothers are), I still believe in things like elves and wishing on the new moon and four leaf clovers and listening to the sea from a big conch shell."

IONESCO, Eugene   1912-

PERSONAL: Born November 26, 1912, in Bucharest, Romania; now a French citizen; son of Eugene and Marie-Therese Ionesco; married Rodika, 1936; children: Marie-

EUGENE IONESCO

. . . here is your fruit juice, here are your rolls, here is your toast, here is your butter, here is your orange marmalade, here is your strawberry jam, here are your fried eggs, here is your ham, and here is your little girl. ■ (From *Story Number 1* by Eugene Ionesco. Illustrated by Etienne Delessert.)

France. *Education:* Educated in Bucharest and Paris; holds license es lettres, agrege de lettres. *Home:* 14, rue de Rivoli, Paris 4, France.

CAREER: Professor of French in Romania, 1936-39; worked for publisher in France; now full-time writer. *Awards, honors:* Chevalier des Arts et lettres, 1961; *Story Number 3* was a Children's Book Showcase title, 1972; Jerusalem Prize, 1973.

WRITINGS: Plays, five volumes translated by Donald Watson: (volume 1: "The Chairs," "The Bald Prima Donna," "The Lesson," "Jacques"; volume 2: "Amadee," "The New Tenant," "Victims of Duty"; volume 3: "The Killer," "Improvisation," "Maid to Marry"; volume 4: "Rhinoceros," "The Leader," "The Future is in Eggs''; volume 5: "Exit the King," "The Motor Show," "Foursome"), Calder, 1958-63; *Four Plays: The Bald Soprano; The Lesson; Jack, or, the Submission; The Chairs,* translated by Donald M. Allen, Grove, 1958; *Story Number 3,* Harlin Quist, 1971. (For complete list of writings see *Contemporary Authors,* volume 9-10.) Author of ballet, "Apprendre a Marcher," performed by Ballets Modernes de Paris. Contributor to *Les Lettres nouvelles, Les Lettres francaises, Encore, Evergreen Review,* and other publications.

FOR MORE INFORMATION SEE: Theatre Arts, March, 1958, July, 1958; Harper's Bazaar, May, 1958; Mid-Century Drama, by Laurence Kitchin, Faber, 1960; Time, December 12, 1960; Mademoiselle, April, 1961; Horizon, May, 1961; Four Playwrights and a Postscript: Brecht, Ionesco, Beckett, Genet, by David I. Grossvogel, Cornell University Press, 1962; Livres de France, October, 1963; Times Literary Supplement, 1963, page 658; New York Review of Books, July 9, 1964; New York Times Book Review, May 2, 1971, November 7, 1971.

JARMAN, Rosemary Hawley 1935-

PERSONAL: Born April 27, 1935, in Worcester, England; daughter of Charles (a master butcher) and Josephine (Hawley) Smith; divorced. Education: Until the age of eleven was educated solely by maternal grandmother, a former headmistress at British schools; attended high school in Worcester. Residence: Worcestershire, England. Agent: E.P.S. Lewin & Partners, 1 Grosvenor Court, Sloane St., London S.W.1, England.

CAREER: Worcestershire County Council, local government officer, 1960-68. Singer, specializing in lieder and oratorio work, and cellist. Member: Society of Authors, Richard III Society. Awards, honors: First Novel Award of Silver Quill (author's club), 1971, for We Speak No Treason.

WRITINGS—Novels: We Speak No Treason (Literary Guild selection), Little, Brown, 1971; The King's Grey Mare, Little, Brown, 1973. Contributor of short stories to Woman and other periodicals.

WORK IN PROGRESS: A novel about Katherine de Valois and the Valois-Tudor connections; a novel about German occupation of the Channel Islands in the 1940's.

SIDELIGHTS: "Motivation: An obsession with correctitude in English history and a compulsion to challenge the Tudor-oriented propaganda in connection with the Wars of the Roses, particularly Richard III of England. Historical research immensely important in all areas."

FOR MORE INFORMATION SEE: Bookseller, January 16, 1971, February 6, 1971; Observer (magazine section), March 14, 1971; Life, September 10, 1971; Time, January 3, 1972, August 27, 1973; Horn Book, April, 1972.

JARRELL, Randall 1914-1965

PERSONAL: Surname accented on second syllable; born May 6, 1914, in Nashville, Tenn.; son of Owen and Anna (Campbell) Jarrell; married Mary Eloise von Schrader, November 8, 1952. Education: Vanderbilt University, A.B., 1935, A.M., 1938. Address: 5706 South Lake Dr., Greensboro, N.C.

CAREER: Kenyon College, Gambier, Ohio, instructor, 1937-39; University of Texas, Austin, instructor in English, 1939-42; Sarah Lawrence College, Bronxville, N.Y., instructor in English, 1946-47; Princeton University, Princeton, N.J., visiting fellow in creative writing, 1951-52; Woman's College of the University of North Carolina (now University of North Carolina at Greensboro), associate professor, 1947-51, 1953-54, professor of English, 1958-65. Taught at the Salzburg Seminar in American Civilization, Salzburg, Austria, 1948; visiting professor, Princeton University, 1951-52, University of Illinois, 1953; consultant in poetry to the Library of Congress, 1956-58; George Elliston Lecturer, University of Cincinnati, 1958-65; Phi Beta Kappa visiting scholar, 1964-65. Military service: U.S. Army Air Forces, 1942-46; became celestial navigation tower operator. Member: Academy of American Poets (chancellor), National Institute of Arts and Letters, Phi Beta Kappa. Awards, honors: Guggenheim fellowship in poetry, 1946; Levinson prize, 1948; Oscar Blumenthal prize, 1951; National Institute of Arts and Letters grant, 1951; National Book Award, 1961, for The Woman at the Washington Zoo; O. Max Gardner award, 1962; D.II.L., Bard College, 1962; Ingram-Merrill Literary award, 1965; fellow, Indiana University School of Letters; The Juniper Tree was selected a Children's Book Showcase Title, 1974.

WRITINGS: (Contributor) Five Young American Poets, New Directions, 1940; Blood for a Stranger (poems), Harcourt, 1942; Little Friend, Little Friend (poems), Dial, 1945; Losses (poems), Harcourt, 1948; (translator) Ferdinand Gregorovius, The Ghetto and the Jews of Rome, Schocken, 1948; The Seven-League Crutches (poems), Harcourt, 1951; Poetry and the Age (criticism), Knopf, 1953; Pictures from an Institution (novel), Knopf, 1954; Selected Poems, Knopf, 1955; (editor) The Anchor Book of Stories, Doubleday Anchor, 1958; Uncollected Poems, (Cincinnati), 1958.

RANDALL JARRELL

The Woman at the Washington Zoo (poems and translations), Atheneum, 1960; (editor) *The Best Short Stories of Rudyard Kipling,* Doubleday, 1961; *A Sad Heart at the Supermarket* (essays and fables), Atheneum, 1962; (translator) Ludwig Bechstein, *The Rabbit Catcher,* Macmillan, 1962; (translator) Jakob Grimm, *The Golden Bird,* Macmillan, 1962; (editor) Rudyard Kipling, *The English in England,* Doubleday, 1963; editor) R. Kipling, *In the Vernacular: The English in India,* Doubleday, 1963; (editor) *Six Russian Short Novels,* Doubleday, 1963; *The Gingerbread Rabbit* (juvenile), Macmillan, 1963; *The Bat Poet* (juvenile), Macmillan, 1964; (translator) Anton Chekhov, "The Three Sisters," produced at Morosco Theatre, 1964; *The Lost World* (new poems), Macmillan, 1965, with an appreciation by Robert Lowell, Collier Books, 1966; *The Animal Family* (juvenile), illustrated by Maurice Sendak, Pantheon, 1965; *Randall Jarrell, 1914-1965,* edited by Lowell, Peter Taylor, Robert Penn Warren, Farrar, Straus, 1968; *Complete Poems,* Farrar, Straus, 1968; (translator) Goethe, "Faust," *Part I,* Farrar, 1971; (translator) *Snow White and the Seven Dwarfs* (illustrated by Nancy Ekholm Burkert), Farrar, Straus, 1972; (with Lore Segal) *The Juniper Tree* (illustrated by Maurice Sendak; ALA Notable Book), Farrar, Straus, 1973.

There was a lifeboat stranded at its edge: inside the boat something was crying. ■ (From *The Animal Family* by Randall Jarrell. Illustrated by Maurice Sendak.)

Was acting literary editor of *The Nation;* poetry critic, *Partisan Review,* 1949-51, *Yale Review,* 1955-57; member of editorial board, *American Scholar,* 1957-65. Contributor to *New Republic, New York Times Book Review,* and other publications.

SIDELIGHTS: Mrs. Jarrell acknowledges that her husband "had never failed or been clumsy at anything [he'd] ever done." His memory was exceptional. His wife reports that "like those grandmothers who can quote the context of the Bible wherever you open it and let your hand fall, Randall dazzled me by doing this with *Remembrance of Things Past*. . . .A game with him was to turn on the FM and guess what the music was, . . .and often he could say after one bar, Mahler! Strauss!" He could identify painters with equal facility, and sports cars. He once said that "the public has an unusual relationship to the poet: it doesn't even know that he is there." And so the majority of his friends, he believed, were the half-tamed creatures in the woods; he himself was a bat, and lived the bat-poet. Shortly before he was struck by a car and killed he suffered a nervous breakdown.

His wife writes: "Before the worst of it happened, he was granted a few magic weeks of Lisztian virtuosity when nothing in his lectures or readings was veiled to him any longer, and when everything his heart desired seemed possible. Poems flew at him, quatrains, haiku, aphorisms, parts of poems. Ideas for poems finally beat at his head like many wings." Jarrell once defined a good poet as "someone who manages, in a life time of standing out in thunderstorms, to be struck by lightning five or six times; a dozen or two dozen times and he is great." Jarrell, standing in a faerie landscape, was struck so perhaps six times.

A memorial gathering of eleven poets, including Robert Lowell, John Berryman, Robert Penn Warren, Richard Wilbur, and Stanley Kunitz, was held at Yale University, February 28, 1966.

FOR MORE INFORMATION SEE: Edward Hungerford, editor, *Poets in Progress,* Northwestern University Press, 1962, new edition, 1967; Howard Nemerov, *Poetry and Fiction,* Rutgers University Press, 1963; *New York Times,* October 16, 1965, March 2, 1966; *Commentary,* February, 1966; *Reporter,* September 8, 1966; *Harper's,* April, 1967; *Carleton Miscellany,* winter, 1967; *Partisan Review,* winter, 1967; Robert Lowell, Peter Taylor, and Robert Penn Warren, editors, *Randall Jarrell: 1914-1965,* Farrar, Straus, 1967; Karl Shapiro, *Randall Jarrell,* Library of Congress, Gertrude Clarke Whittall Poetry and Literature Fund, 1967; *Time,* September 15, 1967; *Third Book of Junior Authors,* edited by de Montreville and Hill, H. W. Wilson, 1972; *New York Times Book Review,* November 4, 1973; *New York,* November 26, 1973; *Saturday Review,* December 4, 1973.

(Died October 14, 1965)

JENKINS, Marie M(agdalen)   1909-
(Sister Mary Scholastica; W. S. Markins, a pseudonym)

PERSONAL: Born September 26, 1909, in Eldorado, Ill.; daughter of B. Robert (a teacher and salesman) and Clara Ann (Rhine) Jenkins. *Education:* Phillips University, A.B., 1929; Catholic University of America, M.S., 1951; University of Oklahoma, Ph.D., 1961. *Politics:* Republican. *Religion:* Roman Catholic. *Home:* Route 1, Box 113, Hinton, Va. 22831. *Office:* Department of Biology, Madison College, Harrisonburg, Va. 22801.

MARIE M. JENKINS

CAREER: Teacher in elementary and secondary schools of Oklahoma, 1931-42; St. Joseph's Convent, Tulsa, Okla., professed nun of Benedictine Order with religious name of Sister Mary Scholastica, 1942-57; as nun taught in Catholic high school in Tulsa, Okla., 1944-48, 1949-52, and at Benedictine Heights College, Guthrie, Okla., 1952-55; Benedictine Heights College, Tulsa, Okla., registrar, 1956-57; University of Oklahoma, Norman, instructor in zoology, 1960-62; Madison College, Harrisonburg, Va., associate professor, 1962-67, professor of biology, 1967—. *Member:* American Society of Zoologists, American Association for the Advancement of Science, American Microscopical Society, Society of Children's Book Writers, Southwestern Association of Naturalists, Virginia Academy of Science, Sigma Xi, Phi Sigma, Skyline Kennel Club (charter member; former secretary). *Awards, honors:* Grants from Virginia Academy of Science, 1963, Sigma Xi, 1964, 1966, and U.S. Public Health Service, 1966-69.

WRITINGS: (Contributor) William Corning and Stanley Ratner, editors, *Chemistry of Learning: Invertebrate Research,* Plenum, 1967; *Moon Jelly Swims Through the Sea* (juvenile), Holiday House, 1969; *Animals Without Parents* (juvenile), Holiday House, 1970; (contributor) Libbie H. Hyman, editor, *Biology of the Turbellaria,* McGraw, in press; *The Curious Mollusks* (juvenile), Holiday House, 1972. Contributor of about twenty research papers to scientific journals and articles to *Worm Runner's Digest.* Under pseudonym W. S. Markins, co-author of weekly column, "Kennel Corner," in *News-Leader,* 1971-73. Member of editorial board, *Journal of Biological Psychology.*

WORK IN PROGRESS: Continuing research and writing on reproductive activity correlated with ageing in the planarian, *Dugesia dorotocephala;* a juvenile book on comparative embryology, publication by Holiday House expected in late 1974.

SIDELIGHTS: Marie Jenkins lives alone on a ten-acre wooded tract at the foot of a mountain rise in Virginia. She raises, trains, and exhibits German shepherds, still is active in Catholic church affairs, and "very interested in conservation, but feels too strongly about it to write on it."

"I began reading when I was three and have read voraciously ever since. I earned my first money, a nickel, about that time by reading from a speller for a lady who came to visit my mother. When I was twelve, my teacher wrote on the board the names of all her pupils and, after each one, the profession or career each individual wished to follow. Without hesitation I told her, "A writer and artist." She thought I wanted to be an expert in penmanship and insisted, on learning the truth of the matter, in changing "writer" to "author". I didn't like the change then, and still don't. I have no idea why.

"I wrote poems during most of my teens—two or three hundred of them. A few were published but none were purchased. My father insisted I become a teacher so I could earn my living. I took the courses and obtained a lifetime certificate but refused to use it for a couple of years until the depression came along, and I had to choose between teaching and eating or not teaching and not eating. I have taught ever since, and have never wanted to. I retired in the spring of 1974. I enjoy teaching as long as I am telling people something interesting but I heartily detest drills, tests, exams, committee meetings, counselling, extra-curricular activities, teacher's meetings, professional journals, books on methods, and all the other non-interesting paraphernalia of the teaching profession. I have taught every grade, without exception, from kindergarten through graduate college work, and have taught every basic high-school subject.

"I have written sporadically all these years but no one ever accepted anything I sent in—probably because I wasn't really interested in writing for magazines. I didn't enjoy reading magazines of any kind and it follows that any thing I would write for them would have little enthusiasm to bolster it. I love to read books, particulary Gothics, books on nature and tales of interesting personal experiences. I am especially fond of books for children and teen-agers, my favorites in this area being mystery stories and books on animals, especially dogs.

"In 1966, I received a $50,000 three-year research grant from Health, Education and Welfare (HD-02217). It was MOST unsatisfactory. Because of all the red tape involved, I had even less time than before to spend on research. I got so fed up I decided it was high time to get seriously started in doing what I'd always wanted to do: write. I enrolled in a correspondence course with the University of Oklahoma and about half-way through it I decided I just couldn't wait another minute to start writing. I was about half-way through a book on one of my favorite subjects, planarians, so I sent a couple of chapters, together with a letter, to Edward Lindemann at Holiday House. He wasn't interested in that book but he was interested in my doing one on

Usually he ate snails, or crabs and other crustaceans, but he had found none for a long time and he was very hungry. ■ (From *Moon Jelly* by Marie M. Jenkins. Illustrated by Rene Martin.)

another subject. The result was Moon Jelly (1969). I have written two more books for him and am under contract for a fourth, but I still can't get him to let me do a book on planarians. I'll never be satisfied until I get one or two done; one for children 6-10, and another for older youngsters. (I finally finished the writing course a year late.)"

JOHNSON, Elizabeth   1911-

PERSONAL: Born October 10, 1911, in Swampscott, Mass.; daughter of Fred May and Elizabeth (Lewis) Johnson. *Education:* Wellesley College, A.B., 1933; Simmons College, B.S., 1935. *Home:* 42 Walker Rd., Swampscott, Mass. *Office:* Lynn Public Library, North Common St., Lynn, Mass.

CAREER: Public Library, Rochester, N.Y., children's librarian, 1935-37; Public Library, Lynn, Mass., supervisor, work with children, 1937—. *Member:* American Library Association, Women's National Book Association.

WRITINGS: The Little Knight, Little, Brown, 1957; *The Three-in-One Prince,* Little, Brown, 1961; *No Magic, Thank You,* Little, Brown, 1964; *Stuck with Luck,* Little, Brown, 1967; *All in Free but Janey,* Little, Brown, 1968; *Break a Magic Circle* (Child Study Association book list), Little, Brown, 1971.

With his bicycle basket full of dog, lunch, book and leprechaun, Tom pedaled out from town toward the park. ■ (From *Stuck with Luck* by Elizabeth Johnson. Illustrated by Trina Schart Hyman.)

ELIZABETH JOHNSON

SIDELIGHTS: "Because I was a storyteller in the public library, I was very interested in fairy stories and stories of magic. My very first book, *The Little Knight*, was because I couldn't find any story where a princess did anything interesting. I was sure there must have been one somewhere who had spunk, so I made her up! Once someone likes something you've written it's a great incentive to keep on writing. So that's how it all happened."

FOR MORE INFORMATION SEE: Horn Book, October, 1971.

JOHNSON, Gaylord   1884-

PERSONAL: Born February 8, 1884, in Adrian, Mich.; son of Jacob Schuyler (a dentist) and Celeste (Barrette)

The big surprise in the animal kingdom is the Hippopotamus. It is distantly related to our everyday barnyard hog. ■ (From *The Story of Animals* by Gaylord Johnson. Illustrated by Don Bolognese.)

Johnson; married Alice Bagley Hall (a Christian Science practitioner), August 31, 1947. *Education:* University of Michigan, student, 1902-04. *Politics:* Republican. *Religion:* Christian Scientist. *Home:* 11 Fifth Ave., New York, N.Y. 10003.

CAREER: Copy writer, specializing in mail order copy for books and educational courses, with five advertising agencies in New York, N.Y., 1920-47, with agency in Minneapolis, Minn., 1947-48; independent consultant on mail order advertising copy, 1948—. Author and illustrator.

WRITINGS—All self-illustrated, except as indicated: *The Star People,* Macmillan, 1921; *The Sky Movies,* Macmillan, 1922; *Nature's Program,* Doubleday, 1926; *The Stars for children* (contains *The Star People* and *The Sky Movies*), Macmillan, 1934; *Discover the Stars,* Leisure League of America, 1935, revised edition (with Irving Adler) published as *Discover the Stars: A Beginner's Guide to the Science of Astronomy and the Earth Satellite,* Sentinel Books, 1954; *Hunting with the Microscope,* Leisure League of America, 1936, revised edition (with Maurice Bleifeld and Charles Tanzer) published as *Hunting with the Microscope: A Beginner's Guide to Exploring the Micro-World of Plants and Animals,* Sentinel Books, 1956; *The Story of Earthquakes and Volcanoes,* Messner, 1938; *How Father Time Changes the Animals' Shapes,* Messner, 1939; *Our Solar System,* Doubleday, 1955; *The Story of Animals: Mammals Around the World,* illustrated by Don Bolognese, Harvey House, 1958; *The Story of Planets, Space and Stars,* illustrated by Frank Angelini, Harvey House, 1959. Contributor of some forty articles on astronomy and natural history to *Popular Science Monthly,* 1932-39.

WORK IN PROGRESS: Biographies of Antoni Van Leeuwenhoek, Robert Hooke, and Christopher Wren; research on Lafayette's triumphal tour of United States in 1824-25; research for brief biographies of Biblical characters.

HOBBIES AND OTHER INTERESTS: Watercolor painting; Biblical archaeology and its effects on Bible history.

146

JOHNSON, William Weber 1909-

PERSONAL: Born December 18, 1909, in Mattoon, Ill.; son of Finis Ewing (a railroadman) and Jessie (Weber) Johnson; married second wife, Elizabeth Ann McMurray, October 7, 1951; children: (first marriage) Peter W., Jane (Mrs. Ronald Jones); stepchildren: Richard Ellegood. *Education:* De Pauw University, B.A., 1932; University of Illinois, M.A., 1933. *Politics:* Democratic. *Religion:* Unitarian Universalist. *Address:* Box 3056, Warner Springs, Calif. 92086. *Office:* Department of Journalism, University of California, Los Angeles, Calif. 90024.

CAREER: Newspaper reporter in Decatur, Ill., 1933-34; reporter and city editor, Urbana and Decatur, Ill., 1934-37; Associated Press, reporter, Detroit, Mich., 1937-39; N.W. Ayer, Inc., writer and public relations adviser, Chicago, Ill., and New York, N.Y., 1939-40; Time, Inc., New York, N.Y., contributing editor, 1940-43, war correspondent in Europe, 1944-45, bureau chief (sometimes of combined *Life* and *Time* bureaus), in Mexico City, 1945-47, Buenos Aires, 1947-48, Dallas, 1948-53, Boston, 1954-57, correspondent, Beverly Hills, Calif. 1958-61; University of California, Los Angeles, professor of journalism, 1961—. *Awards, honors:* Mentioned in (British) dispatches twice while war correspondent; Guggenheim fellowship to write *Kelly Blue,* 1959; Commonwealth Club gold medal for non-fiction, 1909.

WRITINGS: *Sam Houston, the Tallest Texan* (juvenile),

WILLIAM WEBER JOHNSON

Random House, 1953; *The Birth of Texas* (juvenile), Houghton, 1960; *Captain Cortes Conquers Mexico* (juvenile), Random House, 1960; *Kelly Blue* (biography), Doubleday, 1960; *Mexico,* Time/Life Books, 1961; *The Andean Republics,* Time/Life Books, 1965; *Heroic Mexico,* Doubleday, 1968; *Baja California,* Time/Life, 1972; *The Story of Sea Otters,* Random House, 1973; *The Forty Niners,* Time/Life, 1974. Contributor to periodicals, including *Holiday, Saturday Evening Post, Life en Espanol, New York Times Book Review, West, Westways, Nature/Science Yearbook, Smithsonian.*

WORK IN PROGRESS: Biography of Hernan Cortes.

SIDELIGHTS: "Have been writing since mid-teens. Early efforts mainly fiction and poetry, wholly unsuccessful. Experience as journalist helped establish career as non-fiction writer."

HOBBIES AND OTHER INTERESTS: History, nature and photography—"latter two often combined."

JONES, Adrienne 1915-

PERSONAL: Born July 28, 1915, in Atlanta, Ga.; daughter of Arthur Washington and Orianna (Mason) Applewhite; married Richard Morris Jones, 1939; children: Gregory, Gwen. *Education:* Educated at Theosophical School of the Open Gate and in Beverly Hills, Calif., public schools; largely self-educated. *Politics:* Liberal Democrat. *Religion:* Grew up a Theosophist; later Episcopalian; more recently Unitarian-Universalist. *Home:* 24491 Los Serranos Dr., Laguna Niguel, Calif. 92677.

CAREER: Professional free-lance writer and novelist; has also worked as an office and managerial worker, cattle rancher, and with youth groups. Speaker at conferences, schools, libraries, and writers' groups. *Member:* P.E.N., American Civil Liberties Union, National Association for the Advancement of Colored People, Audubon Society, Southern California Council on Literature for Children and Young People, California Writers Guild, Southern Christian Leadership Conference. *Awards, honors:* Southern California Council on Children and Young People award for "best book by a Southern California author," 1972, for *Another Place, Another Spring.*

WRITINGS: *Thunderbird Pass,* Lippincott, 1952; *Where Eagles Fly,* Putnam, 1957; *Ride the Far Wind* (juvenile) Little, Brown, 1964; *Wild Voyageur: Story of a Canada Goose* (juvenile), Little, Brown, 1966; *Sail, Calypso!* (juvenile), Little, Brown, 1968; *Another Place, Another Spring,* Houghton, 1971; *Hawk* (short story), Bank Street College of Education, 1972; *My Name is Gnorr with an Unsilent G* (short story), Bank Street College of Education, 1972; *Old Witch Hannifin and Her Shoonaget* (short story), Bank Street College of Education, 1972; *Niki and Albert and the Seventh Street Raiders,* Bank Street College of Education, 1972; *Who Needs a Hand to Hold?,* Bank Street College of Education, 1973; *The Mural Master,* Houghton, 1974; *So, Nothing Is Forever,* Houghton, 1974. Excerpts from books anthologized in *Bright Horizons: A Collection,* Scott, Foresman, 1969, and in *On the Edge,* Ginn, 1970.

ADRIENNE JONES

CAREER: Became cartoonist at seventeen, drawing for *Berliner Tageblatt, Berliner Morgenpost,* and magazines in Germany, 1921-36; cartoonist and reporter for *Praeger Tagblatt* and *Czesko Slovo* in Czechoslovakia, 1936-39; cartoonist for *London Sketch, Blighty,* and *Everybody's* in England, and reporter for *Glasgow Herald* in Scotland, 1939-46; came to United States in 1946 and worked as writer and artist on comic strips for Dell magazines; now writer and illustrator of children's books. *Awards, honors:* Gold Medal Junior Book Award of Boys' Clubs of America, for *The Adventure of Light, 1958.*

WRITINGS: *The Haunted Department Store,* Collins; *Nothing to Wear but Clothes,* Aladdin, 1953; *The Mailbox Takes a Holiday,* Macmillan, 1953; *Nothing to Eat but Food,* Aladdin, 1954; *Hinkeldinkl,* Macmillan, 1955; *The Wishing Shoe,* Abelard, 1955; *Up the Trail and Down the Street,* Macmillan, 1956; *The Sweetest Story Ever Told,* Sterling, 1956; *Read All About It,* Prentice-Hall, 1957; *The Day It Happened,* Macmillan, 1958; *The Adventure of Light,* Prentice-Hall, 1958; *The March of Trade,* Prentice-Hall, 1960; *The Story of Sports,* Dodd, 1960; *Sports, Sports Everywhere,* Dodd, 1962; *Time to Spare,* Prentice-Hall, 1962; *Walls, Gates and Avenues,* Prentice-Hall, 1964; *Any Mail For Me?,* Dodd, 1964; *Count Carrot,* Holiday, 1966; *No Place Too Far,* Dodd, 1967; *Atu, the Silent One,* Holiday, 1967; *A Day Around the World,* Abelard, 1968; *The Story of the Three R's,* Prentice-Hall, 1970; *People and Things in Early Greece,* Grosset, 1971; *The Story of Things,* Prentice-Hall, 1972; *A Place to Stay,* Dodd, 1973; *To Carry and to Hold,* Dodd, 1975. Contributor to *Story Parade.*

WORK IN PROGRESS: Research on the historical background of the Bill of Rights for a series of short stories; a novel set in the 40's, prior to World War II.

SIDELIGHTS: "My endeavor is to learn and understand the feelings and reasons behind the human act, the human mind and heart. In my writing the effort is to portray the brotherhood and friendship that is found in its most vital and active form in the world of the young, yet to understand, and reveal the personal tragedies and failures which are so much a part of life. I have chosen to write mainly for young people, as this is the nearest one can come to touching the future. To me it is the most exciting field of writing." Ms. Jones' books have been published in Germany, Austria, Denmark, the Netherlands, Italy, and Japan.

HOBBIES AND OTHER INTERESTS: Travel, books, music, beach-rambling, mountaineering, conservation activities, conversation.

FOR MORE INFORMATION SEE: *Horn Book,* February, 1972, June, 1974.

JUPO, Frank J. 1904-

PERSONAL: Born February 28, 1904, in Dessau, Germany; son of Max and Rosa Potzernheim; married October 28, 1944; wife's name, Edith. *Education:* Attended schools in Dessau. *Home:* 99-72 66th Rd., Forest Hills, N.Y.

SIDELIGHTS: "My original wish was to become a journalist. I did not attend art school, but my first handiest means of expression was doing cartoons. After some newspaper writing (in German) in Prague, Czechoslovakia, and cartooning as a refugee in wartime England, I started writing and illustrating children's books at the plea of a publisher who had lost most of his writers to the draft.

"My first books were picture books, but I was pushed by an immense curiosity to find out how man lived in times past and in countries far away, and wanting to share this knowledge, started writing the kind of books I write now.

But, overturned by messengers afraid of losing their livelihood, or used for garbage disposals, the first appearance of the mailbox was only a limited success. ■ (From *Any Mail for Me?* by Frank Jupo. Illustrated by the author.)

"To have the books just the way I want them, I do it all: from conceiving the idea to doing the dummy, plus writing the captions—and, of course, the text—and choosing the type, and, naturally, doing the illustrations.

"My working habits include a regular, six days a week: getting up at six, starting work at eight, a three hour break for lunch and—at least—one hour's walk. I then continue to work until five or six. I'm in best condition early in the morning. I do lots of research—pictorial and otherwise and plenty of reading—historical and biographical—squeezing in six weeks of travel to outlandish places."

HOBBIES AND OTHER INTERESTS: The sea; social history, customs, and costumes.

FRANCIS KALNAY

KALNAY, Francis   1899-

PERSONAL: Surname is pronounced *Kal*-nay; born July 18, 1899, in Budapest, Hungary; came to United States, 1919; divorced; children: Elizabeth Tagora, Maria Peti, Peter. *Education:* Attended Nautical Academy. *Home:* 25005 Outlook Dr., Carmel, Calif. 93921.

CAREER: Has been farmer, journalist, actor, and done educational film work. *Military service:* U.S. Army, 1941-45. *Awards, honors: Chucaro, Wild Pony of the Pampa* received a *New York Herald Tribune* Children's Spring Book Festival Award, 1958, and was a Newbery Medal Honor Book.

WRITINGS: (Editor with Richard Collins) *The New America: A Handbook of Necessary Information for Aliens, Refugees, and New Citizens,* Greenberg, 1941; *Chucaro, Wild Pony of the Pampa* (juvenile), Harcourt, 1958; *The Richest Boy in the World* (autobiographical juvenile), Harcourt, 1959; *It Happened in Chichipica* (juvenile), Harcourt, 1971. Contributor of articles on gastronomy to *House Beautiful.*

WORK IN PROGRESS: A book for young children with Sierra Madre setting; short stories on adult theme.

SIDELIGHTS: "Love the open road, a well equipped kitchen and my children and grandchildren. When at home in Carmel, Calif., divide my time between my study and my garden. The latter gets most attention."

FOR MORE INFORMATION SEE: Horn Book, October, 1971.

FRANK JUPO

On market days the afternoon bus for the state capitol was so packed that it appeared ready to burst at the seams. ▪ (From *It Happened in Chichipica* by Francis Kalnay. Illustrated by Charles Robinson.)

KELLY, Ralph
See GEIS, Darlene

KINDRED, Wendy (Good) 1937-

PERSONAL: Born December 19, 1937, in Detroit, Mich.; daughter of Charles Roger and Ida (Berndt) Good; married, 1960 (divorced, 1968); children: Audrey Lauren and Jessica Berit (twins). *Education:* Student at Western College for Women, 1955-56, and University of Vienna, 1956-57; University of Chicago, B.F.A., 1959, M.F.A., 1963. *Home:* 9 Alfred St., Fort Kent, Me. 04743. *Office:* University of Maine, Fort Kent, Mc. 04743.

CAREER: High school teacher of art in Harvey, Ill., 1960-62; School of Fine Arts, Addis Ababa, Ethiopia, teacher of art history and graphics, 1965-69; University of Maine at Fort Kent, assistant professor of art, 1973—. Children's Community Workshop School, New York, coordinator, 1971. Painter and graphic artist; writer and illustrator of children's books. *Awards, honors:* Weekly Reader Children's Book Club fellowship to Bread Loaf Writers' Conference, 1971; Fehsenfeld Award for painting, Indiana Artists Exhibition at Indianapolis Museum of Art, 1973.

WRITINGS–Self-illustrated: *Negatu in the Garden*, McGraw, 1971; *Ida's Idea*, McGraw, 1972; *Lucky Wilma*, Dial, 1973.

WENDY KINDRED

Negatu began to wish he had somebody to play with, so he looked in the window to see what Yeshi and Phyllis and Tina were doing. ■ (From *Negatu in the Garden* by Wendy Kindred. Illustrated by the author.)

SIDELIGHTS: Lived in Ethiopia, where her children were born, for five years, and has also lived in Greece, Austria, and France.

FOR MORE INFORMATION SEE: Horn Book, April, 1973.

KING, Cynthia 1925-

PERSONAL: Born August 27, 1925, in New York, N.Y.; daughter of Adolph (a metallurgical engineer) and Elsie (a psychologist; maiden name, Oschrin) Bregman; married Jonathan King (an architect), July 26, 1944; children: Gordon, Austin, Nathaniel. *Education:* Attended Bryn Mawr College, 1943-44, University of Chicago, 1944-46, New York University Writers Workshop, 1967-69. *Home:* 680 Flintdale, Houston, Tex. 77024.

CAREER: Hillman Periodicals, New York, N.Y., associate editor, 1946-51; Fawcett Publications, New York, N.Y., managing editor, 1951-56; The Awty School, Houston, Tex., teacher of creative writing, 1973—; *Member:* Associated Authors of Children's Literature.

WRITINGS: In the Morning of Time: The Story of the Norse God Balder (juvenile), Four Winds, 1970. Contributor of articles and stories to periodicals. Editor, *Greenacres Gazette;* book reviewer, *Houston Chronicle,* 1971-72.

WORK IN PROGRESS: Fiction for young readers; synthesis of teaching experiences for adults.

SIDELIGHTS: "Over the years my major interests have changed and grown to include reading, working, and writing about and for children of various ages, and their relationship to fantasy and realities of their lives. It was with this in mind that I became interested in fictionalizing the body of Norse mythology, which seemed to allow expression of common angers and frustrations that 'realistic' fiction could not. I have traveled some in Europe and particularly the time I spent in Scandinavia and Finland affected my literary ambitions. I believe that children respond totally to high quality prose or poetry, and if it is lacking, interest wanes."

FOR MORE INFORMATION SEE: Library Journal, May 15, 1970; *Horn Book,* August, 1970.

KLEIN, Norma 1938-

PERSONAL: Born May 13, 1938, in New York, N.Y.; daughter of Emanuel (a psychoanalyst) and Sadie (Frankel) Klein; married Erwin Fleissner (a biochemist), July 27, 1963; children: Jennifer Luise, Katherine Nicole. *Education:* Cornell University, student, 1956-57; Barnard College, B.A. (cum laude), 1960; Columbia University, M.A., 1963. *Politics:* Democrat. *Religion:* None. *Home:* 29 West 96th St., New York, N.Y. 10025. *Agent:* (juvenile books) Elaine Markson, 44 Greenwich Ave., New York, N.Y. 10011; (adult books) Cyrilly Abels, 119 West 57th St., New York, N.Y. 10019.

CAREER: Free-lance writer. *Member:* Phi Beta Kappa.

WRITINGS: Love and Other Euphemisms (novel and five short stories), Putnam, 1972; *Mom, the Wolfman and Me* (juvenile novel), Pantheon, 1972; *Girls Can Be Anything* (Junior Literary Guild selection), Dutton, 1973; *It's Not What You Expect* (juvenile novel), Pantheon, 1973; *If I Had It My Way* (juvenile), Pantheon, 1973; *Give Me One Good Reason* (adult), Putnam, 1973; *Taking Sides* (juvenile), Pantheon, 1974; *Confessions of an Only Child* (juvenile), Pantheon, 1974; *Dinosaur's Housewarming Party* (Junior Literary Guild selection), Crown, 1974; *Naomi in the Middle* (juvenile), Dial, 1974; *A Train for Jane* (juvenile), Feminist Press, 1974; *Sunshine* (novelization of TV movie), Avon, 1974; *Coming to Life* (adult), Simon & Schuster, 1974. Work is anthologized in *Prize Stories 1963: The O. Henry Awards; Prize Stories 1968: The O Henry Awards; The Best American Short Stories of 1969.* Contributor of about sixty short stories to magazines, including *Sewanee Review, Mademoiselle, Prairie Schooner,* and *Denver Quarterly.*

WORK IN PROGRESS: Untitled juvenile novel.

SIDELIGHTS: "I was born and have lived all my life in New York City, a city I still love. My parents are Jewish but not religious, left-wing politically, open-minded. I have one brother, sixteen months younger than myself who is a social worker. I attended private schools, Dalton from the age of three to thirteen, Elizabeth Irwin High School, both

NORMA KLEIN

We brought the hot dogs and potato chips and some orange punch into our tents and ate in there. We pretended William was a wild beast since he kept lurking outside the tent, sniffing the hot dogs. ■ (From *Confessions of an Only Child* by Norma Klein. Illustrated by Richard Cuffari.)

coeducational and progressive. I spent my freshman year of college at Cornell, then transferred to Barnard where I graduated cum laude, Phi Beta Kappa in 1960. I was a Russian major in college, mainly due to my love of Chekhov, and went on to receive an M.A. in Slavic Languages from Columbia in 1963. I took writing courses in college, from W. D. Snodgrass at Cornell and George P. Elliott and Robert Pack at Barnard. In 1958 I published my first short story and have since published about sixty of them, mainly in literary quarterlies such as *The Sewanee Review* and *Denver Quarterly,* a few in the big magazines such as *Mademoiselle* and *Cosmopolitan.* Several of these stories were anthologized, in *Prize Stories of 1963, Prize Stories of 1968, Prize Stories of 1974 (O. Henry Awards),* and *The Best American Short Stories of 1969.*

"At the age of twenty-one, while studying at Barnard, I met my husband, a research biochemist. We have two daughters. In the decade from 1960 to 1970, I mainly devoted myself to writing short stories. But I found it was impossible to get a short story collection published without having written a novel. So, in 1970 I wrote a novel, *Pratfalls,* which was finally published with five of my already published short stories. I gradually became converted to writing novels and imagine that I will not return to short stories for a long time. It saddens me that there is so little interest in stories in America today, but I've decided not to spend my life fighting it.

"I began writing children's books after reading the millionth picture book to my older daughter and figuring I would like to give it a try. An agent suggested that I would have an easier time getting a novel for eight-to-twelve-year olds accepted than a picture book so I wrote one, *Mom, The Wolfman and Me.* I found I enjoyed writing for children very much, partly perhaps because I got such a warm response to *Mom.* I've since had many children's books published and hope to do more.

"I hope to continue writing both adult and juvenile fiction. What appeals to me in the latter is the opportunity to write for different age groups, from picture books to teenage novels. I find having children, observing them, is invaluable in this regard. I also find that a 100-page manuscript, a length I find very congenial, is considered a novel in children's books and can be published on its own. What draws me most, however, is that I feel the children's book field has been and is still, very weighed down by taboos on many subjects, on abortion, sex, the human body, etc. I feel one could write a book a year till one was just touching on each of these taboos. As a feminist, I especially want to write for girls, but girls who are active intellectually, who are strong, interesting people. I'd like parents and adults in general to be portrayed in children's books as they are, with faults, as children really see them. I'd like all this to be done nondidactically, humorously in books that are fun to read and I hope not just me but many others will make the same effort since it's so important. We need books where children masturbate, think about their parents sex lives, enjoy the physical sensations provided by their bodies. We need books that are non-punitive, open, honest. There aren't enough, not nearly.

"My own life is quiet, middle class. We live on the West Side of Manhattan in a six-room apartment, near Central Park where we play tennis. I write every morning 9-12, then go out for lunch with friends, walks, shopping. I usually come home in the late afternoon, play with the children, cook.

"As a teenage, I traveled to Europe a fair amount, on bicycle trips to France (The Experiment in International Living), to England, to Russia during a Youth Festival (1957). But I haven't been back since my honeymoon in 1963. We usually spend a month during the summer in the town where my husband grew up, Aurora, in upstate New York. It's peaceful and very pleasant.

"I studied French for many years, Russian, Czech, German but am afraid to speak any of them. I used to be able to read French and Russian, but am not sure I'd remember.

"I read constantly, love fiction, hate non-fiction. My favorites are, after Chekhov: Jane Austen, E. M. Forster, Philip Roth (his early work), Joyce Carol Oates, (her stories, her novels are too violent for my taste), Trollope, Shaw, Oscar Wilde, Dostoevsky, Margaret Drabble, Shirley Hazzard, Edna O'Brien, Alison Lurie, Sue Kaufman, Seymour Epstein, Gilliam Tindall, Andrea Newman, L. Woiwode....In children's books I like Judy Blume, Paul Zindel, Constance C. Greene, E. B. White, Louise Fitzhugh, Noel Streatfield, Laura Ingalls Wilder, Astrid Lindgren, Elizabeth Enright, Paula Fox. In general, I guess I prefer realistic fiction, humorous if possible, not autobiographical sounding."

FOR MORE INFORMATION SEE: Horn Book, February, 1973; *Junior Literary Guild Catalogue,* March, 1973; *New York Times Book Review,* June 3, 1973.

KNUDSON, R. R.
See KNUDSON, Rozanne

KNUDSON, Rozanne   1932-
(R. R. Knudson)

PERSONAL: Surname is pronounced Nude-son; born June 1, 1932, in Washington, D.C.; daughter of James K. (a lawyer) and Ruth (Ellsworth) Knudson. *Education:* Brigham Young University, B.A., 1954; University of Georgia, M.A., 1955; Stanford University, Ph.D., 1967. *Politics:* Liberal. *Religion:* Church of Jesus Christ of Latter-Day Saints (Mormon). *Home:* 73 The Boulevard, Sea Cliff, Long Island, N.Y. 11579. *Agent:* McIntosh & Otis, Inc., 18 East 41st St., New York, N.Y. 10017.

CAREER: Teacher of English at public high schools in Florida, 1957-60; Purdue University, Lafayette, Ind., assistant professor of English, 1965-67; Hicksville Schools, Hicksville, N.Y., supervisor of English, 1967-70; City University of New York, York College, Jamaica, N.Y., assistant professor of English, 1970-72; full-time writer, 1972—. Visiting instructor at University of Lethbridge, summer, 1969. *Member:* National Council of Teachers of English, Authors League of America, American Civil Liberties Union.

WRITINGS—Under name R. R. Knudson, except as noted: (Under name Rozanne Knudson; with Arnold L.

Lazarus) *Selected Objectives for the English Language Arts, Grades 7-12,* Houghton, 1967; (editor with P. K. Ebert) *Sports Poems,* Dell, 1971; *Zanballer* (teen novel), Delacorte, 1972; *Jesus Song* (teen novel), Delacorte, 1973; *You Are the Rain* (teen novel), Delacorte, 1974; *Fox Running* (teen novel), Harper, 1975. Contributor to *Books for You,* revised edition, Washington Square Press, 1971, and to education and library journals. Co-editor, *Quartet,* 1966-68.

WORK IN PROGRESS: Zanbanger, a sequel to *Zanballer; I Came to Love, I Came Into My Own,* a novel for adults.

SIDELIGHTS: "I have never wanted to be a writer. I would much rather read and do, at the rate of usually two books a day, mostly fiction and poetry. I consider myself a friend of writers, buy tons of books, hound librarians and English teachers to supply me. I live with May Swenson so have even met lots of writers, all of whom I lionize.

"I started writing to survive in the publish-or-perish business of professoring: articles for professional journals, reviews, ghost writing for full professors who helped pay my way through graduate schools." On the advice of an editor at Delacorte, Miss Knudson wrote her football novel, *Zanballer,* and completed it in 38 days. "It's an autobiography and led to my downfall as a professor ('fiction doesn't count' I was told by a dean). I'm now a full-time writer until I run out of savings."

FOR MORE INFORMATION SEE: Publishers' Weekly, April 16, 1973.

ROZANNE KNUDSON

Manfred: You should cast aside silly ball games and turn to less aggressive, less tomboyish pursuits. Zan: Like what . . . sir! Manfred: Well, dear, if you must be a sports fan, why not join the cheerleaders. ■ (From *Zanballer* by R. R. Knudson. Jacket designed by Paul Bacon.)

LATTIMORE, Eleanor Frances 1904-

PERSONAL: Born June 30, 1904, in Shanghai, China; daughter of American nationals, David (a professor at Chinese universities, later at Dartmouth college) and Margaret (Barnes) Lattimore; married Robert Armstrong Andrews (a free-lance writer and designer), November 29, 1934 (died, 1963); children: Peter van Etten, Michael Cameron. *Education:* Educated at home by father; studied art at California School of Arts and Crafts, 1920-22, at Art Students League and Grand Central School of Art, New York, N.Y., 1924. *Home:* 307 Romany Rd., Lexington, Ky. 40502.

CAREER: Grew up in China, spent a year in Switzerland as a child, and came to United States with parents in 1920; after art school worked as a free-lance artist until 1930; writer of children's stories, and illustrator, mainly of own books, 1930—. Work exhibited in group shows at galleries in Boston, New York, and Charleston, S.C., and represented in permanent collections of libraries throughout the United States.

WRITINGS—Self-illustrated juveniles, all published by Morrow except as otherwise indicated: *Little Pear: The*

Story of a Little Chinese Boy, Harcourt, 1931; *Jerry and the Pusa*, Harcourt, 1932; *The Seven Crowns*, Harcourt, 1933; *Little Pear and His Friends*, Harcourt, 1934; *Turkestan Reunion*, Day, 1934; *The Lost Leopard*, Harcourt, 1935; *The Clever Cat*, Harcourt, 1936; *Junior, a Colored Boy of Charleston*, Harcourt, 1938; *Jonny*, Harcourt, 1939.

The Story of Lee Ling, Harcourt, 1940; *The Questions of Lifu: A Story of China*, Harcourt, 1942; *Storm on the Island*, Harcourt, 1942; *Peachblossom*, Harcourt, 1943; *First Grade*, Harcourt, 1944; *Bayou Boy*, 1946, *Jeremy's Isle*, 1947, *Three Little Chinese Girls*, 1948, *Davy of the Everglades*, 1949, *Deborah's White Winter*, 1949.

Christopher and His Turtle, 1950, *Indigo Hill*, 1950, *Bells for a Chinese Donkey*, 1951, *The Fig Tree*, 1951, *Lively Victoria*, 1952, *Jasper*, 1953, *Wu, the Gatekeeper's Son*, 1953, *Holly in the Snow*, 1954, *Diana in the China Shop*, 1955, *Willow Tree Village*, 1955, *Molly in the Middle*, 1956, *Little Pear and the Rabbits*, 1956, *The Journey of Ching Lai*, 1957, *The Monkey of Crofton*, 1957, *Fair Bay*, 1958, *Happiness for Kimi*, 1958, *The Fisherman's Son*, 1959, *The Youngest Artist*, 1959.

Beachcomber Boy, 1960, *The Chinese Daughter*, 1960, *Cousin Melinda*, 1961, *The Wonderful Glass House*, 1961, *The Bittern's Nest*, 1962, *Laurie and Company*, 1962, *Janetta's Magnet*, 1963, *The Little Tumbler*, 1963, *Felicia*, 1964, *The Mexican Bird*, 1965, *The Bus Trip*, 1965, *The Search for Christina*, 1966, *The Two Helens*, 1967, *Bird Song*, 1968, *The Girl on the Deer*, 1969.

The Three Firecrackers, 1970, *More About Little Pear*, 1971, *A Similar Face*, 1973.

As Josephine looked over the stair rail she saw a light switched on below. It was not the hall light that was usually kept burning, but a flashlight. . . . ■ (From *The Girl on the Deer* by Eleanor Frances Lattimore. Illustrated by the author.)

Illustrator: Bertha Metzger, *Picture Tales from the Chinese*, Stokes, 1934; E. Freivogel, *All Around the City*, Missionary Education Movement, 1938.

Contributor of short stories to *Jack and Jill*, *Story Parade*, *Trailways*, *American Junior Red Cross Magazine*, and *Christian Science Monitor*.

SIDELIGHTS: Miss Lattimore's books have been translated for publication abroad, transcribed into Braille.

FOR MORE INFORMATION SEE: Junior Book of Authors, edited by Kunitz and Haycraft, H. W. Wilson, 1934, new edition, 1951; Bertha E. Miller, *Illustrators of Children's Books 1946-56*, Horn Book, 1958.

ELEANOR FRANCES LATTIMORE

LAURENCE, Ester Hauser 1935-

PERSONAL: Born July 27, 1935, in Charleston, N.Y.; daughter of John and Edna (Stead) Hauser; married Joseph P. Laurence (a geophysicist), June 17, 1955; children: Daniel, William, John and Jeff (twins). *Education:* University of Wisconsin, B.S., 1957. *Politics:* Democrat. *Religion:* Unitarian Universalist. *Home:* 2858 Stevens St., Madison, Wis. 53705.

There were yummy-looking horns of different sizes. But B-9 didn't eat any of them. ■ (From *B-9 The Hungry Metal Eater* by Ester Hauser Laurence. Illustrated by Ron Bradford.)

ESTER HAUSER LAURENCE

CAREER: During her college days worked as cashier in a cafeteria and tended the Wisconsin seismograph station. Madison Interracial Study Group, co-chairman, 1969. Teaches writing, University of Wisconsin extension, 1972—. *Member:* Wisconsin Fellowship of Poets, Council for Wisconsin Writers, Madison Area Writers' Workshop. *Awards, honors:* Honorable mention for children's book, Council for Wisconsin Writers, 1970.

WRITINGS: We're Off to Catch a Dragon (juvenile), Abingdon, 1969; *B-9 The Hungry Metal Eater* (easy reader), Rand McNally, 1972.

WORK IN PROGRESS: No-Hassle Bread Making; several juveniles.

SIDELIGHTS: Ms. Laurence has made up fantasy songs and stories as long as she can remember. She feels that it is significant that she was "a welfare kid and a foster child," mentioning this in the hope that it may encourage some other disadvantaged child to achieve his goal.

FOR MORE INFORMATION SEE: Horn Book, December, 1969.

LESLIE, Robert Franklin   1911-

PERSONAL: Born October 21, 1911, in Dublib, Tex.; son of Frank and Anna May (Morrison) Leslie; married Lea Rochat, September 13, 1937. *Education:* University of California, Santa Barbara, B.A., 1939; University of Southern California, M.A., 1942. *Politics:* Republican. *Religion:* Episcopalian. *Home:* 4555 Longridge Ave., Sherman Oaks, Calif. 91403.

CAREER: Teacher of French, Spanish, Latin, and English at high school level in schools in Pasedena, North Holly-wood, and Carpinteria, Calif., 1939-72. Conductor of photographic tours throughout Latin America, Canada, American Southwest, Europe, and Asia, 1946-68. *Wartime service:* American Red Cross field director in Philippines and Japan, 1945-46. *Member:* P.E.N. (treasurer of Los Angeles chapter, 1972). *Awards, honors:* Southern California Council on Literature for Children and Young People Award for notable book, 1970, for *The Bears and I.*

WRITINGS: Read the Wild Water: 780 Miles by Canoe Down the Green River, Dutton, 1966; *High Trails West,* Crown, 1967; *The Bears and I: Raising Three Cubs in the North Woods,* Dutton, 1968; *Wild Pets: Firsthand Account of Wild Animals as Pets, Guests, and Visitors,* Crown, 1970; *Wild Burro Rescue,* Childrens Press, 1973. Contributor to *Reader's Digest* and other national magazines

WORK IN PROGRESS: Two books for Children's Press, both wild animal stories set in the Canadian northwoods.

SIDELIGHTS: Leslie, of Scottish and Cherokee Indian ancestry, has explored wilderness regions of western Canada and the United States, and Mexico, living for long periods of time in remote woodland, desert, and mountain fastness. He has canoed most rivers and many back-country lakes in the western United States and Canada, hiked thousands of miles along western trail systems, and climbed mountains in North America, Japan, and Europe, including the Schwartz face of the Matterhorn.

As an amateur archaeologist, Leslie has amassed a large collection of Indian relics and lore. As an ecologist, he lectures and writes about preservation of desert, mountain, and forest wilderness areas. As a photographer, he has

ROBERT FRANKLIN LESLIE

When exposed boulders were scattered throughout the channel as are shown here, we walked the canoes through. ▪ (From *Read the Wild Water* by Robert Franklin Leslie.)

shown movies nationally on television and has conducted photography tours throughout Southwestern Indian reservations, Mexico, Canada, and Europe.

The Bears and I has been optioned for filming by Walt Disney Productions.

HOBBIES AND OTHER INTERESTS: Leather carving, wood sculpture.

LIVELY, Penelope 1933-

PERSONAL: Born March 17, 1933, in Cairo, Egypt; married Jack Lively (a university teacher), June 27, 1957; children: Josephine, Adam. *Education:* St. Anne's College, B.A., 1956. *Home and office:* Rectory Farmhouse, Church Hanborough, Oxford, England. *Agent:* Murray Pollinger, 11 Long Acre, London WC2E 9LH, England.

CAREER: Free-lance writer. *Member:* Society of Authors. *Awards, honors:* Book World's Children's Spring Book Festival Award, 1973, for *The Driftway;* Carnegie Medal, 1973, for *The Ghost of Thomas Kempe.*

WRITINGS: Astercote, Heinemann, 1970, Dutton, 1971; *The Whispering Knights,* Heinemann, 1971; *The Wild Hunt of the Ghost Hounds* (Junior Literary Guild selection), Hei3emann, 1971, Dutton, 1972; *The Driftway,* Heinemann, 1972, Dutton, 1973; *The Ghost of Thomas Kempe* (Junior Literary Guild selection), Heinemann, 1973; (contributor) *My England,* Heinemann, 1973; *The House in Norham Gardens,* Dutton, 1974; *Boy Without a Name,* Heinemann, 1974.

SIDELIGHTS: Penelope Lively was born in Cairo and spent her childhood in Egypt, visiting England several times, until the outbreak of World War II made such trips impossible. When she was twelve, the war ended and she went to England to stay. "It seemed very strange, lush and

green and cool. I felt like a visitor and had a nostalgia for the places where I had been a child that was almost a physical pain, but that is quite gone now. I have grown my own roots, and an attachment to the landscape and atmosphere of midland England that is perhaps the stronger for being acquired."

On returning to England, Ms. Lively was sent to a boarding school where she endured five desperately unhappy years. "English boarding schools can be barbaric institutions, and mine was a particularly misguided place. I liked reading and was quite prepared to learn; the school aimed at turning out competent hockey and lacrosse players and did not encourage other activities." At eighteen, she went to St. Anne's College, Oxford, where she spent three happy and rewarding years reading history.

After earning her degree in 1954, she was a research assistant in Oxford and then married Jack Lively, at that time a research fellow at St. Antony's College. Their daughter, Josephine, was born in 1958, and their son, Adam, in 1961. The Livelys moved from Oxford to Swansea University, next to Sussex University, and then, six years ago, they returned to Oxford where Mr. Lively is Fellow in Politics at St. Peter's College.

Penelope Lively has been writing for only a few years. With her children in school, she began to explore Oxfordshire and to read about local history and folklore. "This sparked off something in me that has given rise to five

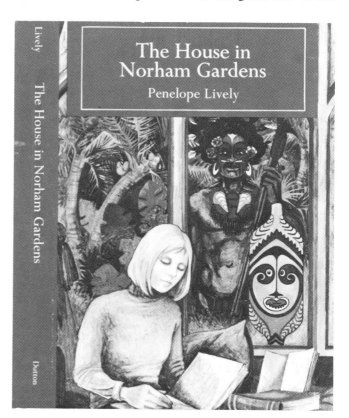

The year is 1900: in England Victoria is queen. The man is remote from England in distance by half the circumference of the world: in understanding, by five thousand years. ▪ (From *The House in Norham Gardens* by Penelope Lively. Jacket painting by Alexy Pendle.)

books for children. They are all deeply rooted in the English landscape and are all, in different ways, concerned with the permanence of place and the strong feeling of continuity that haunts the English countryside and expresses itself so variously—physically in the very structure of fields, roads, woods, and buildings; and imaginatively in the folklore and mythology.''

FOR MORE INFORMATION SEE: Times Literary Supplement, April 4, 1970; *Spectator,* May 9, 1970; *Books and Bookmen,* May, 1970; *Horn Book,* April, 1971, August, 1972, June, 1973; *Junior Literary Guild Catalogue,* March, 1972, September, 1973.

LONDON, Jane
See GEIS, Darlene

LOVELACE, Delos Wheeler   1894-1967

PERSONAL: Born December 2, 1894, in Brainerd, Minn.; son of Mortimer and Josephine (Wheeler) Lovelace; married Maud Palmer Hart (a writer), November 29, 1917; children: Merian (Mrs. Englebert Kirchner). *Education:* University of Minnesota, student, 1916-17; special studies at Cambridge University, 1919, and Columbia University, 1921. *Politics:* Republican. *Religion:* Episcopalian. *Home:* 774 West Eighth St., Claremont, Calif. *Agent:* Nannine Joseph, 200 West 54th St., New York, N.Y. 10019.

CAREER: Reporter with *Fargo Courier News,* Fargo, N.D., 1913-14, *Minneapolis Daily News,* Minneapolis, Minn., 1914-15; reporter, then night editor for *Minneapolis Tribune,* Minneapolis, Minn., 1915-17, 1919-20, and *New York Daily News,* New York, N.Y., 1920-31; *New York Sun,* New York, N.Y., assistant city editor, 1928-50, *New York World-Telegram and Sun,* New York, N.Y., staff writer, 1950-52. *Military service:* U.S. Army, American Expeditionary Forces, World War I; second lieutenant. *Member:* University Club (Claremont, Calif.).

WRITINGS: Rockne of Notre Dame (juvenile), Putnam, 1931; *King Kong* (novelization of the radio script by Edgar Wallace and Merian C. Cooper), Grosset & Dunlap, 1932; (with wife, Maud Hart Lovelace) *One Stayed at Welcome* (novel), Day, 1934; (with M. Lovelace) *Gentlemen from England* (novel), Macmillan, 1937; (with M. Lovelace) *The Golden Wedge* (juvenile), Crowell, 1942; *General "Ike" Eisenhower, Statesman and Soldier of Peace* (juvenile), Crowell, 1944, reissued as *"Ike" Eisenhower,* 1952, 3rd revised edition, 1959; *Journey to Bethlehem* (novel), Crowell, 1953; *That Dodger Horse* (juvenile), Crowell, 1956. Excerpts from book on Eisenhower included in *Youth Decides,* Row, Peterson & Co., 1952, *Journey into America,* Houghton, 1956, *All Around America,* Scott, 1959. Contributor of short stories to *Saturday Evening Post, Ladies' Home Journal, Country Gentleman, American,* other magazines; author of syndicated column, "Who's News Today," 1943-47.

WORK IN PROGRESS: Historical novel.

FOR MORE INFORMATION SEE: New York Times, January 20, 1967; *Publishers' Weekly,* February 13, 1967.

(Died January 17, 1967)

PETER LOWRY

LOWRY, Peter   1953-

PERSONAL: Born March 6, 1953, in Berkeley, Calif.; son of Ritchie Peter (a professor) and Betty (Trishman) Lowry. *Education:* Harvard University, student, 1971-73. *Politics:* Democrat. *Religion:* None. *Home:* 79 Moore Rd., Wayland, Mass. 01778. *Office:* Porter Sargent, Inc., 11 Beacon St., Boston, Mass. 02108.

CAREER: While student at Harvard worked as bartender in private homes, 1971-72, traveling editor, summer, 1972, and office boy in patent law firm, Boston, Mass., 1972-73; Porter Sargent, Inc. (publisher), Boston, Mass., member of editorial staff, 1973—. *Member:* Boston Authors Club.

WRITINGS: (With Field Griffith) *Model Rocketry: Hobby of Tomorrow* (teen book), Doubleday, 1972; (Scandinavian editor) *Let's Go: A Student Guide to Europe,* Dutton, 1973. Contributor of articles to *Seventeen,* articles, reviews, and photographs to *New York Times,* reviews and photographs to *Boston Globe,* and photographs to *Washington Post* and other newspapers.

WORK IN PROGRESS: Project assistant on book, *The Double Dealer,* financed by youth grant of National Endowment for the Humanities, completion expected in 1974.

SIDELIGHTS: "Motivation: fame and fortune." As a high school student Lowry won two awards from the Deep South Writers' Conference—fourth place nationally in poetry, 1968, and first place nationally in journalism, 1970. He has traveled in most countries of Europe and in New Zealand, Samoa, and Tahiti.

LUZZATI, Emanuele 1912-

PERSONAL: Born June 6, 1921, in Genoa, Italy; son of Guido and Fernanda Vita (Finzi) Luzzati. *Education:* Ecole des Beaux Arts, Lausanne, Switzerland, Diploma, 1945. *Religion:* Jewish. *Home:* Via Caffaro 12A, Genoa, Italy.

CAREER: Stage designer, designer of animated cartoons, and ceramic artist, 1945—. Has done more than 200 designs for theater sets, primarily for Italian theaters, including La Scala at Milan, but also for Chicago Lyric Opera, the Glyndebourne Festival Opera in London, the English Opera Group, and for productions in Paris, Munich, and Lisbon; director as well as designer of animated cartoons he has produced in Rome, Italy; his ceramics and decorations have been commissioned for the "Leonardo da Vinci" and other Italian luxury liners. *Awards, honors:* His animated cartoon, "The Thieving Magpie," was nominated for an Academy Award in Hollywood, 1966; also honored for his work at the Bratislava Illustration Biennal, 1967; Moscow Art Festival first prize, 1973, and Academy Award nomination, 1974, both for "Pulcinella."

EMANUELE LUZZATI

WRITINGS—Self-illustrated: (Adapted) Giovanni Boaccaccio, *Chichibio and the Crane,* Obolensky, 1961; *I Paladini di Francia: Ovvero il Tradimento di Gano Dimaganza* (title means "The Paladius of France: Or the Betrayal of Gano Dimaganza"), Mursia, 1962; *LaGaza ladra* (title means "The Thieving Magpie"), Mursia, 1964, produced as an animated cartoon; (adapted) *Ali Baba e i Quaranta Ladroni,* Emme Edizioni, 1968, translation by Robert Mann published as *Ali Baba and the Forty Thieves,* Pantheon, 1969; (adapted from a medieval puppet show) *Ronald and the Wizard Calico,* Hutchinson, 1969. Also illustrator of Gianni Rodari's *Castello di carte,* Mursia, 1963; *Pulcinella,* Emme Edizioni, 1971, translation published as *Punch and the Magic Fish,* Pantheon, 1972; *The Magic Flute,* Basil Blackwell, 1971; *Iviaggi oi Marco Polo* (Marco Polo travels), Emme Edizioni, 1972; *Luccellin bel Verde* (Italian tales), Edizioni Einaudi, 1972; *Bimbo Recita,* Emme Edizioni, 1973; *Il Principe Granchio* (Italian tales), Edizioni Einaudi, 1974.

FOR MORE INFORMATION SEE: Times Literary Supplement, October 16, 1969; *New York Times Book Review,* May 7, 1972.

LYNCH, Lorenzo 1932-

PERSONAL: Born May 27, 1932; son of Ollie (a railroad worker) and Clara (Oliver) Lynch; married Catherine Lockett, November, 1956; children: Walter, Christopher, Andrew, Eyvette, Angela. *Education:* Took correspondence course from Art Instruction, Inc., Minneapolis, 1946-50; attended Art Students League, New York, 1950 and School of Visual Arts, New York, 1956-60. *Home:* 99 Powell St., Brooklyn, N.Y. 11212. *Office:* 298 Fifth Ave., New York, N.Y. 10001.

CAREER: Fisher Advertising, Brooklyn, N.Y., staff artist, 1961-65; Olivetti & Underwood, New York, N.Y., staff artist, 1966-67; Martins Department Store, Brooklyn, N.Y., production manager, 1967-68; opened Annivette Studios, New York, N.Y., 1968, artist, 1968—. *Military service:* U.S. Army, 1953-55.

WRITINGS: The Hot Dog Man (juvenile), Bobbs, 1970; *The Black is Beautiful Beauty Book,* Prentice-Hall, 1974.

WORK IN PROGRESS: What Does A City Dog Do All Day?, a picture book.

SIDELIGHTS: "I've always been interested in writing since reading Richard Wright's *Black Boy* when I was a child. I feel that writing, art and acting are very much in tune with each other."

FOR MORE INFORMATION SEE: The Illustrator, Spring, 1974.

MANUSHKIN, Fran(ces) 1942-

PERSONAL: Surname is pronounced Ma-*nush*-kin; born November 2, 1942 in Chicago, Ill.; daughter of Meyer (a furniture salesman) and Beatrice (Kessler) Manushkin. *Education:* Studied at University of Illinois and Roosevelt

University; Northeastern Illinois State Teacher's College, B.A., 1964. *Home:* 121 East 88th St., New York, N.Y. 10028. *Office:* Harper & Row Publishers, Inc., 10 East 53rd St., New York, N.Y. 10022.

CAREER: Elementary teacher in Chicago, Ill., 1964-65; went to New York, N.Y., and worked about six months at Doubleday Bookstore and about six months as tour guide at Lincoln Center for Performing Arts; Holt, Rinehart & Winston, Inc., New York, N.Y., secretary to college psychology editor, 1967-68; Harper & Row Publishers, Inc., New York, N.Y., 1968—, started as secretary, now associate editor, Harper Junior Books, 1973—. *Member:* Sierra Club.

WRITINGS: Baby (picturebook illustrated by Ronald Himler), Harper, 1972; *Bubblebeath* (picturebook illustrated by Himler), Harper, 1974.

WORK IN PROGRESS: Two more picturebooks, *Shirleybird* and an untitled book, both for Harper.

FRAN MANUSHKIN

SIDELIGHTS: "Think most children's books are bland, lacking vitality and spark. I am most interested in fantasy—what *could* happen and the feelings that reveals about people's needs and hopes.

"I very much enjoy reading fiction and poetry (favorites are Colette, Ruth Krauss, James Agee, Charlotte Zolotow, Maurice Sendak, Virginia Woolf, Japanese and Chinese poetry and artwork). Enjoy bicycling, playing guitar, cooking, yoga, daydreaming, watching children, keeping my plants alive, going to museums and movies."

She also does volunteer work at Lighthouse for the Blind and Rusk Institute for Physical Therapy.

FOR MORE INFORMATION SEE: New York Times Book Review, May 7, 1972; *Horn Book,* June, 1972.

MARKINS, W. S.
See JENKINS, Marie M.

MATHIS, Sharon Bell   1937-

PERSONAL: Born February 26, 1937, in Atlantic City, N.J.; daughter of John Willie and Alice Mary (Frazier) Bell; married Leroy Franklin Mathis, July 11, 1957; children: Sherie, Stacy, Stephanie. *Education:* Morgan State College, B.A., 1958. *Religion:* Roman Catholic. *Residence:* Washington, D.C. *Agent:* Marilyn Marlow, Curtis Brown Ltd., 60 East 56th St., New York, N.Y. 10022.

SIDELIGHTS: "I write to *salute* the strength in Black children and to say to them, 'Stay strong, stay Black and stay alive.'

Mrs. Tracy was growing a baby. She fed the baby very carefully.
■ (From *Baby* by Fran Manushkin. Illustrated by Ronald Himler.)

SHARON BELL MATHIS

"James Baldwin said it eloquently: 'By the time he's six years old the Black child already senses the danger this country is preparing for him. . . .'"

FOR MORE INFORMATION SEE: New York Times, March 27, 1970; *Jet,* April 23, 1970; *Washington Post,* March 21, 1971; *Black World,* August, 1971, May 1973, May 1974; *Horn Book,* August, 1971, February, 1973, April, 1974, June, 1974; *Redbook,* August 1972; *New York Times Book Review,* September 10, 1972; *Ebony,* December, 1972; *Essence,* April, 1973; *Jet,* May 2, 1974.

Lilly Etta laughed to see a round earring on one side and a flat one on the other side. But that night Lilly Etta got up once again and stayed up a long time. ■ (From *Sidewalk Story* by Sharon Bell Mathis. Illustrated by Leo Carty.)

CAREER: Children's Hospital of District of Columbia, Washington, interviewer, 1958-59; teacher in parochial elementary school in Washington, D.C., 1959-65; Stuart Junior High School, Washington, D.C., special education teacher, 1965—. Howard University, Washington, D.C., writer in residence, 1972-74. Writer in charge of children's literature division, Washington, D.C. Black Writers Workshop, 1970-73. Member of board of advisers of lawyers committee of District of Columbia Commission on the Arts, 1972—; member of Black Women's Community Development Foundation, 1973—. *Awards, honors:* Award from Council on Interracial Books for Children, 1970, for *Sidewalk Story;* awards from *New York Times* and American Library Association, 1972, for *Teacup Full of Roses;* fellowship from Wesleyan University and Weekly Readers Book Club, awarded at Bread Loaf Writer's Conference, 1970; Coretta Scott King Award, runner-up, 1973, for *Teacup Full of Roses;* Coretta Scott King Award, 1974, for *Ray Charles.*

WRITINGS—For children: *Brooklyn Story,* Hill & Wang, 1970; *Sidewalk Story* (Child Study Association book list), Viking, 1971; *Teacup Full of Roses* (Ala Notable Book; Child Study Association book list), Viking, 1972; *Ray Charles,* Crowell, 1973; *Listen for the Fig Tree,* Viking 1974; *The Hundred Penny Box,* Viking, 1975. Author of "Ebony Juniors Speak!," a monthly column in *Ebony, Jr!* and "Society and Youth," a bi-weekly column in *Liteside.*

WORK IN PROGRESS: Sammy's Baby, a children's book, publication by Viking expected in 1976; a book on voter registration, Viking, 1976.

EDITH MAXWELL

MAXWELL, Edith 1923-

PERSONAL: Born March 12, 1923, in Newburgh, N.Y.; daughter of James A. (a civil engineer) and Theodora (Bowerman) Smith; married Robert W. Maxwell (a stockbroker), October 18, 1945; children: Mary Christine (Mrs. Robert Hevener), Margaret, Jeanne. *Education:* Student at Mount St. Mary's Academy, Newburgh, 1936-40, and Russell Sage College, 1940-42. *Politics:* Republican. *Religion:* Episcopalian. *Home:* 20 Redwood Dr., Hillsborough, Calif. 94010. *Agent:* Edith Margolis, Lenninger Literary Agency, Inc., 437 Fifth Ave., New York, N.Y. 10016.

CAREER: Began writing in the 1940's, selling her first short stories to pulp magazines. Has been Travelers Aid volunteer at San Francisco Airport and worked with Crippled Children's Auxiliary and Peninsula Children's Theatre. *Member:* Junior League (San Francisco).

WRITINGS: Just Dial a Number (Junior Literary Guild selection), Dodd, 1971. Contributor of short stories to magazines and children's plays produced by Peninsula Children's Theatre. Editor, "The Corral" *Junior League Magazine,* of Fort Worth, Texas, 1956-59.

WORK IN PROGRESS: Research in group encounter sessions as possible theme of juvenile novel.

SIDELIGHTS: "I grew up in the Hudson Valley town of Newburgh, New York, with a strong Quaker background tempered by the Catholic teachings of the Dominican sisters of Mount Saint Mary's—a unique but broadening religious background. I always enjoyed writing, particularly those back-to-school themes about What I Did Last Summer. They were never remotely concerned with what I had actually done, only with what I wished I'd done. Book reports and factual writing came harder. I made my first fiction sale while a student at Mount Saint Mary's—ghostwriting love letters for my classmates to send to cadets at nearby West Point. The going price, I recall, was twenty-five cents a letter. When this venture came to the Sisters' attention, they registered strong disapproval. My beloved English teacher, Sister Agnus Alma, objected to the letters on the grounds that the whole project lacked common honesty. Besides, she felt they were grossly overpriced.

"Later, as a student at Russell Sage College in Troy, New York, I continued to work at writing—but not very hard, because I was busy living and learning. It wasn't until after I married and our first daughter was born that I settled down to the task of trying to sell.

"I have never held to the theory that one can write for oneself. If a fictional experience isn't shared—which means published—it remains rather like the sound of one hand clapping. So, with joyous innocence I started submitting short stories to the *Saturday Evening Post* and the old *Collier's* Magazine. They came bouncing back like yo-yo balls. The pile of rejection slips grew alarmingly high, and I grew very discouraged. Then, while attending a Writer's Conference at the University of Oklahoma, I met and talked with a group of very bright and articulate editors of pulp magazines. I had never considered writing for the pulps, but came home from that conference determined to try. I did, and I sold. I was a published writer! I made an artistic display of my pulp magazine sales on the coffee table, much to my family's embarrassment. But I thought it was beautiful.

"Learning to write in the pulps is not for everyone, I know. But if one is so inclined, the knowledge and experience gained is worth more than a dozen creative writing courses. This is only my personal opinion, and I know many would not agree.

"I continued writing short stories and gradually began to sell to better markets. My agent (by some miracle I found an agent) often remarked that my short stories sounded like chapters of a novel, and urged me to try a novel. But it seemed such an impossibly long task, I could not face up to it. I wrote *Just Dial a Number* as a long short story. My agent returned it *telling* (not urging) me to make it into a novel. By that time, the hard part was over, so writing the book was fun. I did not write the book for teenagers, I wrote it about teenagers. The decision to market it in the juvenile field was my agent's, who is far wiser about these things than I. The decision to publish was Dodd's—to whom I will be eternally grateful for having the courage to publish a virtually unknown author.

"I am working on my second teenage novel, this time consciously writing for teenagers. Perhaps this is my natural field, I do not know. I fell into it by accident. I do know I have a pretty much unshared opinion that today's teenagers are not a separate species of man, requiring a special kind of insight and understanding. They are young people, playing their game in a whole new ball park, under a whole new set of rules. So it would follow that their responses would be, at times, unfathomable to the older generation.

164

"I have an almost total recall of that dark, fearful, almost claustrophobic world of adolescence when not only is the world pouring sensory perceptions into you, but your own response to this world is unknown, unrehearsed, often unexpected. All of which brings me to the point that there is a universality in human experience which gives me— a middle-aged housewife—the courage to reach back into the twilight of a former self and write about a group to which I no longer belong.

"As for writing in general, my greatest enemy is myself. I am a hopeless extrovert; I need people. After a long, lonely stint at the typewriter I develop a fearful case of cabin fever and have to go play in a bridge tournament where the combat is raw and real.

"I favor writing on a schedule—which I don't do. I favor working from an outline—which I can't do. I do it all wrong and backwards. Yet if I hang loose and write from the heart, I know there's always the chance that I might get lucky and write something I didn't know I knew. And that's a beautiful experience."

FOR MORE INFORMATION SEE: Junior Literary Guild Catalogue, March, 1971.

McCAIN, Murray (David, Jr.) 1926-

PERSONAL: Born December 28, 1926, in Newport, N.C.; son of Murray David (farmer) and Toye (Garner) McCain. *Education:* University of North Carolina, A.B., 1949. *Politics:* Democrat. *Agent:* Candida Donadio, Lantz-Donadio, 111 West 57th St., New York, N.Y. *Office:* Bantam Books, 666 Fifth Ave., New York, N.Y. 10019.

MURRAY McCAIN

GOATS aren't allowed in libraries. DO YOU KNOW WHY?

(From *Books!* by Murray McCain. Illustrated by John Alcorn.)

CAREER: American Broadcasting Co., New York, N.Y., film editor, 1951-54; Appleton-Century-Crofts, New York, editor, 1955-58; Criterion Books, New York, editor 1959-60; Bantam Books, New York, executive managing editor, 1960—. *Military service:* U.S. Army, 1946-47, became technician (fourth class).

WRITINGS: Books!, Simon & Schuster, 1962; *Writing!,* Farrar, Straus, 1964; *The Boy Who Walked Off The Page,* Dutton, 1969.

WORK IN PROGRESS: Several children's books.

SIDELIGHTS: "Learning to read was probably the most

important thing that ever happened to me, after being born. Since then I have been both occupied and preoccupied with the problems of reading and writing. Of course, there are many other ways to communicate, but these have special interest for me. It is no coincidence that all three of my published books are about the give and take between writer and reader.

"If I could ever manage to tell a fairly long, good story well, I think I would be able to die happy. A good story has more of the elements of magic in it than anything else I know, so you can see that what I really want to be is a magician."

MEHDEVI, Alexander (Sinclair) 1947-

PERSONAL: Born June 9, 1947, in Mazatlan, Mexico; son of Mohamed (an Iranian diplomat) and Anne-Marie (an American; maiden name, Sinclair) Mehdevi. *Education:* Attended schools in England, 1957-59, Madrid, 1959-60, Vienna, 1961-62, Abadan, Iran, 1962, American International School in Vienna, 1962-65, and Amherst College, 1965-66; Diplomatic Academy of Vienna, Zertifikat (M.A. equivalent), 1970; further study at Sorbonne, University of Paris, 1970, and University of Geneva, 1971. *Religion:* None. *Home:* 357 West 84th St., New York, N.Y. 10024. *Office:* Rizzoli International Bookstore, 712 Fifth Ave., New York, N.Y.

CAREER: Interrupted studies to write, 1967-68; while attending University of Paris taught English with audiovisual

ALEXANDER MEHDEVI

materials to adults at Centre d'Etudes Linguistiques, 1970; simultaneous interpreter for United Nations conferences at Palais des Nations, Geneva, 1971; taught English and German with conventional methods and audiovisual materials at Centre d'Etudes Linguistiques and Centre d'Enseignement Technique de Banque, Paris, 1972; in charge of children's books at Rizzoli International Bookstore, New York, 1973—.

WRITINGS: Bungling Pedro and Other Majorcan Tales (retold), Knopf, 1970; *Tales from Underground,* Macmillan, 1974; *The Flowers of Majorca,* Macmillan, 1974. Contributor to *Moneysworth, Children's Digest* and *Nuevos Horizontes.*

WORK IN PROGRESS: Compiling the first foreign-language catalogue of children's books for U.S. publication; writing a series of anthropomorphic tales about insects.

SIDELIGHTS: A pocketbook edition of *Bungling Pedro* is to be published in German by Fischer Taschenbuch Verlag. Some of the tales were included in condensed form earlier in a German textbook. Mehdevi speaks, writes, and reads fluently in four languages—English, Spanish, French, and German—and also speaks and reads Italian. He says that he would like to teach children's literature.

FOR MORE INFORMATION SEE: Horn Book, April, 1971.

MORRIS, Robert A(da) 1933-

PERSONAL: Born November 15, 1933, in Charlottesville, Va.; son of Charles Everett and Amy (Ada) Morris; married Sally Ward Warburton (a secretary), October 18, 1962; children: Everett Ashley. *Education:* University of Delaware, B.A., 1958; University of Hawaii, M.S., 1966; State University of New York Veterinary College at Cornell University, candidate for D.V.M., 1970—. *Home:* 1489 Coddington Rd., Brooktondale, N.Y. 14817.

CAREER: Waikiki Aquarium, Honolulu, Hawaii, assistant director, 1963-65; Marineland of Florida, St. Augustine, curator, 1965-66; New York Aquarium, New York, N.Y., curator, 1966-70. Leader of New York Aquarium expeditions to collect white whales in Hudson Bay, 1967, and first narwhale from above Arctic Circle, 1969; underwater diver. *Military service:* U.S. Navy, 1952-54. *Member:* International Association for Aquatic Animal Medicine, Explorers Club (New York). *Awards, honors: Seahorse* was a Children's Book Showcase title, 1973.

WRITINGS: (Author of introduction) Reginald Dutta, *Tropical Fish,* Octopus Books, 1971; *Seahorse* (juvenile), Harper, 1972. Contributor of scientific and popular articles to periodicals, including *Animal Kingdom, Pacific Science, Norwegian Whaling Gazaeete,* and *Tropical Fish Hobbyist.*

WORK IN PROGRESS: A book on dolphins for Harper's "Science I Can Read" series; a juvenile book on sharks.

FOR MORE INFORMATION SEE: Life, September 26, 1969; *Horn Book,* December, 1972.

Soon there are hundreds of baby seahorses in the water. They are as long as their father's nose. ■ (From *Seahorse* by Robert A. Morris. Illustrated by Arnold Lobel.)

MOSEL, Arlene (Tichy) 1921-

PERSONAL: Surname is pronounced Mo-*zel;* born August 27, 1921, in Cleveland, Ohio; daughter of Edward J. (an engraver) and Marie (Fingulin) Tichy; married Victor H. Mosel (a sales engineer), December 26, 1942; children: Nancy Mosel Farrar, Joanne, James. *Education:* Ohio Wesleyan University, B.A., 1942; Western Reserve University (now Case Western Reserve University), M.S.L.S., 1959. *Religion:* Lutheran. *Home:* 3343 Braemar Rd., Shaker Heights, Ohio 44120.

CAREER: Enoch Pratt Free Library, Baltimore, Md., assistant in children's department; Case Western Reserve University, Cleveland, Ohio, associate professor of library science. Assistant coordinator of Children's Services, Cuyahoga County Public Library. *Awards, honors: Tikki Tikki Tembo* was an American Library Association Notable Book, 1968; *The Funny Little Woman* was an Honor Book in Hans Christian Andersen International Children's Book Awards, 1974.

WRITINGS: (Reteller) *Tikki Tikki Tembo* (illustrated by Blair Lent), Holt, 1968; (reteller) *The Funny Little Woman* (*Horn Book* honor list; ALA Notable Book; illustrated by Lent), Dutton, 1972.

SIDELIGHTS: "As a librarian, my greatest pleasure came from telling stories and planning story-hour programs. My books have grown from these experiences. I am intrigued with stories that have a quiet subtle humor—they are a challenge to the story-teller. Children are always eager for the unexpected and a chance to laugh.

"My career as a librarian must have been contagious, for I now have two daughters who are librarians. One is a children's librarian in Indianapolis and the other is a law librarian in a law school. I have a teen-age son at home—which is an extraordinary experience."

FOR MORE INFORMATION SEE: New York Times Book Review, March 17, 1968; *Book World,* May 5, 1968; *Commonweal,* May 24, 1968; *Junior Literary Guild Catalogue,* September, 1972; *Times Literary Supplement,* June 26, 1969; *Horn Book,* December, 1972; MacCann and Richard, *The Child's First Books,* H. W. Wilson, 1973.

ARLENE E. MOSEL

The Old Man with the Ladder hurried as fast as his old legs could carry him. ■ (From *Tikki Tikki Tembo* by Arlene Mosel. Illustrated by Blair Lent.)

Something about the Author

MURRAY, (Judith) Michele (Freedman) 1933-1974

PERSONAL: Born April 25, 1933, in Brooklyn, N.Y.; daughter of Aaron (a government clerk) and Mollie (Giseu) Freedman; married James Murray (an administrative officer with District of Columbia government), January 29, 1955; children: David, Jonathan, Sarah, Matthew. *Education:* American University, student, 1951-53; New School for Social Research, B.A., 1954; University of Connecticut, M.A., 1956. *Religion:* Jewish, converted to Catholicism, 1953. *Home:* 9816 Parkwood Dr., Bethesda, Md. 20014.

CAREER: Instructor in English at Annhurst College, Putnam, Conn., 1956-57, Georgetown University, Washington, D.C., 1957-59, and Catholic University of America, Washington, D.C., 1959-60; Howard University, Washington, D.C., instructor in humanities, 1965-66; *National Observer,* Silver Spring, Md., book review editor, 1972-74. *Member:* Nova.

WRITINGS: Nellie Cameron (Child Study Association book list), Seabury, 1971; *The Crystal Nights* (young adult), Seabury, 1973; (editor) *A House of Good Proportion: Images of Women in Literature,* Simon & Schuster, 1973; *The Great Mother and Other Poems,* Sheed & Ward,

Nellie never wanted to let go of Sundays, no matter what. But there was Monday morning like a slap at the beginning of the week, harder than ever to bear after the lazy, sweet summer habits. ▪ (From *Nellie Cameron* by Michele Murray. Illustrated by Leonora E. Prince.)

1974. About sixty poems have been published in little literary magazines, 1965—; regular contributor to *National Catholic Reporter.*

WORK IN PROGRESS: A book of criticism; *Dacia's War,* a children's novel; sixteen of her private journals from 1948-74 may be published.

SIDELIGHTS: "Love to write and always wanted to be a writer. I believe in the value of the artist of integrity in a time of literary careerism and try to bring to my children's books the aesthetic quality of the best fiction for adults in depth, complexity and writing style."

FOR MORE INFORMATION SEE: Junior Literary Guild Catalogue, March, 1971; *New York Times Book Review,* September 16, 1973; *National Observer,* March 23, 1974.

(Died March 14, 1974)

NESPOJOHN, Katherine V(eronica) 1912-

PERSONAL: Born June 25, 1912, in Bridgeport, Conn.; daughter of Oliver Francis (a production engineer) and Nora (Herlihy) Merillat; married Joseph B. Nespojohn (a postal employee), August 13, 1948; children: Nora Mary. *Education:* Teachers College, Columbia University, B.S., 1938, M.A., 1942; further study at University of California, Berkeley, 1942, and Fairfield University, 1965-68. *Religion:* Roman Catholic. *Home:* 1057 Fairfield Beach Rd., Fairfield, Conn. 06430. *Agent:* Florence Alexander, 50 East 42nd St., New York, N.Y.

MICHELE MURRAY

CAREER: Elementary and high school teacher in Stratford, Conn., 1936-46; University of Bridgeport, Bridgeport, Conn., instructor in biology, creative writing, and journalism, 1942-49; teacher in elementary and high school in Fairfield, Conn., 1943-53, science consultant, 1953-68. *Member:* National Education Association, Connecticut Education Association, Fairfield Education Association, Association of Retired Teachers of Connecticut.

WRITINGS—Juvenile: *Animal Eyes,* Prentice-Hall, 1965; *Worms,* Watts, 1972.

WORK IN PROGRESS: Animal Ears, completion expected in 1975.

FOR MORE INFORMATION SEE: New York Times Book Review, May 7, 1972; *Bridgeport Sunday Post,* October, 1972.

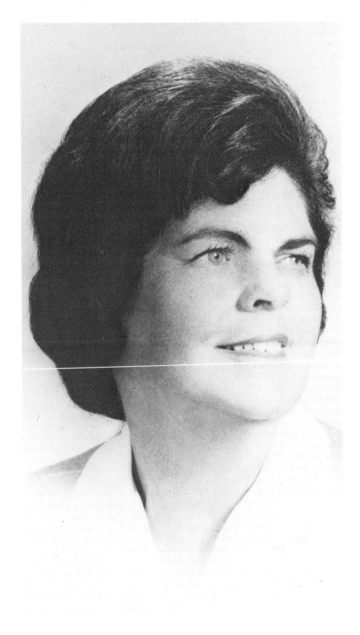

KATHERINE NESPOJOHN

IB OHLSSON by Ohlsson

OHLSSON, Ib 1935-

PERSONAL: Born August 9, 1935, in Copenhagen, Denmark. *Education:* Attended public school in Copenhagen, 1952, and School of Decorative and Applied Arts, Copenhagen, 1952-56. *Residence and studio:* New York, N.Y.

CAREER: Worked in Copenhagen, Denmark, 1955-60, first as apprentice, then as designer of educational charts and manuals for Danish Civil Defense Corps., and freelance illustrator and designer, 1957-60; designer of packaging for Walter Dorwin Teague, Inc., New York, N.Y., and Thomas Laufer, Assoc., Sausalito, Calif., 1960-61; free-lance illustrator and designer for book and magazine publishers and business firms, New York, N.Y., 1962—. *Awards, honors:* Lewis Carroll Shelf Award, 1971, for *The Nonsense Book; Farewell to the Farivox* was a Children's Book Showcase Title, 1973.

ILLUSTRATOR: Samuel S. Vaughan, *The Two-Thirty Bird,* Norton, 1965; Marilyn Sachs, *Laura's Luck,* Doubleday, 1965; M. Jean Craig, *The Long and Dangerous Journey,* Norton, 1965; Jay Williams, *Philbert the Fearful,* Norton, 1966; Agnes McCarthy, *Room Ten,* Doubleday, 1966; Felice Holman, *Professor Diggins' Dragons,* Macmillan, 1966; Marguerite Walters, *City-Country ABC,* Doubleday, 1966; Edward Fenton, *The Big Yellow Balloon,* Doubleday, 1967; Bette Distler, *Timothy Tuneful,* Macmillan, 1968; Borghild Margarethe Dahl, *Rikk of the Rendal Clan,* Dutton, 1968; Verna Aardema, *Tales for the Third Ear,* Dutton, 1969; Charles E. Alverson, *Bears Don't Cry,* Dutton, 1969.

Susan Meyers, *Mysterious Bender Bones,* Doubleday, 1970; Duncan Emrich, *Nonsense Book* (ALA Notable Book), Four Winds, 1970; Richard E. Cheney, *Really Eager and the Glorious Watermelon Contest,* Dutton, 1970; Edith Unnerstad, *Mickie,* Four Winds, 1971; Harry Hartwick, *Farewell to the Farivox,* Four Winds, 1972; Duncan Emrich, *The Hodgepodge Book: An Almanac of American Folklore,* Four Winds, 1972; Wallis Kendal, *Just Gin,* Viking, 1973; Lillian Moore, *Spooky Rhymes and Riddles,* Scholastic Book Services, 1973.

Also illustrator for Reader's Digest Book Division, *Newsweek, Woman's Day, Good Housekeeping,* and *New York Times.*

FOR MORE INFORMATION SEE: Illustrators of Children's Books, 1957-1966, Horn Book, 1968.

OLSCHEWSKI, Alfred (Erich) 1920-

PERSONAL: Surname is pronounced Ol-*chef*-ski; born March 8, 1920, in Gumbinnen, Germany; son of Otto (building superintendent) and Lydia (Fabricius) Olschewski; married Evelyn Druyer Dunn (communications administrator), August 25, 1968. *Education:* Studied at Academy of Art, Duesseldorf, Germany, and Handwerk und Kunst, Kassel, Germany. *Home:* 77 Nagog Hill Rd., Acton, Mass. 01720.

CAREER: Free-lance illustrator, designer, and teacher, 1969—. Colibris Editora Ltd., Rio de Janeiro, Brazil, illustrator and designer, 1954-59; Bolta Products, Lawrence, Mass., textile designer, 1961-69. *Member:* Cambridge Art Association, Copley Society of Boston, De Cordova Museum.

WRITINGS—Self-illustrated children's books: *The Wheel Rolls Over,* Little, Brown, 1962; *We Fly,* Little, Brown, 1967; *Winterbird,* Houghton, 1969.

ALFRED OLSCHEWSKI

Illustrator: Freya Littledale, *The Magic Tablecloth,* Scholastic Book Services, 1972.

SIDELIGHTS: "My books derive from my own experiences and interests. Every writer, for adults and children, must write out of the world he knows if he is to be honest with himself and his audience. I like working for children. Their minds are open and their reactions are honest.

"As for how I write. Being basically an artist, I see my stories in pictures first, block out the art, and then write the words to go with it."

(From *Winterbird* by Alfred Olschewski. Illustrated by the author.)

ORGEL, Doris 1929-
(Doris Adelberg)

PERSONAL: Surname is pronounced Or-gel; born February 15, 1929, in Vienna, Austria; daughter of Ernest and Erna (Ehrmann) Adelberg; married Shelley Orgel (a psychiatrist and psychoanalyst), June 25 1949; children: Paul, Laura, Jeremy. Education: Radcliffe College, student, 1946-48; Barnard College, B.A. (cum laude), 1950. Politics: Democrat. Religion: Jewish (non-practicing). Home: 33 Stonybrook Rd., Westport, Conn. 06880. Agent: Curtis Brown Ltd., 60 East 56th St., New York, N.Y. 10022.

CAREER: Employed in magazine and book publishing fields prior to 1955; author and translator of children's books. Member: Authors Guild, P.E.N., Phi Beta Kappa.

Awards, Honors: Lewis Carroll Shelf Award, 1960, for translation of Dwarf Long-Nose; her retelling of Little John, illustrated by Anita Lobel, received first prize in picture-book division at Book World's Children's Spring Book Festival, 1972.

WRITINGS: Sarah's Room, Harper, 1963; (under name Doris Adelberg) Grandma's Holidays, Dial, 1963; (under name Doris Adelberg) Lizzie's Twins, Dial, 1964; The Good-Byes of Magnus Marmalade, Putnam, 1966; Cindy's Snowdrops, Knopf, 1966; Cindy's Sad and Happy Tree, Knopf, 1967; In a Forgotten Place, Knopf, 1967; On the Sand Dune, Harper, 1968; Whose Turtle?, World Publishing, 1968; Phoebe and the Prince, Putnam, 1969; Merry, Rose and Christmas-Tree June, Knopf, 1969; Next Door to Xanadu, Harper, 1969; The Uproar, McGraw, 1970; The Mulberry Music, Harper, 1971; Bartholomew, We Love You!, Knopf, 1973.

Fairy tales and other stories retold: Clemens Brentano, The Tale of Gockel, Hinkel and Gackeliah, Random House, 1961; Clemens Brentano, Schoolmaster Whackwell's Won-

. . . they had been picking cucumbers for their supper when the storm had come along. ■ (From Baron Munchausen retold by Doris Orgel. Selected and illustrated by Willi Baum.)

derful Sons, Random House, 1962; Wilhelm Hauff, *The Heart of Stone,* Macmillan, 1964; Richard Wagner, *Lohengrin,* Putnam, 1966; Wilhelm Hauff, *A Monkey's Uncle,* Farrar, Straus, 1969; E.T.A. Hoffman, *The Child From Far Away,* Addison-Wesley, 1971; Rudolf E. Raspe, *Baron Munchausen: 15 Truly Tall Tales,* Addison-Wesley, 1971; Theodor Storm, *Little John,* Farrar, Straus, 1972.

Translator: Wilhelm Hauff, *Dwarf Long-Nose,* Random House, 1960; Walter Grieder, *The Enchanted Drum,* Parents' Magazine Press, 1969; Mira Lobe, *The Grandma in the Apple Tree,* McGraw, 1970. Reviewer of children's books for *New York Times.*

WORK IN PROGRESS: Some Magic Powers, a novel for children nine-to-twelve.

SIDELIGHTS: Doris Orgel's first original book, *Sarah's Room,* has been published in England and, in German translation, in Switzerland. Maurice Sendak, Erik Blegvad, Leonard Weisgard, Ati Forberg, and Anita Lobel are among the well-known illustrators of her books.

HOBBIES AND OTHER INTERESTS: Reading novels, weeding, tennis, listening to music, traveling.

FOR MORE INFORMATION SEE: New York Times Book Review, July 9, 1967; *Punch,* November 29, 1967; *Library Journal,* July, 1968, September, 1970; *Saturday Review,* September 13, 1969; *Horn Book,* February, 1970, December, 1970, April 1972; *Publishers' Weekly,* March 5, 1973.

OSMOND, Edward   1900-

PERSONAL: Born May 6, 1900, in Orford, Suffolk, England; son of Percy Herbert (a clergyman, Church of England) and Agnes (Sadler) Osmond; married Constance M. Biggs (now an author and artist under name Laurie Osmond), November 12, 1927; children: Christine Gillian. *Education:* Educated privately; studied art at the Polytechnic, London, England, 1917-24, Art Teachers Diploma, 1924, Diploma in Art History (London), 1924. *Home:* Downland Cottage, Lullington Close, Seaford, Sussex, England.

CAREER: Free-lance illustrator, 1928—; author, illustrator, and designer of children's books. Part-time art teacher at the Department of Art and Design, College of Further Education, Hastings, England; former art teacher at The Polytechnic, London, England. *Member:* Society of Industrial Artists, Society of Authors. *Awards, honors:* Carnegie Medal of Library Association (for outstanding children's book of the year by a British subject) for *A Valley Grows Up,* 1954.

WRITINGS—All self-illustrated, some also designed: *A Valley Grows Up,* Oxford University Press, 1953; "Animals of the World" series, Clarendon Press, 1953-56; *Houses,* Batsford, 1956; *Villages,* Batsford, 1957; *Towns,* Batsford, 1958; "Animals of Britain" series, Clarendon Press, 1959-62; *From Drumbeat to Ticker Tape,* Hutchinson, 1960; *The Artist in Britain,* Studio Books, 1961; *People of the Desert,* Odhams, 1963; *People of the Jungle Forest,* Odhams, 1963; *People of the Grasslands,* Odhams, 1964; *People of the Arctic,* Odhams, 1964; *People of the High Mountains,* Odham, 1965; *People of the Lonely Mountain,* Odhams, 1965; *Animals of Central Asia,* Abelard, 1967.

WORK IN PROGRESS: A broad outline of Western art on a cause and effect approach for older children and students.

SIDELIGHTS: Writes for children from eight-nine upwards. His theory on children's books: they should be produced while the writer is, himself, learning about their subject matter—that this imparts some hidden excitement which may infect the reader. He thinks that ideally the book should be written, illustrated, and designed by the same person.

PAGE, Eileen
See HEAL, Edith

PENDERY, Rosemary (Schmitz)

PERSONAL: Born in Elgin, Ill.; daughter of Theodore William and Phyllis (Schickler) Schmitz; married John Manning Pendery (self-employed), July 11, 1965; children: Samantha Sue; foster children: nine. *Education:* University of California, Santa Barbara, B.A., 1962; University of California, Los Angeles, graduate study, 1965. *Address:* P.O. Box 149, De Funiak Springs, Fla. 32433.

CAREER: Private tutor at levels through high school in De Funiak Springs, Fla., and Santa Monica, Calif., 1962—; teacher of piano privately in De Funiak Springs, Fla., 1972—. Has done demonstration and master teaching in

ROSEMARY PENDERY

Andy was sitting on the back porch. He felt very sad. He tried and tried to think of a good home for his frog. ■ (From *A Home for Hopper* by Rosemary Pendery. Illustrated by Robert Quackenbush.)

kindergarten and elementary grades in public and private schools of California; director of Santa Monica Head Start program, 1966, and volunteer chairman of De Funiak Springs Head Start program, 1973. *Member:* Delta Phi Upsilon, Pilot Club.

WRITINGS: A Home for Hopper (juvenile), Morrow, 1971.

SIDELIGHTS: "My husband and I love to travel, back pack, hike, and camp. We enjoy riding bicycles and motor bikes, swimming and playing tennis. I am especially interested in the special needs of the slow learner and the emotionally disturbed child."

FOR MORE INFORMATION SEE: New York Times Book Review, Children's Books Section, May 2, 1971.

PIRO, Richard   1934-

PERSONAL: Born July 18, 1934, in Somerville, Mass.; son of James (a printer) and Louise (Capone) Piro. *Education:* Boston University, B.Mus., 1956, M.Mus., 1962. *Politics:* Independent. *Religion:* None. *Home:* 2906 Forest Ave., Berkeley, Calif. 94705. *Office: Vector* Magazine, 83 Sixth St., San Francisco, Calif. 94103.

Richard Piro directing "Fiddler on the Roof": "It was the idea of a black Fiddler on the Roof that had captured imaginations. Professionalism cautioned that this idea alone was not sufficient nourishment to entertain and hold an audience for two and a half hours." ▪ (From *Black Fiddler* by Richard Piro. Jacket photo by Dan O'Neil IV.)

CAREER: Junior High School teacher of music and drama in New York, N.Y., 1963-73; *Vector,* San Francisco, Calif., editor, 1973—. Member of San Francisco Opera Co., San Francisco Symphony Chorus, and Oakland Symphony Chorus. *Military service:* U.S. Army, 1956-58. *Awards, honors: Black Fiddler* was an American Library Association Notable Book, 1972.

WRITINGS: Black Fiddler, Morrow, 1971. Regular contributor to journals of Music Educators National Conference and American Theatre Association.

WORK IN PROGRESS: A film script of *Black Fiddler.*

FOR MORE INFORMATION SEE: Horn Book, August, 1971.

POWERS, Margaret
See HEAL, Edith

PUGH, Ellen T(iffany)   1920-

PERSONAL: Surname rhymes with "dew"; born June 2, 1920, in Cleveland, Ohio; daughter of Clarence Romaine (a railroad man) and Margaret May (Williams) Tiffany; married David Benjamin Pugh (a college administrator), July 3,

ELLEN T. PUGH

176

At first, it seemed the young man had released nothing into Elin's hand, and there were understanding nods. Of course, such an undesirable person would have nothing fit to give a princess, let alone moon snow. ▪ (From *More Tales from the Welsh Hills* by Ellen Pugh. Illustrated by Joan Sandin.)

1949. *Education:* Western Reserve University, B.A., 1943, B.S. in L.S., 1945; Northwestern University, M.A., 1947. *Politics:* Democrat. *Religion:* Unitarian Universalist. *Home:* Southwest 600 Crestview, Apt. 15, Pullman, Wash. 99163. *Agent:* Ruth Cantor, 156 Fifth Ave., New York, N.Y. 10010. *Office:* Holland Library, Pullman, Wash. 99163.

CAREER: Teacher of courses in English or creative writing at various colleges, including Pennsylvania State University, University Park, 1948-49, and Queens College, Charlotte, N.C., 1954-55; Cincinnati Public Library, Cincinnati, Ohio, branch librarian, 1955-58; University of Nebraska, Lincoln, order librarian, 1958-63; University of Oregon, Eugene, catalog librarian, 1963-65; University of Rochester, Rochester, N.Y., catalog librarian, 1965-68;

Washington State University, Holland Library, Pullman, serials librarian, 1969—. *Member:* American Library Association, Spokane Writers Guild (vice-president, 1973—), Spiritual Frontiers Fellowship.

*WRITINGS—*Youth books: *Tales from the Welsh Hills* (retold), Dodd, 1968; *Brave His Soul: The Story of Prince Madog of Wales and His Discovery of America in 1170* (Junior Literary Guild selection), Dodd, 1970; *More Tales from the Welsh Hills* (retold), Dodd, 1971.

WORK IN PROGRESS: Yulen's Wonderful Journey, a legend of pacific Northwest Indians; several other fiction and nonfiction projects.

SIDELIGHTS: "My Welsh background (my mother's side, and my husband) supplied the motive for my first three books. Now I am interested in working with American history, especially that of the American West and Northwest. There are many comic, heroic, and tragic sagas yet untold.

"Teacher and librarian friends tell me youngster's aren't interested in the past of their country; only in things of the moment; but I can't—or won't—believe that. Only by knowing what *has* happened can one understand what *is* happening and predict what *will* happen. This is the field I wish to work in, mainly, on both juvenile and adult levels."

FOR MORE INFORMATION SEE: Horn Book, October, 1971.

PURSCELL, Phyllis 1934-

PERSONAL: Born December 18, 1934, in Fort Dodge, Iowa; daughter of H. Lynn (a physicist) and Georgia (Williams) Bloxom; married Delano Purscell (owner of a retail business), December 23, 1954; children: Lynne, Benjamin, Laura, Andrea. *Education:* Student at Dana College, 1952, Municipal University of Omaha, 1953, and Iowa State Teachers College, 1953-54. *Address:* R.D. 2, Box 211, Monroe, N.Y. 10950. *Agent:* Robert P. Mills, 156 East 52nd St., New York, N.Y. 10022.

CAREER: Elementary teacher in Atwood, Calif., 1954-55, and Council Bluffs, Iowa, 1955-58. *Member:* New York Civil Liberties Union, Monroe Peace Council.

*WRITINGS—*Juvenile: *Old Boy's Tree House and Other "Deep Forest" Tales* (illustrated by Ursula Arndt), Weybright & Talley, 1968.

QUACKENBUSH, Robert M(ead) 1929-

PERSONAL: Born July 23, 1929, in Hollywood, Calif.; son of Roy Maynard (an engineer) and Virginia (Arbogast) Quackenbush; married Margery Clouser, July 3, 1971. *Education:* Art Center College of Design, B.A., 1956. *Home:* 308 East 79th St. New York, N.Y. 10021. *Office:* 236 East 78th St., New York, N.Y. 10021.

CAREER: Scandanavian Airlines System, in United States and Stockholm, Sweden, advertising art director, 1956-61; free-lance illustrator, painter, and writer, 1961—; Robert

Quackenbush Gallery, New York, N.Y., owner and teacher of art classes, 1968—. *Military service:* U.S. Army, 1951-53. *Awards, honors:* American Institute of Graphic Arts Fifty Best Books award, 1963, for *Poems for Galloping;* Society of Illustrators citations, 1967, for *If I Drove a Truck,* and 1969, for *Little Hans* and *The Pilot.*

WRITINGS—Self-illustrated children's books: (Compiler) *Poems for Counting,* Holt, 1963; (compiler) *Poems for Galloping,* Holt, 1963; *Old MacDonald Had a Farm,* Lippincott, 1972; *Go Tell Aunt Rhody,* Lippincott, 1973; *She'll Be Comin' 'Round the Mountain,* Lippincott, 1973; *Clementine,* Lippincott, 1974.

Illustrator; all children's books: Miriam B. Young *Billy and Milly,* Lothrop 1963; Inez Rice, *A Long, Long Time,* Lothrop, 1963; Hans Christian Andersen, *The Steadfast Tin Soldier,* Holt, 1964; Oscar Wilde, *The Selfish Giant,* Holt, 1965; Marie Halun Bloch, *The Two Worlds of Damyan,* Atheneum, 1966; Robin McKown, *Rakoto and the Drongo Bird,* Lothrop, 1966; McKown, *The Boy Who Woke Up in Madagascar,* Putnam, 1966; Guy de Maupassant, *The Diamond Necklace,* Watts, 1967; Mary K. Phelan, *Election Day,* Crowell, 1967; Anthony Rowley, *A Sunday in Autumn,* Singer, 1967; Margaretha Shemin, *Mrs. Herring,* Lothrop, 1967; Miriam B. Young. *If I Drove a Truck,* Lothrop, 1967; Lilian L. Moore, *I Feel the Same Way* (Junior Literary Guild selection), Atheneum, 1967; Irma S. Black, *Busy Winds,* Holiday House, 1968; James Fenimore Cooper, *The Pilot,* Limited Editions Club, 1968; Eleanor L. Clymer, *Horatio* (Junior Literary Guild selection), Atheneum, 1968; Stephen Crane, *The Open Boat,* Watts 1968; Herman Melville, *Billy Budd, Foretopsman,* Watts, 1968; Mariana Prieto, *When the Monkeys Wore Sombreros,* Harvey House, 1969; Natalie S. Carlson, *Befana's Gift,* Harper, 1969; Era K. Evans, *The Dirt Book: An Introduction to Earth Science,* Little, Brown, 1969; Oscar Wilde, *Little Hans, the Devoted Friend,* Bobbs-Merrill, 1969.

Georgess McHargue, *The Baker and the Basilisk* (Junior Literary Guild selection), Bobbs-Merrill, 1970; Meriam B. Young, *If I Flew a Plane,* Lothrop, 1970; Leonore Klein, *D is for Rover,* Harvey House, 1970; Irma S. Black, *Busy Seeds,* Holiday House, 1970; Charlotte Zolotow, *You and*

(From *There'll be a Hot Time in the Old Town Tonight* by Robert Quackenbush. Illustrated by the author.)

ROBERT QUACKENBUSH

Me, Macmillan, 1970; John Stewart, *The Key to the Kitchen,* Lothrop. 1970; Miriam B. Young, *Beware the Polar Bear,* Lothrop, 1970; Guy Daniels, translator, *The Peasant's Pea Patch,* Delacorte, 1971; Lini R. Grol, *The Bellfounder's Sons,* Bobbs-Merrill, 1971; Rosemary Pendery, *A Home for Hopper,* Morrow, 1971; Harry S. George, *Demo of 70th Street,* Walck, 1971; Jeanette S. Lowrey, *Six Silver Spoons,* Harper, 1971; Julian May, *Blue River,* Holiday House, 1971; Miriam B. Young, *If I Drove a Car,* Lothrop, 1971; Miriam B. Young, *If I Sailed a Boat,* Lothrop, 1971; George Mendoza, *The Scribbler,* Holt, 1971; Miriam B. Young, *If I Drove a Train,* Lothrop, 1972; Ann Cooke, *Giraffes at Home,* Crowell, 1972; Mindel Sitomer and Harry Sitomer, *Lines, Segments and Polygons,* Crowell, 1972; Miriam B. Young, *If I Drove a Tractor,* Lothrop, 1973; Miriam B. Young, *If I Rode a Horse,* Lothrop, 1973; Berniece Freschet, *Prong-Horn on the Powder River,* Crowell, 1973; Jane Yolen, *Wizard Islands,* Crowell, 1973; John F. Waters, *Steal Harbor,* Warne, 1973; Miriam B. Young, *If I Drove a Bus,* Lothrop, 1973; Miriam B. Young, *If I Rode an Elephant,* Lothrop, 1974; Eleanor Clymer, *Leave Horatio Alone,* Atheneum, 1974; Miriam B. Young, *If I Rode a Dinosaur,* Lothrop, 1974; Mason Weems, *Life of Washington,* Limited Editions Club, 1974.

SIDELIGHTS: Quackenbush (a Dutch name originally meaning "duck in the bush") has had exhibits of his art work in leading museums of the U.S., including the Whitney Museum and the Philadelphia Academy of Fine Arts.

"My basic teaching premise stems from my belief that everyone has a unique story to present and to share with children . . . whether it is told with pictures or with words or both. To awaken these stories within my students, I begin by having them draw or write about the rooms they slept in as children. It is truly exciting to watch people discover their childhood worlds again."

QUAMMEN, David 1948-

PERSONAL: Born February 24, 1948, in Cincinnati, Ohio; son of W. A. and Mary (Egan) Quammen. *Education:* Yale University, B.A., 1970; Oxford University, B. Litt., 1973. *Agent:* Owen Laster, Wiliam Morris Agency, 1350 Avenue of the Americas, New York, N.Y. 10019.

CAREER: Writer.

WRITINGS: To Walk the Line (*School Library Journal* book list; novel), Knopf, 1970. Also author of a screen adaptation of *Absalom, Absalom!* neither published nor produced.

WORK IN PROGRESS: Jane Austen: A biography; an untitled novel.

SIDELIGHTS: Quammen describes his novel as dealing "with the birth, growth, and death of a friendship between a white ivy leaguer and a black militant, and is intended to map the gradual convergence of two radically different consciousnesses. As a first draft, it came at the reader in alternating chapters of first person narration by Tyrone, the black, and John, the white. . . (My novel then) went into a straight third person narrative form, and became more modest and, I think, more honest in the process. I was probably not bringing off the projection of Tyrone's consciousness, and in the final form I am not pretending to. The more striking overall affect was sacrificed to greater tightness, reality, and (hopefully) line-by-line, thought-by-thought integrity."

Quammen lists his favorite novelists as Faulkner, Warren, Beckett, and Kafka.

FOR MORE INFORMATION SEE: Library Journal, October 7, 1970; *Best Sellers,* December 15, 1970.

RABE, Berniece (Louise) 1928-

PERSONAL: Surname rhymes with "Abe"; born January 11, 1928, in Parma, Mo.; daughter of Grover Cleveland (a farmer) and Martha (Green) Bagby; married Walter Henry Rabe (vice-president of Precision Diamond Tool Co.), July 30, 1946; children: Alan Walter, Brian Cleve, Clay Victor, Dari Mari. *Education:* Early schooling ended with eighth grade; National College of Education, B.A., 1963; graduate study at Northern Illinois University and (currently) at Roosevelt University. *Religion:* Church of Jesus Christ of Latter-Day Saints (Mormon). *Home:* 860 Willow Lane, Sleepy Hollow, Ill. 60118. *Agent:* Patricia S. Myrer, McIntosh & Otis, Inc., 18 East 41st St., New York, N.Y. 10017.

CAREER: Model with Patricia Stevens Model Agency, Chicago, Ill., 1945-46; teacher and tutor in special education classes, Elgin, Ill., 1963-67. Teacher-trainer with Chicago Stake of Church of Jesus Christ of Latter-Day Saints. *Member:* Fox Valley Writers (member of executive board), Off Campus Writers (member of executive board). *Awards, honors:* Novel awards at Indiana University Writers' Conference and Judson Writers' Conference for manuscript of *Rass;* a chapter of *Rass* received first prize for short story in Chicago Fine Arts competition.

WRITINGS: Rass (juvenile novel), Thomas Nelson, 1973; *Naomi,* Nelson, 1975. Contributor of stories to children's magazines.

WORK IN PROGRESS: Two picture books; two juvenile novels, *Secret Teacher* and *Secret of Strongbox.*

SIDELIGHTS: "I've been a story-spinner by birthright but never aspired to write until I was past forty and had something I wanted to share with a greater audience than the groups I'd lectured before over the years. My husband suggested the writing media."

FOR MORE INFORMATION SEE: Publishers' Weekly, April 16, 1973.

BERNIECE RABE

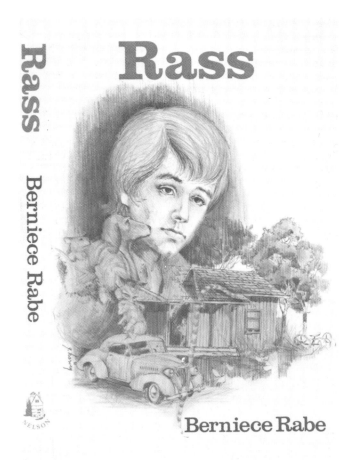

Dad was proud of the horses he broke in to do his bidding, and Rass wanted nothing more than that Dad should be proud of him, too. Trouble was, he was no horse. ∎ (From *Rass* by Berniece Rabe. Jacket designed by Gerry Harvey.)

REED, Gwendolyn 1932-

PERSONAL: Born June 27, 1932, in Louisville, Ky.; daughter of Henry Morrison (a businessman) and Cecelia (Zawatski) Reed. *Education:* Louisville Collegiate School, graduate, 1950; Radcliffe College, B.A., 1954. *Residence:* New York, N.Y. *Agent:* Marilyn Marlow, Curtis Brown Ltd., 60 East 56th St., New York, N.Y. 10022.

CAREER: Worked for Institute of International Education, New York, N.Y., 1956-58, and Museum of Fine Arts, Boston, Mass., 1959-61; Grolier, Inc., New York, N.Y., associate editor of *Book of Knowledge,* 1961-63.

WRITINGS—All for young people: (Editor with Sara Hannum) *Lean Out of the Window: An Anthology of Modern Poetry,* Atheneum, 1965; (editor) *Out of the Ark: An Anthology of Animal Verse* (ALA Notable Book), Atheneum, 1968; *The Sand Lady,* Lothrop, 1968; *Adam and Eve,* Lothrop, 1968; (editor) *Bird Songs* (poems), Atheneum, 1969; *When the Assyrians Came Down from the Trees,* Lothrop, 1969; *The Talkative Beasts: Myths, Fables, and Poems of India,* Lothrop, 1969; (editor) *Songs the Sandman Sings,* Atheneum, 1969; (editor) *Beginnings,* Atheneum, 1971.

FOR MORE INFORMATION SEE: Young Readers' Review, June, 1968, November, 1968; *Horn Book,* December, 1969.

RICHOUX, Pat(ricia) 1927-

PERSONAL: Surname is pronounced Ri-*shue;* born November 1, 1927, in Omaha, Neb.; daughter of Howard Julius (a telephone engineer) and Louise (Kinney) Platt; married Henry J. Richoux (a college electronics teacher), August 8, 1947; children: Howard N., David M., John M.,

She had missed the count for her pivot right turn. . . . Mark, pivoting correctly two counts later, had called his warning as he passed, but it was too late. She had marched clear out of formation, heading for Pasadena. ■ (From *Follow the Leader* by Pat Richoux. Illustrated by George Porter.)

Donna L. *Education:* Doane College, student, 1945-47. *Religion:* Congregational. *Home:* 6652 Richmond Ave., Richmond, Calif. 94805.

PAT RICHOUX

WRITINGS: A Long Walk on a Short Dock (juvenile), Morrow, 1969; *Follow the Leader* (juvenile), Morrow, 1971; *The Stardust Kid* (adult novel), Putnam, 1973.

SIDELIGHTS: As a Navy wife, 1947-59, Ms. Richoux lived in Hawaii and Guam. The background for *Long Walk* was drawn from her own childhood summers on Lake Okoboji in northern Iowa.

The musical background for her second and third books came from playing the sax and clarinet in a high school band, also in local "semi-pro" dance bands in Omaha during the World War II era.

RIDGE, Antonia (Florence)

PERSONAL: Born in Amsterdam, Holland. *Education:* Educated in schools in Holland, England, and France. *Home:* 5 Cranbrook Dr., Esher, Surrey KT10 8DL, England.

CAREER: Author of books, plays, and songs; writes and broadcasts for British Broadcasting Corp., especially on "Woman's Hour." *Member:* Woman's Press Club of London Ltd., Radio Writers Association, Song Writers Guild of Great Britain Ltd., Writers' Guild of Great Britain, French Society of Authors. *Awards, honors:* Citoyenne d'Honneur, Town of St. Etienne, 1967; gold medal and Diplome d'honneur, Meilleurs Ouvriers de France, 1967; Best Radio Drama Script award, Writers' Guild of Great Britain, 1969, for "The Little French Clock."

WRITINGS: The Handy Elephant, and Other Stories, Faber, 1946; *Rom-Bom-Bom, and Other Stories,* Faber, 1946; *Hurrah for Muggins, and Other Stories,* Faber, 1947; *Endless and Company,* Faber, 1948; *Galloping Fred,* Faber, 1950; *Leave It to the Brooks,* National Magazine Co., 1950; *Jan and His Clogs,* Roy, 1951; *Family Album,* Harper, 1952; *Puppet Plays for Children,* Transatlantic, 1953; *Cousin Jan,* Faber, 1954; *Six Radio Plays,* E. J. Arnold, 1954; *By Special Request,* Faber, 1958; *Jan Klaassen Cures the King,* Faber, 1952, reissued as *The Poppenkast; or, How Jan Klaassen Cured the Sick King,* 1958, reissued as *How Jan Klaassen Cured the King: A Play for Children,* 1969; *Grandma Went to Russia,* Faber, 1959; *Never Run from the Lion, and Another Story,* Faber, 1958, Walck,

ANTONIA RIDGE

1959; (editor) Dorothy McCall, *A String of Beads,* Faber, 1961, Transatlantic, 1962; (with Mies Boyhuys) *The Little Red Pony,* Harrap, 1960, Bobbs-Merrill, 1962; *The Thirteenth Child,* Faber, 1962, published in America as *The Royal Pawn,* Appleton, 1963; (with Bouhuys) *Hurrah for a Dutch Birthday,* Faber, 1964; *For Love of a Rose,* Faber, 1965; (translator and adapter) Norbert Casteret, *Mission Underground,* Harrap, 1968; (with Bouhuys) *Melodia: a Story from Holland,* Faber, 1969; "The Little French Clock" (radio play), first broadcast by British Broadcasting Corp., 1969.

Writing for British Broadcasting Corp. programs includes talks, stories, and serials, radio and television plays for adults and children, history scripts for schools programs, talks broadcast to France on "Ici Londres." Also writer of plays for Hogarth Puppets, songs, English lyrics of songs and "Stories-in-Song" for Obernkirchen Children's Choir, including English words for "The Happy Wanderer." Contributor of articles and stories to *Woman's Journal, Woman, My Home, Argosy* (England), *Good Housekeeping, Woman's Mirror,* and *Woman's Weekly.*

SIDELIGHTS: A film, "Das Schone Abenteur," is an adaptation of the German edition of *Family Album;* radio and television plays for adult and children are regularly repeated in France, Germany, Italy, Switzerland, Yugoslavia, Belgium, the Scandinavian countries, and Greece; books have been translated into several languages and serialized in European magazines and newspapers.

FOR MORE INFORMATION SEE: Times Literary Supplement, January 12, 1967, October 16, 1969.

ROBINSON, Jean O. 1934-

PERSONAL: Born August 19, 1934, in La Crosse, Wis.; daughter of Henry Adam (a hardware merchant) and Amanda (Lueck) Kroner; married Donald W. Robinson (an art director), March 12, 1955; children: Lindsey Jean, Carol Elizabeth. *Education:* Wisconsin State College—La Crosse, student, 1953-54. *Religion:* Lutheran. *Home:* 18 Mercer Hill Rd., Ambler, Pa. 19002.

CAREER: WKBT Television, La Crosse, Wis., copywriter, 1954-55; KTRI Radio, Sioux City, Iowa, copywriter, 1955-56; KSTP Radio & Television, Minneapolis, Minn., copywriter, 1956-57; has also worked as a library assistant in La Crosse, Wis., and in Minneapolis, Minn., where she was a church librarian for six years; writer.

WRITINGS: Francie (juvenile novel), Follett, 1970; *The Secret Life of T. K. Dearing* (Junior Literary Guild selection), Seabury, 1973; *The Strange, But Wonderful Cosmic Awareness of Duffy Moon* (juvenile novel), Seabury, 1974. Contributor of other short fiction and nonfiction magazine pieces in *Modern Bride, Weight Watchers, Camping Journal, Girltalk, Lady's Circle, Ingenue, American Girl, Practical English, Modern People, Jack and Jill, Child Life,* and many others.

JEAN O. ROBINSON

Take our club flag, for instance. It was one of Mom's best white towels, which should give you an idea of how low I would stoop to get what I needed. ■ (From *The Secret Life of T. K. Dearing* by Jean Robinson. Illustrated by Charles Robinson.)

WORK IN PROGRESS: Another juvenile novel; assorted magazine articles.

SIDELIGHTS: "My daughters claim that they are the only kids in school whose mother cannot write a simple excuse note without revising it three or four times and typing it up double-spaced with wide margins.

"*The Secret Life of T. K. Dearing* was an entry on a 3 x 5 file card for a long time before he actually came to life. Then, for a brief moment, he emerged in one of my short stories, though under a different name. Finally I knew he would wait no longer. T. K. wanted his story told; what's more, *he* would do the telling. From that moment on, I had no rest. T. K. took over my typewriter, he answered the phone, I could even hear him (and his grandfather) talking in my mind when I was trying to sleep. He dictated to me the details of his life, his family, his neighborhood. All I was required to do was walk in the woods and locate his clubhouse.

"Never before have I been so completely taken over by a character. If I took a break from my typewriter to visit a friend, T. K. would have a bit of dialogue he would insist be written down the minute I walked into my friend's house. Toward the end of the book I even sprained my ankle, tuning in to T. K. when I should have been watching some steps."

FOR MORE INFORMATION SEE: *Junior Literary Guild Catalogue,* March, 1973; *Publishers' Weekly,* March 5, 1973.

ROBINSON, Joan (Mary) G(ale Thomas) 1910- (Joan Gale Thomas)

PERSONAL: Born 1910, in Gerrard's Cross, Buckinghamshire, England; daughter of George Gale (a barrister-at-law and solicitor) and Beatrice Amy (a barrister-at-law; maiden name, Cuff) Thomas; married second husband, Richard Gavin Robinson (a writer and illustrator), 1941; children: Deborah, Susanna. *Education:* Educated in private schools in England; also studied at Chelsea Illustrators Studio. *Home:* Unicorn House, Burnham Market, King's Lynn Norfolk, England and 39 South Hill Park, London N.W.3, England.

JOAN G. ROBINSON

CAREER: Writer and illustrator of children's books, 1939—. *Member:* Society of Authors, National Book League, P.E.N.

WRITINGS—Under name Joan Gale Thomas, all self-illustrated: *A Stands for Angel,* Mowbray, 1939 (published in America as *A Is for Angel,* Lothrop, 1953); *Our Father,* Mowbray, 1940; *If Jesus Came to My House,* Mowbray, 1941, Lothrop, 1951; *Christmas,* Mowbray, 1946; *My Garden Book,* Mowbray, 1947; *God of All Things,* Mowbray, 1948; *One Little Baby,* Mowbray, 1950, Lothrop, 1956; *Ten Little Angels,* Mowbray, 1951; *The Happy Year,* Mowbray, 1953; *If I'd Been Born in Bethlehem,* Mowbray, 1953; *I Ask a Blessing,* Mowbray, 1955; *Where Is God?,* Mowbray, 1957, Lothrop, 1959; *The Christmas Angel,* Mowbray, 1961; *Seven Days,* Mowbray, 1964.

Under name of Joan G. Robinson, all self-illustrated: *Debbie Robbie's Day Nursery,* University of London Press, 1950; *Susie at Home,* Harrap, 1953; *Teddy Robinson,* Harrap, 1953; *More About Teddy Robinson,* Harrap, 1954; *Teddy Robinson's Book,* Harrap, 1955; *Dear Teddy Robinson,* Harrap, 1956; *Mary-Mary,* Harrap, 1957; *More Mary-Mary,* Harrap, 1958; *Another Teddy Robinson,* Harrap, 1960; *Madam Mary-Mary,* Harrap, 1960; *Keeping Up with Teddy Robinson,* Harrap, 1964; *Mary-Mary Stories* (includes *Mary-Mary, More Mary-Mary,* and *Madam Mary-Mary*), Harrap, 1965, Coward, 1968.

Author only: (With Gale Young) *Monsieur Charbon,* Harrap, 1962; *When Marnie Was There,* Collins, 1967, Coward, 1968; *Charley* (ALA Notable Book), Collins, 1969, Coward, 1970; *The House in the Square,* Collins, 1972.

Illustrator only: *Carol Book,* Mowbray, 1959.

WORK IN PROGRESS: Another children's novel.

SIDELIGHTS:. "There must be some advantages in not being good at school—I went to seven and was hopeless in each. One reason might be that nothing is expected of you. Another that one develops some small line of one's own which somehow sidesteps the competitive world. I drew. I painted Christmas cards. In time I wrote simple verses for very small children so as to have something to illustrate. These developed into a whole series of little books. I illustrated other people's stories, and when these did not please me, I wrote my own.

"Not wanting to aspire too high, I wrote about a teddy bear. It was not easy—I was very slow, putting a lot into it. Then came another series about a little girl, the smallest and most insignificant of a large family, who always came out on top. By this time illustrating seemed a mug's game. Writing was everything. Dare I write a novel? I did for ten-to-twelve-year olds. Much went into it of the solitary child, for some of us are always solitary children, even though we are of four, as I was. Two more books about loners followed, not I hope without their humor, and this brings me up to the present time. Now . . ."

Ms. Robinson prefers writing to illustrating. She writes slowly, aiming in secular books at striking a balance between entertaining the children and not boring the parents

"When I'm a lady I shall always make raw cakes"

(From *Mary-Mary Stories* by Joan G. Robinson. Illustrated by the author.)

to death if they read aloud. Her major concern in religious books is "no guilt—no strings attached to God's love," the result she believes of her own non-conformist childhood. "I never passed an exam, never mastered long division, and am still inclined to discover platitudes with great enthusiasm thinking I've invented them. I can also sit up all night talking."

FOR MORE INFORMATION SEE: Boris Ford, *Young Writers, Young Readers,* Hutchinson, 1960; Margery Fisher, *Intent Upon Reading,* Brockhampton Press, 1961; Brian Doyle, *The Who's Who of Children's Literature,* Schocken, 1968; *Horn Book,* August, 1970.

ROBOTTOM, John 1934-

PERSONAL: Born January 8, 1934, in Birmingham, England; son of Albert (an engineer) and Kathleen (Carlisle) Robottom; married Molly Barber (a lecturer), November 11, 1956; children: Ellen, Sally, Robert. *Education:* University of Birmingham, B.A. (honors), 1956. *Home:* 11 Knutswood Close, King's Heath, Birmingham, England.

CAREER: Teacher in secondary schools, 1956-65; Bingley College of Education, Yorkshire, England, lecturer in his-

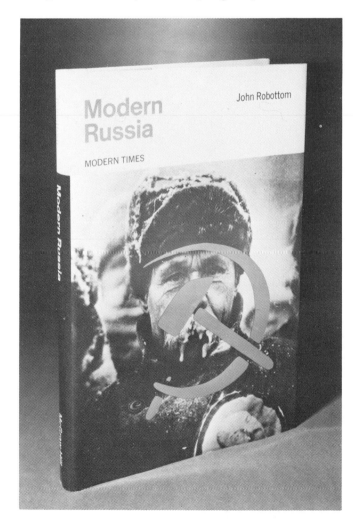

tory, 1966-68; Crewe College of Education, Crewe, England, senior lecturer in history, 1968-73, principal lecturer in history, 1973-74; British Broadcasting Corporation, Midland's division, education officer, 1974—.

WRITINGS: Modern China: China in Revolution, Longmans, Green, 1967, published in America as *China in Revolution,* McGraw, 1969; *Modern Russia,* Longmans, Green, 1969; (editor) *Making the Modern World,* Longmans, Green, 1970; *Twentieth Century China,* Wayland, 1971; *Making the Nineteenth Century: Britain,* Longmans, Green, 1974.

WORK IN PROGRESS: Books on nineteenth-century European history for use in English schools; documentary source material for study of Russian and Chinese history.

SIDELIGHTS: "My principal area of interest lies in the production of material on history for children (14-16). I do much writing and lecturing on this subject. My chief secondary interest is travel, especially in Eastern Europe. I speak French and Serbo-Croatian, both badly.

"I believe in history as a core element in a sound general education and have not lost faith in its potential as a means of improving understanding between groups and between nations. Much of my present work is founded upon the enjoyment of ten years teaching in different United Kingdom secondary schools."

ROCKWELL, Thomas 1933-

PERSONAL: Born March 13, 1933, in New Rochelle, N.Y., son of Norman (an artist) and Mary (Barstow) Rockwell; married Gail Sudler (an artist), July 16, 1955; children: Barnaby, Abigail. *Education:* Bard College, B.A., 1956. *Home address:* R.D.3, Lauer Rd., Poughkeepsie, N.Y., 12603. *Agent:* Joan Raines, Theron Raines Agency, 244 Madison Ave., New York, N.Y.

WRITINGS: Rackety-Bang (juvenile; illustrated by his

THOMAS ROCKWELL

"E-nor-muss. . . . Miss Kinnell, it's a stupid word. Why don't they just say 'big'? I don't see why the people who write these dumb books always have to use such big words. . . ." ■ (From *Squawwwk* by Thomas Rockwell. Illustrated by Gail Rockwell.)

wife, Gail Rockwell), Pantheon, 1969; *Norman Rockwell's Hometown* (juvenile; illustrated by his father, Norman Rockwell), Windmill Books, 1970; *Humpf!* (juvenile, illustrated by Muriel Batherman), Pantheon, 1971; *Squawwwk!* (juvenile, illustrated by Gail Rockwell), Little, Brown, 1972; *The Neon Motorcycle* (juvenile, illustrated by Michael Horen), Watts, 1973.

SIDELIGHTS: "I began reading to my son, Barnaby, when he was about three years old from the *Oxford Book of Nursery Rhymes,* edited by Iona and Peter Opie. The nursery rhymes interested and excited me—there was such a variety among the poems—character sketches, stories, prayers, riddles, nonsense, fantasy, all sorts of rhymes and rhythms. I couldn't resist trying a few myself. From there I went on to stories and picture books."

ROTHMAN, Joel 1938-

PERSONAL: Born April 6, 1938, in New York, N.Y.; son of David and Gladys Rothman; married Katy Hidalgo (a teacher), April, 1960; married second wife, Marilyn Amsel (a teacher), January 31, 1971; children: (first marriage) Ivan, Andrea. *Education:* Brooklyn College of the City University of New York, B.A., 1962; Hunter College of the City University of New York, M.S., 1965; Columbia University, further study. *Politics:* "Depends." *Home:* 3 Sheridan Sq., New York, N.Y. 10014.

CAREER: Professional musician (percussionist), 1953—, and publisher of his own percussion method books; teacher of music, science, and reading in elementary schools of New York, N.Y., 1962—.

Some people dine by candlelight. ■ (From *Night Lights* by Joel Rothman. Illustrated by Joe Lasker.)

JOEL ROTHMAN

WRITINGS—Juvenile: (With Ruthven Tremain) *Secrets with Ciphers and Codes,* Macmillan, 1969; (with Bruce Roberts) *At Last to the Ocean; The Story of the Endless Cycle of Water,* Crowell-Collier, 1971; *Night Lights,* Albert Whitman, 1972; *A Moment in Time,* Scroll Press, 1972; *I Can Be Anything You Can Be,* Scroll Press, 1973; *Once There Was a Stream,* Scroll Press, 1973; *Which One is Different?,* Doubleday, 1974; *The Artcyclopedia,* Elizabeth Press, 1974. Writer of more than ninety manuals on percussion methods, 1961-72.

RUSKIN, Ariane   1935-

PERSONAL: Born September 18, 1935, daughter of Simon L. (a physician) and Frances (Reder) Ruskin; married Michael Batterberry, May, 1968. *Education:* Barnard College, B.A., 1955; New Hall, Cambridge University, M.A., 1957. *Home:* 1100 Madison Ave., New York, N.Y. 10023.

CAREER: Dancer with Marquis de Cuevas Ballet, Paris, France, 1955; editorial work with United Nations, New York, N.Y., 1961; now free-lance writer. *Member:* Phi Beta Kappa.

WRITINGS: The Pantheon Story of Art for Young People, Pantheon, 1964; *Spy for Liberty* (life of Beaumarchais), Pantheon, 1965; *Nineteenth Century Art,* McGraw, 1968; *Seventeenth and Eighteenth Century Art,* McGraw, 1969;

Reprinted by permission of McGraw-Hill Book Company.

(with Michael Batterberry) *Greek and Roman Art*, McGraw, 1970; *Art of the High Renaissance*, McGraw, 1970; *Prehistoric Art and Ancient Art of the Near East*, McGraw, 1971; (with Michael Batterberry) *Primitive Art*, McGraw, 1971; (with Michael Batterberry) *To Picasso With Love*, Abrams, 1971; *Art and History*, Watts, 1972; *On the Town in New York*, Scribner, 1973; (with Michael Batterberry) *History in Art*, Watts, 1974; *Pantheon Story of American Art*, Pantheon, 1975. Contributor to *Wine and Food*. Contributing editor, *Harpers Bazaar*, 1972-74.

SIDELIGHTS: Speaks French and Spanish; has reading knowledge of Greek and Latin.

SCAGNETTI, Jack   1924-

PERSONAL: Born December 24, 1924, in Piney Fork, Ohio; son of Quinto and Albina (Tardella) Scagnetti; married, 1950 (divorced); children: Kimberly, Craig. *Education:* Graduated from high school in Detroit, Mich., 1943 ("considerable self-education via actually writing, plus reading"). *Home and office:* 4634 Kraft, North Hollywood, Calif. 91602.

CAREER: Started writing at age thirteen, helped by sister who was a society editor; reporter and editor for weekly newspapers in Detroit, Mich., and concurrently public relations director for private athletic club in Detroit, 1948-57; publicity director and promotion manager for chain of seventeen bowling centers, Norwalk, Calif., 1958-65; chief editor, *Popular Hot Rodding* (magazine), Los Angeles, Calif., 1966-68; free-lance magazine and publicity writer and photographer, Sherman Oaks, Calif., 1968—. Copywriter and editorial director for automotive advertising agency, Detroit, 1953-54. *Military service:* U.S. Army, 1943-46.

WRITINGS: (With George Barris) *Famous Custom and Show Cars* (Junior Literary Guild Selection), Dutton, 1973; (with Mac Hunter) *Golf for Beginners*, Grosset, 1973; (with Count Yogi) *Five Simple Steps to Perfect Golf*, Nash Publishing, 1973; (with George Barris) *Cars of the Stars*, Jonathan David, 1974. Contributor of more than six hundred articles to *Cars, Hi-Performance, Inside Golf, Cars, GolfGuide,* and other magazines; also writer and editor of 24 special single-subject "one-shot" magazines in auto and golf field. Contributing editor, *Motor Life*, 1958-61.

WORK IN PROGRESS: Books on a famous golfer, on golf instruction, and Rudolph Valentino; movie stars nostalgia photo books.

JACK SCAGNETTI

KEN SCHIFF

SCHIFF, Ken(neth Roy) 1942-

PERSONAL: Born August 3, 1942, in New York, N.Y.; son of Louis (a banker) and Alice (Neubauer) Schiff. *Education:* Grinnell College, B.A., 1964; Columbia University, M.A., 1966. *Home:* 12 Summer St., Somerville, Mass. 02143.

CAREER: *Westport News,* Westport, Conn., sports editor, 1964-65; Globe Book Co., New York, N.Y., an editor, 1966-73; permanent substitute junior high school teacher of social studies, Newton, Mass., 1973; Boston Center for Adult Education, Boston, Mass., instructor in creative writing, 1972—; Massachusetts Institute of Technology, Boston, humanities instructor, 1974. *Awards, honors: Passing Go* was nominated for a National Book Award.

WRITINGS: Passing Go (novel; ALA Notable Book), Dodd, 1972; *American Popular Culture,* Learning Trends, *in press.*

SCHNEIDER, Herman 1905-

PERSONAL: Born May 31, 1905, in Kreschov, Poland; son of Louis (a tailor) and Leah (Feldman) Schneider; married Natalie Shmerler, August 19, 1931 (divorced, 1941); married Nina Zimet (a writer), June 29, 1941; children: (first marriage) Robert; (second marriage) Susan Schneider Colchie, Lucy; (stepson) Steven. *Education:* City University of New York, City College, B.S., 1928, M.S., 1930. *Religion:* Jewish. *Home:* 21 West 11th St., New York, N.Y. 10011.

CAREER: New York (N.Y.), public schools, teacher, 1928-48, science supervisor, 1948-53; Bank St. College, New York, N.Y., member of faculty, 1941-46. Consultant for 52 filmstrips associated with the *Heath Science Series* published by University Films, Inc. *Member:* National Education Association, National Science Teachers Association, American Association for the Advancement of Science (fellow), Council for Elementary Science International, Association for the Education of Teachers in Science, National Association of Science Writers, New York Academy of Science. *Awards, honors:* Litt.D., Fairleigh Dickinson University, 1967.

WRITINGS: Everyday Machines and How They Work, Whittlesey House, 1950; *Everyday Weather and How It Works,* Whittlesey House, 1951, 3rd edition, 1963; (compiler with Julius Schwartz) *Growing Up With Science Books* (New York), c. 1959.

With wife, Nina Schneider—all juveniles: *How Big Is Big?: From Stars to Atoms, a Yardstick for the Universe,* W. R. Scott, 1946, revised edition, 1950; *Let's Find Out,* W. R. Scott, 1946; *Now Try This,* W. R. Scott, 1947, reissued as *Now Try This to Move a Heavy Load: Push, Pull and Lift,* 1963 (published in England as *Push, Pull, and Lift,* Brockhampton Press, 1960); *Let's Look Inside Your House: A Picture-Science Book About Water, Heat and Electricity,* W. R. Scott, 1948; *Heat and Electricity,* W. R. Scott, 1948; *How Your Body Works,* introduction by Milton I. Levine, W. R. Scott, 1949.

Let's Look Under the City: Water, Gas, Waste, Electricity, Telephone, W. R. Scott, 1950, revised edition, 1954; *Plants in the City,* John Day, 1951, revised edition, Faber, 1953; *You Among the Stars,* W. R. Scott, 1951; *Follow the Sunset,* Doubleday, 1952; *Rocks, Rivers and the Changing Earth: A First Book About Geology,* W. R. Scott, 1952; *Your Telephone and How It Works,* Whittlesey House, 1952, 3rd edition, 1965; *More Power to You: A Short History of Power from the Windmill to the Atom,* W. R. Scott, 1953, also published as *More Power to You: From Windmills to Atomic Energy,* E. M. Hale, 1953; *Science Fun with Milk Cartons,* Whittlesey House, 1953; *Heath Elementary Science,* Heath, Book 1: *Science for Work and Play,* Book 2: *Science for Here and Now,* Book 3: *Science Far and Near,* Book 4: *Science in Your Life,* Book 5: *Science in Our World,* Book 6: *Science for Today and Tomorrow,* 1954-55, 2nd edition published as *Heath Science Series* with additional titles, Book 7: *Science in the Space Age,* Book 8: *Science and Your Future,* 1961, 3rd edition, 1968 (series published in England as *Elementary Science,* Harrap, 1954-55, 2nd edition, 1961); *Let's Find Out About Electricity* (includes kit to make working models

NINA & HERMAN SCHNEIDER

of a telegraph set, lighthouse, 4-way traffic signal, and TV theatre), Grosset, 1956; *Let's Find Out About the Weather* (includes kit to make working models of a barometer, weather vane, air current and air speed indicators, humidity gauge, and weather house), Grosset, 1956; (editor) Eunice Holsaert, *Life in the Arctic,* Harvey House, 1957; (editor) Eunice Holsaert, *Life in the Tropics,* Harvey House, 1957; *Science Around You,* Harrap, 1966.

WORK IN PROGRESS: A revision, with wife, Nina Schneider, of *Heath Science Series,* grades 1-6.

SCHOLASTICA, Sister Mary
See JENKINS, Marie M.

SHAW, Ray

PERSONAL: Surname is legally Shaw; Daughter of David and Lillian (Levinson) Shaw; married Eugene O. Rappaport (a medical doctor; deceased); children: Lee, Faith. *Education:* Attended New York University and Northwestern University. *Home:* 255 West 90th St., New York, N.Y. 10024.

CAREER: Sculptor, free-lance photographer, and writer; has sculpted the hands of many celebrities, including those of Bernard Baruch, Lauren Bacall, Irving Berlin, Margaret Bourke-White, Jack Dempsey, General James Doolittle, Albert Einstein, Mischa Elman, Helen Hayes, Joe Louis, Clare Booth Luce, President Prado of Peru, Franklin D. Roosevelt, Archbishop Fulton J. Sheen, Lowell Thomas, Margaret Truman, Sir Ernest McMillan, Fritz Reiner, and George Szell; has exhibited sculpture and photographs in numerous cities throughout United States, and covered photo assignments in many foreign countries for UNICEF, the World Bank, International Business Machines Corp., and others. *Member:* Overseas Press Club, Women's Press Club of New York.

WRITINGS: Catnips, Essandess, 1970; (with Charlotte Zolotow) *A Week in Lateef's World: India,* Crowell Collier, 1971; *The Nutcracker* (photo-story of the ballet), Prentice-Hall, 1971; *New York for Children,* Dutton, 1972; *How to Find Those Great Overseas Jobs,* Award Books, 1972; *Candle Art,* Morrow, 1973; *Washington for Children,* Scribner, 1975. Contributor of articles to *Musical America, Family Circle, Maclean's* (Canada), *American Magazine, Charm,* and other periodicals.

Something about the Author

RAY SHAW

WORK IN PROGRESS: A Week in Tooran's World: Iran, and *A Week in a Zuni Indian Child's World,* both for Crowell Collier; research on a book on Tibet; compiling photos to illustrate Walt Whitman's poetry.

SIDELIGHTS: Ms. Shaw has traveled in Algeria, Denmark, Egypt, Syria, Israel, Jordan, Lebanon, England, Iceland, Ireland, India, Iran, Morocco, Switzerland, Tunisia, Turkey, Mexico and other countries on photo-journalistic assignments; she is presently awaiting word on a trip to China to execute book assignments. Ms. Shaw's sculpture of the hands of President Roosevelt is on permanent exhibit at the Hyde Park Library.

HOBBIES AND OTHER INTERESTS: The dance, cooking.

SHULMAN, Alix Kates 1932-

PERSONAL: Born August 17, 1932, in Cleveland, Ohio; daughter of Samuel S. (an attorney) and Dorothy (Davis) Kates; married Marcus Klien, April 19, 1953; married second husband, Martin Shulman, June 19, 1959; children: (second marriage) Teddy, Polly. *Education:* Bradford Junior College, A.A., 1951; Western Reserve University, B.A., 1953; graduate study at Columbia University, 1953-54, and New York University, 1960-61. *Residence:* New York, N.Y. *Agent:* Ellen Levine, Curtis Brown Ltd., 60 East 56th St., New York, N.Y. 10022.

Everyone knew that Lisa was the best finder in the playground. (From *Finders Keepers* by Alix Shulman. Illustrated by Emily McCully.)

CAREER: Writer. *Member:* Feminists on Children's Media, Society of Magazine Writers.

WRITINGS: Bosley on the Number Line (juvenile), McKay, 1970; (contributor) Sookie Stambler, editor, *Women's Liberation: A Blueprint for the Future,* Ace Books, 1970; (editor) *The Traffic in Women and Other Essays,* Times Change Press, 1970; *Awake or Asleep* (juvenile), Addison-Wesley, 1971; *To the Barricades: The Anarchist Life of Emma Goldman* (juvenile), Crowell, 1971; (contributor) Vivian Gornick and B. K. Moran, editors, *Women in Sexist Society: Studies in Power and Powerlessness,* Basic Books, 1971; *Finders Keepers* (juvenile), Bradbury, 1972; *Memoirs of an Ex-Prom Queen* (novel), Knopf, 1972; (editor) *Red Emma Speaks: Selected Writings and Speeches of Emma Goldman,* Random House, 1972. Contributor to *Redbook, Evergreen Review, Atlantic Monthly,* and to feminist journals.

SILVER, Ruth
See CHEW, Ruth

SIMON, Joe
See SIMON, Joseph H.

SIMON, Joseph H. 1913-
(Joe Simon)

PERSONAL: Born October 11, 1913, in Rochester, N.Y.; son of Harry (a tailor) and Rose (Kurland) Simon; married wife, Harriet, May 18, 1946; children: Jon, James, Melissa, Gail, Lori. *Education:* Attended Syracuse University. *Politics:* Independent. *Religion:* Jewish. *Home:* 11 Arbutus Lane, Stony Brook, N.Y., 11790.

CAREER: Rochester Journal American, Rochester, N.Y., artist-writer, 1933-36; Syracuse Journal American, Syracuse, N.Y., art editor, writer, 1936-38; *Syracuse Herald,* Syracuse, N.Y., artist-writer, 1938-39; editor, Goodman Publications and Crestwood Publications, 1946-68, Harvey Publications, 1945—, National Periodicals and Pyramid Publications, 1968-70, all in New York, N.Y. Publisher, Mainline Publications and Pastime Publications; Bursten, Phillips & Newman Advertising, Great Neck, N.Y., art director. *Military service:* U.S. Coast Guard, 1942-45.

WRITINGS—under name Joe Simon; all self-illustrated: *Incurably Sick,* Avon, 1962; *Look Who's Talking,* W.W.R., Inc., 1964; *A Funny Thing Happened to Me on the Way to Tel Aviv,* All American Printing Co., 1967; (editor) *Ensicklopedia,* Pyramid Publications, 1970.

Creator of Captain America and many other comic book heroes; originator of "Young Romance" comic books and *Sick* Magazine.

WORK IN PROGRESS: A book on dog breeding for the family, self-illustrated, entitled *Home Bred;* memoirs of the early years of comic books.

HOBBIES AND OTHER INTERESTS: Breeding great danes; politics.

FOR MORE INFORMATION SEE: Jules Feiffer, *The Great Comic Book Heroes,* Dial, 1965.

SOMMER, Elyse 1929-

PERSONAL: Born January 26, 1929, in Frankfurt, Germany; daughter of Julius (a businessman) and Meta (Bluethenthal) Vorchheimer; married Mike Sommer (a salesman), May 24, 1952; children: Paul, Joellen. *Education:* New York University, B.Sc., 1949. *Address:* P.O. Box E, Woodmere, N.Y. 11598.

CAREER: Elyse Sommer, Inc. (literary agency), Woodmere, N.Y., owner and president, 1952—. Teacher of crafts in high school and adult education classes; also teacher of adult illiterates. *Member:* American Crafts Council, Long Island Craftsmen's Guild.

WRITINGS: Decoupage Old and New, Watson-Guptill, 1971; *The Bread Dough Craft Book,* Lothrop, 1972; (with daughter, Joellen Sommer) *Sew Your Own Accessories,* Lothrop, 1972; *Designing Without Outs,* Lothrop, 1973; *Rock and Stone Craft,* Crown, 1973; *Make It With Burlap,* Lothrop, 1973; *Contemporary Costume Jewelry: A Multi-media Approach,* Crown, 1974; (with husband, Mike Sommer) *Creating with Driftwood and Weathered Wood,* Crown, 1974; (with Mike Sommer) *A New Look at Crochet,* Crown, 1975. Contributor to *Writer's Digest* and *Creative Crafts.* Formerly wrote monthly newsletter for writers.

WORK IN PROGRESS: Art from Felt, for Crown; *Primer of Patchwork, Applique, and Quilting,* for Lothrop.

SIDELIGHTS: "I have tried in all my books to inspire the reader not so much to learn to make things but to learn to see artistic possibilities in all sorts of materials. To me the important self-development for a craftsman, young or old, is to be able to see something more than a stone or a shape. The execution of the idea is fun, the finished product is satisfying, but most importantly the creative craftsman has learned to look at something in a new way.

"Hopefully this will then be applied to other aspects of life . . . looking at people, listening to words in a way that reaches below the obvious surface. For those who copy step-by-step, and there will always be those, I've tried to set standards of good taste to offset some of the plastic, artsy-craftsy horrors foisted on the public by the mass producers."

Her husband does the photographs for her books, and has become co-author on all adult books.

FOR MORE INFORMATION SEE: Horn Book, October, 1972.

STEVENS, Peter
See GEIS, Darlene

STEWART, Robert Neil 1891-1972

PERSONAL: Born August 8, 1891, in Edinburgh, Scotland; son of John Charles and Anna (Babington) Stewart; married Georgette Hambachidze, April 20, 1917; children: Nino, Danah. *Education:* Attended Harrow School and Royal Military College (now Academy) at Sandhurst. *Home:* Kinlochmoidart, Fort William, Scotland.

CAREER: British Army, 1911-21, 1939-45, retired as major general. Served in France 1914-16, the Balkans, 1916-18, Caucasia, 1918-19, Great Britain, 1939-45. *Awards, honors*—Military: Order of British Empire, Military Cross (twice), Legion d'Honneur, Order of the Falcon (Iceland).

WRITINGS: Experiment in Angling, and Some Essays, Northern Chronicle Office, 1947; *Casting Around,* Thomas Nelson, 1948; *Rivers of Iceland,* Icelandic Government, 1950; *Running Silver,* W. & R. Chambers, 1952; *Open Spaces,* Thomas Nelson, 1953; *Boys' Book of Angling,* W. & R. Chambers, 1955; *Boy's Book of Boats,* W. & R. Chambers, 1956; *Dogs of the Northern Trails,* W. & R. Chambers, 1956; *Boys' Book of the Deep Sea,* W. & R. Chambers, 1957; *Boys' Book of the Jungle,* W. & R.

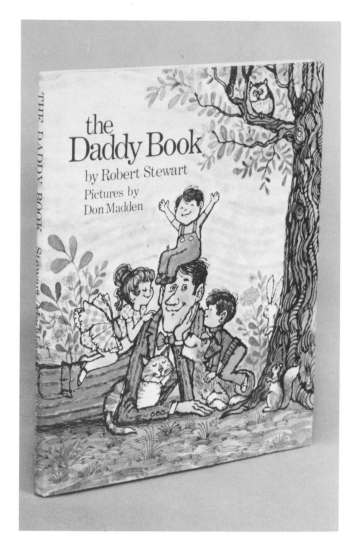

Chambers, 1958; *Boys' Book of the Yukon,* W. & R. Chambers, 1959; *Unsung Trails,* W. & R. Chambers, 1960; (with Moray MacLaren) *Fishing as We Find It,* Stanley Paul, 1960; *Salmons and Trout: Their Habits and Haunts,* W. & R. Chambers, 1963; *A Living from Lobsters,* Fishing News, 1971.

(Died June 21, 1972)

STONE, Eugenia   1879-1971
(Gene Stone)

PERSONAL: Born May 11, 1879, in Gold Hill, Nev.; daughter of William Hamilton (an attorney) and Cassaline (Mara) Stone. *Education:* Studied at University of California and University of Southern California. *Politics:* Democrat. *Home:* 294 North Raymond Ave., Pasadena, Calif. 91103.

CAREER: Onetime teacher in public schools in Nevada and California; Railroad and Public Service Commission of Nevada, assistant secretary, 1913-19; free-lance writer, mostly of books for young people, 1920-71.

WRITINGS: (Under name Gene Stone) *Sagebrush Stories,* Crowell, Volume I: *Jane and the Owl,* 1920, Volume II: *The Adventures of Jane,* 1921; (under name Gene Stone) *Cousin Nancy,* Crowell, 1920; (under name Gene Stone) *The Story of Thomas Jefferson,* Barse & Hopkins, 1922; *Big Wheels Rolling,* Caxton, 1942; *Freemen Shall Stand,* Thomas Nelson, 1944; *Robin Hood's Arrow,* Wilcox & Follett, 1948; *Secret of the Bog,* Holiday House, 1948; *Page Boy for King Arthur,* Wilcox & Follet, 1949, reissued as *Page Boy of Camelot,* Scholastic Book Services, 1972; *Sagebrush Filly* (Junior Literary Guild selection), Knopf, 1950; *Squire for King Arthur,* Wilcox & Follett, 1955; *Magpie Hill,* Watts, 1958; *Tall Sails to Jamestown,* Macrae Smith, 1967.

WORK IN PROGRESS: Wild Marjoram, a historical novel; *Swimmer in the Rain;* "Panorama," a dramatic poem; "The Sorcerer," an epic poem based on Chinese ancient love story and comedy.

FOR MORE INFORMATION SEE: Young Wings, February, 1951.

(Died, 1971)

The three craned their necks, teetering on the fence rail. Lying in the back of the buckboard was something furry and brownish. ■ (From *Sagebrush Filly* by Eugenia Stone. Illustrated by Earl Mayan.)

STONE, Gene
See STONE, Eugenia

SUBOND, Valerie
See GRAYLAND, Valerie

SWARTHOUT, Kathryn   1919-

PERSONAL: Born January 8, 1919, in Columbus, Mont.; daughter of Lige Hood and Blair (Cox) Vaughn; married Glendon Fred Swarthout (a professor of English and writer), December 28, 1940; children: Miles Hood. *Education:* Ward-Belmont, A.A., 1938; University of Michigan, A.B., 1940; Michigan State University, M.A., 1956. *Religion:* Protestant. *Home:* 5045 Tamanar Way, Scottsdale, Ariz. 85253. *Agent:* William Morris Agency, 1350 Avenue of the Americas, New York, N.Y. 10019.

CAREER: Teacher in elementary grades, 1954-59; writer for children. *Member:* League of Women Voters.

WRITINGS—Juvenile books with husband, Glendon Swarthout: *The Ghost and the Magic Saber,* Random House, 1963; *Whichaway,* Random House, 1966; *The Button Boat,* Doubleday, 1969; *TV Thompson,* Doubleday, 1972; *Whales To See The*, Doubleday, 1975.

FOR MORE INFORMATION SEE: Horn Book, February, 1970.

KATHRYN SWARTHOUT

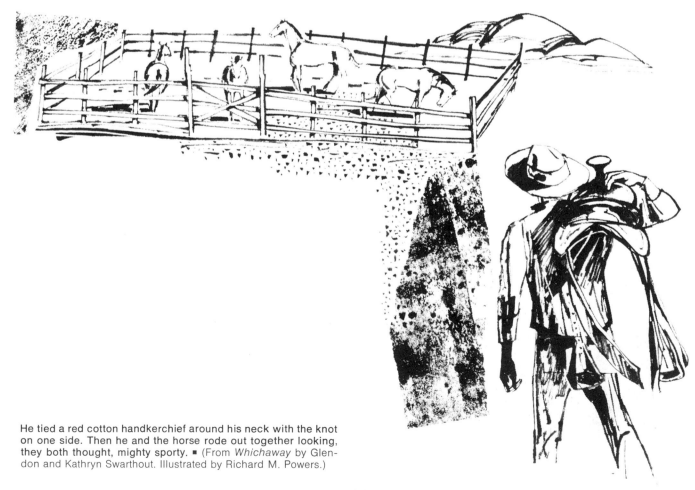

He tied a red cotton handkerchief around his neck with the knot on one side. Then he and the horse rode out together looking, they both thought, mighty sporty. ■ (From *Whichaway* by Glendon and Kathryn Swarthout. Illustrated by Richard M. Powers.)

SYPHER, Lucy Johnston 1907-

PERSONAL: Born August 6, 1907, in Wales, N.D.; daughter of George H. (a banker) and Caroline (Gale) Johnston; married Wylie Sypher (an author and professor), August 31, 1929; children: G. Wylie, Gale Sypher Jacob. *Education:* University of North Dakota, A.B., 1927; Tufts University, M.A., 1929. *Home:* 60 Williston Rd., Auburndale, Mass. 02166.

CAREER: Lasell Junior College, Auburndale, Mass., instructor in English and lecturer in current affairs, 1929-69. *Member:* Phi Beta Kappa.

WRITINGS: The Edge of Nowhere, Atheneum, 1972; *Cousins and Circuses,* Atheneum, 1974; *The Spell of the Northern Lights,* Atheneum, in press.

WORK IN PROGRESS: A fourth volume in the series.

SIDELIGHTS: "Cousins and Circuses, like *The Edge of Nowhere,* tells about my life nearly sixty years ago in the village of Wales, North Dakota. How much of the story is true? Almost everything and almost everybody. You can find Wales on the map, and if you went there today, you'd see my family house, still standing at the Edge of Nowhere.

"My mother, a musician, and my father, a college professor, moved to Wales for my father's health. There my mother continued to make music for everybody, and my father ran a small bank, knew every farmer for miles

"The snow must be higher than they are—it'll be like a tunnel to the house." ■ (From *The Edge of Nowhere* by Lucy Johnston Sypher. Illustrated by Ray Abel.)

around, and continued to teach, his own children and everyone else's. My older brother Amory could outtalk anyone he met and was afraid of nothing, while I was shy and timid.

"Topsy was my trick dog. And my best friend, one of three girls in a Canadian minister's family, was Gwendolyn. Her small brother had three royal names. Other people may be a blend of two or three people that I remember, and I had to imagine one man I'd heard of and never seen. My ten cousins, mostly boys, have their own names and all behave like themselves.

"In 1916 my brother and his friends dug a cave in the backyard, a deep pit that they sometimes forgot to cover! Nearby was a tiny stone house for my club. The cave and the stone house are gone, but they were as real then as our Fourth of July fireworks, our day at the county fair, and the Chautauqua programs in the big tent on Main Street.

"Summer and winter, such a village had threatening or tragic events—fierce blizzards, uncontrollable fires with no fire department, violent summer windstorms, and epidemics

LUCY JOHNSTON SYPHER

of crippling infantile paralysis. We knew about the lawbreakers who were never caught, and we couldn't save the child who died because there was no doctor.

"Yet *Cousins and Circuses* is mostly about our good times. In 1916 we drove five hundred miles to Minneapolis for my mother's family reunion. The trip took four days each way. We followed trails of striped paint on fenceposts, we pushed ourselves out of mudholes, and we slept wherever we could, even if the hotel had bedbugs.

"I remember watching the biggest circus in the world with my grandfather, and I still have his tall desk-secretary and the 1820 newspaper I found in it, with a secret recipe for happiness. But the best of the trip was coming home, catching sight of Wales elevators and our cottonwoods. My shout at the end of the book is in my exact words—my mother never forgot them: 'Dear old Wales!'"

FOR MORE INFORMATION SEE: Washington Post ("Children's Book World"), November 5, 1972; *Horn Book,* April, 1973, June, 1974.

TEALE, Edwin Way 1899-

PERSONAL: Born June 2, 1899, in Joliet, Ill.; son of Oliver Cromwell and Clara Louise (Way) Teale; married Nellie Imogene Donovan, 1923; children: David Allen (killed in action, Germany, 1945). *Education:* Earlham College, A.B., 1922; Columbia University, A.M., 1927. *Home and Office:* "Trail Wood," Hampton, Conn.

EDWIN WAY TEALE

This praying mantis, rearing above the leaves of a garden plant, suggests some prehistoric dinosaur with bony armor and spiked forelegs. ▪ (From *Grassroot Jungles* by Edwin Way Teale. Photograph by the author.)

CAREER: Friends University, Wichita, Kan., instructor in English and public speaking, and editorial assistant, 1922-27; *Popular Science Monthly,* feature writer, 1928-41; freelance writer, 1941—. *Military Service:* U.S. Army, World War I. *Member:* Thoreau Society (president, 1958), New York Entomological Society (president, 1944), Brooklyn Entomological Society (president, 1949-53), New York Academy of Sciences (fellow), American Association for the Advancement of Science (fellow), Royal Photographic Society (associate), Explorers Club (New York), American Ornithologists' Union. *Awards, honors:* John Burroughs Medal; Christopher Medal; Indiana Authors Day award; Garden Club of America, Sarah Chapman Francis Medal, 1965; honorary LL.D., Earlham College, 1957; Pulitzer Prize for general nonfiction, 1966, for *Wandering Through Winter.*

WRITINGS: The Book of Gliders, Dutton, 1930; *Grassroot Jungles,* Dodd, 1937; *The Junior Book of Insects,* Dutton, 1939; *The Boy's Book of Photography,* Dutton, 1939; *The Golden Throng,* Dodd, 1940, 2nd Edition, 1961; *New Horizons,* Dodd, 1942; *Byways to Adventure,* Dodd, 1942; *Dune Boy,* Dodd, 1943; *The Lost Woods,* Dodd, 1945; *Days without Time,* Dodd, 1948; (editor) *The Insect World of J. Henri Fabre,* Dodd, 1949; *North With The Spring,* Dodd, 1951; *Green Treasure* (anthology), Dodd, 1952; *Circle of the Seasons,* Dodd, 1953; (editor) John Muir, *Wilderness World,* Houghton, 1954; *Insect Friends* (juvenile), Dodd, 1955; *Autumn Across America,* Dodd, 1956; *Adventures in Nature,* Dodd, 1959; *Journey Into Summer,* Dodd, 1960; *The Lost Dog* (juvenile), Dodd, 1961; *The Strange Lives of Familiar Insects,* Dodd, 1962;

(editor) *The Thoughts of Thoreau,* Dodd, 1962; *Audubon's Wildlife,* Viking, 1964; *Wandering Through Winter,* Dodd, 1965; *Springtime In Britain,* Dodd, 1970; *Photographs of American Nature,* Dodd, 1972; *A Naturalist Buys an Old Farm,* Dodd, 1974.

WORK IN PROGRESS: Three books: an autobiography and two on nature subjects.

SIDELIGHTS: Teale has traveled twenty thousand miles gathering material for fourth book in his "Seasons" series. His other books have been translated into a total of ten languages, and transcribed by the Library of Congress into Braille for the blind. Nature study and photography are his most absorbing interests, and he has taken more than twenty thousand pictures of natural history subjects. Some have been exhibited in the Royal Photographic Society salon, London, in South Africa, and other parts of the world.

FOR MORE INFORMATION SEE: Third Book of Junior Authors, edited by de Montreville and Hill, H. W. Wilson, 1972.

THOMAS, Joan Gale
See ROBINSON, Joan G.

TODD, Anne Ophelia
See DOWDEN, Anne Ophelia

TRESSELT, Alvin   1916-

PERSONAL: Surname is pronounced *Treh*-celt; born September 30, 1916, in Passaic, N.J.; son of Alvin and Eliza- beth Ellen (Thaller) Tresselt; married Blossom Budney (also a writer of children's books), April 9, 1949; children: Ellen Victoria, India Rachel. *Education:* Graduate of high school in Passaic. *Politics:* Democrat. *Home:* R.D.3, West Redding, Conn. 06896. *Office:* Parents' Magazine Press, 52 Vanderbilt Ave., New York, N.Y. 10017.

CAREER: "From 1934 I did a miscellaneous number of jobs typical of a young fellow trying to make a living during the depression, up until 1942. For reasons of health, I was rejected by the army and I did various defense jobs until 1946 when I joined B. Altman's & Co. (New York, N.Y.) in the interior display department. Later I went into the advertising department, doing home furnishings copy writing." *Humpty Dumpty's Magazine,* New York, N.Y., editor, 1952-65; Parents' Magazine Press, New York, N.Y., editor, 1965-67, executive editor and vice-president, 1967-74; free lance writer and editor, 1974—. *Awards, honors: White Snow, Bright Snow,* illustrated by Roger Duvoisin, won the American Library Association's Caldecott Medal, 1948; *Bonnie Bess, the Weathervane Horse,* illustrated by Marilyn Hafner, won first prize in picturebook division of *New York Herald Tribune's* Children's Spring Book Festival, 1949. Irma Simonton Black Award, 1973, for *The Dead Tree.*

WRITINGS—All for children: *Rain Drop Splash* (Caldecott honor book; illustrated by Leonard Weisgard), Lothrop, 1946; *Johnny Maple Leaf,* Lothrop, 1948; *White Snow, Bright Snow,* Lothrop, 1948; *The Wind and Peter,* Oxford University Press, 1948; *Bonnie Bess, the Weathervane Horse,* Lothrop, 1949, reissued with new illustrations done by Eric Blegvad, Parents' Magazine Press, 1970; *Sun Up,* Lothrop, 1949; *Follow the Wind,* Lothrop, 1950; *Little Lost Squirrel,* Grosset, 1950; *Hi Mister Robin,* Lothrop, 1950;

A chicken looked into the egg. ■ (From *The World in the Candy Egg* by Alvin Tresselt. Illustrated by Roger Duvoisin.)

ALVIN TRESSELT

Autumn Harvest, Lothrop, 1951; *The Rabbit Story,* Lothrop, 1952; *Follow the Road,* Lothrop, 1953; *I Saw the Sea Come In,* Lothrop, 1954; *Wake Up Farm,* Lothrop, 1955; *Wake Up City,* Lothrop, 1956; *Frog in the Well,* Lothrop, 1958; *Smallest Elephant in the World,* Knopf, 1959.

Timothy Robbins Climbs the Mountain, Lothrop, 1960; *Under the Trees and Through the Grass,* Lothrop, 1962; *Elephant Is Not a Cat,* Parents' Magazine Press, 1962; *How Far is Far?,* Parents' Magazine Press, 1964; *The Mitten,* Lothrop, 1964; *Hide and Seek Fog* (Caldecott honor book; illustrated by Roger Duvoisin), Lothrop, 1965; *A Thousand Lights and Fireflies,* Parents' Magazine Press, 1965; *The World in the Candy Egg,* Lothrop, 1967; *The Old Man and the Tiger,* Grosset, 1967; *Fox Who Traveled,* Grosset, 1968; (with Nancy Cleaver) *The Legend of the Willow Plate,* Parents' Magazine Press, 1968; *It's Time Now!,* Lothrop, 1969; *The Beaver Pond,* Lothrop, 1970; *Stories from the Bible,* Coward, 1971; *The Dead Tree* (ALA Notable Book), Parents' Magazine Press, 1972.

Editor (English rewrite, working from a literal translation of the Japanese, except where noted)—All published by Parents' Magazine Press: *Tears of the Dragon,* 1967; *Crane Maiden,* 1968; *Fisherman Under the Sea,* 1969; *Witch's Magic Cloth,* 1969; *Rolling Rice Ball,* 1969; *Eleven Hungry Cats,* 1970; *A Sparrow's Magic,* 1970; *Gengorah and the Thunder God,* 1970; *Land of Lost Buttons,* 1970; *Ogre and His Bride,* 1971; *Lim Fu and the Golden Mountain,* 1971; *Little Mouse Who Tarried,* 1971; *Humpty Dumpty's Bedtime Stories,* 1971; (adapted from German) *Wonder Fish from the Sea,* 1971.

SIDELIGHTS: Most of Tresselt's books have been illustrated by Roger Duvoisin. In 1972 their combined books went over a million copies sold. Other prominent artists who have illustrated his books are Leonard Weisgard, Joseph Lowe, and Milton Glazer.

FOR MORE INFORMATION SEE: More Junior Authors, edited by Muriel Fuller, H.W. Wilson, 1963; *Saturday Review,* February 18, 1967; *Young Readers' Review,* May, 1967; *Christian Science Monitor,* May 4, 1967; *New York Times Book Review,* April 14, 1968, May 7, 1972; *Book World,* May 5, 1968; Lee Bennet Hopkins, *Books Are By People,* Citation, 1969; *Horn Book,* October, 1969, April, 1971, April, 1973; *Library Journal,* September, 1970.

TYLER, Anne   1941-

PERSONAL: Born October 25, 1941, in Minneapolis, Minn.; daughter of Lloyd Parry (a chemist) and Phyllis (Mahon) Tyler; married Taghi Modarressi (a psychiatrist), May 3, 1963; children: Tezh, Mitra (daughters). *Education:* Duke University, B.A., 1961; Columbia University, graduate study in Russian, 1961-62. *Religion:* Quaker. *Residence:* Baltimore, Md. *Agent:* Diarmuid Russell, 551 Fifth Ave., New York, N.Y. 10017.

CAREER: Duke University Library, Durham, N.C., Russian bibliographer, 1962-63; McGill University Law Library, Montreal, Quebec, Canada, assistant to the librarian, 1964-65.

ANNE TYLER

WRITINGS: If Morning Ever Comes, Knopf, 1964; *The Tin Can Tree,* Knopf, 1965; *A Slipping Down Life* (ALA Notable Book), Knopf, 1970; *The Clock Winder,* Knopf, 1972; *Celestial Navigation,* Knopf, 1974. Short stories in *Post, Seventeen, New Yorker, Critic, Antioch Review,* and *Southern Review.*

SIDELIGHTS: Spent childhood in a Utopian community in North Carolina. Speaks Persian; expects permanent residence will be Iran, her husband's country.

ULLMAN, James Ramsey   1907-1971

PERSONAL: Born November 24, 1907, in New York, N.Y.; son of Alexander F. and Eunice (Ramsey) Ullman; married Ruth Fishman, 1930; married Elaine Luria, 1946; married Marian Blinn, 1961; children: (first marriage) James R., Jr., William A. *Education:* Phillips Academy, Andover, student, 1922-25; Princeton University, B.A., 1929. *Home:* 168 Marlborough St., Boston, Mass. 02116. *Agent:* Harold Matson Co., 22 East 40th St., New York, N.Y. 10016.

CAREER: Newspaper reporter and feature writer, 1929-32; theatrical producer, New York, N.Y., 1933-37, and co-producer of Sidney Kingsley's "Men in White," Pulitzer Prize play, 1934; executive of Works Progress Administration Federal Theater project, 1938-39; self-employed writer, 1939-71. *Military service:* American Field Service, Volunteer Ambulance Corps, attached to British 8th Army in Africa, 1942-43; became lieutenant. *Member:* Authors Guild of America, P.E.N., Overseas Press Club, American Alpine Club, Princeton Club of New York, Explorers Club.

WRITINGS: Mad Shelley, Princeton University Press, 1930; *The Other Side of the Mountain,* Carrick, 1938; *High Conquest,* Lippincott, 1941; *The White Tower,* Lippincott, 1945; (editor) *Kingdom of Adventure: Everest,* Sloanc, 1947; *River of the Sun,* Lippincott, 1950; *Windom's Way,* Lippincott, 1952; *Island of the Blue Macaws,* Lippincott, 1953; *The Sands of Karakorum,* Lippincott, 1953; *Banner in the Sky,* Lippincott, 1954; *The Age of Mountaineering,* Lippincott, 1954; (with Tenzing Norgay) *Tiger of the*

For one flashing, timeless instant on that forlorn and timeless mountainside he looked into a man's eyes, and everything that the man was was there. He saw it all now, naked and manifest before him: the fear and the pride and the bottomless sterility of pride; the despairing lonely hunger of the unloving and unloved; the will to conquer and the will to die . . . ▪ (From the movie *"The White Tower,"* © 1949 by RKO Radio Pictures, Inc.)

JAMES RAMSEY ULLMAN

Snows, Putnam, 1955; *The Day on Fire,* World Publishing, 1958; *Down the Colorado,* Houghton, 1960; *Fia Fia,* World Publishing, 1962; *Where the Bong Tree Grows,* World Publishing, 1963; *Americans on Everest,* Lippincott, 1964; (with Al Dinhofer) *Caribbean Here and Now,* Macmillan, 1968; *Straight Up,* Doubleday, 1968; *And Not to Yield,* Doubleday, 1970. Contributor of fiction and nonfiction to *Holiday, Saturday Evening Post, Life, Sports Illustrated, Horizon, Saturday Review,* and other national magazines.

WORK IN PROGRESS: Pieces on Antarctic and Congo.

SIDELIGHTS: A world traveler and mountaineer, Ullman was a member of the first American expedition to Mount Everest in the spring of 1963. Participated in civil rights freedom march, Montgomery, Ala., March, 1965. Seven of his books, *High Conquest, The White Tower, River of the Sun, Windom's Way, Banner in the Sky, The Day on Fire,* and *And Not to Yield,* have been sold for motion pictures.

FOR MORE INFORMATION SEE: Variety, June 23, 1971; *Time,* July 5, 1971.

(Died, June 20, 1971)

VIORST, Judith

PERSONAL: Born in Newark, N.J.; daughter of Martin (an accountant) and Ruth (Ehrenkranz) Stahl; married Milton Viorst (a writer); children: Anthony, Nicholas, Alexander. *Education:* Rutgers University, B.A. (with honors). *Religion:* Jewish. *Home:* 3432 Ashley Ter. N.W., Washington, D.C. 20008. *Agent:* Robert Lescher, 155 East 71st St., New York, N.Y. 10027.

CAREER: Poet, journalist, author of children's books. Contributing editor, *Redbook* Magazine. *Member:* Phi Beta Kappa. *Awards, honors:* Emmy Award, 1970, for poetic monologs written for CBS special, "Annie, The Women in the Life of a Man."

WRITINGS: The Village Square (poems), Coward, 1965; *It's Hard to Be Hip Over Thirty, and Other Tragedies of Married Life* (poems), World Publishing, 1968; (with husband, Milton Viorst) *The Washington, D.C. Underground Gourmet,* Simon & Schuster, 1970; *People and Other Aggravations* (poems), World Publishing, 1971; *Yes, Married: A Saga of Love and Complaint* (collected prose pieces), Saturday Review Press, 1972.

Juvenile fiction: *Sunday Morning,* Harper, 1968; *I'll Fix Anthony,* Harper, 1969; *Try It Again, Sam: Safety When You Walk,* Lothrop, 1970; *The Tenth Good Thing About Barney* (Junior Literary Guild selection), Atheneum, 1971; *Alexander and the Terrible, Horrible, No Good, Very Bad Day* (Junior Literary Guild selection), Atheneum, 1972; *My Mama Says There Aren't Any Zombies, Ghosts, Vampires, Creatures, Demons, Monsters, Fiends, Goblins, or Things* (Junior Literary Guild selection), Atheneum, 1973; *Rosie and Michael,* Atheneum, in press.

Juvenile nonfiction: (Editor with Shirley Moore) *Wonderful World of Science,* Science Service, 1961; *Projects: Space,* Washington Square Press, 1962; *One Hundred and Fifty Science Experiments, Step-by-Step,* Bantam, 1963; *Natural World,* Bantam, 1965; *The Changing Earth,* Bantam, 1967.

Author of syndicated column for Washington Star Syndicate, 1970-72, and of regular column for *Redbook,* 1972—. Author of poetic monologs for television. Contributor of poems and articles to *New York, New York Times, Holiday, Venture, Washingtonian,* and other periodicals.

SIDELIGHTS: Judith Viorst started writing when she was seven: "terrible poems about dead dogs, mostly." She had always wanted to write publishable poems and children's books, but she had no success until she began writing about herself, her husband, her marriage, and her children.

"It's quite terrific to be a working mother whose research, for the most part, consists of hanging around the house. Since my husband also works at home (and can make lunch) it's altogether a very pleasant arrangement. He is the harshest critic and greeter and encourager of my books and without him there wouldn't be any. Not one word I wrote was ever published until we were married.

"Most of my children's books are for or about my own children, and mostly they're written to meet certain needs. For instance, when Anthony was mercilessly persecuting his younger brother I decided to write *I'll Fix Anthony* to cheer up Nick. When a lot of questions about death were being raised around our house, my struggle for a way to respond to those questions resulted in the Barney book. I observed that the concept of 'I'm Having a bad day' seemed to help adults get through those bad days a little better and so I wrote about such a day for Alexander, who was having a lot of them. For Nick, who used to be scared of monsters and doubtful of his mother's infallibility (he's recovered from the former but not the latter), I wrote *My Mama Says*."

FOR MORE INFORMATION SEE: McCall's, September, 1969; Selma G. Lanes, *Down the Rabbit Hole*, Atheneum, 1971; *Life*, December 17, 1971; *Horn Book*, April, 1972; *Junior Literary Guild Catalogue*, September, 1972, September, 1973; *Washington Post* ("Children's Book World"), November 5, 1972; *Saturday Review/World*, December 4, 1973.

JUDITH VIORST

I couldn't have some cream cheese on my sandwich because, she said, there wasn't any more. And then I found the cream cheese under the lettuce in back of the Jello, So. . . . ■ (From *My Mama Says There Aren't any Zombies, Ghosts, Vampires, Creatures, Demons, Monsters, Fiends, Goblins, or Things* by Judith Viorst. Illustrated by Kay Chorao.)

WARBLER, J. M.
See COCAGNAC, A. M.

WEIL, Lisl

PERSONAL: Lisl rhymes with "easel," and Weil rhymes with "style"; born in Vienna, Austria; came to United States, 1939; naturalized citizen, 1944; married Julius Marx (deceased). *Education:* Educated in Vienna. *Home:* 25 Central Park W., New York, N.Y. 10023.

CAREER: Author and illustrator; worked in various fields of illustration in Europe and United States before finding "that I can give my best by working for children." Has performed with Little Orchestra Society of New York at young people's concerts in Carnegie Hall and Philharmonic Hall since the late 1940's, illustrating the story of the music being played; also has appeared with Boston Pops Orchestra, the Chicago, Detroit, Indianapolis, and Baltimore symphony orchestras, and on television specials; had weekly television show, "Children's Sketch Book," produced by National Broadcasting Co., 1963-64.

WRITINGS—Self-illustrated: (Reteller) *Jacoble Tells the Truth,* Houghton, 1946; *Happy ABC,* World Publishing, 1946; *Bill the Brave,* Houghton, 1948.

Pudding's Wonderful Bone, Crowell, 1956; *I Wish, I Wish,* Houghton, 1957; *The Busiest Boy in Holland,* Houghton, 1959.

Bitzli and the Big Bad Wolf, Houghton, 1960; *Mimi,* Houghton, 1961; *The Lionhearted One,* Houghton, 1962; (reteller) *The Sorcerer's Apprentice: A Musical Picture Story* (based on music by Paul Dukas with transcriptions for piano by David Shapiro), Little, Brown, 1962; *The Happy Ski ABC,* Putnam, 1964; *Eyes So-Big,* Houghton, 1964; *Happy Birthday in Barcelona,* Houghton, 1965; (reteller) *The Fantastic Toy Shop* (musical story-ballet; music

LISL WEIL

202

The traveling circus gypsies have come to the farm. ■ (From *Melissa* by Lisl Weil. Illustrated by the author.)

adapted by David Shapiro), Abelard, 1966; *Melissa*, Macmillan, 1966; *Melissa's Friend Fabrizzio*, Macmillan, 1967; *The Story of Smetana's "The Bartered Bride,"* Putnam, 1967; *Shivers and the Case of the Secret Hamburgers*, Houghton, 1967; *Alphabet of Puppy Care*, Abelard, 1968; (reteller) *The Golden Spinning Wheel: An Old Bohemian Folk Tale* (music of Antonin Dvorak adapted by David Shapiro), Macmillan, 1969; *King Midas' Secret and Other*

Follies, McGraw, 1969; *Things That Go Bang*, McGraw, 1969; *Out and In*, Scholastic Book Services, 1969.

The Hopping Knapsack, Macmillan, 1970; *The Wiggler*, Houghton, 1971; *Monkey Trouble*, Scholastic Book Services, 1972; *Fat Ernest*, Parents' Magazine Press, 1973; *The Funny Old Bag*, Parents' Magazine Press, 1973; *The Little Chestnut Tree Story*, Scholastic Book Services, 1973;

Walt and Pepper, Parents' Magazine Press, 1974; *Ralphi Rhino* (Junior Literary Guild selection), Walker, 1974.

Illustrator: Marion Moss, *Doll House,* World Publishing, 1946; Dori Furth, *Back in Time for Supper,* McKay, 1947; *The Thirsty Lion,* Crowell, 1949.

Ruth Langland Holberg, *Catnip Man,* Crowell, 1951; Henry Steele Commager, *Chestnut Squirrel,* Houghton, 1952; Christine N. Govan, *The Super-Duper Car,* Houghton, 1952; Ruth Corabel Simon, *Mat and Mandy and the Little Old Car,* Crowell, 1952; Ruth Langland Holberg, *Three Birthday Wishes,* Crowell, 1953; Ruth Corabel Simon, *Mat and Mandy and the Big Dog, Bigger,* Crowell, 1954; Elizabeth Duryea, *The Long Christmas Eve,* Houghton, 1954; Dorris W. Hendrickson, *Breakneck Hill,* Follett, 1954; Pamela Brown, *Windmill Family,* Crowell, 1955; Marion Flood French, *Mr. Bear Goes to Boston,* Follett, 1955; *Let's Cook without Cooking,* Crowell, 1955; *Tony for Keeps,* Winston, 1955; *A House for Henrietta,* Crowell, 1958; Emilie Warren McLeod, *Clancy's Witch,* Atlantic-Little, Brown, 1959.

Little Witch, Scholastic, 1961; Mary Elting, *Miss Polly's Animal School,* Grosset, 1961; Helen Diehl Olds, *What Will I Wear?,* Knopf, 1961; *Upstairs and Downstairs,* Crowell, 1962; *Gates Readers,* Macmillan, 1962; *Sheep Ahoy,* Houghton, 1963; *Betsy and Tacy Go Uptown,* Houghton, 1963; *Tommy Goes Shopping and Nancy Cooks,* American Book Corp., 1963; Alice Low, *A Day of Your Own: Your Birthday,* Random House, 1964; Lucretia Peabody Hale, *Stories from the Peterkin Papers,* Scholastic Book Services, 1964; Margaret V. D. Bevans, *"I Wonder Why?" Thought the Owl,* Putnam, 1965; Aileen Lucia Fisher, *Human Rights Day,* Crowell, 1966.

Sesyle Joslin, *Doctor George Owl,* Houghton, 1970; *Kate,* Scholastic Book Services, 1970; *Faces and Places,* Scholastic Book Services, 1971; Marjorie W. Sharmat, *51 Sycamore Lane,* Macmillan, 1971; Eda J. Le Shan, *What Makes Me Feel This Way? Growing Up with Human Emotions,* Macmillan, 1972; *A Visit with Rosalind,* Macmillan, 1972; *Told Under the City Umbrella,* Macmillan, 1972; *A Time to Shout,* Scholastic Book Services, 1973; *Master of All Masters,* Scholastic Book Services, 1973; *The Little Store on the Corner,* Scholastic Book Services, 1973; *Katie and Those Boys,* Scholastic Book Services, 1974; *Clara Bolton,* Scholastic Book Services, 1974; *Your First Pet,* Macmillan, 1974; *Mindy,* Macmillan, 1974.

Also illustrator of "What Is?" series, by Lee P. McGrath and Joan Scobey, published by Essandess: *What Is a Father?,* 1968; *What Is a Mother?,* 1968; *What Is a Sister?,* 1969; *What Is a Grandmother?,* 1970; *What Is a Brother?,* 1970; *What Is a Grandfather?,* 1970; *What Is a Friend?,* 1971; *What Is a Pet?,* 1971.

SIDELIGHTS: "Already as a small child I loved to draw and to dance and I loved music. Showing talent as early as I could hold a crayon, my wonderful parents started my education in the arts. I was fortunate to have excellent teachers that stressed expression of feelings and the close relationship and rhymes that are present in the arts and in life around us.

"Doing children's books and performing at Young People's

Concerts, illustrating the music played on the stage, is no work but greatest joy for me. I love to draw happy and funny things. And I hope that with my stories I can give my readers and listeners something to think about too. Upon invitations I have given countless chalk-talks for children and their elders at schools and library meetings around the country. [For concerts] my life-sized drawings with colored chalks are done in perfect rhythm. It all is choreographed with movements and so becomes a real picture-ballet. It is my very own way of making my audiences listen with their eyes as well as their ears.

"One of my books, *The Sorcerer's Apprentice,* has been made into a sound movie by the Weston Woods Studios, in which I am drawing the pictures to the music, just as I do on the concert stages."

FOR MORE INFORMATION SEE: Illustrators of Children's Books 1946-1956, Horn Book, 1958; *Times Literary Supplement,* May 25, 1967; *Illustrators of Children's Books 1957-1966,* Horn Book, 1968; *Library Journal,* May 15, 1969, July, 1969, May 15, 1970; *New York Times Book Review,* May 2, 1971; *Christian Science Monitor,* May 2, 1973.

WOLKSTEIN, Diane   1942-

PERSONAL: Born November 11, 1942, in New York, N.Y.; daughter of Harry W. (a certified public accountant) and Ruth (Barenbaum) Wolkstein; married Bernard Zucker

(a gem merchant), September 7, 1969; children: Rachel Cloudstone. *Education:* Smith College, B.A., 1964; studied pantomime in Paris, 1964-65, Bank Street College of Education, M.A., 1967. *Religion:* Jewish. *Home:* 10 Patchin Pl., New York, N.Y. 10011. *Agent:* Marilyn Marlow, 60 East 56th St., New York, N.Y. 10022.

CAREER: Hostess of bi-weekly radio show, "Stories from Many Lands with Diane Wolkstein," WNYC-radio, New York, N.Y., 1967—. Bank Street College, New York, N.Y., instructor in storytelling and children's literature, 1970—; leader of storytelling workshops for librarians and teachers. *Awards, honors:* New York Academy of Sciences Children's Science Book honorable mention, 1973, for *8,000 Stones.*

WRITINGS: 8,000 Stones, Doubleday, 1972; *The Cool Ride in the Sky,* Knopf, 1973. Contributor of articles to *Wilson Library Bulletin* and *School Library Journal.*

SIDELIGHTS: Ms. Wolkstein was guest storyteller at the John Masefield Storytelling Festival in Toronto, 1972, has recorded stories for Canadian Broadcasting Corporation radio and TV, and has told stories in cities of Europe. She has recorded "Tales of the Hopi Indians," 1972, "California Fairy Tales," 1972, and "Eskimo Stories: Tales of Magic," 1974, for Spoken Arts.

HOBBIES AND OTHER INTERESTS: Travel, gardening in New York City.

FOR MORE INFORMATION SEE: New York Times, July 15, 1968; *New York Daily News,* August 24, 1973; *New York Times Book Review,* September 30, 1973; *Saturday Review/World,* December 4, 1973.

The courtiers came out of the palace, and soon a huge noisy crowd formed around the animal. ▪ (From *8,000 Stones* by Diane Wolkstein. Illustrated by Ed Young.)

YAMAGUCHI, Marianne (Illenberger) 1936-

PERSONAL: Born January 10, 1936, in Cuyahoga Falls, Ohio; daughter of Arthur Max (a lawyer) and Esther (Lind) Illenberger; married John Tohr Yamaguchi (an economic consultant, demographer, and writer), September 10, 1960; children: Esme Turid, Kara Elizabeth. *Education:* Bowling Green State University, student, 1954-57; Rhode Island School of Design, B.F.A., 1960. *Home:* Flat 1, 44 Milson Rd., Cremorne Point, New South Wales, 2090, Australia.

CAREER: High school art teacher in Australia.

WRITINGS—Self-illustrated: (Compiler) *Finger Plays,* Holt, 1970.

Illustrator: Tohr Yamaguchi, *The Golden Crane,* Holt, 1963; Tohr Yamaguchi, *Two Crabs in the Moonlight,* Holt, 1965; Yoshika Uchida, *The Sea of Gold,* Scribner, 1965; J. R. Larson, *Palace in Bagdad,* Scribner, 1966; Eric C. Roies, *Running Wild,* Angus & Robertson, 1972; Eric C. Roies, *The River,* Angus & Robertson, 1973.

MARIANNE YAMAGUCHI

WORK IN PROGRESS: Writing and illustrating a book.

SIDELIGHTS: The Yamaguchis lived in New York City for seven years before his work took them to Australia.

FOR MORE INFORMATION SEE: Third Book of Junior Authors, edited by de Montreville and Hill, H. W. Wilson, 1972.

YEP, Laurence M(ichael)   1948-

PERSONAL: Born June 14, 1948, in San Francisco, Calif.; son of Thomas G. (a postal clerk) and Franche (Lee) Yep. Education: Marquette University, student, 1966-68; University of California, Santa Cruz, B.A., 1970; State University of New York at Buffalo, Ph.D., 1974. Home: 921 Populus Pl., Sunnyvale, Calif. 94086. Agent: Lurton Blassingame, 60 East 42nd St., New York, N.Y. 10017.

MEMBER: Science Fiction Writers of America. Awards, honors: Book-of-the-Month Club writing fellowship, 1970.

WRITINGS: Sweetwater (juvenile science fiction novel), Harper, 1973. Stories included in the collections: World's

Best Science Fiction, Ace Books, 1969; Quark #2, Paperback Library, 1971; Protostars, Ballantine, 1971; The Demon Children, Avon, 1973; Strange Bedfellows, Random House, 1973; Last Dangerous Visions, Harper, in press. Contributor to science fiction magazines, including Worlds of If and Galaxy.

WORK IN PROGRESS: A juvenile book about the first Chinese aviator who flew in 1909 near Oakland Calif.; a cycle of stories "dealing with the beautiful and terrible ways in which our future experience of the stars will transform our ancient myths"; his doctoral dissertation on Quentin Compson.

SIDELIGHTS: "I was raised in a black ghetto but commuted to a grammar school in Chinatown in San Francisco so that I did not really meet White Culture until I went to high school. In a sense I have no one culture to call my own since I exist peripherally in several. However, in my writing I can create my own."

FOR MORE INFORMATION SEE: Publishers' Weekly, April 16, 1973.

LAURENCE M. YEP

I don't know what he was looking for, but he studied me for a long time. His myriad eyes reflected my image so I saw a hundred Tyrees—each a perfect miniature. ■ (From *Sweetwater* by Laurence Yep. Illustrated by Julia Noonan.)

207

YOUNG, Miriam 1913-1974

PERSONAL: Born February 26, 1913, in New York, N.Y.; daughter of Frank A. (an actor) and Myrtle (an actress; McKenley) Burt; married Walter Young (an artist), September 7, 1934; children: Peter, Nancy, Barry. *Education:* Attended Erasmus Hall HIgh School, Brooklyn, N.Y., and then Columbia University. *Home:* Lake Katonah, Katonah, N.Y. 10536. *Agent:* Diarmuid Russell, Russell & Volkening, Inc., 551 Fifth Ave., New York, N.Y. 10017.

CAREER: Writer, principally for children.

WRITINGS—Adult: *Mother Wore Tights* (nonfiction), McGraw, 1944; *Heaven Faces West* (fiction), Appleton, 1948.

Juvenile: *Prace, a Carousel Horse,* Crowell, 1950; *Georgie Finds a Grandpa,* Golden Press, 1954; *Five Pennies to Spend,* Golden Press, 1955; *Marco's Chance,* Harcourt, 1959; *Up and Away!,* Harcourt, 1960; *The Most Beautiful Kitten,* Lantern Press, 1961; *The Dollar Horse,* Harcourt, 1961; *Please Don't Feed Horace,* Dial, 1961; *The Secret of Stone House Farm,* Dial, 1963; *Miss Suzy,* Parents' Magazine Press, 1964; *Jellybeans for Breakfast,* Parents' Magazine Press, 1968; *Billy and Milly,* Lothrop, 1968; *A Bear Named George,* Crown, 1969; *The Witchmobile,* Lothrop, 1969; *If I Drove a Truck,* Lothrop, 1969; *If I Flew a Plane,* Lothrop, 1970; *Slow as a Snail, Quick as a Bird,* Lothrop, 1970; *Something Small,* Putnam, 1970; *Can't You Pre-*

MIRIAM YOUNG

tend?, Putnam, 1970; *Beware the Polar Bear,* Lothrop, 1970; *Peas in a Pod,* Putnam, 1970; *If I Drove a Car,* Lothrop, 1971; *If I Sailed a Boat,* Lothrop, 1971; *If I Drove a Train,* Lothrop, 1972; *Christy and the Cat Jail,* Lothrop, 1972; *Miss Suzy's Easter Surprise,* Parents' Magazine Press, 1972; *King Basil's Birthday,* Watts, 1973; *Witch's Garden* (juvenile novel), Atheneum, 1973; *If I Drove a Tractor,* Lothrop, 1973; *If I Rode a Horse,* Lothrop, 1973; *If I Drove a Bus,* Lothrop, 1973; *If I Rode an Elephant,* Lothrop, 1974; *If I Rode a Dinosaur,* Lothrop, 1974; *Miss Suzy's Birthday,* Parents' Magazine Press, 1974; *Truth and Consequences,* Four Winds, in press; *So What, if it's Raining,* Parents' Magazine Press, in press.

WORK IN PROGRESS: Several picture books (illustrated by others); a suspense novel for young people; "a book for eight-to-twelve age readers about a girl whose father was a preacher and whose grandfather was a gambler and race-track man, which is a fictionalized account of my mother's childhood in San Francisco in 1895."

SIDELIGHTS: "My husband is an artist and paints as steadily as I write, which is every day except when we are traveling. We travel quite a bit in Europe and are especially fond of the French countryside.

"My parents were on the stage and their experiences, and my own, traveling with them as a backstage baby, was the basis of my book *Mother Wore Tights* which was made into a major motion picture. I started writing at boarding school, writing plays with my roommate who was also the daughter of an actress. These plays were always comedies, and I still like to put comedy in my books whenever possible. In the 'If I Drove' series, for instance, there is one doublepage spread in each book that is nonsensical or just for fun.

"Children who write letters to me or who ask questions when I give talks at schools, etc., always want to know: Where do you get your ideas. I always answer: 'Ideas come from life. I never just sit down to write thinking, I want to write a story; what shall it be? I am too fascinated by real people and real events to want to make them up completely. Of course, these events and people are usually changed beyond recognition. But they provide the necessary spark that sets the story afire. In *Here Lies Kimberly Jones,* for instance, something that happened with one of my children was the kernel around which the rest of the story was formed. In *Slow as a Snail, Quick as a Bird,* I used my own experiences raising Monarch butterflies. In *Christy and the Cat Jail,* I combined all the cats we have had into one.'

"Our house is set on the shore of a lake, and that type of community is featured in several of my books. I enjoy writing for various age groups. Turning from picture books to books for older readers makes a nice change. But in any case, I enjoy it."

Mother Wore Tights was filmed by 20th-Century Fox in 1947.

FOR MORE INFORMATION SEE: Book World, October 26, 1969; *New York Times Book Review,* November 9, 1969; *Horn Book,* October, 1972, June 6, 1973; *Time,* September 23, 1974; *Variety,* September 25, 1974.

(Died September 12, 1974)

The grass at the foot of the maple was filled with fresh green clover. Miss Suzy picked enough for a wreath and sat looking around. ■ (From *Miss Suzy's Easter Surprise* by Miriam Young. Illustrated by Arnold Lobel.)

No home town, no home. But at home in any town. That was the trouper. ■ (From the movie
''Mother Wore Tights,'' © 1947 by 20th Century-Fox.)

Something about the Author

ZALBEN, Jane Breskin 1950-

PERSONAL: Born April 21, 1950, in New York, N.Y.; daughter of Murry (a certified public accountant) and Mae (a librarian; maiden name, Kirshbloom) Breskin; married Steven Zalben (a former mathematics teacher, now studying architecture), December 25, 1969. *Education:* High School of Music and Art, New York, student, 1964-67; Queen's College, Flushing, B.A., 1971; Pratt Institute, study at Graphics Center, 1971-72. *Home:* 156-12 71st Ave., Kew Garden Hills, N.Y. 11367.

CAREER: Dial Press, New York, N.Y., assistant to art director of children's book department, 1971-72; Thomas Y. Crowell Co., New York, N.Y., free-lance book designer, 1972; painter, etcher, lithographer, and illustrator.

WRITINGS—Self-illustrated juveniles: *Cecilia's Older Brother,* Macmillan, 1973; *Lyle and Humus,* Macmillan, 1974; *The Ballad of Basil and Hillary, and Friends,* Macmillan, in press.

Illustrator: Jan Wahl, *Jeremiah Knucklebones,* Holt, 1974.

SIDELIGHTS: "I naturally draw from my life, past and present for my children's books and try to feel what a child feels when I write. I love plants and animals very much and I own about 75 or so plants. I also love to cook exotic foods."

FOR MORE INFORMATION SEE: Horn Book, June, 1973; *London Times,* November, 1973; *Kirkus,* July, 1974.

JANE BRESKIN ZALBEN

And finally they thought of stamp collecting. ■ (From *Cecilia's Older Brother* by Jane Breskin Zalben. Illustrated by the author.)

SOMETHING ABOUT THE AUTHOR

CUMULATIVE INDEXES, VOLUMES 1-7
Illustrators and Authors

ILLUSTRATIONS INDEX

(In the following index, the number of the volume in which an illustrator's work appears is given *before* the colon, and the page on which it appears is given *after* the colon. For example, a drawing by Adams, Adrienne appears in Volume 2 on page 6, and another drawing by her appears in Volume 3 on page 80.)

AUTHORS INDEX

(In the following index, the number of the volume in which an author's sketch appears is given *before* the colon, and the page on which it appears is given *after* the colon. For example, the sketch of Aardema, Verna, appears in Volume 4 on page 1).